Introduction to Choreographies

In concurrent and distributed systems, processes can complete tasks together by playing their parts in a joint plan. The plan, or protocol, can be written as a choreography: a formal description of the overall behaviour that processes should collaborate to implement, like authenticating a user or purchasing an item online. Formality brings clarity, but not only that. Choreographies can contribute to important safety and liveness properties.

This book is an ideal introduction to theory of choreographies for students, researchers, and professionals in computer science and applied mathematics. It covers languages for writing choreographies and their semantics, and principles for implementing choreographies correctly. The text treats the study of choreographies as a discipline in its own right, following a systematic approach that starts from simple foundations and proceeds to more advanced features in incremental steps. Each chapter includes examples and exercises aimed at helping with understanding the theory and its relation to practice.

FABRIZIO MONTESI is Professor of Computer Science at the University of Southern Denmark. He is a Villum Young Investigator and recipient of several awards for science and innovation, including the EAPLS Best PhD Dissertation Award and the Best Thesis in ICT Award from the General Confederation of Italian Industry.

Introduction to Choreographies

FABRIZIO MONTESI

University of Southern Denmark

CAMBRIDGE
UNIVERSITY PRESS

Shaftesbury Road, Cambridge CB2 8EA, United Kingdom

One Liberty Plaza, 20th Floor, New York, NY 10006, USA

477 Williamstown Road, Port Melbourne, VIC 3207, Australia

314–321, 3rd Floor, Plot 3, Splendor Forum, Jasola District Centre, New Delhi – 110025, India

103 Penang Road, #05–06/07, Visioncrest Commercial, Singapore 238467

Cambridge University Press is part of Cambridge University Press & Assessment,
a department of the University of Cambridge.

We share the University's mission to contribute to society through the pursuit of
education, learning and research at the highest international levels of excellence.

www.cambridge.org
Information on this title: www.cambridge.org/9781108833769
DOI: 10.1017/9781108981491

First published 2023

A catalogue record for this publication is available from the British Library.

A Cataloging-in-Publication data record for this book is available from the Library of Congress.

ISBN 978-1-108-83376-9 Hardback

Contents

Illustrations

Notations

$s \xrightarrow{\vec{\mu}} s'$	There is an execution from s to s' with trace $\vec{\mu}$	47
$\twoheadrightarrow$	A multi-step transition relation	47
$s \xrightarrow{\vec{\mu}}$	The state s has the trace $\vec{\mu}$	47
$s \xnrightarrow{\vec{\mu}}$	The state s does not have the trace $\vec{\mu}$	47
P	A process term	56
p!	Send a message to p	56
p?	Receive a message from p	56
SimpleProc	The language of Simple Processes	56
N	A network	57
SimpleNet	The set of networks in Simple Processes	57
supp	The function that maps functions to their supports	57
p[P]	The atomic network that returns P for p	57
$N \mid M$	The parallel composition of N and M	58
$N \setminus \mathsf{p}$	The network obtained by removing p as running process from N	67
$\vec{\mathsf{p}}$	A sequence of process names	69
$N\!\restriction_{\{\mathsf{p}_1,\dots,\mathsf{p}_n\}}$	The restriction of N to $\{\mathsf{p}_1,\dots,\mathsf{p}_n\}$	69
$N\!\restriction_{\mathsf{p}_1,\dots,\mathsf{p}_n}$	Shortcut for $N\!\restriction_{\{\mathsf{p}_1,\dots,\mathsf{p}_n\}}$	69
$[\![C]\!]_\mathsf{p}$	The projection of choreography C on process p	77
$[\![C]\!]$	The endpoint projection (EPP) of choreography C	78
Var	The set of (local) variables	95
x	A variable (used in local stores and expressions)	95
Val	The set of (local) values	95
v	A value (used in local stores and expressions)	95
I	An instruction, either in a choreographic or a process language	95
$I; C$	Do I and then C, in a choreographic language	95
$\mathsf{p}.e \to \mathsf{q}.x$	Process p communicates the evaluation of e to q, which stores it in variable x	95
e	A (local) expression	95
$\mathsf{p}.x := e$	Process p evaluates e and stores the result in x	95
$f(\vec{e})$	The invocation of function f with the evaluations of $\vec{e}$ as arguments	96
f	A function name	96
StatefulChor	The language of Stateful Choreographies	96
σ	A process store	98
PStore	The set of process stores	98
$\sigma[x \mapsto v]$	The store obtained from σ by updating the value for variable x to v	98
Σ	A choreographic store	98
$\Sigma[\mathsf{p}.x \mapsto v]$	The choreographic store obtained from Σ by updating the value for variable x of process p to v	98
$\sigma \vdash e \downarrow v$	The expression e is evaluated to v under σ	99
$\langle C, \Sigma \rangle$	A configuration in Stateful Choreographies	100

Introduction
Alice, Bob, Concurrency, and Distribution

The Importance of Protocols

Two aspects have become pervasive in modern computing: *concurrency*, the performance of multiple tasks at a time; and *distribution*, the usage of components located on different communicating devices. Even mobile phones and tiny single-board computers feature multiple processing units of different kinds, with purposes that go from generic computing to more specialised ones such as artificial intelligence and computer graphics. Computer networks are getting bigger than ever with the rise of the World Wide Web, telecommunications, cloud computing, edge computing, and the Internet of Things. This transformation has caused an explosion in the number of computer programs that communicate with each other over networks – the Internet alone connects billions of devices already.

On one hand, modern computer networks and their applications have become the drivers of our technological advancement. They enable better citizen services, new kinds of industry, new ways to connect socially, and even better health with smart medical devices. On the other hand, these systems and their software are increasingly complex because services depend on other services to function. For example, the website of a national service for citizens might depend on an external identification service to verify that the user can access a certain document. The user's web browser, the website, and the identification service are thus integrated: they communicate with each other to reach the goal of providing authenticated access to documents. In concurrent and distributed systems, the heart of integration is the notion of *protocol*: a document that prescribes the communications that the involved parties should perform in order to reach a goal. We will also refer to communications as interactions.

It is important that protocols are clear and precise. If they are ambiguous, designers of different parts of the same system might interpret the same protocol differently. Different interpretations usually lead to errors and errors can have dire consequences in this setting: applications hanging, data corruption, information leaks, and so forth. The more we equip programmers with solid methods for defining and implementing protocols correctly, the more likely they are to succeed at integrating the different parts of concurrent and distributed systems correctly. The ultimate quest is to increase the intelligibility, reliability, effectiveness, and transparency of these systems, as well as to make people more productive in building them. It is this quest that makes the discipline of interaction worth studying.

Computer scientists and mathematicians might get a familiar feeling when presented with the necessity of achieving both clarity and precision in writing. A computer scientist could point out that we need a good *language* to write protocols. A mathematician could say that we need a good *notation*.

From Protocols to Choreographies

Needham and Schroeder [1978] introduced an interesting notation for writing protocols. A communication of a message M from the participant A to the participant B is written

$$A \rightarrow B : M.$$

To define a protocol where A sends a message M to B and then B passes the same message to another participant C, we can just compose communications in a sequence:

$$A \rightarrow B : M$$
$$B \rightarrow C : M.$$

This is called Alice and Bob notation, due to a presentational style found in security research: the participants A and B represent the fictional characters Alice and Bob, respectively, who follow a protocol to perform some task. There might be more participants, like C in our example – typically a shorthand for Carol or Charlie. The first mention of Alice and Bob appeared in the seminal paper by Rivest and colleagues [1978] on their public-key cryptosystem:

'For our scenarios we suppose that A and B (also known as Alice and Bob) are two users of a public-key cryptosystem.'

We ourselves will use fictional characters like Alice and Bob often in this book.

Over the years, researchers and developers created many more protocol notations. Some of these notations are visual rather than textual, like Message Sequence Charts [International Telecommunication Union 1996]. The message sequence chart of our protocol with Alice, Bob, and Charlie looks as follows.

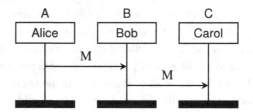

This visual representation (as a message sequence chart) is equivalent to our previous textual representation (in Alice and Bob notation) in the sense that they contain the same information. Intuitively, both notations follow the same style: they define a protocol from the point of view of an external observer, which sees the interactions performed by the participants. In this book, the protocol definitions given in this style are called *choreographies*.

In the beginning of the 2000s, researchers and practitioners started working on languages for writing choreographies that offer more features, for example:

- Including functions for computing the data to be transmitted.
- Nested protocols – that is, the ability to call another protocol as a procedure.
- Manipulating the local memory stores of participants.

We call languages designed for writing choreographies *choreographic languages*.

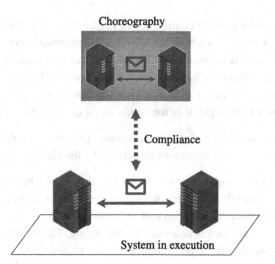

Figure 0.1 An abstract depiction of the property of choreography compliance: the interactions that take place among participants should follow the choreography that has been agreed upon. At the top, the blueprint represents a choreography that prescribes a message communication between two computers (represented by the full arrow with the envelope). At the bottom is the real system where the communication takes place. Compliance (represented by the dashed arrow) guarantees that the real system execution matches the expectations written in the choreography.

Choreographic languages have been adopted in different contexts. In 2005 the World Wide Web Consortium (W3C) – the international standard organisation for the Web – published the Web Services Choreography Description Language (WS-CDL), a language for defining interactions among web services [W3C 2005]. Later, in 2011, the Object Management Group (OMG) – a global consortium for technological standards – introduced choreographies in their notation for business processes (BPMN) [Object Management Group 2011]. The usage of choreographies has been advocated also when dealing with the development of *microservices*, whereby applications are fine-grained compositions of independently executable distributed services [Dragoni et al. 2017]. This momentum has pushed for (and is still pushing for) a lot of research on both the theory of choreographies and its application to programming [Ancona et al. 2016; Hüttel et al. 2016; Giallorenzo et al. 2021]. Alice and Bob are in the spotlight.

Choreography Compliance

Choreographies allow software developers and system designers to formalise an agreement on how the participants of a system should interact. The next step is to develop software and/or hardware that animates each participant according to such agreement. That is, when the implementations of all participants are run together, their joint execution should give rise to the interactions expected by the choreography. When this is the case, we say that the system of participants complies with the choreography, or that the system has the property of *choreography compliance*. (In the literature, compliance is also called *conformance*.)

We depict choreography compliance in Figure 0.1, for a simple distributed system with two participants. At the top we have the choreography agreed upon, depicted as the 'blueprint' that defines the expected communications between the two participants (represented by the computers). At the bottom we have the implementations of the two participants, which are running together and communicating. The property of compliance (represented by the dashed vertical arrow) can then be thought of as the combination of the following two conditions:

1. The system enacts only the communications prescribed by the choreography.
2. Vice versa, the communications prescribed by the choreography are enacted by the system.

Violating the first condition would mean that the system behaves unexpectedly: the system is 'unsound'. Conversely, violating the second condition would mean that the system does not do all that it is supposed to do: the system is 'incomplete'.[1]

Achieving compliance is notoriously challenging. This is not very surprising because coding concurrent systems is hard: programmers have to reason about all the possible ways in which the different participants might interact under all possible schedulings of their actions, which leads quickly to an explosion of the number of cases to be considered [O'Hearn 2018]. The issue is appropriately named the *state explosion problem* in computer science [Clarke & Grumberg 1987; Valmari 1996; Clarke et al. 2011]. It follows that concurrency can look deceptively simple, but in reality even small programs that look innocuous at first sight might yield undesired *emergent behaviour* (the behaviour that emerges from running these programs together). Indeed, programmers do not excel at dealing intuitively with concurrency and distribution, experts included [Lu et al. 2008; Leesatapornwongsa et al. 2016]. Furthermore, achieving choreography compliance is getting more pressing and difficult in practice: with the passing of time, computer networks are getting bigger and including more participants. This trend calls for principles of broad applicability.

The challenge posed by choreography compliance implies that we cannot merely stop at designing precise languages and notations for choreographies. We have to go further and develop rigorous methods for reasoning about the construction of compliant implementations. Motivated by this realisation, researchers have developed several approaches for formally relating choreographies to implementations. As a consequence, choreographic languages are typically designed such that choreographies are mechanically readable, amenable to mathematical reasoning, and used in computer programs [Ancona et al. 2016].

Choreographies in Practice

Some of the methods developed for expressing choreographies and achieving choreography compliance carry principles that can be used on multiple levels. For a programmer, these principles constitute a mental toolbox for the effective development of concurrent and distributed software. The same principles form the backbone of powerful tools, which provide automated or semi-automated help towards the goal of guaranteeing compliance. We now mention some of the most important application strategies for choreographic languages that have been developed so far.

---

[1] The second condition can be relaxed to allow for systems that do not implement everything prescribed by the choreography while retaining some of the key benefits of the choreographic approach. We discuss this aspect in Chapter 12, after our technical presentation.

Documentation and Specification

The most immediate application of choreographic languages is to reduce ambiguity in the documentation and specification of concurrent and distributed systems [W3C 2005; Object Management Group 2011]. The clarity of choreographies can help with choosing which design best suits the requirements at hand or developing standards for cross-team collaboration.

Furthermore, as we are going to see in this book, some choreographic languages guarantee desirable properties, for example, related to system progress (*liveness* properties). Writing a specification in one such language can therefore be used to prove that the specification respects these properties.

Compilation

Some choreographic languages support the automatic compilation of code for each participant described in a choreography, which then implements correctly what the participant should do [Montesi 2013; Ancona et al. 2016; Autili et al. 2020; Giallorenzo et al. 2021]. This idea has several lines of application.

Scaffolding The generation of skeleton implementations of each participant described in the choreography [Mendling & Hafner 2008; Carbone and Montesi 2013]. Typically, these skeletons are programs with details that need to be filled in, like how the data to be communicated are computed and transformed. Developers are then responsible for manually completing these programs with the missing details. This method has been particularly relevant in the setting of choreographic languages for web services [Object Management Group 2011; W3C 2005].

Libraries The generation of software libraries, which developers can modularly compose and invoke within their applications to make sure that they are following the choreography correctly [Giallorenzo et al. 2020]. For example, a service provider can use this technology to publish a library that clients can adopt to interact correctly with the provided service. While this method might be interesting for any concurrent and distributed system, it is particularly useful for systems that include multiple vendors or implementation technologies, as in cloud computing, edge computing, the Internet of Things, and microservices [Dragoni et al. 2017].

Connectors Choreographies can define protocols for integrating already existing components over a network. These components can be, for example, functions, objects, or services [Carbone and Montesi 2013; Dalla Preda et al. 2017; Scalas et al. 2017; Autili et al. 2020; Giallorenzo et al. 2020]. From the choreography, we can then generate distributed code that steers each component correctly to achieve the desired integration. This application is relevant for different settings, including cloud computing, edge computing, and business processes.

Parallel Algorithms Parallel algorithms, where independent tasks are computed in parallel, can be expressed as choreographies as well [Ng & Yoshida 2015; Cruz-Filipe & Montesi 2016]. In this case, compilation yields distributed software that, when run with the input required by the algorithm, returns the expected result. This application is particularly useful for high-performance computing (HPC) and distributed computation in general.

Verification

Another popular avenue of application for choreographies is the verification of code that already exists. There are two main trends, depending on whether verification takes place before or during execution.

Runtime Verification Given a choreography, we can equip each participant in a system with a monitoring tool which checks that all incoming and outgoing communications comply with what is written in the choreography [Castellani et al. 2016; Neykova et al. 2017].

Static Verification Given a choreography and some existing code for a specific participant, it is possible to automatically analyse the code to check whether it complies with the choreography [Honda et al. 2016; Scalas et al. 2019; Miu et al. 2021]. Choreographic languages can be computationally complete, making the static verification problem undecidable in general. Therefore, static verification typically comes at the cost of weakening the expressivity of the choreographic language or the correctness guarantees provided by choreography compliance.

The applications that we have described require having a choreography, which is usually written manually. When the code of a system is already written, there are methods for the semi-automated or automated reconstruction of a choreography from the programs of participants [Alur et al. 2003; Lange & Tuosto 2012; Lange et al. 2015; Cruz-Filipe et al. 2017; Carbone et al. 2018]. *Choreographic round-trip engineering* is a development process that combines methods for going back and forth between choreographies and participant implementations [Montesi 2013; Carbone et al. 2018]. The former and the latter can be seen as two views that need to be kept in sync. In choreographic round-trip engineering, developers can edit any of the two views and then use (semi-)automated methods to refresh the other. More details and pointers for further reading are given in Chapter 12.

Why This Book

Applications of choreographies rely on a clear understanding of what choreographies are and how choreography compliance can be achieved. Having resources for achieving such an understanding is therefore important, both for revealing how existing tools work under the hood, and for the future development of new technologies and the field of choreography-based development in general. However, at the time of this writing, literature on choreographies consists mainly of research articles that focus on specific developments and are intended for expert readers. There is no well-organised presentation of the key ideas of choreographies aimed at newcomers. This is what motivated the writing of this book, which aims to fill this gap.

More specifically, this book is an introduction to the theory of choreographies and the principles of choreography compliance. We will see how a *semantics* of choreographies can be mathematically defined by using logical methods, which will provide us with an interpretation of what running a protocol means. We will also expose the principles of how choreographies can be correctly implemented in the real world, by defining a translation of choreographies into models of executable programs. Paraphrasing, we are going to study how the Alices and Bobs that participate in a computer system can follow their intended choreographies.

Acknowledgements

I would like to thank the many colleagues – too many to mention here – with whom I have discussed and shared insights on choreographic languages and related topics over the years. The understanding that I gained from these discussions has been invaluable in the process of writing this book.

I am very grateful to the following people for interesting discussions and helpful comments on different contents of this book: Marco Carbone, Ilaria Castellani, Luís Cruz-Filipe, Ornela Dardha, Mariangiola Dezani-Ciancaglini, Simon Fowler, Saverio Giallorenzo, Eva Graversen, Thomas Hildebrandt, Ivan Lanese, Marco Peressotti, Valentino Picotti, Nobuko Yoshida, Gianluigi Zavattaro, and Olaf Zimmermann. Special thanks to Davide Sangiorgi for his advice on the publication of this book.

This book grew out of my teaching experience, which motivated me to explore how different features of choreographies can be presented in a coherent framework. In particular, I would like to extend a special thanks to the students at the University of Southern Denmark who have studied choreographies with me. The experience of interacting with students of different fields (computer science, mathematics, and engineering) played an important role in lowering reading prerequisites and influenced the presentation of several concepts in this book.

I extend my gratitude to the whole team at Cambridge University Press who helped with making the book a reality, in particular David Tranah and Anna Scriven. Thank you also to Johanne Aarup Hansen for her illustration of choreographies, which is part of the cover.

Finally, I would like to thank Maja Dembić for her encouragement and support throughout the process of writing this book.

This Book

Purpose, Audience, and Approach

The aim of this book is to introduce the reader to the theory of choreographies. For newcomers entirely unfamiliar with the idea of choreographies, the goal is to equip them with a fresh perspective on how we can abstract, design, and reason about concurrent and distributed systems. The book explains what choreographies are, how they can be modelled mathematically, and how they can be related to compliant implementations.

The intended primary audience consists of professionals and students in the areas of computer science and engineering, but the book is also designed to be approachable to mathematicians (willing to become) familiar with context-free grammars. Researchers can use the book to acquire the necessary knowledge for advancing the state of the art or for applying choreographies in other contexts. Lecturers should find the book useful in the preparation and execution of courses. Students should be helped in their learning by the rigorous and systematic presentation of the theory. Software architects, developers, and engineers can benefit from the insights in this book to improve their skills regarding integration protocols and the implementation of choreography-based tools. Project leaders can gain a fundamental understanding of the key issues behind systems based on choreographies and how to talk about them.

Pedagogically, the book follows an iterative approach. It starts with a very simple choreographic language and then progressively extends it with more sophisticated features like memory stores and recursion. Each chapter includes examples and exercises aimed at helping with understanding the theory and its relation to practice. Comprehensiveness is not an objective: we will not present features to capture all possible protocols. References to other relevant techniques and further developments are given where appropriate, sometimes in the text but mostly in Chapter 12.

Prerequisites

To read this book, you should be familiar with the basics of:

- The theories of sets, functions, and relations.
- Discrete structures like graphs and trees.
- The induction proof technique, including structural induction.
- Context-free grammars.

It is also assumed that the reader is familiar with the notion of concurrency and the basic intuition of how distributed systems are programmed. Relevant books for covering these topics include [Hopcroft et al. 2003; Tanenbaum & van Steen 2007; Franklin & Daoud 2010; Rosen & Krithivasan 2012; Cormen et al. 2022]. These prerequisites are attainable in most computer science BSc degrees.

To study choreographies, we are going to define choreographic languages and then write choreographies as terms of these languages. The syntax of languages is going to be defined using context-free grammars. To give meaning to choreographies, we are going to extensively use Plotkin's structural approach to operational semantics [Plotkin 2004].

The rules defining the semantics of choreographies are going to be rules of inference, borrowing from logical methods and deductive systems in particular. Knowing formal systems based on rules of inference is an advantage, but not a requirement for reading this book: Chapter 1 provides a brief introduction to the essential knowledge on these systems that we need for the rest of the book. The reader familiar with inference systems (including admissible rules) can safely skip the first chapter and jump straight to Chapter 2.

An important aspect of choreographies is determining how they can be executed correctly in concurrent and distributed systems, in terms of independent programs for *processes*. To model process programs, we will borrow techniques from the area of process calculi. We will introduce the necessary notions on process calculi as we go along, so knowing this area is not a requirement for reading this book. The reader familiar with process calculi will recognise that we borrow many ideas from Milner's seminal *Calculus of Communicating Systems* [Milner 1980].

Structure of the Book

This book is structured in three parts, each one consisting of different chapters:

- Part I introduces a minimal language for defining choreographies and the core theory for relating choreographies to compliant systems of processes.
- Part II extends the choreographic language with standard features from the world of computation: memory, choices, and recursion. This allows for modelling more realistic scenarios.
- Part III presents other extensions and variations of the theory which deal with more specific aspects of some concurrent and distributed systems like asynchronous communication. It also provides references to articles for further reading.

Every chapter contains exercises, which the reader is suggested to solve right where they are presented. For the exercises marked with ↪, a solution is given in the Solutions chapter at the end of this book. The reader is invited to try the exercise first and check the solution later: the solution is provided as a baseline for comparison and as a way to get inspiration in case of getting stuck. Some exercises are marked with !, which indicates that they might be more involved.

Online Resources

A web page containing general information, errata, and additional resources is available. At the time of this writing, it is reachable at

https://fabriziomontesi.com/introduction-to-choreographies/.

Part I

Foundations

Introduction to Part I

Part I establishes the foundations for the study of choreographies. The focus is on minimality: the choreographies in this part are simple, but they will suffice to explore all the core components of what a choreography means and how it can be implemented. Simplicity should not be confused with triviality: as we will see, simple choreographies are enough to unravel all the core concepts connected to choreographies and choreography compliance. These concepts are many, and we shall be particularly careful in formulating them as generally as reasonably possible – that is, assuming as little as possible. Aside from such carefulness being general good practice, this will pay off tremendously in the next parts of the book, where we will study additional features that allow for modelling more sophisticated scenarios: these features will build modularly on top of what we establish in this part.

To define the meaning of choreographies and their implementations, we will use the formalism of inference systems, which is presented in Chapter 1. Then, in Chapter 2, we introduce a language for writing choreographies and explore its meaning.

The essence of choreographies is the notion of communication, which is offered as a linguistic construct in our choreographic language. In real systems, communication is obtained by executing programs that perform compatible actions for exchanging data over a shared medium (like send and receive actions over a network channel). The crux of implementing a system that follows a choreography correctly is thus to write process programs that, when executed, will perform their respective actions at the right time such that they enact the choreography together. We present a language for modelling such programs in Chapter 3. As we shall see, writing process programs is not as straightforward as writing choreographies. Mistakes can cause systems to encounter safety issues, like processes trying to use the network in conflicting ways, or liveness issues, like processes getting stuck forever. These issues are both recurring and hard to deal with in the world of concurrency and distribution, but it will turn out that studying how to implement a choreography correctly can help with these problems as well.

Our development will culminate in Chapter 4, where we will present endpoint projection: a mapping from choreographies to process programs given as a recursive function. Endpoint projection reveals the essence of how choreographies can be translated into working implementations. We will prove that endpoint projection is correct in the sense that the process programs that it returns implement exactly the communications prescribed by the input choreography. In other words, endpoint projection guarantees choreography compliance.

Last but not least, we will find that the correctness of endpoint projection has important implications: all systems that consist of code generated by endpoint projection are free from the aforementioned safety and liveness issues. Intuitively, this is because a choreography cannot describe unsafe or stuck systems by design. The syntax of choreographies does not even allow for writing these mistakes. This design feature is a hallmark of the choreographic approach and one of the key aspects that makes theory of choreographies worthy of study.

1 Inference Systems

Before venturing into the study of choreographies, in this chapter we are going to familiarise ourselves with the formalism used throughout this book: *inference systems*. Inference systems are widely used in the fields of formal logic and programming languages, among others [Girard et al. 1989; Buss 1998].

An inference system is a set of *inference rules*. An inference rule has the form

$$\frac{\text{Premise 1} \quad \text{Premise 2} \quad \cdots \quad \text{Premise } n}{\text{Conclusion}} \text{ NAME},$$

which reads 'If all the premises Premise 1, Premise 2, ..., and Premise n hold, then Conclusion holds'. Premise 1, Premise 2, ..., Premise n, and Conclusion are mathematical statements, called *propositions*, and the label NAME is the name of the rule. The horizontal line is a visual aid to separate the premises from the conclusion.

Every inference rule has exactly one conclusion. By contrast, an inference rule can have any number of premises, including none at all. Rules without premises are called *axioms*, and their conclusions always hold.

1.1 Example: Modelling Flight Connections with Inference Rules

1.1.1 Expressing a Connected Graph with Axioms

Let us jump straight into an example and develop our first inference rules. Examine the graph displayed in Figure 1.1, which presents possible flight connections between cities. It is directed and connected. We are going to capture this graph as an inference system and then use the system to answer a few questions, like whether it is possible to fly from a given city to another.[1]

First, we need to establish the forms that propositions can take in rules. A way of expressing the graph in Figure 1.1 is to say that the following propositions hold.

- There is a connection from Odense to Rome.
- There is a connection from Rome to Sydney.
- There is a connection from Sydney to Tokyo.
- There is a connection from Tokyo to New York.
- There is a connection from New York to Rome.

---

[1] This example is inspired by Pfenning's lecture notes on deductive inference, where he uses inference rules to reason about graphs [Pfenning 2012].

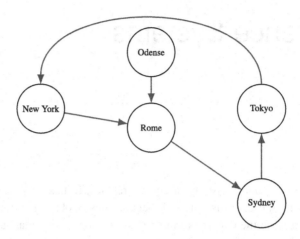

Figure 1.1 A directed graph representing flight connections between some cities.

To save ink, we can abbreviate each proposition of the form 'there is a connection from A to B' to 'conn(A, B)', for any cities A and B. The previous list can therefore be written as:

- conn(Odense, Rome)
- conn(Rome, Sydney)
- conn(Sydney, Tokyo)
- conn(Tokyo, New York)
- conn(New York, Rome).

Now that we know which propositions should hold, we write an axiom for each one of them. The axioms are given next. We name each axiom with the initials of the two cities that it connects.

$$\frac{}{\text{conn(Odense, Rome)}}\ \text{OR} \qquad \frac{}{\text{conn(Rome, Sydney)}}\ \text{RS} \qquad \frac{}{\text{conn(Sydney, Tokyo)}}\ \text{ST}$$

$$\frac{}{\text{conn(Tokyo, New York)}}\ \text{TN} \qquad \frac{}{\text{conn(New York, Rome)}}\ \text{NR}$$

These five axioms capture the structure of the graph in Figure 1.1. In the next section, we shall define rules that tell us how to use this information to deduce new propositions.

1.1.2 Schematic Variables

Consider the problem of checking whether it is possible to fly from one city to another, possibly involving intermediate stops. In graph theory terminology, this is the problem of checking whether there exists a walk between two cities. For example, we can see that there is a walk from Tokyo to New York without going through intermediate stops and that there is a walk from Tokyo to Rome by going through New York. For any two cities A and B, we abbreviate propositions of the form 'there is a walk from A to B' to 'walk(A, B)'. Thus, walk(Tokyo, New York) and walk(Tokyo, Rome) hold.

To capture walks, we could proceed just like we did for direct flight connections. That is, we could define an axiom for each walk-proposition that should hold. If we proceeded in this way, however, the inference system would remain a mere collection of predetermined facts that we

$$\frac{}{\text{conn(Odense, Rome)}} \text{ OR} \qquad \frac{}{\text{conn(Rome, Sydney)}} \text{ RS} \qquad \frac{}{\text{conn(Sydney, Tokyo)}} \text{ ST}$$

$$\frac{}{\text{conn(Tokyo, New York)}} \text{ TN} \qquad \frac{}{\text{conn(New York, Rome)}} \text{ NR}$$

$$\frac{\text{conn}(A, B)}{\text{walk}(A, B)} \text{ DIR} \qquad \frac{\text{walk}(A, B) \quad \text{walk}(B, C)}{\text{walk}(A, C)} \text{ COMP}$$

Figure 1.2 An inference system for flights.

had to figure out by ourselves, working outside of the system. In other words, the system would not help us in deducing new facts, but rather require us to determine all valid facts in advance. What we are going to do instead is to define rules that allow us to *deduce* that a walk exists.

Let **City** be the set of cities that we are considering:

$$\textbf{City} \triangleq \{\text{Odense, Rome, Sydney, Tokyo, New York}\},$$

where the symbol $\triangleq$ stands for 'is defined as'.[2] In the rest of this chapter, we write A, B, and C for variables that range over elements of **City**. That is, A, B, and C carry the assumption that $A, B, C \in$ **City**.

The simplest kind of walk is without intermediate stops. Formally, for any A and B: if there is a direct connection from A to B, then there is a walk from A to B. Equivalently, using our abbreviations: if conn(A, B), then walk(A, B). We can express this elegantly with the following rule, called DIR (for direct connection).

$$\frac{\text{conn}(A, B)}{\text{walk}(A, B)} \text{ DIR}$$

We read rule DIR exactly as 'if conn(A, B), then walk(A, B)'. (The name DIR stands for direct.)

Rule DIR introduces a new ingredient that we have not seen yet in the context of inference rules: rules can have variables. In this case, rule DIR has the variables A and B. Variables in rules are typically called *schematic variables* [Buss 1998].

Rule DIR can be used to deduce walks that consist of one step. Of course, in general walks might consist of multiple steps. To infer those, we can use this intuitive principle of composition: if there is a walk from A to B and there is a walk from B to C, then there is a walk from A to C (that goes through B). That is to say, we can compose a walk from smaller walks. We represent this principle as the following rule (COMP is short for compose).

$$\frac{\text{walk}(A, B) \quad \text{walk}(B, C)}{\text{walk}(A, C)} \text{ COMP}$$

Our axioms for connections and the rules DIR and COMP form a system for deducing walks of any length. The whole system is displayed in Figure 1.2 for reference. In the next section, we explore how systems like this can be used.

---

[2] For our purposes, we might just as well say that **City** is the set of all existing city names, or even the set of all strings. The important assumption is that **City** contains the cities that our inference system talks about. We choose to use the smallest set that respects this assumption for the sake of simplicity.

1.2   Derivations

Inference systems come into action through the concept of *derivation*. A derivation is a formal proof that uses the rules of an inference system to reach a conclusion.

1.2.1   Combining Rules

Suppose that we wanted to answer this question:

Is there a walk from Odense to Rome?

By our notation from Section 1.1, this is equivalent to asking:

Does the proposition walk(Odense, Rome) hold?

Using rule DIR from the inference system in Figure 1.2, we can prove that this is indeed the case under a certain assumption:

1. Assume conn(Odense, Rome).
2. By rule DIR, replacing variable A with Odense and variable B with Rome, we deduce from conn(Odense, Rome) that walk(Odense, Rome).

This proof is a derivation. There is a standard notation to display this kind of proof much more concisely which relies on the notation of inference rules. In this case, we can express the proof as

$$\frac{\text{conn(Odense, Rome)}}{\text{walk(Odense, Rome)}} \text{ DIR}, \tag{1.1}$$

which tells us succinctly how walk(Odense, Rome) can be derived from the assumption conn (Odense, Rome) by invoking rule DIR. We call the invocation of a rule in a derivation a *rule application*. In a rule application, variables of the rule being applied can be instantiated (in this case, A and B are instantiated to Odense and Rome).

Assumptions of a derivation are also called *hypotheses* or *premises*. For example, we might say that the derivation in (1.1) has conn(Odense, Rome) as a hypothesis or premise.

Our proof of walk(Odense, Rome) can be strengthened: it starts by assuming that conn(Odense, Rome), but this assumption can actually be proved by rule OR. Here is a derivation of walk(Odense, Rome) that does not have any assumptions.

1. By rule OR, we have that conn(Odense, Rome).
2. By rule DIR, replacing variable A with Odense and variable B with Rome, we deduce from conn(Odense, Rome) that walk(Odense, Rome).

This derivation combines the rules OR and DIR. Specifically, we have applied rule OR to obtain the premise of DIR (where its variables have been replaced with the appropriate cities) and then applied rule DIR to reach our desired conclusion. We can display this proof in the notation for derivations as follows.

$$\frac{\dfrac{}{\text{conn(Odense, Rome)}} \text{ OR}}{\text{walk(Odense, Rome)}} \text{ DIR} \tag{1.2}$$

The horizontal bar notation for inference rules shows its best when we construct derivations like this: the composition of (applications of) OR and DIR is made visually evident by placing the conclusion of the former as the premise of the latter. This tells us where the premise for the application of DIR comes from.

As usual with mathematical proofs, it is important to point out whether a derivation has assumptions and what they are. The same concern applies when we discuss whether a proposition can be concluded. We say that a proposition is *derivable* from some assumptions if it is the conclusion of a derivation with those assumptions. According to the derivation in (1.1), the proposition walk(Odense, Rome) is derivable from the assumption conn(Odense, Rome). When a proposition is the conclusion of a derivation with no assumptions, we simply say that the proposition is derivable. The derivation in (1.2) shows that the proposition walk(Odense, Rome) is derivable. In the remainder, unless we explicitly point out otherwise, we discuss derivations without assumptions. Since derivations are proofs, we also say that a proposition is *provable* whenever it is derivable.

1.2.2 Derivations As Trees

The derivations that we have seen so far use rules with at most one premise, which made those derivations take the shape of a chain of rule applications. This is just a special case of the general shape of derivations. In general, derivations are trees.

As an example, say that we wanted to derive walk(Odense, Sydney) – meaning we want to find a derivation without assumptions that concludes that proposition. Rule DIR is not sufficient anymore since, if we try to apply it, we get stuck quite early:

$$\frac{\text{conn(Odense, Sydney)}}{\text{walk(Odense, Sydney)}} \text{ DIR}.$$

In this derivation, we are left with the assumption conn(Odense, Sydney), which we have no way of getting rid of because it cannot be derived with any of the rules in Figure 1.2. Rule COMP is more promising: by instantiating its variables A with Odense, B with Rome, and C with Sydney, we get the derivation

$$\frac{\text{walk(Odense, Rome)} \quad \text{walk(Rome, Sydney)}}{\text{walk(Odense, Sydney)}} \text{ COMP},$$

which has walk(Odense, Rome) and walk(Rome, Sydney) as assumptions. These assumptions are easy to solve: for the first, we can just reuse the derivation from (1.2); for the second, we follow the same strategy as for the first but with a different axiom at the end. We obtain the derivation

$$\frac{\dfrac{\overline{\text{conn(Odense, Rome)}} \text{ OR}}{\text{walk(Odense, Rome)}} \text{ DIR} \quad \dfrac{\overline{\text{conn(Rome, Sydney)}} \text{ RS}}{\text{walk(Rome, Sydney)}} \text{ DIR}}{\text{walk(Odense, Sydney)}} \text{ COMP}. \tag{1.3}$$

The derivation in (1.3) can be faithfully represented as a tree where the application of rule COMP is the root. We can depict this by drawing a tree where the premise of each rule application in the derivation has an edge that points to the rule application used to prove that premise, as follows.

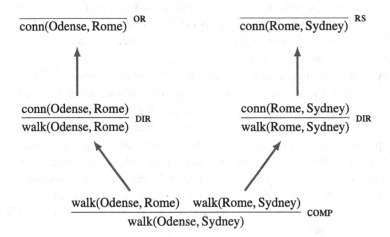

The visual style that we used for derivations until now and the tree-based one just displayed are interchangeable since they represent the same objects. In general, any derivation is a directed rooted tree (a tree with directed edges and a designated root node), where:

- Each rule application in the derivation is a node.
- The root is the rule application at the bottom of the derivation.
- Each edge connects a rule application to another rule application used to prove a premise of the former.

The observation that derivations are trees is useful because we get that standard notions about trees immediately apply to derivations. For instance, we have that:

- The *size* of a derivation $\mathcal{D}$, written size($\mathcal{D}$), is the number of nodes (rule applications) in the derivation.
- The *height* of a derivation, written height($\mathcal{D}$), is the number of nodes that we encounter in the longest path from the root to a leaf.

Furthermore, the observation gives us a sense of direction: we say that a derivation *ends* with its root since it is the step that gives us the conclusion of the derivation.

1.2.3　Searching for Derivations

When working with inference systems, constructing a proof that a proposition holds corresponds to constructing a derivation. The problem of finding a derivation that concludes a given proposition is called *proof search* in the literature.

Inference systems support an elegant method to look for derivations, which works from the bottom up. We start by building the derivation from the conclusion, and then we match the shape of any proposition that we have to prove to restrict the set of possible rules that we have to consider in order to continue.

Say, for example, that we wanted to prove the proposition walk(New York, Tokyo). First of all, we look for rules that could possibly conclude a walk-proposition. The only two rules in Figure 1.2 that can conclude a proposition of this type are DIR and COMP, so we immediately get to know that any derivation of this proposition must necessarily end with (have at the bottom) an application of one of these two rules. This restricts the set of candidate rules to start with from seven down to two, but it does not give us a preference among them: we have to pick one, and if we fail with the one that we choose, we will have to try with the other. We perform these attempts in the next two paragraphs.

Attempt with Rule DIR

We observe that rule DIR is simpler than rule COMP for two reasons. First, it has only one premise while COMP has two. Second, its premise is of the form conn(A, B), which can only be derived by using one of the five axioms, so it will be easy to check out if it holds. Thus, it makes sense to try rule DIR first. We get the derivation

$$\frac{\text{conn(New York, Tokyo)}}{\text{walk(New York, Tokyo)}} \text{ DIR}.$$

To continue in our derivation, we need to find a rule that can conclude conn(New York, Tokyo). Unfortunately, there is no such rule in Figure 1.2, so our attempt at deriving walk(New York, Tokyo) by using rule DIR has failed. (We have already encountered a similar situation in Section 1.2.2, where we wanted to derive walk(Odense, Sydney).)

Attempt with Rule COMP

Since rule DIR cannot help us in starting the search for our derivation, applying rule COMP is the only possibility left. Rule COMP is defined as

$$\frac{\text{walk}(A, B) \quad \text{walk}(B, C)}{\text{walk}(A, C)} \text{ COMP}.$$

Clearly, since we want to conclude walk(New York, Tokyo), we should instantiate A with New York and C with Tokyo. But we have no indication on what we should choose as B. We informally depict the situation as follows, where we write B? for 'we do not know what B should be'.

$$\frac{\text{walk(New York, } B?) \quad \text{walk}(B?, \text{Tokyo})}{\text{walk(New York, Tokyo)}} \text{ COMP}$$

At this point, we could proceed by brute force: try out all possible cities for B and see whether we can complete our derivation. Some cities are more promising than others, though. For example, we can see that deriving a walk from New York to Rome is easy, thanks to the rules NR and DIR. Let us then choose Rome as B. We reach the derivation

$$\frac{\text{walk(New York, Rome)} \quad \text{walk(Rome, Tokyo)}}{\text{walk(New York, Tokyo)}} \text{ COMP}.$$

In other words, we have reduced the problem of deriving walk(New York, Tokyo) to the problems of deriving walk(New York, Rome) and of deriving walk(Rome, Tokyo).

We deal with deriving the first premise by recursively applying our method for proof search: we check which rules could possibly apply, in this case rules DIR and COMP, and then try rule DIR first because it is simpler. By rule DIR we can extend our derivation as follows.

$$\frac{\dfrac{\text{conn(New York, Rome)}}{\text{walk(New York, Rome)}} \text{ DIR} \quad \text{walk(Rome, Tokyo)}}{\text{walk(New York, Tokyo)}} \text{ COMP}.$$

We are left with the task of deriving conn(New York, Rome) in the left branch, which we can do by applying axiom NR:

$$
\cfrac{\cfrac{\quad}{\text{conn(New York, Rome)}}\ \text{NR}}{\text{walk(New York, Rome)}}\ \text{DIR} \qquad \text{walk(Rome, Tokyo)}
$$
$$
\overline{\qquad\qquad\qquad\qquad \text{walk(New York, Tokyo)}\qquad\qquad\qquad\qquad}\ \text{COMP} \quad .
$$

We still have to derive the second premise of our application of rule COMP, walk(Rome, Tokyo). Applying our method to this proposition, we end up again in the case where we need to use rule COMP. Let us choose Sydney as an intermediate city:

$$
\cfrac{\text{conn(New York, Rome)}}{\text{walk(New York, Rome)}}\ \text{DIR} \quad \cfrac{\text{walk(Rome, Sydney)} \quad \text{walk(Sydney, Tokyo)}}{\text{walk(Rome, Tokyo)}}\ \text{COMP}
$$
$$
\overline{\qquad\qquad\qquad\qquad \text{walk(New York, Tokyo)}\qquad\qquad\qquad\qquad}\ \text{COMP} \quad .
$$

Thus, we are left with the task of deriving walk(Rome, Sydney) and walk(Sydney, Tokyo). This is easy since these pairs are connected directly:

$$
(1.4)
$$

The derivation in (1.4) is proof that walk(New York, Tokyo) holds in the inference system in Figure 1.2.

1.2.4 Formal Definition

Definition 1.1 (Derivation)   We formalise the notion that derivations are trees and then present some useful notation. Recall that an inference system is a set of inference rules, and let p range over propositions. Let S be an inference system and $\{p_1, \ldots, p_k\}$ be a set of propositions for some natural number k such that $k \geq 0$. Then a finite directed rooted tree (a finite tree with directed edges and a root) is a derivation in S with hypotheses $p_1, \ldots, p_k$ if, for every node n in the tree:

- n is an application of a rule in S;
- for each premise p in n, either $p \in \{p_1, \ldots, p_k\}$ (p is one of the hypotheses) or there is an edge from n to another node n' such that n' has p as conclusion.

Derivations are ranged over by $\mathcal{D}, \mathcal{E}, \mathcal{F}$. It is often useful to indicate the conclusion of a derivation, so we introduce the notation $\mathcal{D} :: p$ to denote a derivation $\mathcal{D}$ with conclusion p. If there is a derivation $\mathcal{D} :: p$ with hypotheses $p_1, \ldots, p_n$, we say that p can be derived from $p_1, \ldots, p_n$.

Remark 1.2   Extending what we discussed at the end of Section 1.2.1, we adopt the convention that, when we write about derivations and derivable propositions, there are no hypotheses unless they are explicitly shown or discussed.

Example 1.1 Let $\mathcal{D}$ be the derivation in (1.3):

$$\mathcal{D} \triangleq \cfrac{\cfrac{}{\text{conn(Odense, Rome)}} \text{ OR}}{\cfrac{\text{walk(Odense, Rome)}}{}} \text{ DIR} \quad \cfrac{\cfrac{}{\text{conn(Rome, Sydney)}} \text{ RS}}{\text{walk(Rome, Sydney)}} \text{ DIR}}{\text{walk(Odense, Sydney)}} \text{ COMP}.$$

Therefore, we can write $\mathcal{D} :: \text{walk(Odense, Sydney)}$.

Exercise 1.1 Derive walk(New York, Sydney) using the system in Figure 1.2. (Recall that, by Remark 1.2, the derivation cannot have hypotheses.)

Exercise 1.2 Derive walk(Odense, New York) from the hypothesis walk(Odense, Sydney) using the system in Figure 1.2.

Exercise 1.3 ($\hookrightarrow$) In rule applications, different schematic variables can be instantiated with the same value. Derive walk(New York, New York) using the system in Figure 1.2.
   (Hint: In rule COMP, nothing forbids A from being the same as C.)

1.2.5 Subderivations

Just like trees have subtrees, derivations have subderivations. Specifically, for any derivations $\mathcal{D}$ and $\mathcal{D}'$, we say that $\mathcal{D}'$ is a *subderivation* of $\mathcal{D}$ if the sets of nodes and edges of $\mathcal{D}'$ are respectively subsets of the sets of nodes and edges of $\mathcal{D}$.

By definition of subderivation, any derivation $\mathcal{D}$ is a subderivation of itself. Sometimes excluding this case is useful. Given a derivation $\mathcal{D}$, we say that $\mathcal{D}'$ is a *strict subderivation* of $\mathcal{D}$ if the sets of nodes and edges of $\mathcal{D}'$ are respectively strict subsets of the sets of nodes and edges of $\mathcal{D}$.

As an example, let $\mathcal{D}$ be again the derivation of walk(Odense, Sydney) from (1.3):

$$\mathcal{D} \triangleq \cfrac{\cfrac{\cfrac{}{\text{conn(Odense, Rome)}} \text{ OR}}{\text{walk(Odense, Rome)}} \text{ DIR} \quad \cfrac{\cfrac{}{\text{conn(Rome, Sydney)}} \text{ RS}}{\text{walk(Rome, Sydney)}} \text{ DIR}}{\text{walk(Odense, Sydney)}} \text{ COMP}.$$

The following derivations are all (strict) subderivations of $\mathcal{D}$.

$$\mathcal{E} \triangleq \cfrac{\cfrac{}{\text{conn(Odense, Rome)}} \text{ OR}}{\text{walk(Odense, Rome)}} \text{ DIR}$$

$$\mathcal{E}' \triangleq \cfrac{}{\text{conn(Odense, Rome)}} \text{ OR}$$

$$\mathcal{F} \triangleq \cfrac{\cfrac{}{\text{conn(Rome, Sydney)}} \text{ RS}}{\text{walk(Rome, Sydney)}} \text{ DIR}$$

$$\mathcal{F}' \triangleq \cfrac{}{\text{conn(Rome, Sydney)}} \text{ RS}$$

It is often useful to see a derivation as a composition of other derivations. The latter are then subderivations of the former. For example, we can rewrite $\mathcal{D}$ as a derivation that composes $\mathcal{E}$ to prove the left premise walk(Odense, Sydney) for the application of rule COMP. This composition can be expressed concisely using the notation for derivations as follows.

$$\mathcal{D} = \cfrac{\mathcal{E} \qquad \cfrac{\cfrac{\text{conn(Rome, Sydney)}}{} \; \text{RS}}{\text{walk(Rome, Sydney)}} \; \text{DIR}}{\text{walk(Odense, Rome)} \qquad \qquad \qquad \text{walk(Odense, Sydney)}} \; \text{COMP} \qquad (1.5)$$

In (1.5), the writing $\overset{\mathcal{E}}{\text{walk(Odense, Rome)}}$ is used to denote that we have 'plugged in' the derivation $\mathcal{E}$ to prove the premise walk(Odense, Rome) for the application of rule COMP. We graphically represent this operation in (1.6).

$$\mathcal{D} = \qquad$$

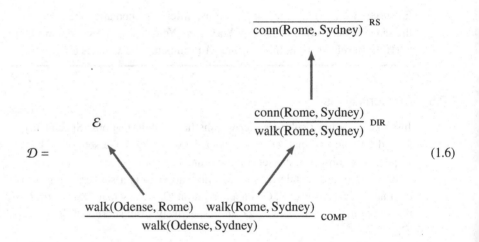

$$(1.6)$$

All the derivations shown next are equal to $\mathcal{D}$.

$$\mathcal{D} = \cfrac{\overset{\mathcal{E}}{\text{walk(Odense, Rome)}} \qquad \overset{\mathcal{F}}{\text{walk(Rome, Sydney)}}}{\text{walk(Odense, Sydney)}} \; \text{COMP}$$

$$\mathcal{D} = \cfrac{\cfrac{\overset{\mathcal{E}'}{\text{conn(Odense, Rome)}}}{\text{walk(Odense, Rome)}} \; \text{DIR} \qquad \cfrac{\cfrac{\text{conn(Rome, Sydney)}}{} \; \text{RS}}{\text{walk(Rome, Sydney)}} \; \text{DIR}}{\text{walk(Odense, Sydney)}} \; \text{COMP}$$

$$\mathcal{D} = \cfrac{\cfrac{\overset{\mathcal{E}'}{\text{conn(Odense, Rome)}}}{\text{walk(Odense, Rome)}} \; \text{DIR} \qquad \overset{\mathcal{F}}{\text{walk(Rome, Sydney)}}}{\text{walk(Odense, Sydney)}} \; \text{COMP}$$

$$\frac{}{\text{conn(Odense, Rome)}}\ \text{OR} \qquad \frac{}{\text{conn(Rome, Sydney)}}\ \text{RS}$$

$$\frac{}{\text{conn(New York, Rome)}}\ \text{NR} \qquad \frac{}{\text{conn(Tokyo, New York)}}\ \text{TN} \qquad \frac{}{\text{conn(Sydney, Tokyo)}}\ \text{ST}$$

$$\frac{\text{conn}(A, B)}{\text{conn}(B, A)}\ \text{SYM} \qquad \frac{\text{conn}(A, B)}{\text{walk}(A, B)}\ \text{DIR} \qquad \frac{\text{walk}(A, B) \quad \text{walk}(B, C)}{\text{walk}(A, C)}\ \text{COMP}$$

Figure 1.3 An inference system for flights with symmetric connections.

Likewise, we can decompose $\mathcal{E}$ and $\mathcal{F}$ as follows.

$$\mathcal{E} = \frac{\dfrac{}{\text{conn(Odense, Rome)}}\ \text{OR}}{\text{walk(Odense, Rome)}}\ \text{DIR} = \frac{\dfrac{\mathcal{E}'}{\text{conn(Odense, Rome)}}}{\text{walk(Odense, Rome)}}\ \text{DIR}$$

$$\mathcal{F} = \frac{\dfrac{}{\text{conn(Rome, Odense)}}\ \text{OR}}{\text{walk(Rome, Odense)}}\ \text{DIR} = \frac{\dfrac{\mathcal{F}'}{\text{conn(Rome, Odense)}}}{\text{walk(Rome, Odense)}}\ \text{DIR}$$

When there is an edge from the root of a derivation to another (sub)derivation, we say that the latter is an *immediate subderivation* of the former. For example, $\mathcal{E}$ and $\mathcal{F}$ are immediate subderivations of $\mathcal{D}$, $\mathcal{E}'$ is an immediate subderivation of $\mathcal{E}$, and $\mathcal{F}'$ is an immediate subderivation of $\mathcal{F}$.

Exercise 1.4 Consider the system in Figure 1.3. Compared to the system in Figure 1.2, this system includes the additional rule SYM. Given a connection, the rule concludes a connection in the opposite direction. Intuitively, this means that the graph of connections is undirected in this system: flight connections go both ways.

Derive walk(Odense, Odense).

Exercise 1.5 Show that, for any $A \in$ **City**, the proposition $\text{walk}(A, A)$ is derivable in the system in Figure 1.3.

1.2.6 Derivations and Induction

Derivations play well with the principle of induction, which comes in handy when proving properties about an inference system. As trees, derivations have a clear recursive structure: a derivation can be either an application of an axiom or a composition of (sub)derivations. Inference rules can be seen as operators for constructing derivations. Graphically speaking (for derivations with no hypotheses):

- The application of an axiom, say AXIOM, with conclusion p is a derivation that consists of a single node:

$$\frac{}{p}\ \text{AXIOM}.$$

$$\frac{}{\text{conn(Odense, Rome)}} \text{ OR} \qquad \frac{}{\text{conn(Rome, Sydney)}} \text{ RS}$$

$$\frac{}{\text{conn(New York, Rome)}} \text{ NR} \qquad \frac{}{\text{conn(Tokyo, New York)}} \text{ TN} \qquad \frac{}{\text{conn(Sydney, Tokyo)}} \text{ ST}$$

$$\frac{\text{conn}(A, B)}{\text{walk}(A, B, 1)} \text{ DIR-W} \qquad \frac{\text{walk}(A, B, n) \quad \text{walk}(B, C, m)}{\text{walk}(A, C, n + m)} \text{ COMP-W}$$

Figure 1.4 An inference system for weighted flight walks.

- Let $\mathcal{D}_1, \ldots, \mathcal{D}_n$ be derivations that respectively conclude $p_1, \ldots, p_n$. We can compose these derivations in a larger derivation by applying a rule, say RULE, that has $p_1, \ldots, p_n$ as premises:

$$\frac{\begin{array}{ccc} \mathcal{D}_1 & & \mathcal{D}_n \\ p_1 & \cdots & p_n \end{array}}{p} \text{ RULE}.$$

For example, suppose that we had two derivations $\mathcal{D} :: \text{walk(Odense, Rome)}$ and $\mathcal{E} :: \text{walk(Rome, Sydney)}$ in the system in Figure 1.2. We can apply rule COMP in Figure 1.2 to compose these derivations into a new derivation that contains them:

$$\frac{\begin{array}{cc} \mathcal{D} & \mathcal{E} \\ \text{walk(Odense, Rome)} & \text{walk(Rome, Sydney)} \end{array}}{\text{walk(Odense, Rome)}} \text{ COMP}.$$

To exemplify the usage of these principles, we introduce the system in Figure 1.4, which replaces rules DIR and COMP from the system in Figure 1.2 with the variations DIR-W and COMP-W. The rules DIR-W and COMP-W act like their originals with the extra feature that they measure the length of walks: walks are weighted with each connection having weight 1. A proposition $\text{walk}(A, B, n)$ means that it is possible to walk from A to B by going through exactly n direct connections, where n is a natural number. In rule DIR-W, from the premise that there is a connection from A to B, we deduce that there is a walk of length 1 from A to B. In rule COMP-W, from the premises that there is a walk from A to B of length n and that there is a walk from B to C of length m, we conclude that there is a walk from A to C of length $n + m$.

Example 1.2 The following derivation revisits the derivation in (1.3) of a path from Odense to Sydney in the system in Figure 1.4.

$$\frac{\dfrac{}{\text{conn(Odense, Rome)}} \text{ OR}}{\dfrac{\text{walk(Odense, Rome, 1)}}{} \text{ DIR-W}} \qquad \frac{\dfrac{}{\text{conn(Rome, Sydney)}} \text{ RS}}{\dfrac{\text{walk(Rome, Sydney, 1)}}{} \text{ DIR}}$$
$$\frac{}{\text{walk(Odense, Sydney, 2)}} \text{ COMP-W}$$

The walk-propositions that we can derive with the system in Figure 1.4 are more informative than the walk-propositions that we can derive with the system in Figure 1.2, since they add the length information. However, intuitively, any walk has a length even if it is not explicitly indicated: for any walk between two cities derived using the rules in Figure 1.2, there should be a length such that we can derive a walk between the same cities using the rules in Figure 1.4. Let us state this formally:

Proposition 1.3   Let $\mathcal{D}$ be a derivation in the system in Figure 1.2. For any $A, B \in$ **City**:

1. If $\mathcal{D}$ concludes conn(A, B), then there exists a derivation $\mathcal{E} :: $ conn(A, B) in the system in Figure 1.4.
2. If $\mathcal{D}$ concludes walk(A, B), then there exist a natural number n and a derivation $\mathcal{E} :: $ walk (A, B, n) in the system in Figure 1.4.

Proposition 1.3 can be proved by induction. Since derivations are recursively defined trees built by composing (smaller) derivations with rule applications, there are different options regarding how we could proceed by induction. These include the size, height, or structure of the derivation. We take the opportunity to refresh memory on proofs by induction and, at the same time, exemplify the related techniques in the setting of inference systems. In particular, we show two proofs: one based on size and one based on structure. We use *strong induction* in the former and *structural induction* in the latter.[3] The two techniques give us different induction hypotheses for the induction steps, which we spell out explicitly. (An overview of the induction principles used in this book can be found in Rosen & Krithivasan [2012].)

Proof of Proposition 1.3 (by induction on the size of $\mathcal{D}$)   We proceed by strong induction on the size of $\mathcal{D}$. The base case is therefore when $\mathcal{D}$ has size 1 (the smallest possible). The case in which $\mathcal{D}$ has greater size is the induction step. In that case, strong induction gives us as an induction hypothesis that Proposition 1.3 holds for all smaller derivations.

We have the following cases.

Case 1 (Base Case) $\mathcal{D}$ has size 1. The only way to construct a derivation of size 1 is to apply one of the axioms. Therefore, $\mathcal{D}$ is an application of an axiom and concludes a proposition conn(A, B) for some A and B. Since the systems in Figures 1.2 and 1.4 have the same axioms, the derivation $\mathcal{D}$ is also a derivation in the system in Figure 1.4. Thus, the thesis follows by setting $\mathcal{E}$ to be $\mathcal{D}$: $\mathcal{E} \triangleq \mathcal{D}$.

Case 2 (Induction Step) $\mathcal{D}$ has size $k + 1$, for $k \geq 1$. By strong induction, the induction hypothesis is that the statement of Proposition 1.3 holds for all derivations of size less than k (all derivations smaller than $\mathcal{D}$).

We now proceed by cases on which rule is applied at the end of $\mathcal{D}$ – that is, the rule applied in the root of $\mathcal{D}$. Since $\mathcal{D}$ has size greater than 1, it must end with either an application of rule DIR or rule COMP. We get the following (sub)cases.

Case 2.1 $\mathcal{D}$ ends with an application of DIR:

$$\mathcal{D} = \frac{\dfrac{\mathcal{D}'}{\text{conn}(A, B)}}{\text{walk}(A, B)} \text{ DIR}$$

for some $\mathcal{D}'$. Observe that size$(\mathcal{D}') = k$, since $\mathcal{D}$ consists exactly of $\mathcal{D}'$ and an application of rule DIR. Thus, by induction hypothesis, we have that there exists $\mathcal{E}'$ such that $\mathcal{E}' :: $ conn(A, B) in the system in Figure 1.4. The thesis now follows by rule DIR-w for $n \triangleq 1$:

$$\mathcal{E} \triangleq \frac{\dfrac{\mathcal{E}'}{\text{conn}(A, B)}}{\text{walk}(A, B, 1)} \text{ DIR-w} \quad .$$

---

[3] Strong induction is also called complete induction in the literature.

Case 2.2 $\mathcal{D}$ ends with an application of COMP:

$$\mathcal{D} = \frac{\overset{\mathcal{D}'}{\text{walk}(A,C)} \quad \overset{\mathcal{D}''}{\text{walk}(C,B)}}{\text{walk}(A,B)} \;\text{COMP}$$

for some $\mathcal{D}'$, $\mathcal{D}''$, and C. Similarly to the previous case, observe that $\mathcal{D}'$ and $\mathcal{D}''$ are strictly smaller than $\mathcal{D}$. Thus, by induction hypothesis, we have that:

- There exist i and $\mathcal{E}'$ :: walk(A,C,i) in the system in Figure 1.4.
- There exist j and $\mathcal{E}''$ :: walk(C,B,j) in the system in Figure 1.4.

The thesis now follows by rule COMP-W for $n \triangleq i + j$:

$$\mathcal{E} \triangleq \frac{\overset{\mathcal{E}'}{\text{walk}(A,C,i)} \quad \overset{\mathcal{E}''}{\text{walk}(C,B,j)}}{\text{walk}(A,B,i+j)} \;\text{COMP-W} \qquad \qquad \square$$

Reasoning on the size of $\mathcal{D}$ gave us nested subcases for each rule that can be applied to build a derivation of that size. This is an indication that dealing directly with the structure of the derivation might yield a simpler proof (without case nesting). Let us see what happens if we revisit the proof by using structural induction on the derivation of interest.

Proof of Proposition 1.3 (by induction on the structure of $\mathcal{D}$)   By induction on the structure of $\mathcal{D}$, we have a case for each possible way in which $\mathcal{D}$ can be constructed.

Applications of axioms are base cases. We treat all of them as a single case: they are all solved in the same way.

Applications of inference rules that compose subderivations are inductive steps. In these cases, the induction hypothesis is that the statement of Proposition 1.3 holds for all the subderivations being composed (all the immediate subderivations of $\mathcal{D}$).

Case 1 $\mathcal{D}$ is an application of an axiom. Since the systems in Figures 1.2 and 1.4 have the same axioms, the thesis follows by $\mathcal{E} \triangleq \mathcal{D}$ (the derivation $\mathcal{D}$ is also a derivation in the system in Figure 1.4).

Case 2 $\mathcal{D}$ ends with an application of rule DIR. That is,

$$\mathcal{D} = \frac{\overset{\mathcal{D}'}{\text{conn}(A,B)}}{\text{walk}(A,B)} \;\text{DIR}$$

for some $\mathcal{D}'$.

By induction hypothesis we have that there exists conn(A,B) :: $\mathcal{E}'$ in the system in Figure 1.4. The thesis follows by rule DIR-W for $n \triangleq 1$:

$$\mathcal{E} \triangleq \frac{\overset{\mathcal{E}'}{\text{conn}(A,B)}}{\text{walk}(A,B,1)} \;\text{DIR-W.}$$

Case 3 $\mathcal{D}$ ends with an application of rule COMP. That is,

$$\mathcal{D} = \frac{\overset{\mathcal{D}'}{\text{walk}(A,C)} \quad \overset{\mathcal{D}''}{\text{walk}(C,B)}}{\text{walk}(A,B)} \;\text{COMP}$$

for some $\mathcal{D}'$, $\mathcal{D}''$, and C. By induction hypothesis on the subderivations $\mathcal{D}'$ and $\mathcal{D}''$, we get that:

- There exist i and $\mathcal{E}'$ :: walk(A, C, i) in the system in Figure 1.4.
- There exist j and $\mathcal{E}''$ :: walk(C, B, j) in the system in Figure 1.4.

The thesis now follows by rule COMP-W for $n \triangleq i + j$:

$$\mathcal{E} \triangleq \dfrac{\overset{\mathcal{E}'}{\text{walk}(A, C, i)} \quad \overset{\mathcal{E}''}{\text{walk}(C, B, j)}}{\text{walk}(A, B, i + j)} \text{ COMP-W} \qquad \square$$

One might argue that the second proof is slightly more elegant for the following reasons.

- The second proof is more direct: it does not present the case nesting of the first proof. Induction on the structure of the derivation immediately puts us on the right track, giving us cases depending on how the derivation ends. In the inductive step of the first proof, we had to observe by ourselves that we could proceed by subcases on the last applied rule.
- The second proof is also more minimalistic: it uses a weaker induction hypothesis, which applies only to the immediate subderivations of $\mathcal{D}$ instead of all smaller derivations (as in the first proof).

Nevertheless, the two proofs of Proposition 1.3 are very similar. Other possibilities include using the height of derivations or the principle of *mathematical induction*. The reader is invited to check this in the next exercise.

Exercise 1.6 Prove Proposition 1.3 by strong induction on the height of $\mathcal{D}$. Then try to prove it again by using mathematical induction instead of strong induction. That is, the induction hypothesis in the inductive step should be that the statement of the proposition holds for all derivations of height precisely height$(\mathcal{D}) - 1$ (all derivations one step shorter than $\mathcal{D}$). Does the proof get easier or harder?

Exercise 1.7 ($\hookrightarrow$) Prove that the system in Figure 1.4 calculates weights faithfully, meaning that, for any A, B, n, and derivation $\mathcal{D}$ in the system in Figure 1.4, if $\mathcal{D}$ concludes walk(A, B, n) then $\mathcal{D}$ contains exactly n applications of axioms (or, equivalently, $\mathcal{D}$ has exactly n leaves).

(Hint: it might be helpful to prove the statement for $n = 1$ first and then use this result in the proof for any n.)

Remark 1.4 In the remainder, we invoke induction by stating that we proceed by induction on a natural number or a structure. In the former case, we are implicitly referring to mathematical or strong induction (depending on what induction hypothesis is used in the proof). In the latter case, we are implicitly referring to structural induction.

1.3   Underivable Propositions

To ascertain that a proposition holds in an inference system, we can simply derive it. Checking that the derivation is correct is a mechanical exercise: we have to check that each node of the derivation is an application of a rule in the inference system under consideration. This method serves the purpose of showing that a proposition holds. In this section, we discuss the dual problem: proving that a proposition certainly *does not* hold.

Proving that a proposition does not hold in an inference system is done by showing that the proposition is *underivable* – that is, it cannot be derived. How can we prove that a proposition cannot be derived, exactly? This can be tricky because it requires reasoning about all the possible derivations that could potentially conclude the proposition of interest and showing that none of those derivations can actually be built.

Let us consider a simple example first: showing that conn(Odense, New York) cannot be derived in the system in Figure 1.2. This is easy by case exhaustion. We observe that any derivation concluding a proposition of that shape must consist of an application of one of the axioms, and the only axiom that can conclude a conn-proposition with Odense in the first position is OR. However, OR, our only possibility, concludes conn(Odense, Rome). Hence, conn(Odense, New York) cannot be derived.

A more interesting exercise is showing that conn(Odense, New York) cannot be derived in the system in Figure 1.3. The problem is that rule SYM can make our search for possible derivations go on indefinitely. First, we observe that the only rules in Figure 1.3 that can have a conclusion of the form conn(A, B) are the axioms and rule SYM. None of the axioms can be applied for A = Odense and B = New York, as in our case. Thus, any derivation $\mathcal{D}$ of conn(Odense, New York) would necessarily have to be structured as follows, for some $\mathcal{D}'$.

$$\mathcal{D} = \frac{\overset{\mathcal{D}'}{\text{conn(New York, Odense)}}}{\text{conn(Odense, New York)}} \text{ SYM}$$

The question now is whether $\mathcal{D}'$ :: conn(New York, Odense) actually exists. Again we end up observing that the only possible way for $\mathcal{D}'$ to end is with an application of rule SYM, so the derivation $\mathcal{D}$ necessarily has the following form, for some $\mathcal{D}''$.

$$\mathcal{D} = \frac{\dfrac{\overset{\mathcal{D}''}{\text{conn(Odense, New York)}}}{\text{conn(New York, Odense)}} \text{ SYM}}{\text{conn(Odense, New York)}} \text{ SYM}$$

We got back to where we started from: to show that no $\mathcal{D}$ like this exists, we have to prove that conn(Odense, New York) is *underivable* – that is, there is no $\mathcal{D}''$ that concludes conn(Odense, New York). The derivation $\mathcal{D}''$ can be expanded just like we did for $\mathcal{D}$, so by proceeding like this we would never finish our proof:

$$\mathcal{D} = \frac{\dfrac{\dfrac{\dfrac{\dfrac{\vdots}{\text{conn(Odense, New York)}} \text{ SYM}}{\text{conn(New York, Odense)}} \text{ SYM.}}{\text{conn(Odense, New York)}} \text{ SYM}}{\text{conn(New York, Odense)}} \text{ SYM}}{\text{conn(Odense, New York)}}$$

However, we can build a proof by contradiction based on the size of derivations.

Proposition 1.5   There exists no derivation $\mathcal{D}$ of conn(Odense, New York) in the system in Figure 1.3.

Proof   We proceed by contradiction: we assume that conn(Odense, New York) is derivable and then show that this assumption leads to a contradiction.

$$\frac{}{\text{conn(Odense, Rome)}} \text{ OR} \qquad \frac{}{\text{conn(Rome, Sydney)}} \text{ RS}$$

$$\frac{}{\text{conn(Tokyo, New York)}} \text{ TN} \qquad \frac{}{\text{conn(Sydney, Tokyo)}} \text{ ST}$$

$$\frac{\text{conn}(A, B)}{\text{conn}(B, A)} \text{ SYM} \qquad \frac{\text{conn}(A, B)}{\text{walk}(A, B, 1)} \text{ DIR-W} \qquad \frac{\text{walk}(A, B, n) \quad \text{walk}(B, C, m)}{\text{walk}(A, C, n + m)} \text{ COMP-W}$$

Figure 1.5 An inference system for weighted flight walks, with symmetry but without a connection from New York to Rome.

Assume that conn(Odense, New York) is derivable. This means that there are some derivations (at least one) that conclude it. Since all derivations are finite, among these derivations there must be at least one derivation M that is minimal, meaning that no other derivation of conn(Odense, New York) is strictly smaller than M.

We now prove that M actually cannot exist – hence, there cannot be any derivation of conn(Odense, New York) at all.

Since conn(Odense, New York) cannot be concluded with any other rule than SYM, it must be the case that:

$$M = \frac{\begin{array}{c} M' \\ \hline \text{conn(New York, Odense)} \end{array}}{\text{conn(Odense, New York)}} \text{ SYM}$$

for some M'. By similar reasoning, it must be that M' ends with an application of SYM, so we get:

$$M = \frac{\dfrac{\begin{array}{c} M'' \\ \hline \text{conn(Odense, New York)} \end{array}}{\text{conn(New York, Odense)}} \text{ SYM}}{\text{conn(Odense, New York)}} \text{ SYM}$$

for some M''. Observe that M'' is a strict subderivation of M, so size(M'') < size(M). This contradicts that M is a minimal proof, so M cannot exist. □

Exercise 1.8 ($\hookrightarrow$)   Show that there is no biggest derivation of walk(New York, New York) in the system in Figure 1.2. In other words, show that for any derivation $\mathcal{D}$ :: walk(New York, New York), there exists another derivation $\mathcal{E}$ :: walk(New York, New York) such that size($\mathcal{E}$) > size($\mathcal{D}$).

(Hint: proceed by showing that given any derivation $\mathcal{D}$ :: walk(New York, New York), there exists a bigger derivation that has $\mathcal{D}$ as strict subderivation.)

Exercise 1.9   Consider the system in Figure 1.5. Compared to the system in Figure 1.4, we added rule SYM and removed the connection from New York to Rome. Prove that it is not possible to derive walk(New York, Rome, 1) in this system.

Exercise 1.10   Prove that walk(Tokyo, Odense, 2) is underivable in the system in Figure 1.5.

$$\frac{}{\text{conn(Odense, Rome)}} \text{ OR} \qquad \frac{}{\text{conn(Rome, Sydney)}} \text{ RS}$$

$$\frac{}{\text{conn(New York, Rome)}} \text{ NR} \qquad \frac{}{\text{conn(Tokyo, New York)}} \text{ TN} \qquad \frac{}{\text{conn(Sydney, Tokyo)}} \text{ ST}$$

$$\frac{\text{conn}(A, B)}{\text{walk}(A, B)} \text{ DIR} \qquad \frac{\text{conn}(A, B) \quad \text{walk}(B, C)}{\text{walk}(A, C)} \text{ STEP}$$

Figure 1.6 An alternative inference system for flights.

1.4   Admissible and Derivable Rules

Consider the inference system in Figure 1.6. It is like the system in Figure 1.2, but rule COMP is replaced by rule STEP. The rules COMP and STEP differ only in their first premise: rule COMP requires a walk from A to B, whereas rule STEP requires a direct connection from A to B.

Rule STEP changes the way in which we search for and build derivations: walks are searched by identifying the starting connection (first premise) and then recursively looking for the rest of the walk (second premise). By contrast, with rule COMP, we arbitrarily 'split' the walk that we are trying to find into two subwalks that we then recursively look for (first and second premises); whether the first walk consists of one or many connections is entirely up to us.

In a sense, rule STEP is more efficient than rule COMP because it saves us from applying the last connection in a walk. Recall the derivation in Equation 1.3:

$$\frac{\dfrac{}{\text{conn(Odense, Rome)}} \text{ OR}}{\text{walk(Odense, Rome)}} \text{ DIR} \quad \frac{\dfrac{}{\text{conn(Rome, Sydney)}} \text{ RS}}{\text{walk(Rome, Sydney)}} \text{ DIR}}{\text{walk(Odense, Sydney)}} \text{ COMP} \qquad (1.7)$$

With rule STEP, we can derive the same walk with a smaller derivation:

$$\frac{\dfrac{}{\text{conn(Odense, Rome)}} \text{ OR} \quad \dfrac{\dfrac{}{\text{conn(Rome, Sydney)}} \text{ RS}}{\text{walk(Rome, Sydney)}} \text{ DIR}}{\text{walk(Odense, Sydney)}} \text{ STEP} \qquad (1.8)$$

Can we then say that rule STEP is better than rule COMP? Not really, because rule COMP has its own big advantage: it gives us a modular way of composing walks. This allows us to reuse derivations of walks that we have made in the past. For example, say that there exist $\mathcal{D}$ :: walk(Odense, Sydney) and $\mathcal{E}$ :: walk(Sydney, Tokyo). (We actually know this by (1.7) and a subderivation in (1.4), respectively.) By rule COMP, we can immediately conclude walk(Odense, Tokyo). Notice that, in order to do this, we do not need to know anything more about $\mathcal{D}$ and $\mathcal{E}$ than their conclusions. By contrast, rule STEP would not be directly applicable in this situation and would force us to find a derivation of walk(Odense, Tokyo).

Given the differences between the rules COMP and STEP, it is interesting to ask whether they affect the power of the inference system in terms of derivability:

- If we added rule STEP to the system in Figure 1.2, could we derive anything new?
- Vice versa, if we added rule COMP to the system in Figure 1.6, could we derive anything new?

The next two subsections are dedicated to answering these questions. It will turn out that the answer to both of them is, in fact, no. Rule STEP would be redundant in the system that has rule

COMP, and vice versa. The two systems in Figures 1.2 and 1.6 can derive exactly the same set of propositions – those that can be derived by a system with both rule STEP and rule COMP.

There is a technical name for inference rules that are redundant with respect to derivability: admissible rules. We write that an inference rule, say

$$\frac{p_1 \cdots p_n}{p} \text{ RULE},$$

is *admissible* if its conclusion p is derivable whenever its premises $p_1, \ldots, p_n$ are derivable in the inference system of interest. In other words: if there exist derivations of $p_1, \ldots, p_n$, then there exists a derivation of p. Whenever this holds, we also say that the system *admits* the rule. We use a dashed line to distinguish rules that we know to be admissible.

We now proceed to proving that rule STEP is admissible in the system with rule COMP (Section 1.4.1), and vice versa (Section 1.4.2).

1.4.1 Derivable Rules

To prove that rule STEP is admissible in the system in Figure 1.2, we show that it is a *derivable rule* in that system. A derivable rule is a special instance of an admissible rule: all derivable rules are admissible, but not vice versa.

We say that an inference rule, say

$$\frac{p_1 \cdots p_n}{p} \text{ RULE},$$

is derivable if there is a derivation of p with hypotheses $p_1, \ldots, p_n$ using the other rules in the system of reference. This implies that the rule is admissible: once derivations of $p_1, \ldots, p_n$ are given, the derivation of the rule can be used to reach the conclusion p (we are going to exemplify this reasoning for rule STEP). Here in particular, we are interested in showing that given the premises of rule STEP as hypotheses, we can always build a derivation of the conclusion of rule STEP using the rules in Figure 1.2.

Proposition 1.6 The rule

$$\frac{\text{conn}(A, B) \quad \text{walk}(B, C)}{\text{walk}(A, C)} \text{ STEP}$$

is derivable in the system in Figure 1.2.

Proof We apply the rules DIR and COMP to obtain a derivation of walk(A, C) from the hypotheses conn(A, B) and walk(B, C):

$$\frac{\dfrac{\text{conn}(A, B)}{\text{walk}(A, B)} \text{ DIR} \quad \text{walk}(B, C)}{\text{walk}(A, C)} \text{ COMP} . \tag{1.9}$$

□

The derivation in (1.9) justifies that rule STEP is admissible. Given any two derivations $\mathcal{D} ::$ conn(A, B) and $\mathcal{E} ::$ walk(B, C) where $A, B, C \in$ **City**, then walk(A, C) is derivable because of the following derivation:

$$\frac{\dfrac{\begin{array}{c} \mathcal{D} \\ \text{conn}(A, B) \end{array}}{\text{walk}(A, B)} \text{ DIR} \quad \begin{array}{c} \mathcal{E} \\ \text{walk}(B, C) \end{array}}{\text{walk}(A, C)} \text{ COMP} .$$

Derivable rules enjoy the property that they are stable under extension of the inference system. In the case of rule STEP: if we added more rules to the system in Figure 1.2, rule STEP would remain derivable because its proof of derivability depends only on the presence of rules DIR and COMP.

Another important property of derivable rules is that their applications can be modularly replaced with the derivation used to prove that the rule is derivable, instantiating variables appropriately. By modularly here, we mean that the derivations used to prove the premises of the derivable rule are left untouched. For example, we can define the following transformation based on the derivation in (1.9) ($\to$ here means 'is rewritten to').

$$
\cfrac{\overset{\mathcal{D}}{\text{conn}(A,B)} \quad \overset{\mathcal{E}}{\text{walk}(B,C)}}{\text{walk}(A,C)}\ \text{STEP} \quad \to \quad \cfrac{\cfrac{\overset{\mathcal{D}}{\text{conn}(A,B)}}{\text{walk}(A,B)}\ \text{DIR} \quad \overset{\mathcal{E}}{\text{walk}(B,C)}}{\text{walk}(A,C)}\ \text{COMP} \tag{1.10}
$$

Consider now this derivation of a multi-hop flight from Odense to Tokyo:

$$
\cfrac{\cfrac{}{\text{conn}(\text{Odense, Rome})}\ \text{OR} \quad \cfrac{\cfrac{}{\text{conn}(\text{Rome, Sydney})}\ \text{RS} \quad \cfrac{\cfrac{}{\text{conn}(\text{Sydney, Tokyo})}\ \text{RS}}{\text{walk}(\text{Sydney, Tokyo})}\ \text{DIR}}{\text{walk}(\text{Rome, Tokyo})}\ \text{STEP}}{\text{walk}(\text{Odense, Tokyo})}\ \text{STEP} \quad .
$$

To translate this derivation into a derivation in the system in Figure 1.2, we can just rewrite each application of rule STEP as indicated by (1.10). Since the transformation does not affect the rest of the derivation, the order in which we pick and rewrite these applications does not matter – in fact, we could rewrite all of them simultaneously. For instance, here is the result of replacing the top-right occurrence of STEP first:

$$
\cfrac{\cfrac{}{\text{conn}(\text{Odense, Rome})}\ \text{OR} \quad \cfrac{\cfrac{\cfrac{}{\text{conn}(\text{Rome, Sydney})}\ \text{RS}}{\text{walk}(\text{Rome, Sydney})}\ \text{DIR} \quad \cfrac{\cfrac{}{\text{conn}(\text{Sydney, Tokyo})}\ \text{ST}}{\text{walk}(\text{Sydney, Tokyo})}\ \text{DIR}}{\text{walk}(\text{Rome, Tokyo})}\ \text{COMP}}{\text{walk}(\text{Odense, Tokyo})}\ \text{STEP} \quad .
$$

And here is the result of replacing also the occurrence at the bottom of the derivation:

$$
\cfrac{\cfrac{\cfrac{}{\text{conn}(\text{Odense, Rome})}\ \text{OR}}{\text{walk}(\text{Odense, Rome})}\ \text{DIR} \quad \cfrac{\cfrac{\cfrac{}{\text{conn}(\text{Rome, Sydney})}\ \text{RS}}{\text{walk}(\text{Rome, Sydney})}\ \text{DIR} \quad \cfrac{\cfrac{}{\text{conn}(\text{Sydney, Tokyo})}\ \text{ST}}{\text{walk}(\text{Sydney, Tokyo})}\ \text{DIR}}{\text{walk}(\text{Rome, Tokyo})}\ \text{COMP}}{\text{walk}(\text{Odense, Tokyo})}\ \text{COMP} \tag{1.11}
$$

The derivation in (1.11) is valid in the system in Figure 1.2.

Exercise 1.11 Prove that the rule

$$
\cfrac{}{\text{walk}(\text{Sydney, New York})}\ \text{SN}
$$

is derivable in the system in Figure 1.6.

Exercise 1.12 Prove that the rule

$$\frac{\text{walk}(A, B) \quad \text{conn}(B, C)}{\text{walk}(A, C)} \quad \text{STEP-ALT}$$

is derivable in the system in Figure 1.2.

Exercise 1.13 Prove that the rule

$$\frac{\text{walk}(A, B) \quad \text{walk}(B, C) \quad \text{walk}(C, D)}{\text{walk}(A, D)} \quad \text{COMP-ALT}$$

is derivable in the system in Figure 1.2.

1.4.2 Admissible Rules

We now move to proving that rule COMP is admissible in the system with rule STEP.

Recall the definition of rule COMP:

$$\frac{\text{walk}(A, B) \quad \text{walk}(B, C)}{\text{walk}(A, C)} \quad \text{COMP} .$$

As a first attempt, we can try the same strategy that we followed in Section 1.4.1: proving that rule COMP is derivable, by deriving the conclusion walk(A, C) from the hypotheses walk(A, B) and walk(B, C) using the rules in Figure 1.6. Unfortunately, we reach a dead end pretty quickly. The only way to build a path with multiple connections is by using rule STEP, which requires a conn-proposition as premise. But our only available hypotheses are walk-propositions, and we have no rule that allows us to conclude a conn-proposition from a walk-proposition.

We resort to a different proof technique whereby we use induction to reason about all the possible ways in which the premises of rule COMP might have been derived.

Proposition 1.7 The rule

$$\frac{\text{walk}(A, B) \quad \text{walk}(B, C)}{\text{walk}(A, C)} \quad \text{COMP}$$

is admissible in the system in Figure 1.6.

Proof Let $\mathcal{D}$ and $\mathcal{E}$ be, respectively, the derivations in the system in Figure 1.6 of the two premises walk(A, B) and walk(B, C). We have to prove that there exists a derivation $\mathcal{F} :: \text{walk}(A, C)$ in the same system.

We proceed by induction on the structure of $\mathcal{D}$. Since $\mathcal{D}$ concludes a walk-proposition, it can end with either an application of rule DIR or an application of rule STEP.

Case 1 $\mathcal{D}$ ends with an application of rule DIR:

$$\mathcal{D} = \frac{\begin{array}{c} \mathcal{D}' \\ \text{conn}(A, B) \end{array}}{\text{walk}(A, B)} \quad \text{DIR}$$

for some $\mathcal{D}'$. This is the base case, and the thesis follows by rule STEP:

$$\mathcal{F} \triangleq \frac{\begin{array}{cc} \mathcal{D}' & \mathcal{E} \\ \text{conn}(A, B) & \text{walk}(B, C) \end{array}}{\text{walk}(A, C)} \quad \text{STEP} .$$

Case 2 $\mathcal{D}$ ends with an application of rule STEP:

$$\mathcal{D} = \frac{\overset{\mathcal{D}'}{\text{conn}(A, B')} \quad \overset{\mathcal{D}''}{\text{walk}(B', B)}}{\text{walk}(A, B)} \text{ STEP}$$

for some B', $\mathcal{D}'$, and $\mathcal{D}''$. Since $\mathcal{D}''$ is an immediate subderivation of $\mathcal{D}$, we can apply the induction hypothesis to $\mathcal{D}''$ :: walk(B', B) and $\mathcal{E}$ :: walk(B, C), obtaining that there exists $\mathcal{G}$ :: walk(B', C). Then we get to the thesis by constructing the following derivation:

$$\mathcal{F} \triangleq \frac{\overset{\mathcal{D}'}{\text{conn}(A, B')} \quad \overset{\mathcal{G}}{\text{walk}(B', C)}}{\text{walk}(A, C)} \text{ STEP} \, .$$

□

Rule COMP does not enjoy the properties of stability and modular replacement that we presented for derivable rules. The proof of Figure 1.6 analyses all the possible cases in which a derivation is constructed, and therefore it needs to be revisited in case any new rules are added to the inference system. It is also evident that the derivations of the premises of rule COMP are not reused as they are. Indeed, eliminating applications of rule COMP from a derivation can result in deep rewritings, as we show in the next example.

Example 1.3   Consider the following derivation.

$$\mathcal{H} \triangleq \frac{\overset{\mathcal{H}'}{\text{walk(Odense, Sydney)}} \quad \overset{\mathcal{H}''}{\text{walk(Sydney, Tokyo)}}}{\text{walk(Odense, Tokyo)}} \text{ COMP}$$

The subderivations $\mathcal{H}'$ and $\mathcal{H}''$ are defined as:

$$\mathcal{H}' \triangleq \frac{\dfrac{\overline{\text{conn(Odense, Rome)}} \text{ OR}}{\text{walk(Odense, Rome)}} \text{ DIR} \quad \dfrac{\overline{\text{conn(Rome, Sydney)}} \text{ RS}}{\text{walk(Rome, Sydney)}} \text{ DIR}}{\text{walk(Odense, Sydney)}} \text{ COMP}$$

$$\mathcal{H}'' \triangleq \frac{\dfrac{\overline{\text{conn(Sydney, Tokyo)}}}{\text{}} \text{ ST}}{\text{walk(Sydney, Tokyo)}} \text{ DIR} \, .$$

By Proposition 1.7, walk(Odense, Tokyo) is derivable in the system with rule STEP (Figure 1.6). We show how to use the proof of Proposition 1.7 to reconstruct the derivation that justifies this claim.

The statement of Proposition 1.7 assumes that the two premises of rule COMP are proven in the system with rule STEP. This is not the case for $\mathcal{H}$ because the derivation of the first premise – $\mathcal{H}'$ – contains an application of rule COMP. Therefore we start by eliminating the application of COMP in $\mathcal{H}'$.

Let us execute the reasoning in the proof of Proposition 1.7 on derivation $\mathcal{H}'$. The variables in the proof get instantiated as follows.

$$A \triangleq \text{Odense} \quad B \triangleq \text{Rome} \quad C \triangleq \text{Sydney}$$

$$\mathcal{D} \triangleq \frac{\overline{\text{conn(Odense, Rome)}} \text{ OR}}{\text{walk(Odense, Rome)}} \text{ DIR} \quad \mathcal{E} \triangleq \frac{\overline{\text{conn(Rome, Sydney)}} \text{ RS}}{\text{walk(Rome, Sydney)}} \text{ DIR}$$

Hence, we fall into Case 1: $\mathcal{D}$, the derivation of the first premise of $\mathcal{H}'$, ends with an application of rule DIR. Let $\mathcal{F}'$ be the derivation constructed by the proof:

$$\mathcal{F}' \triangleq \frac{\dfrac{}{\text{conn(Odense, Rome)}} \text{ OR } \dfrac{\dfrac{}{\text{conn(Rome, Sydney)}} \text{ RS}}{\text{walk(Rome, Sydney)}} \text{ DIR}}{\text{walk(Odense, Sydney)}} \text{ STEP} \; .$$

We can replace $\mathcal{H}'$ with $\mathcal{F}'$ in $\mathcal{H}$, obtaining:

$$\frac{\begin{array}{cc} \mathcal{F}' & \mathcal{H}'' \\ \text{walk(Odense, Sydney)} & \text{walk(Sydney, Tokyo)} \end{array}}{\text{walk(Odense, Tokyo)}} \text{ COMP} \qquad (1.12)$$

Since $\mathcal{F}'$ and $\mathcal{H}''$ are in the system with rule STEP, we can now execute the proof of Proposition 1.7 on the derivation in (1.12). The variables in the proof are now instantiated as follows.

$$A \triangleq \text{Odense} \quad B \triangleq \text{Sydney} \quad C \triangleq \text{Tokyo} \quad \mathcal{D} \triangleq \mathcal{F}' \quad \mathcal{E} \triangleq \mathcal{H}''$$

We fall into Case 2 because the derivation of the first premise ends with an application of rule STEP. The proof now invokes the induction hypothesis to derive walk(Rome, Tokyo) by using the derivations of walk(Rome, Sydney) and walk(Sydney, Tokyo) – that is,

$$\frac{\dfrac{\dfrac{}{\text{conn(Rome, Sydney)}} \text{ RS}}{\text{walk(Rome, Sydney)}} \text{ DIR} \qquad \begin{array}{c} \mathcal{H}'' \\ \text{walk(Sydney, Tokyo)} \end{array}}{\text{walk(Rome, Tokyo)}} \text{ COMP} \qquad (1.13)$$

Invoking the induction hypothesis corresponds to executing recursively the reasoning of the proof to the derivation in (1.13). Since the derivation of the first premise ends with an application of rule DIR, we fall into Case 1 and obtain:

$$\mathcal{G} \triangleq \frac{\dfrac{}{\text{conn(Rome, Sydney)}} \text{ RS} \qquad \begin{array}{c} \mathcal{H}'' \\ \text{walk(Sydney, Tokyo)} \end{array}}{\text{walk(Rome, Tokyo)}} \text{ STEP} \; .$$

We are now back to completing the execution of the reasoning in (1.13) for the derivation in (1.12). The proof constructs the derivation

$$\mathcal{F} \triangleq \frac{\dfrac{}{\text{conn(Odense, Rome)}} \text{ OR } \begin{array}{c} \mathcal{G} \\ \text{walk(Rome, Tokyo)} \end{array}}{\text{walk(Odense, Sydney)}} \text{ STEP} \; ,$$

which is in the system in Figure 1.6. We can verify this by expanding $\mathcal{G}$:

$$\mathcal{F} = \frac{\dfrac{}{\text{conn(Odense, Rome)}} \text{ OR } \dfrac{\dfrac{}{\text{conn(Rome, Sydney)}} \text{ RS} \quad \dfrac{\dfrac{}{\text{conn(Sydney, Tokyo)}} \text{ ST}}{\text{walk(Sydney, Tokyo)}} \text{ DIR}}{\text{walk(Rome, Tokyo)}} \text{ STEP}}{\text{walk(Odense, Tokyo)}} \text{ STEP} \; .$$

Exercise 1.14   Rework the proof of Proposition 1.7 such that it proceeds by induction on the height of the derivation $\mathcal{D}$ – height($\mathcal{D}$) – instead of its structure.

Exercise 1.15   Prove that the rule

$$\frac{\text{walk}(A, B) \quad \text{conn}(B, C)}{\text{walk}(A, C)} \text{ STEP-ALT}$$

is admissible in the system in Figure 1.6.

1.4.3   Taking Stock

Proposition 1.6 tells us that adding rule STEP to the system in Figure 1.2 does not add any expressive power, in the sense that any proposition that can be derived in this extended system could already be derived with the rules in Figure 1.2. Since STEP is derivable in the system in Figure 1.2, we can see it as a modular shortcut that can be defined in that system: in a derivation, we can always apply rule STEP with the reassurance that we can replace such application with a derivation that shows how it can be implemented in terms of the other rules in Figure 1.2. The procedure for eliminating an application of rule STEP is a simple expansion.

Likewise, Proposition 1.7 tells us that adding rule COMP does not add any expressive power to the system in Figure 1.6. However, rewriting a derivation to eliminate applications of rule COMP might require inspecting and altering the structure of the entire derivation (as shown in Example 1.3). This is why rule COMP is not stable under extensions of the inference system: adding a new rule would introduce new cases for the rewriting of the derivation, which we would need to prove we can deal with.

In a nutshell:

- Admissible rules do not add expressive power – that is, they do not affect the set of derivable propositions. However, they can be convenient shortcuts.
- All derivable rules are also admissible rules.
- Derivable rules remain derivable even if we add new rules to the inference system. This is not true in general for all admissible rules.

2 Simple Choreographies

Now that we have familiarised ourselves with inference systems, we proceed to using them in the study of choreographies. We start in this chapter by building a language called Simple Choreographies – a formal choreographic language that allows for writing (simple) choreographies and inferring their meaning. We will add further features to our language in the other chapters by building on top of the basic concepts established here.

The cornerstone of our study will be the notion of *process*, which captures the Alices and Bobs that we talked about in the Preface. Processes are independent participants in a choreography; they can perform local computation and interact with other processes by communicating with them. From the perspective of computer systems, processes are abstract representations of computer programs executed concurrently; each process possesses its own control state and memory.

Example 2.1 We informally introduce a choreography for an online bookstore, which will serve as a running example in this and some of the following chapters. The choreography involves two processes, called Buyer and Seller. Essentially, Buyer interacts with Seller to obtain the price of a book that Seller offers. The choreography consists of the following sequence of steps.
1. Buyer communicates the title of a book that they wish to buy to Seller.
2. Seller replies to Buyer with the price of the book.

2.1 Syntax

We first define the *syntax* of Simple Choreographies, which determines the set of choreographies that can be written in the language.

Let **PName** be an infinite set of *process names*, ranged over by p, q, r, s, and so forth. The syntax of Simple Choreographies is given by the context-free grammar displayed in Backus-Naur Form (BNF) in Figure 2.1, where the symbol C ranges over choreographies. Let **SimpleChor** be the language of the grammar – that is, the set of all terms that can be derived from the symbol C. In other words, **SimpleChor** is the set of all choreographies that can be written in Simple Choreographies.

$$C ::= p \rightarrow q; C \mid 0$$

Figure 2.1 Syntax of Simple Choreographies.

The grammar is defined such that a choreography can take two forms.

- The *terminated choreography* **0**, which is the choreography that prescribes no interactions.
- A *communication* term p → q; *C* (also called *interaction*). This is a communication from some process p to some other process q. The choreography continues, then, as specified by the subterm *C*. We call *C* the *continuation* of the term.

We assume that communications are always between different processes: for every p and q, whenever we write p → q, we require p ≠ q.

Example 2.2   Recall the informal sequence of steps that we described for the online bookstore scenario in Example 2.1:

1. Buyer communicates the title of a book that they wish to buy to Seller.
2. Seller replies to Buyer with the price of the book.

The following choreography formalises this protocol.

$$\text{Buyer} \to \text{Seller}; \text{Seller} \to \text{Buyer}; \mathbf{0}$$

Note that what we have is actually a rather coarse abstraction of what we described in Example 2.1 because we are not formalising *what* is being sent from a process to another. For example, the informal description states that Buyer sends 'the title of a book that they wish to buy' to Seller in the first interaction, but our choreography does not define this part. It simply states that Buyer sends some unspecified message to Seller and that Seller replies to Buyer afterwards. We are going to explore how to define the content of messages in Chapter 5.

Exercise 2.1 (↪)   Write a choreography for the following *ring protocol* among Alice, Bob, and Charlie.

1. Alice communicates a message to Bob.
2. Bob communicates a message to Charlie.
3. Charlie communicates a message to Alice.

We are going to use this choreography in other exercises in this chapter.

Exercise 2.2   Write a choreography for the following *scatter protocol*, where Alice communicates a message to Bob and Charlie.

1. Alice communicates a message to Bob.
2. Alice communicates a message to Charlie.

2.2   Semantics

We move to defining an *operational semantics* for Simple Choreographies – that is, an operational interpretation of what a choreography means in terms of the interactions that it prescribes. Our objective is to formalise the execution of a choreography. We use one of the most established

$$\frac{}{\mathsf{p} \to \mathsf{q}; C \xrightarrow{\mathsf{p} \to \mathsf{q}} C} \text{ COM} \qquad \frac{C \xrightarrow{\mu} C' \quad \{\mathsf{p}, \mathsf{q}\} \,\#\, \mathrm{pn}(\mu)}{\mathsf{p} \to \mathsf{q}; C \xrightarrow{\mu} \mathsf{p} \to \mathsf{q}; C'} \text{ DELAY}$$

Figure 2.2 Semantics of Simple Choreographies.

approaches to define this kind of interpretation (perhaps *the* most established approach), called labelled transition systems.

Definition 2.1 (Labelled Transition System (LTS))   A labelled transition system is a triple $(S, L, \longrightarrow)$ where S is the set of *states*, L is the set of *transition labels*, and $\longrightarrow \subseteq S \times L \times S$ is the *transition relation*.

We range over states (elements of S) with s, s', and so forth, and labels (elements of L) with μ, μ', and so forth. Intuitively, labels represent what we can observe about the step from one state into another. We adopt the standard shorthand notation for transitions: we write $s \xrightarrow{\mu} s'$ whenever $(s, \mu, s') \in \longrightarrow$ (read 'the triple (s, μ, s') is an element of $\longrightarrow$'), for some states s and s' in S and label μ in L.

To define an LTS for Simple Choreographies, we follow the structural operational semantics approach by Plotkin [2004]: the behaviour of a choreography is defined in terms of the behaviours of its parts.

Definition 2.2 (LTS for Simple Choreographies)   The lts of Simple Choreographies is the lts $(S, L, \longrightarrow)$, where:

- The set of states S is the set of all choreographies – that is, $S \triangleq \mathbf{SimpleChor}$.
- The set of labels L is defined as the set of all possible communications between any two processes – that is, $L \triangleq \{\mathsf{p} \to \mathsf{q} \mid \mathsf{p}, \mathsf{q} \in \mathbf{PName}\}$.
- The transition relation $\longrightarrow$ is the smallest relation satisfying the inference system in Figure 2.2.

The wording of the last item in Definition 2.2, which defines the transition relation $\longrightarrow$, merits careful consideration. The relation is defined such that it *satisfies* the inference system in Figure 2.2: this means that the relation includes all triples that can be derived in the system. Also, $\longrightarrow$ is the smallest such relation: if a triple cannot be derived in the system, then it is not included. In other words, we are defining the relation as the one that contains exactly (all and only) the triples that can be derived by using the system in Figure 2.2.

We will often refer to the processes mentioned in a transition label. We formalise this concept as a function, pn, which maps each transition label to the set of process names mentioned in the label. Formally, the function pn maps transition labels to sets of process names (subsets of $\mathbf{PName}$) and is defined as follows for any processes p and q:

$$\mathrm{pn}(\mathsf{p} \to \mathsf{q}) \triangleq \{\mathsf{p}, \mathsf{q}\}.$$

For example, $\mathrm{pn}(\mathsf{Buyer} \to \mathsf{Seller}) = \{\mathsf{Buyer}, \mathsf{Seller}\}$.

The inference system that defines the transition relation $\longrightarrow$ has two rules called COM and DELAY. The first models communication while the second allows for concurrent execution. Inference rules for deriving transitions, like COM and DELAY, are also called *transition rules*. We explain them in Sections 2.2.1 and 2.2.1, respectively.

2.2.1   Communication

Rule com is an axiom: it always allows us to execute the first interaction defined in a choreography. In the rule, p, q, and C are all schematic variable, on which we impose no conditions. So the rule works for all process names and choreographies, with one proviso: recall that we assumed $p \neq q$ for all communication terms in Section 2.1, so we inherit this assumption here.

Example 2.3   Consider the choreography from Example 2.2:

$$\text{Buyer} \rightarrow \text{Seller}; \text{Seller} \rightarrow \text{Buyer}; \mathbf{0}.$$

We can derive the following transition.

$$\frac{}{\text{Buyer} \rightarrow \text{Seller}; \text{Seller} \rightarrow \text{Buyer}; \mathbf{0} \xrightarrow{\text{Buyer} \rightarrow \text{Seller}} \text{Seller} \rightarrow \text{Buyer}; \mathbf{0}} \text{ COM}$$

This derivation applies rule com, instantiating its variables thusly: p with Buyer, q with Seller, and C with Seller $\rightarrow$ Buyer; $\mathbf{0}$. The transition that we have derived tells us that the initial choreography can execute a communication from Buyer to Seller (denoted by the label Buyer $\rightarrow$ Seller). The result of the transition is the continuation of the original choreography, for which we can derive a further transition:

$$\frac{}{\text{Seller} \rightarrow \text{Buyer}; \mathbf{0} \xrightarrow{\text{Seller} \rightarrow \text{Buyer}} \mathbf{0}} \text{ COM} \quad .$$

There are no further transitions since we reached term $\mathbf{0}$, for which there are no transition rules.

Exercise 2.3   Repeat the development in Example 2.3 for the choreography that you defined for Exercise 2.1. That is, derive the transition that originates from the choreography, the choreography that it transitions to, and so forth, until the term $\mathbf{0}$ is reached. Then do the same for the choreography that you wrote for Exercise 2.2.

2.2.2   Out-of-Order Execution

The other rule that defines the semantics of Simple Choreographies, rule delay, captures in choreographies the notion that processes are independent of each other.

Before we discuss the formalities of the rule, let us see an example that motivates its presence. Consider the following choreography, where we have two independent buyers, called Buyer_1 and Buyer_2, each communicating with a respective independent seller, Seller_1 and Seller_2.

$$\text{Buyer}_1 \rightarrow \text{Seller}_1; \text{Buyer}_2 \rightarrow \text{Seller}_2; \mathbf{0} \tag{2.1}$$

Notice that the first interaction, $\text{Buyer}_1 \rightarrow \text{Seller}_1$, involves completely different processes than those in the second interaction, $\text{Buyer}_2 \rightarrow \text{Seller}_2$. In other words, in principle, the two interactions are independent of each other. Therefore, there should be no need to wait for the first interaction to be executed before we can observe the second. Rule DELAY addresses this issue by allowing us to derive the following transition.

$$\text{Buyer}_1 \to \text{Seller}_1; \text{Buyer}_2 \to \text{Seller}_2; 0 \xrightarrow{\text{Buyer}_2 \to \text{Seller}_2} \text{Buyer}_1 \to \text{Seller}_1; 0 \qquad (2.2)$$

Rule DELAY allows for delaying the observation of an interaction (in the rule that is the one between p and q), hence its name.[1] In our example, $\text{Buyer}_1 \to \text{Seller}_1$ is postponed to later observation.

This kind of semantics is typically called *out-of-order execution*. The principle is widespread in computing. For example, modern CPUs and language runtimes may change the order in which instructions are executed so as to increase performance, when it is safe to do so. A typical example is the single-threaded imperative code x++; y++;. Since the two increment statements deal with separate variables, the order in which they are performed is uninfluential and the CPU or language runtime may decide to parallelise it. Thus, y might be incremented before x.

Formally, looking at the definition of the rule in Figure 2.2, rule DELAY allows us to observe a transition (the premise $C \xrightarrow{\mu} C'$) performed by the continuation of a communication ($p \to q$ in the conclusion), provided that the transition does not involve any of the processes mentioned in the communication term. This check on the transition is performed by the second premise of the rule, $\{p, q\} \# pn(\mu)$, read 'the processes p and q are not mentioned in μ'. The operator # is just an abbreviation for empty intersection: for any two sets S_1 and S_2, $S_1 \# S_2$ is a shortcut for $S_1 \cap S_2 = \emptyset$, where $\emptyset$ is the empty set as usual.

Example 2.4   The transition in (2.2) can be derived as follows.

$$\cfrac{\cfrac{}{\text{Buyer}_2 \to \text{Seller}_2; 0 \xrightarrow{\text{Buyer}_2 \to \text{Seller}_2} 0} \text{COM} \qquad \{\text{Buyer}_1, \text{Seller}_1\} \# \{\text{Buyer}_2, \text{Seller}_2\}}{\text{Buyer}_1 \to \text{Seller}_1; \text{Buyer}_2 \to \text{Seller}_2; 0 \xrightarrow{\text{Buyer}_2 \to \text{Seller}_2} \text{Buyer}_1 \to \text{Seller}_1; 0} \text{DELAY}$$

Remark 2.3 (Side conditions)   The reader might be puzzled by the fact that the second premise of rule DELAY, $\{p, q\} \# pn(\mu)$, has a form for which we have not specified any inference rules. Indeed, in Example 2.4, we have not derived the required premise $\{\text{Buyer}_1, \text{Seller}_1\} \# \{\text{Buyer}_2, \text{Seller}_2\}$, but simply stated it.

Premises like this are sometimes called *side conditions*, and they express constraints on the schematic variables of a rule – in the case of rule DELAY, the variables of interest for the side condition are p, q, and μ. The rule can be applied only if these constraints are respected.

We could define an explicit inference system for deriving basic facts used as side conditions, such as $\{\text{Buyer}_1, \text{Seller}_1\} \# \{\text{Buyer}_2, \text{Seller}_2\}$. Defining inference systems for this kind of statements is an interesting problem in general, and in fact such systems do exist. However, adding these details would make the system more complicated without adding anything interesting to the formalities that we deal with in this book: we are going to use side conditions only for rather elementary facts.

---

[1] The terminology of 'delaying' actions was previously used in concurrency theory by Merro and Sangiorgi [2004], in the context of process calculi.

Remark 2.4   All mentioned process names (p and q), choreographies (C and C'), and the label μ are schematic variables in rule DELAY (as for rule COM). Henceforth, this is going to be an implicit part of the presentation of inference rules (all elements in the rules will be schematic variables).

Example 2.5   Rule DELAY allows us to go arbitrarily deep in the structure of a choreography, as long as we respect its condition of independence. Consider the following choreography, for some distinct process names p_1, p_2, p_3, q_1, q_2, and q_3.

$$p_1 \to q_1; p_2 \to q_2; p_3 \to q_3; 0 \tag{2.3}$$

By rule DELAY, we can observe the third communication immediately:

$$
\cfrac{
  \cfrac{
    \cfrac{}{p_3 \to q_3; 0 \xrightarrow{p_3 \to q_3} 0} \text{COM}
    \qquad \{p_2, q_2\} \# \{p_3, q_3\}
  }{p_2 \to q_2; p_3 \to q_3; 0 \xrightarrow{p_3 \to q_3} p_2 \to q_2; 0} \text{DELAY}
  \qquad \{p_1, q_1\} \# \{p_3, q_3\}
}{p_1 \to q_1; p_2 \to q_2; p_3 \to q_3; 0 \xrightarrow{p_3 \to q_3} p_1 \to q_1; p_2 \to q_2; 0} \text{DELAY}
$$

Exercise 2.4   Write all the possible transitions of the choreography in (2.3).

The observation made in Example 2.5 can be generalised to choreographies of arbitrary length, as in the following proposition. We use the notation $p_1 \to q_1; \cdots ; p_n \to q_n; C$ to denote a choreography that begins with a sequence of n interaction terms followed by some choreography C, without assuming whether or not the processes in the interactions are all distinct.

Proposition 2.5   For any natural number $n > 0$, the rule

$$
\frac{C \xrightarrow{\mu} C' \quad (\{p_1, q_1\} \cup \cdots \cup \{p_n, q_n\}) \# pn(\mu)}{p_1 \to q_1; \cdots ; p_n \to q_n; C \xrightarrow{\mu} p_1 \to q_1; \cdots ; p_n \to q_n; C'} \text{DELAY-}n
$$

is derivable.

Proof   By induction on n.

Case 1 $n = 1$. We have to prove that the rule

$$
\frac{C \xrightarrow{\mu} C' \quad \{p_1, q_1\} \# pn(\mu)}{p_1 \to q_1; C \xrightarrow{\mu} p_1 \to q_1; C'} \text{DELAY-}1
$$

is derivable. This is exactly rule DELAY. We apply it as follows to obtain the thesis.

$$
\frac{C \xrightarrow{\mu} C' \quad \{p_1, q_1\} \# pn(\mu)}{p_1 \to q_1; C \xrightarrow{\mu} p_1 \to q_1; C'} \text{DELAY}
$$

Case 2 $n = k + 1$ for some $k \geq 1$. We have to prove that the rule

$$\frac{C \xrightarrow{\mu} C' \quad (\{p_1, q_1\} \cup \cdots \cup \{p_k, q_k\} \cup \{p_n, q_n\}) \# \text{pn}(\mu)}{\begin{array}{c} p_1 \to q_1 ; \cdots ; p_k \to q_k ; p_n \to q_n ; C \\ \xrightarrow{\mu} p_1 \to q_1 ; \cdots ; p_k \to q_k ; p_n \to q_n ; C' \end{array}} \text{ DELAY-}n$$

is derivable. Observe that $(\{p_1, q_1\} \cup \cdots \cup \{p_k, q_k\} \cup \{p_n, q_n\}) \# \text{pn}(\mu)$ implies $(\{p_1, q_1\} \cup \cdots \cup \{p_k, q_k\}) \# \text{pn}(\mu)$ and $\{p_n, q_n\} \# \text{pn}(\mu)$. By induction hypothesis, the following rule is derivable.

$$\frac{C \xrightarrow{\mu} C' \quad (\{p_1, q_1\} \cup \cdots \cup \{p_k, q_k\}) \# \text{pn}(\mu)}{p_1 \to q_1 ; \cdots ; p_k \to q_k ; C \xrightarrow{\mu} p_1 \to q_1 ; \cdots ; p_k \to q_k ; C'} \text{ DELAY-}k$$

We can thus combine DELAY-k and DELAY to obtain the thesis:

$$\frac{\dfrac{C \xrightarrow{\mu} C' \quad \{p_n, q_n\} \# \text{pn}(\mu)}{p_n \to q_n ; C \xrightarrow{\mu} p_n \to q_n ; C'} \text{ DELAY} \quad (\{p_1, q_1\} \cup \cdots \cup \{p_k, q_k\}) \# \text{pn}(\mu)}{\begin{array}{c} p_1 \to q_1 ; \cdots ; p_k \to q_k ; p_n \to q_n ; C \\ \xrightarrow{\mu} p_1 \to q_1 ; \cdots ; p_k \to q_k ; p_n \to q_n ; C' \end{array}} \text{ DELAY-}k$$

□

Example 2.6 We can use rule DELAY-3 to derive the transition shown in Example 2.5 more efficiently (recall that p_1, p_2, p_3, q_1, q_2, and q_3 are all distinct):

$$\frac{\dfrac{}{p_3 \to q_3 ; 0 \xrightarrow{p_3 \to q_3} 0} \text{ COM} \quad \{p_1, p_2, q_1, q_2\} \# \{p_3, q_3\}}{p_1 \to q_1 ; p_2 \to q_2 ; p_3 \to q_3 ; 0 \xrightarrow{p_3 \to q_3} p_1 \to q_1 ; p_2 \to q_2 ; 0} \text{ DELAY-3}$$

2.3 Conventions, Notation, and Terminology for Labelled Transition Systems

We introduce some notions that will aid in the presentation and discussion of labelled transition systems throughout the rest of the book. In this section, we consider a generic lts $(S, L, \longrightarrow)$. We use s to range over elements of S and μ to range over elements of L.

2.3.1 Conventions for the Definition of Labelled Transition Systems

In this chapter, we have defined all the components of the lts of Simple Choreographies explicitly: the set of states, the set of labels, and the transition relation. In the next chapters, we adopt a few conventions to tacitly obtain these definitions from a grammar like that in Figure 2.1 and a set of inference rules for the transition relation like that in Figure 2.2. The conventions are:

1. We shall always assume that the set of states of the lts that we are considering is the set of all terms that satisfy the grammar of the choreographic language under study.

2. Given the inference system for a transition relation, we will assume that the set of labels of the lts is the union of all labels that can be instantiated by replacing the schematic variables in the labels used in the rules of the inference system.
3. We will assume that the transition relation is always the smallest relation satisfying the rules of the inference system under consideration.

With these conventions in place, we just need to give the syntax and inference system for transitions of a choreographic language and we will immediately know its lts. This will save us quite a bit of ink in the next chapters, since we will often update the syntax and semantics of choreographies to make them more powerful. For example, to define the syntax and semantics of Simple Choreographies, we would just need to present the syntax in Figure 2.1 and the rules in Figure 2.2. We follow these conventions in the remainder.

2.3.2   Notation and Terminology for Transitions

We adopt additional notation and terminology regarding transitions. Some are borrowed and adapted from automata [Lynch & Tuttle 1987] and process calculi [Milner 1980, 1989; Sangiorgi 2011].

Derivatives

Whenever $s \xrightarrow{\mu} s'$, we say that s' is a μ-*derivative* of s, or sometimes simply that s' is a *derivative* of s (if μ is not relevant).

We write $s \xrightarrow{\mu}$ (read 's can make a transition with label μ') whenever there exists some s' such that $s \xrightarrow{\mu} s'$. Likewise, we write $s \xnrightarrow{\mu}$ (read 's cannot make a transition with label μ') whenever there exists no s' such that $s \xrightarrow{\mu} s'$.

Observe that, in Simple Choreographies, $\mathbf{0} \xnrightarrow{\mu}$ for any label μ. This formalises that $\mathbf{0}$ represents the terminated choreography.

Executions, Traces, and Multi-step Derivatives

For each transition label μ, $\xrightarrow{\mu}$ is the binary relation that relates exactly all states s and s' such that $s \xrightarrow{\mu} s'$. This allows us to borrow notation and terminology for binary relations. For example, if $s_0 \xrightarrow{\mu_1} s_1$ and $s_1 \xrightarrow{\mu_2} s_2$, then we can express the two transitions more succinctly as $s \xrightarrow{\mu_1} s_1 \xrightarrow{\mu_2} s_2$. We can also omit the intermediate state and write $s_0 \xrightarrow{\mu_1}\xrightarrow{\mu_2} s_2$.

More generally, say that there exists a (possibly empty) sequence of transitions from a state s_0:

$$s_0 \xrightarrow{\mu_1} s_1 \cdots \xrightarrow{\mu_n} s_n.$$

This sequence is called an *execution* from s_0 to s_n (when the sequence is empty, $s_0 = s_n$), or simply an execution of s_0. Since an execution can be an empty sequence, every state has an (empty) execution to itself with no transitions; informally, every state can reach itself without doing any work.

Sometimes we just care about the labels of an execution. Whenever there exists an execution $s_0 \xrightarrow{\mu_1} s_1 \cdots \xrightarrow{\mu_n} s_n$, we call the sequence of labels $\mu_1, \ldots, \mu_n$ a *trace* of the state s_0.

In the remainder, we use $\vec{\mu}$ to range over (possibly empty) finite sequences of labels: for every $\vec{\mu}$, $\vec{\mu} = \mu_1, \ldots, \mu_n$ for some $n \geq 0$ and $\mu_1, \ldots, \mu_n$. We write ϵ for the empty sequence. We use the comma notation for composing and extending sequences of labels. In particular, for any label μ and any sequence of labels $\vec{\mu}$ such that $\vec{\mu} = \mu_1, \ldots, \mu_n$ for some $\mu_1, \ldots, \mu_n$, we have the following equalities.

$$\vec{\mu}, \mu = \mu_1, \ldots, \mu_n, \mu$$
$$\mu, \vec{\mu} = \mu, \mu_1, \ldots, \mu_n$$
$$\vec{\mu}, \epsilon = \vec{\mu}$$
$$\epsilon, \vec{\mu} = \vec{\mu}$$

Furthermore, for any two sequences of labels $\vec{\mu}$ and $\vec{\mu}'$ such that $\vec{\mu} = \mu_1, \ldots, \mu_n$ and $\vec{\mu}' = \mu_1', \ldots, \mu_m'$ for some $\mu_1, \ldots, \mu_n$ and $\mu_1', \ldots, \mu_m'$, we have that

$$\vec{\mu}, \vec{\mu}' = \mu_1, \ldots, \mu_n, \mu_1', \ldots, \mu_m'.$$

We write $s \xrightarrow{\vec{\mu}} s'$ when there exists an execution from s to s' with trace $\vec{\mu}$. Whenever this is the case, we say that s' is a $\vec{\mu}$-derivative of s, or simply a *multi-step derivative* of s. The relation $\twoheadrightarrow$ is called the *multi-step transition relation*. Notice that all states are multi-step derivatives of themselves: $s \xrightarrow{\epsilon} s$ for all states s. For any sequence of labels $\vec{\mu}$, the relation $\xrightarrow{\vec{\mu}}$ is a binary relation that relates all states s and s' such that $s \xrightarrow{\vec{\mu}} s'$. A few examples on how the notation can be used:

- $s \xrightarrow{\vec{\mu}} s' \xrightarrow{\vec{\mu}'} s''$ means that $s \xrightarrow{\vec{\mu}} s'$ and $s' \xrightarrow{\vec{\mu}'} s''$.
- $s \xrightarrow{\vec{\mu}} \xrightarrow{\vec{\mu}'} s'$ means that there exists s'' such that $s \xrightarrow{\vec{\mu}} s'' \xrightarrow{\vec{\mu}'} s'$.
- $s \xrightarrow{\vec{\mu}} \xrightarrow{\mu'} s'$ means that there exists s'' such that $s \xrightarrow{\vec{\mu}} s'' \xrightarrow{\mu'} s'$ (shorthand for $s \xrightarrow{\vec{\mu}} s''$ and $s'' \xrightarrow{\mu'} s'$).
- $s \xrightarrow{\mu} \xrightarrow{\vec{\mu}'} s'$ means that there exists s'' such that $s \xrightarrow{\mu} s'' \xrightarrow{\vec{\mu}'} s'$ (shorthand for $s \xrightarrow{\mu} s''$ and $s'' \xrightarrow{\vec{\mu}'} s'$).

The notation $s \xrightarrow{\mu}$ is extended to multi-step transitions. That is, we write $s \xrightarrow{\vec{\mu}}$ whenever there exists some s' such that $s \xrightarrow{\vec{\mu}} s'$, and we write $s \not\xrightarrow{\vec{\mu}}$ whenever there exists no s' such that $s \xrightarrow{\vec{\mu}} s'$.

Example 2.7   Recall the transitions that we derived in Example 2.3:

$$\text{Buyer} \to \text{Seller}; \text{Seller} \to \text{Buyer}; 0 \xrightarrow{\text{Buyer} \to \text{Seller}} \text{Seller} \to \text{Buyer}; 0$$
$$\text{Seller} \to \text{Buyer}; 0 \xrightarrow{\text{Seller} \to \text{Buyer}} 0.$$

With the notation that we have just presented in place, we can show a complete execution of the choreography from Example 2.2 in a single shot:

$$\text{Buyer} \to \text{Seller}; \text{Seller} \to \text{Buyer}; 0 \xrightarrow{\text{Buyer} \to \text{Seller}} \text{Seller} \to \text{Buyer}; 0 \xrightarrow{\text{Seller} \to \text{Buyer}} 0.$$

Sometimes, when presenting an execution, it is useful to point out how the transitions can be derived. To do so, we can write the name of the last applied rule in the derivation of a transition on the side, like this:

$$\text{Buyer} \to \text{Seller}; \text{Seller} \to \text{Buyer}; \mathbf{0}$$

$$\xrightarrow{\text{Buyer} \to \text{Seller}} \text{Seller} \to \text{Buyer}; \mathbf{0} \qquad\qquad \text{by rule COM}$$

$$\xrightarrow{\text{Seller} \to \text{Buyer}} \mathbf{0} \qquad\qquad \text{by rule COM}.$$

We can also abstract from the intermediate state and just focus on the labels:

$$\text{Buyer} \to \text{Seller}; \text{Seller} \to \text{Buyer}; \mathbf{0} \xrightarrow{\text{Buyer} \to \text{Seller}} \xrightarrow{\text{Seller} \to \text{Buyer}} \mathbf{0}. \qquad (2.4)$$

So $\mathbf{0}$ is a multi-step derivative of the choreography $\text{Buyer} \to \text{Seller}; \text{Seller} \to \text{Buyer}; \mathbf{0}$. The execution in (2.4) implies that

$$\text{Buyer} \to \text{Seller}; \text{Seller} \to \text{Buyer}; \mathbf{0} \xrightarrow{\text{Buyer} \to \text{Seller}, \text{Seller} \to \text{Buyer}} \mathbf{0}. \qquad (2.5)$$

The trace shows that we first have an interaction where Buyer sends a message to Seller and then we have an interaction where Seller sends a message to Buyer. That is exactly the communication flow that we wanted in Example 2.1, and there are no other traces. Thus, the formal semantics of the choreography in Example 2.3 matches our informal description in Example 2.2.

For the sake of completeness, these are all the traces of the choreography $\text{Buyer} \to \text{Seller}; \text{Seller} \to \text{Buyer}; \mathbf{0}$:

- ϵ (the empty trace).
- $\text{Buyer} \to \text{Seller}$.
- $\text{Buyer} \to \text{Seller}, \text{Seller} \to \text{Buyer}$.

Example 2.8 Consider again the choreography in (2.1):

$$\text{Buyer}_1 \to \text{Seller}_1; \text{Buyer}_2 \to \text{Seller}_2; \mathbf{0}.$$

This choreography has five traces due to concurrency (the two interactions can be executed in any order).

- ϵ (the empty trace).
- $\text{Buyer}_1 \to \text{Seller}_1$.
- $\text{Buyer}_2 \to \text{Seller}_2$.
- $\text{Buyer}_1 \to \text{Seller}_1, \text{Buyer}_2 \to \text{Seller}_2$.
- $\text{Buyer}_2 \to \text{Seller}_2, \text{Buyer}_1 \to \text{Seller}_1$.

The last two traces are given by the following executions.

$\text{Buyer}_1 \to \text{Seller}_1; \text{Buyer}_2 \to \text{Seller}_2; \mathbf{0}$

$\xrightarrow{\text{Buyer}_1 \to \text{Seller}_1} \text{Buyer}_2 \to \text{Seller}_2; \mathbf{0}$ by rule COM

$\xrightarrow{\text{Buyer}_2 \to \text{Seller}_2} \mathbf{0}$ by rule COM

$\text{Buyer}_1 \to \text{Seller}_1; \text{Buyer}_2 \to \text{Seller}_2; \mathbf{0}$

$\xrightarrow{\text{Buyer}_2 \to \text{Seller}_2} \text{Buyer}_1 \to \text{Seller}_1; \mathbf{0}$ by rule DELAY

$\xrightarrow{\text{Buyer}_1 \to \text{Seller}_1} \mathbf{0}$ by rule COM

Exercise 2.5   Write all the executions of the choreography in (2.3).

The definition of pn is overloaded and extended to sequences of transition labels as follows.

$$\text{pn}(\mu, \vec{\mu}) \triangleq \text{pn}(\mu) \cup \text{pn}(\vec{\mu})$$
$$\text{pn}(\epsilon) \triangleq \emptyset$$

2.3.3   Labelled Transition Systems Generated by States

Building on the concept of derivative, we can define the execution space of a state as a labelled transition system that captures all its possible executions. To this end, we define *generated labelled transition systems (lts)* [Sangiorgi 2011].

Definition 2.6 (Generated Labelled Transition System)   Given a labelled transition system $(S, L, \longrightarrow)$, the labelled transition system generated by a state s has as states the multi-step derivatives of s, as labels the elements of L, and as transitions those in $\longrightarrow$ that relate the multi-step derivatives of s.

The 'given' lts mentioned in the beginning of Definition 2.6 depends on the context. In this chapter, we refer to the lts of Simple Choreographies. We will not point out the given lts explicitly in the remainder, since there is no risk of ambiguity: it is always that of the language under study.

Example 2.9   The choreography from Example 2.2 has three multi-step derivatives: itself, $\text{Seller} \to \text{Buyer}; \mathbf{0}$, and $\mathbf{0}$. The last two multi-step derivatives are given by the following executions:

- $\text{Buyer} \to \text{Seller}; \text{Seller} \to \text{Buyer}; \mathbf{0} \xrightarrow{\text{Buyer} \to \text{Seller}} \text{Seller} \to \text{Buyer}; \mathbf{0}$.
- $\text{Buyer} \to \text{Seller}; \text{Seller} \to \text{Buyer}; \mathbf{0} \xrightarrow{\text{Buyer} \to \text{Seller}} \text{Seller} \to \text{Buyer}; \mathbf{0} \xrightarrow{\text{Seller} \to \text{Buyer}} \mathbf{0}$.

Thus, the lts generated by $\text{Buyer} \to \text{Seller}; \text{Seller} \to \text{Buyer}; \mathbf{0}$ is composed as follows.

- The states are $\text{Buyer} \to \text{Seller}; \text{Seller} \to \text{Buyer}; \mathbf{0}$, $\text{Seller} \to \text{Buyer}; \mathbf{0}$, and $\mathbf{0}$.

- The labels are the labels of the lts of Simple Choreographies.
- The transitions are the following two.
  - Buyer → Seller; Seller → Buyer; $0 \xrightarrow{\text{Buyer→Seller}}$ Seller → Buyer; 0.
  - Seller → Buyer; $0 \xrightarrow{\text{Seller→Buyer}} 0$.

Exercise 2.6   Write the multi-step derivatives of and the lts generated by the choreography that you defined to do Exercise 2.1.

2.3.4   Graphical Representation of Labelled Transition Systems

Labelled transition systems can be represented graphically in a straighforward way. Given an lts $(S, L, \longrightarrow)$, we can visualise it as an edge-labelled directed graph that has the states connected by $\longrightarrow$ as nodes and the elements of $\longrightarrow$ as edges.

Example 2.10   The lts generated by the choreography Buyer → Seller; Seller → Buyer; 0 is visualised by the following graph.

$$\text{Buyer → Seller; Seller → Buyer; } 0$$
$$\downarrow \text{Buyer → Seller}$$
$$\text{Seller → Buyer; } 0$$
$$\downarrow \text{Seller → Buyer}$$
$$0$$

In general, the graphical representation of an lts is complete for transitions but can be incomplete for states and labels: for any lts $(S, L, \longrightarrow)$, the states in S and labels in L that are not used in $\longrightarrow$ do not appear in the graph. In the remainder, when we visualise an lts as a graph, we ignore this aspect: for any language, the set of states and labels is defined separately and is thus clear from the context.

For an lts generated by a choreography, its graphical representation is complete for both transitions and states: since a generated lts has multi-step derivatives as states, all states are used in transitions. It is still incomplete for labels, but again the set of labels will be implicitly clear from the context.

Exercise 2.7   Draw the graphical representation of the lts generated by the choreography that you defined to do Exercise 2.1.

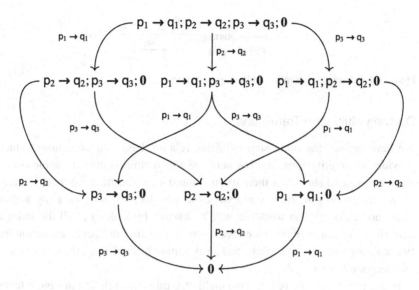

Figure 2.3 Graphical representation of the labelled transition system generated by the choreography $p_1 \to q_1; p_2 \to q_2; p_3 \to q_3; 0$.

Example 2.11   Recall the choreography from (2.3):

$$p_1 \to q_1; p_2 \to q_2; p_3 \to q_3; 0.$$

The graphical representation of the lts generated by this choreography is given in Figure 2.3.

Exercise 2.8   Draw the graphical representations of the labelled transition systems generated by the following choreographies. The purpose of this exercise is mainly to get acquainted with the technicalities of the semantics of Simple Choreographies. However, we describe what the choreographies might represent in practice to provide some intuition.

1. $o_1 \to c_1; o_2 \to c_2; c_1 \to a; c_2 \to a; 0$. This choreography describes a system at a factory where two ordering processes, o_1 and o_2, ask the construction processes c_1 and c_2 to build parts, which are then sent to process a for assembly. Observe how the system can initially execute interactions out of order, but then the collection of parts happens necessarily in sequence because of the ordering enforced by process a.

2. $c \to s_1; c \to s_2; s_1 \to l_1; s_2 \to l_2; 0$. This choreography describes a scenario where a client c sends a command to two independent servers, s_1 and s_2, which then log the received command in their respective logging processes, l_1 and l_2. In this choreography, execution starts necessarily sequentially and then some interactions can be performed out of order later on.

$$\frac{}{s \xrightarrow{\epsilon} s} \text{ REFL} \qquad \frac{s \xrightarrow{\vec{\mu}} s'' \quad s'' \xrightarrow{\mu} s'}{s \xrightarrow{\vec{\mu}\mu} s'} \text{ STEP-R}$$

Figure 2.4 Inference system for multi-step transitions.

2.3.5   Deriving Multi-step Transitions

We have defined the multi-step transition relation based on executions, which is simple and provides an intuitive meaning. Furthermore, this definition gives us some convenient flexibility when we have to show that there exists a multi-step transition from some state s to some state s': we can try to start from s and work our way forward towards s' by adding one transition after another, or we can work our way backwards by looking at all the states of which s' is a derivative. We can even combine executions: if we can construct an execution from s to some s'' (working forwards or backwards) and an execution from s'' to s', then we can join them to obtain an execution from s to s'.

In this subsection, we redefine the multi-step transition relation in a more formal way by using an inference system. This formulation will allow us to reason about multi-step transitions in proofs by using the tools that we have developed so far for derivations. On one hand, to make proofs about all possible multi-step transitions easier, we identify a minimal inference system that consists of just two rules. On the other hand, to retain the aforementioned flexibility in proofs about the existence of some multi-step transitions, we show a few useful rules that are admissible – thus, they can be used without really extending the inference system.

The multi-step transition relation $\twoheadrightarrow$ is the smallest relation that satisfies the inference rules displayed in Figure 2.4. There are only two rules. Rule REFL states that any state is a multi-step derivative of itself. The name REFL stands for reflexivity. Rule STEP-R states that a multi-step transition from a state s to s' that consists of at least one transition with label μ at the end can be derived from a multi-step transition to an intermediate state s'' (first premise) and a transition with label μ from the intermediate state s'' to s'. The name STEP-R stands for 'step right', because the transition step added to the execution is in the right premise.

Example 2.12 The multi-step transition in (2.5) is derivable, as shown in Figure 2.5. (The derivation is displayed rotated for reasons of space.)

The system for deriving multi-step transitions admits some convenient rules, which are displayed in Figure 2.6. Rule STEP-R corresponds to finding multi-step derivatives by working backwards, as we discussed in the previous paragraphs. The rules STEP-L and COMP respectively allow us to work forwards or by composition of executions. Rule SINGLE states that any transition yields an execution consisting of a single step.

$$
\dfrac{
\dfrac{
\dfrac{}{\begin{array}{l}\text{Buyer} \to \text{Seller};\\ \text{Seller} \to \text{Buyer};\\ \mathbf{0}\end{array} \overset{\epsilon}{\twoheadrightarrow} \begin{array}{l}\text{Buyer} \to \text{Seller};\\ \text{Seller} \to \text{Buyer};\\ \mathbf{0}\end{array}}\,\text{REFL}
\qquad
\begin{array}{l}\text{Buyer} \to \text{Seller};\\ \text{Seller} \to \text{Buyer};\\ \mathbf{0}\end{array} \xrightarrow{\text{Buyer}\to\text{Seller}} \begin{array}{l}\text{Seller} \to \text{Buyer};\\ \mathbf{0}\end{array}
}{
\begin{array}{l}\text{Buyer} \to \text{Seller};\\ \text{Seller} \to \text{Buyer};\\ \mathbf{0}\end{array} \overset{\text{Buyer}\to\text{Seller}}{\twoheadrightarrow} \begin{array}{l}\text{Seller} \to \text{Buyer};\\ \mathbf{0}\end{array}
}\,\text{STEP-R}
\qquad
\begin{array}{l}\text{Seller} \to \text{Buyer};\\ \mathbf{0}\end{array} \xrightarrow{\text{Seller}\to\text{Buyer}} \mathbf{0}
}{
\text{Buyer} \to \text{Seller}; \text{Seller} \to \text{Buyer}; \mathbf{0} \overset{\text{Buyer}\to\text{Seller},\text{Seller}\to\text{Buyer}}{\twoheadrightarrow} \mathbf{0}
}\,\text{STEP-R}
$$

Figure 2.5 Derivation of the multi-step transition in (2.5).

$$\dfrac{s \xrightarrow{\mu} s'' \quad s'' \xrightarrow{\vec{\mu}} s'}{s \xrightarrow{\mu,\vec{\mu}} s'} \;\text{STEP-L} \qquad \dfrac{s \xrightarrow{\vec{\mu}} s'' \quad s'' \xrightarrow{\vec{\mu}'} s'}{s \xrightarrow{\vec{\mu},\vec{\mu}'} s'} \;\text{COMP} \qquad \dfrac{s \xrightarrow{\mu} s'}{s \xrightarrow{\mu} s'} \;\text{SINGLE}$$

Figure 2.6 Admissible rules for multi-step transitions. Rule SINGLE is derivable.

Exercise 2.9 Prove that rules STEP-L and COMP in Figure 2.6 are admissible in the system in Figure 2.4. (Hint: recall our study of the system for deriving walks in Chapter 1, in particular the proof of Proposition 1.7.)

Exercise 2.10 Prove that rule SINGLE in Figure 2.6 is derivable in the system in Figure 2.4.

Observe that both STEP-R or STEP-L work as the 'basic' rule for multi-step transitions, in the sense that the rules STEP-R, COMP, and SINGLE are admissible in a system consisting of the rules REFL and STEP-L.

Exercise 2.11 Prove that the rules STEP-R, COMP, and SINGLE are admissible in an inference system that consists of rules REFL and STEP-L.

To summarise:

- When we have to derive a multi-step transition, we can use rules REFL, STEP-L, STEP-R, SINGLE, and COMP.
- When we have to reason about all the possible multi-step transitions that can be derived, it is sufficient to restrict our attention to the system that consists of rules REFL and STEP-R, or the system that consists of rules REFL and STEP-L.

In the remainder, unless otherwise stated, we assume that multi-step transitions are derived by using the system in Figure 2.4 (rules REFL and STEP-R).

Exercise 2.12 Prove that every multi-step transition that can be derived in the system in Figure 2.4 can be derived also in the following system. Then prove that this is no longer the case if any of the three rules in this system is removed.

$$\dfrac{}{s \xrightarrow{\epsilon} s} \;\text{REFL} \qquad \dfrac{s \xrightarrow{\mu} s'}{s \xrightarrow{\mu} s'} \;\text{SINGLE} \qquad \dfrac{s \xrightarrow{\vec{\mu}} s'' \quad s'' \xrightarrow{\vec{\mu}'} s'}{s \xrightarrow{\vec{\mu},\vec{\mu}'} s'} \;\text{COMP}$$

3 Simple Processes

Simple Choreographies is like a (simplistic) high-level programming language. It provides us with a useful abstraction – the communication term $p \to q; C$ – to define interaction protocols. More precisely, the usefulness of this abstraction is that it makes the desired interactions among processes *manifest*: they appear syntactically in the choreography, giving a straightforward interpretation.

In concurrent and distributed systems, each process has its own program run by the computer that hosts it. These *process programs* communicate by executing primitives for sending and receiving messages. For example, a process p can communicate with a process q if the two execute two compatible actions: the process p sends a message to the process q, and the process q receives the message from p. In practical programming frameworks, these instructions are supported by communication channels like sockets, pipes, in-memory objects, and so forth.

Therefore, implementing a choreography requires translating it to appropriate process programs. Other high-level languages face the same challenge: they offer useful abstractions, like functions and objects, but their programs need to be translated to lower-level code that the computer can actually execute, like machine code. In this book, we are interested in bridging the conceptual gap between choreographies and the typical structures of programs that can be run in concurrent systems. If you like, we can think of choreographies as definitions of *what* we want to happen and we can think of process programs as definitions of *how* the processes are going to collectively make it happen.

In this chapter, we introduce Simple Processes: a simple theory of process programs, with its own syntax and semantics. We will use Simple Processes to explore how an interaction protocol defined as a choreography can be implemented by a composition of independent processes that run their own programs. In the next chapter, we will use the intuition gained here to develop an *automatic* translation of choreographies to process programs.

Example 3.1 We give an informal example of process programs by referring to our scenario in Example 2.1. Recall the choreography that we defined for it in Example 2.2:

$$\text{Buyer} \to \text{Seller}; \text{Seller} \to \text{Buyer}; 0.$$

To implement this choreography, we need two process programs: one for process Buyer and one for process Seller.

Informally, a program for Buyer could consist of the following steps.

1. Send a message to Seller.
2. Receive a message from Seller.

$$P, Q, R ::= \text{p!}; P \mid \text{p?}; P \mid \mathbf{0}$$

Figure 3.1 Syntax of Simple Processes.

For Seller, instead, we could use the following program.
1. Receive a message from Buyer.
2. Send a message to Buyer.

3.1   Syntax

We begin by defining the syntax of Simple Processes. This is given by the grammar in Figure 3.1, where P, Q, R range over process terms. Notice that now the word 'process' is overloaded: it can mean either a process name (p) or a process term (P). We will explicitly say which of the two is meant whenever the context does not make it clear.

A process term P can be one of the following.

- The *terminated process* $\mathbf{0}$.
- A *send action* p!; P, read 'send a message to the process called p and then do P'.
- A *receive action* p?; P, read 'receive a message from the process called p and then do P'.

We write **SimpleProc** for the set of all process terms according to the grammar in Figure 3.1. We call process terms also process programs, or simply processes.

The symbol $\mathbf{0}$, which is traditionally used for expressing an inactive term (no-op), is now used to represent both the terminated choreography and the terminated process. The difference will be clear from the context.

Example 3.2   The informal programs for the processes Buyer and Seller in Example 3.1 are written in Simple Processes as follows.
- For Buyer: Seller!; Seller?; $\mathbf{0}$.
- For Seller: Buyer!; Buyer?; $\mathbf{0}$.

Exercise 3.1   Write a process term that formalises the following sequence of actions.
1. Receive a message from Alice.
2. Send a message to Bob.
3. Send a message to Charlie.

3.2   Networks

For processes to be able to communicate, they need to be composed in a system. We call these systems *networks*.

Definition 3.1 (Network)   A network N is a function from process names to process terms:

$$N: \textbf{PName} \longrightarrow \textbf{SimpleProc}.$$

We write **SimpleNet** for the set of all networks.

As we will see formally in our presentation of the semantics of Simple Processes in Section 3.3, the idea is that two processes in a network can communicate whenever they are respectively executing compatible send and receive actions. Before we move to the formalisation of this intuition, however, we introduce terminology and notation to make the treatment of networks more concise.

3.2.1 Support and Running Processes

The *support* of a network N, written supp(N), is the subset of the domain **PName** containing exactly those process names that are not mapped to **0**. In set-builder notation,

$$\text{supp}(N) \triangleq \{ \mathsf{p} \mid N(\mathsf{p}) \neq \mathbf{0} \}.$$

We say that a process p is *running* in a network N if $N(\mathsf{p}) \neq \mathbf{0}$; vice versa, we say that p is not running in N if $N(\mathsf{p}) = \mathbf{0}$. Thus, the support of a network N, supp(N), is also called the set of running processes of N.

In practice, only a finite number of processes are running at a time in a network. Thus, we are going to be interested mostly in networks of this kind. We say that a function N has *finite support* if the set supp(N) is finite.

3.2.2 Notation for Networks

We introduce notation for the definition of networks, inspired by other process models [Milner 1980; Hennessy 2007]. The notation will be useful for making the presentation more terse and for studying properties about the construction of networks.

Terminated Network
The simplest network is the *terminated network* **0**, which maps all process names to the terminated process **0**. Formally, it is defined by the equation

$$\mathbf{0}(\mathsf{p}) \triangleq \mathbf{0} \quad \text{for all } \mathsf{p} \in \textbf{PName}.$$

Again, there will be no ambiguity in using the same symbol **0** as we did for the terminated choreography and process term, since the context will always clarify what we are referring to. On the other hand, **0** gives us a useful mnemonic for an inactive object.

Atomic Networks
An *atomic network* is a network with exactly one running process. We write $\mathsf{p}[P]$ for the atomic network where p is running the term P. Formally, let $\mathsf{p} \in \textbf{PName}$. Then the network $\mathsf{p}[P]$ is defined as the following function.

$$(\mathsf{p}[P])(\mathsf{q}) \triangleq \begin{cases} P & \text{if } \mathsf{q} = \mathsf{p} \\ \mathbf{0} & \text{otherwise} \end{cases}$$

In other words, p[P] is the function that returns P for p, and **0** for all other processes. In this definition, p[P] is wrapped in parentheses purely for presentational reasons: (p[P])(q) is the same as p[P](q).

Example 3.3   The following network has one running process, Buyer, which behaves as defined in Example 3.2.

$$\text{Buyer[Seller!; Seller?; \textbf{0}]}$$

Parallel Composition

Let N and M be networks with disjoint supports – that is, supp(N) # supp(M). Then we write $N \mid M$ for the *parallel composition* of N and M. Formally, $N \mid M$ is defined from N and M as follows.

$$(N \mid M)(\text{p}) \triangleq \begin{cases} N(\text{p}) & \text{if p} \in \text{supp}(N) \\ M(\text{p}) & \text{otherwise} \end{cases}$$

From now on, whenever we write $N \mid M$, we are implicitly assuming that supp(N) # supp(M). Parallel composition is therefore a partial binary operation on networks, since it is undefined for networks whose supports are not disjoint.

Example 3.4   We can use parallel composition to define concisely a network with two running processes, Buyer and Seller, which are executing process terms that implement our bookstore scenario (Example 3.1):

$$\text{Buyer[Seller!; Seller?; \textbf{0}] } \mid \text{ Seller[Buyer?; Buyer!; \textbf{0}]}$$

Example 3.5   Let p, q, and r be some process names. We give a few examples of: parallel compositions that can be written (✓); and parallel compositions that cannot be written (✗) because they violate the condition that the composed networks have disjoint supports.

✓   p[P]|q[Q] can be written for any P and Q. It is the composition of two atomic networks with disjoint supports: p[P], which has {p} as support, and q[Q], which has {q} as support. The support of p[P] | q[Q] is {p, q}.

✓   p[P] | (q[Q] | r[R]) can be written for any P, Q, and R. It is the composition of two networks with disjoint supports: the first, p[P], has {p} as support, and the second, q[Q] | r[R], has {q, r} as support.

✗   p[P] | p[P'] cannot be written for any P and P' such that $P \neq \mathbf{0}$ and $P' \neq \mathbf{0}$, since the two composed networks have overlapping support (both have {p} as support). If either $P = \mathbf{0}$ or $P' = \mathbf{0}$, then the parallel composition can be written, as we show in the next case.

✓   p[P] | p[**0**] can be written for any P. This is a tricky example: while it might appear that we are composing networks with overlapping support, the network p[**0**] has $\emptyset$ as support because p is mapped to the process term **0**.

✗   p[P]|(q[Q]|p[P']) cannot be written for any P, Q, and P' such that $P \neq \mathbf{0}$ and $P' \neq \mathbf{0}$, because the supports of the two composed networks – respectively {p} and {q, p} – overlap (they share p).

✓   p[$\mathbf{0}$] | (p[$\mathbf{0}$] | p[$\mathbf{0}$]) can be written because all the composed networks have $\emptyset$ as support (so all supports are trivially disjoint).

Exercise 3.2   Use the notation explained in this section to write a network of four processes, called p, q, r, and s, such that the processes behave as follows.

- Process p sends a message to q then receives a message from s.
- Process q sends a message to r.
- Process r receives a message from p, receives a message from q, and then sends a message to s.
- Process s receives a message from r then sends a message to p.

Proposition 3.2   For any N and M, supp($N \mid M$) = supp(N) $\cup$ supp(M).

Exercise 3.3 ($\hookrightarrow$)   Prove Proposition 3.2. (Hint: show that all process names in supp($N \mid M$) are necessarily in supp(N) $\cup$ supp(M) and vice versa.)

Parallel composition is right associative. That is, $N_1 \mid N_2 \mid N_3$ is interpreted as $N_1 \mid (N_2 \mid N_3)$.

Remark 3.3   In a network, a process name is effectively the *locations* (or *places*) at which a process program runs. The capability of expressing that computation takes place at difference locations is key to modelling distributed systems. The syntax p[P] is inspired by previous theories that studied locations in depth, like ambient calculi and the distributed π-calculus [Cardelli & Gordon 2000; Hennessy 2007].

3.2.3   Equality of Networks

We will often have to reason about whether two networks are equivalent, in the sense that they both map each process name to the same respective process term. In fact, we will have to do it so frequently that it is convenient to adopt *extensional equality* for networks.

Extensional equality means that two objects are deemed equal if they have the same external properties. For functions, this means that two functions are judged to be equal whenever given the same input they return the same value. Formally, for any two networks N and M, if N(p) = M(p) for all process names p, then $N = M$ ('N is equal to M').

Extensional equality is commonly used in mathematics because it allows us to disregard when functions have been defined differently but yield the same results. However, convenience is balanced by weaker knowledge: whenever we see a proposition of the form $N = M$, we will not know whether or not N and M are actually defined in the same way. It is thus important to point out where extensional equality is used, as we are doing here. Since this knowledge is sufficient for our purposes, we adopt the convenience of extensional equality for networks.[1]

Example 3.6 Consider the network $0 \mid 0$. Is this the same as 0? While the two networks are defined differently, extensional equality answers this question affirmatively: $0 \mid 0 = 0$, because $(0 \mid 0)(p) = 0(p)$ for all p. We can check this by unfolding the definitions of the two networks:

$$(0 \mid 0)(p) = \begin{cases} 0(p) & \text{if } p \in \text{supp}(0) \\ 0(p) & \text{otherwise} \end{cases}$$

$$0(p) = 0 \quad \text{for all } p \in \textbf{PName}.$$

3.2.4 Properties of Parallel Composition

Parallel composition has useful algebraic properties.

Proposition 3.4 The set **SimpleNet** equipped with parallel composition, (**SimpleNet**, $\mid$), is a *partial commutative monoid* with 0 as identity element. That is, it has the following properties.

Identity Element For all N, $N \mid 0 = N$.
Commutativity For all N and M, $N \mid M = M \mid N$.
Associativity For all N_1, N_2, and N_3, $N_1 \mid (N_2 \mid N_3) = (N_1 \mid N_2) \mid N_3$.

Proof We prove each property separately.

Identity Element We need to prove that $(N \mid 0)(p) = N(p)$ for all p. By definition of parallel composition,

$$(N \mid 0)(p) = \begin{cases} N(p) & \text{if } p \in \text{supp}(N) \\ 0(p) & \text{otherwise} \end{cases}.$$

For any p, we have two cases: either $p \in \text{supp}(N)$ or $p \notin \text{supp}(N)$.
If $p \in \text{supp}(N)$, then $(N \mid 0)(p) = N(p)$.
If $p \notin \text{supp}(N)$, then we have that:

$$\begin{aligned} (N \mid 0)(p) = 0(p) \quad &\text{by } p \notin \text{supp}(N) \\ = 0 \quad &\text{by definition of } 0 \\ = N(p) \quad &\text{by } p \notin \text{supp}(N). \end{aligned}$$

---

[1] Choosing the right kind of equality is a recurring topic in logic and programming languages, which has motivated a prolific line of research on sophisticated notions of equivalences. In our case, since networks are functions, extensional equality allows us to ignore irrelevant differences in the definitions of networks. Our development can be reformulated by replacing implicit uses of network equality with explicit mentions of other equivalences that respect the laws that we show in Section 3.2.4, like bisimilarity [Sangiorgi 2011].

Commutativity By definition of parallel composition, we get the following equations.

$$(N \mid M)(p) = \begin{cases} N(p) & \text{if } p \in \text{supp}(N) \\ M(p) & \text{otherwise} \end{cases}$$

$$(M \mid N)(p) = \begin{cases} M(p) & \text{if } p \in \text{supp}(M) \\ N(p) & \text{otherwise} \end{cases}$$

For any p, we have two cases: either $p \in \text{supp}(N)$ or $p \notin \text{supp}(N)$.

If $p \in \text{supp}(N)$, then $(N \mid M)(p) = N(p)$. Also, since parallel composition requires the supports of N and M to be disjoint, we know that $p \notin \text{supp}(M)$. Thus, $(M \mid N)(p) = N(p)$ as well.

Conversely, if $p \in \text{supp}(M)$, then $(M \mid N)(p) = M(p)$. Also, since parallel composition requires the supports of N and M to be disjoint, we know that $p \notin \text{supp}(N)$. Thus, $(N \mid M)(p) = M(p)$ as well.

Associativity By definition of parallel composition, we know that the supports of N_1, N_2, and N_3 are disjoint and we get the following equations.

$$(N_1 \mid (N_2 \mid N_3))(p) = \begin{cases} N_1(p) & \text{if } p \in \text{supp}(N_1) \\ (N_2 \mid N_3)(p) & \text{otherwise} \end{cases}$$

$$((N_1 \mid N_2) \mid N_3)(p) = \begin{cases} (N_1 \mid N_2)(p) & \text{if } p \in \text{supp}(N_1 \mid N_2) \\ N_3(p) & \text{otherwise} \end{cases}$$

For any p, we have two cases: either $p \in \text{supp}(N_1)$ or $p \notin \text{supp}(N_1)$.

If $p \in \text{supp}(N_1)$, then $(N_1 \mid (N_2 \mid N_3))(p) = N_1(p)$. By $p \in \text{supp}(N_1)$ and Proposition 3.2, $p \in \text{supp}(N_1 \mid N_2)$, and thus $((N_1 \mid N_2) \mid N_3)(p) = (N_1 \mid N_2)(p) = N_1(p)$.

If $p \notin \text{supp}(N_1)$, then $(N_1 \mid (N_2 \mid N_3))(p) = (N_2 \mid N_3)(p)$. We have two subcases: either $p \in \text{supp}(N_2)$ or $p \notin \text{supp}(N_2)$. If $p \in \text{supp}(N_2)$, then $(N_2 \mid N_3)(p) = N_2(p)$ and $((N_1 \mid N_2) \mid N_3) = (N_1 \mid N_2)(p)$; by Proposition 3.2, $(N_1 \mid N_2)(p) = N_2(p)$ as well. If $p \notin \text{supp}(N_2)$, then $(N_2 \mid N_3)(p) = N_3(p)$; by $p \notin \text{supp}(N_1)$ (the initial premise in this paragraph), $p \notin \text{supp}(N_2)$ (the premise of this subcase), and Proposition 3.2, we have that $((N_1 \mid N_2) \mid N_3)(p) = N_3(p)$ as well. $\square$

Example 3.7 When reasoning about parallel compositions, Proposition 3.4 allows us to ignore appearances of the identity element, ordering, and nesting.

As examples, consider the following equations, which hold for every process names p, q, and r.

By commutativity:

$$q[p?; 0] \mid p[q!; 0] = p[q!; 0] \mid q[p?; 0]$$

By identity element:

$$p[q!; 0] \mid 0 = p[q!; 0]$$

By associativity:

$$p[q!; r?; 0] \mid (q[p?; 0] \mid r[p!; 0]) = (p[q!; r?; 0] \mid q[p?; 0]) \mid r[p!; 0]$$

By identity element, commutativity, and associativity:

$$(q[p?; 0] \mid r[p!; 0]) \mid (p[q!; r?; 0] \mid 0) = (p[q!; r?; 0] \mid q[p?; 0]) \mid r[p!; 0]$$

Another property of parallel composition is that we can ignore processes mapped to the terminated process term, **0**.

Proposition 3.5   For all N, p, and P, $N \mid p[0] = N$.

Exercise 3.4   Prove Proposition 3.5.

3.2.5   Representing Networks with Finite Supports

Every network with finite support enjoys the property that it is finitely representable by using our notation. In other words, the notation for network is sufficient (or, if you like, complete) for representing all networks with finite support.

Proposition 3.6   Every network N with finite support has a finite representation.

Proof   We show that every N with finite support can be finitely represented as the terminated network **0** or by a finite parallel composition of finitely representable networks.

We have two cases, depending on whether or not supp(N) is empty.

Case 1   supp(N) = $\emptyset$. In this case, $N = $ **0**.
Case 2   supp(N) = $\{p_1, \ldots, p_n\}$ for some process names $p_1, \ldots, p_n$ and natural number $n > 0$. In this case, thanks to the equalities supported by parallel composition,

$$N = p_1[N(p_1)] \mid \cdots \mid p_n[N(p_n)],$$

which is a finite representation, because each $N(p_i)$ is a finite term in the language of Simple Processes.   □

3.3   Semantics

Similarly to what we have done for Simple Choreographies, we equip Simple Processes with a labelled transition system semantics. The idea is that each transition models a step in the execution of a network by matching a send action with a compatible receive action.

Formally, the lts of Simple Processes is given by the inference system displayed in Figure 3.2 – recall our convention for defining an lts from an inference system from Section 2.2. There are two rules, explained in the following two subsections.

$$\frac{}{\text{p[q!; }P] \mid \text{q[p?; }Q] \xrightarrow{\text{p}\rightarrow\text{q}} \text{p[}P] \mid \text{q[}Q]} \text{ COM} \qquad \frac{N \xrightarrow{\mu} N'}{N \mid M \xrightarrow{\mu} N' \mid M} \text{ PAR}$$

Figure 3.2 Semantics of Simple Processes.

3.3.1 Communication

The first rule, called COM, is an axiom: it matches a send action from a process p to a process q with a compatible receive action by process q (which wants to receive from p). The two processes then proceed with their respective continuations (P and Q in the rule).

Example 3.8 Consider the network from Example 3.4:

$$\text{Buyer[Seller!; Seller?; 0]} \mid \text{Seller[Buyer?; Buyer!; 0].}$$

The network matches the left-hand side of the transition in the conclusion of rule COM by instantiating p with Buyer, q with Seller, P with Seller?; 0 and Q with Buyer!; 0. Thus, by rule COM, we can derive the following transition, which gives us the intended communication between Buyer and Seller.

$$\frac{}{\begin{array}{l}\text{Buyer[Seller!; Seller?; 0]}\\\mid \text{Seller[Buyer?; Buyer!; 0]}\end{array} \xrightarrow{\text{Buyer}\rightarrow\text{Seller}} \begin{array}{l}\text{Buyer[Seller?; 0]}\\\mid \text{Seller[Buyer!; 0]}\end{array}} \text{ COM}$$

In rule COM, the sender process appears on the left-hand side of the parallel composition before the transition and the receiver process on the right-hand side. Commutativity of parallel composition allows us to consider also networks in the reverse order, where the receiver appears on the left-hand side and the sender on the right-hand side.

Example 3.9 Consider the derivative of the transition in Example 3.8. By commutativity of parallel composition, it can be rewritten as follows:

$$\text{Buyer[Seller?; 0]} \mid \text{Seller[Buyer!; 0]} = \text{Seller[Buyer!; 0]} \mid \text{Buyer[Seller?; 0].}$$

This means that we can apply COM again to derive a further transition.

$$\frac{}{\text{Buyer[Seller?; 0]} \mid \text{Seller[Buyer!; 0]} \xrightarrow{\text{Seller}\rightarrow\text{Buyer}} \text{Seller[0]} \mid \text{Buyer[0]}} \text{ COM}$$

By Proposition 3.5, the network Seller[0] | Buyer[0] is equal to the terminated network **0**:

$$\text{Seller[0]} \mid \text{Buyer[0]} = \mathbf{0}.$$

Thus, we have the following execution of our initial network from Example 3.4:

Buyer[Seller!; Seller?; **0**] | Seller[Buyer?; Buyer!; **0**]

$\xrightarrow{\text{Buyer}\rightarrow\text{Seller}}$ Buyer[Seller?; **0**] | Seller[Buyer!; **0**]   by rule COM

$\xrightarrow{\text{Seller}\rightarrow\text{Buyer}}$ **0**   by rule COM.

This is the only execution of the network. Observe that the execution matches the transitions of the (only) execution of the choreography that we wanted to implement from Example 2.7:

Buyer → Seller; Seller → Buyer; **0** $\xrightarrow{\text{Buyer}\rightarrow\text{Seller}}$ Seller → Buyer; **0** $\xrightarrow{\text{Seller}\rightarrow\text{Buyer}}$ **0**.

The only difference between the two executions is that the states are different (one has networks, the other choreographies), but otherwise their structures in terms of transitions are indistinguishable.

We are going to generalise this observation and formalise a notion of correct implementation of choreographies in terms of networks in Chapter 4.

Rule COM in Simple Processes bears the same name of the rule for communication in Simple Choreographies (Chapter 2) as a reminder that the two rules model the same aspect (communication), albeit in different languages. This causes no ambiguity since the two rules specify different transition systems that have different syntactic terms.

3.3.2 Parallel Execution

The second rule shown in Figure 3.2, called PAR, allows the two components of a parallel composition to proceed independently: if a network N can perform a transition, then the same transition can be performed by the larger network $N \mid M$. The part of the network not affected by the transition (M) remains unaffected.

Example 3.10   Consider the following network, where the idea is that a Gateway forwards a message from a Client to a Server.

$$\text{Client[Gateway!; }\mathbf{0}] \mid \text{Gateway[Client?; Server!; }\mathbf{0}] \mid \text{Server[Gateway?; }\mathbf{0}] \qquad (3.1)$$

Recall that parallel composition is right-associative. By associativity, the network in (3.1) can be rewritten as follows.

Client[Gateway!; **0**] | Gateway[Client?; Server!; **0**] | Server[Gateway?; **0**]

= (Client[Gateway!; **0**] | Gateway[Client?; Server!; **0**]) | Server[Gateway?; **0**]

Thus, we can derive a transition for the network by using rules PAR and COM:

$$
\frac{\begin{array}{l} \text{Client[Gateway!; 0]} \\ \text{| Gateway[Client?; Server!; 0]} \end{array} \xrightarrow{\text{Client}\to\text{Gateway}} \begin{array}{l} \text{Client[0]} \\ \text{| Gateway[Server!; 0]} \end{array}}{\begin{array}{l} \text{Client[Gateway!; 0]} \\ \text{| Gateway[Client?; Server!; 0]} \\ \text{| Server[Gateway?; 0]} \end{array} \xrightarrow{\text{Client}\to\text{Gateway}} \begin{array}{l} \text{(Client[0]} \\ \text{| Gateway[Server!; 0])} \\ \text{| Server[Gateway?; 0]} \end{array}} \; \text{COM} \atop \text{PAR}
$$

(3.2)

In the application of rule PAR, we have instantiated μ with Client → Gateway, N with

$$\text{Client[Gateway!; 0]} \mid \text{Gateway[Client?; Server!; 0]},$$

and M with Server[Gateway?; 0]. By Proposition 3.5 (and commutativity), we can rewrite the derivative obtained earlier to omit the Client:

$$\text{(Client[0]} \mid \text{Gateway[Server!; 0])} \mid \text{Server[Gateway?; 0]}$$
$$= \text{Gateway[Server!; 0]} \mid \text{Server[Gateway?; 0]}.$$

From the derivative above, we can apply rule COM to obtain a further transition:

$$
\frac{\begin{array}{l} \text{Gateway[Server!; 0]} \\ \text{| Server[Gateway?; 0]} \end{array} \xrightarrow{\text{Gateway}\to\text{Server}} \begin{array}{l} \text{Gateway[0]} \\ \text{| Server[0]} \end{array}}{} \; \text{COM}
$$

(3.3)

Since Gateway[0] | Server[0] = **0**, we have proved that **0** is a multi-step derivative of our initial network:

$$\text{Client[Gateway!; 0]} \mid \text{Gateway[Client?; Server!; 0]} \mid \text{Server[Gateway?; 0]}$$
$$\xrightarrow{\text{Client}\to\text{Gateway}} \text{Gateway[Server!; 0]} \mid \text{Server[Gateway?; 0]}$$
$$\xrightarrow{\text{Gateway}\to\text{Server}} \mathbf{0}.$$

Exercise 3.5 Write a choreography that defines the protocol implemented by the network given in (3.1). The choreography should have exactly one trace – that is, the same trace of the execution shown in Example 3.10.

From now on, we shall use equality laws for networks implicitly. For example, we can simplify the networks in (3.2) directly in the derivation, as follows.

$$\frac{}{\begin{array}{l}\text{Client[Gateway!; 0]}\\ \text{| Gateway[Client?; Server!; 0]}\end{array} \xrightarrow{\text{Client}\rightarrow\text{Gateway}} \text{Gateway[Server!; 0]}} \text{COM}$$

$$\frac{\begin{array}{l}\text{Client[Gateway!; 0]}\\ \text{| Gateway[Client?; Server!; 0]} \xrightarrow{\text{Client}\rightarrow\text{Gateway}} \begin{array}{l}\text{Gateway[Server!; 0]}\\ \text{| Server[Gateway?; 0]}\end{array}\\ \text{| Server[Gateway?; 0]}\end{array}}{} \text{PAR} \qquad (3.4)$$

Similarly, we could just write **0** in the derivative of the conclusion in (3.3), obtaining the terser derivation

$$\frac{}{\text{Gateway[Server!; 0] | Server[Gateway?; 0]} \xrightarrow{\text{Gateway}\rightarrow\text{Server}} \mathbf{0}} \text{COM} \qquad . \qquad (3.5)$$

3.4 Fundamental Properties of the Semantics

In this section, we discuss basic properties of the transition system of Simple Processes, which are fundamental for our later development. This also serves the purpose of gaining familiarity with proofs by induction on the structure of derivations that conclude transitions. We also introduce a practical presentational convention in the proof of the first result (Proposition 3.7).

3.4.1 Transitions and Process Names

A transition never affects processes that do not appear in the label of the transition, in the sense that the corresponding process terms do not change.

Proposition 3.7 For all N, μ, N', and r, if $N \xrightarrow{\mu} N'$ and $r \notin pn(\mu)$, then $N(r) = N'(r)$.

Proof (and a convention on presentation) By structural induction on the derivation of $N \xrightarrow{\mu} N'$. Let $\mathcal{D}$ be this derivation. We have a case for each rule that can be applied last in $\mathcal{D}$.

Case 1 $\mathcal{D}$ ends with an application of rule COM:

$$\mathcal{D} = \frac{}{N \xrightarrow{\mu} N'} \text{COM} \qquad .$$

By the definition of rule COM, this implies that N, μ, and N' are as follows:

$$N = \text{p[q!; } P\text{] | q[p?; } Q\text{]} \qquad \mu = \text{p} \rightarrow \text{q} \qquad N' = \text{p[}P\text{] | q[}Q\text{]}$$

for some p, q, P, and Q. In the remainder, we will encounter many situations like this – that is, proof cases where the last rule application of a derivation gives us information about the structures of the objects of interest. To be more concise, we shall adopt the convention of simply showing the derivation with everything we know from the corresponding rule about the structures of its premises and conclusion. In this case, we would write directly:

$$\mathcal{D} = \frac{}{\text{p[q!; } P\text{] | q[p?; } Q\text{]} \xrightarrow{\text{p}\rightarrow\text{q}} \text{p[}P\text{] | q[}Q\text{]}} \text{COM}$$

for some p, q, P, and Q.

To finish this case, observe that $supp(N) = \{p, q\}$. Also, since $\mu = p \rightarrow q$, we know by hypothesis that $r \neq p, q$ (r is different from p and q). Thus, $N(r) = \mathbf{0}$ and $N'(r) = \mathbf{0}$, and therefore $N(r) = N'(r)$.

Case 2 $\mathcal{D}$ ends with an application of rule PAR:

$$\mathcal{D} = \frac{\overset{\mathcal{D}'}{M_1 \xrightarrow{\mu} M_1'}}{M_1 \mid M_2 \xrightarrow{\mu} M_1' \mid M_2} \text{ PAR}$$

for some $\mathcal{D}'$, M_1, M_2, and M_1'. Notice that we are using the convention explained in the previous case, so we are implicitly saying that by definition of rule PAR we get to know that $N = M_1 \mid M_2$ and $N' = M_1' \mid M_2$. By induction hypothesis on $\mathcal{D}'$, $M_1(\mathsf{r}) = M_1'(\mathsf{r})$ for all $\mathsf{r} \notin \mathrm{pn}(\mu)$. Hence, $(M_1 \mid M_2)(\mathsf{r}) = (M_1' \mid M_2)(\mathsf{r})$. □

3.4.2 Transitions and Process Removal

Proposition 3.7 tells us that the processes not mentioned in the label of a transition remain unaffected by the transition. Building on this result, we can prove the stronger property that all processes not mentioned in a transition are actually not necessary in order to perform the transition. To formulate this property, we introduce an operator for removing processes from (the support of) a network. For any network N and process name p, we write $N \setminus \mathsf{p}$ for the network obtained by updating N to map p to $\mathbf{0}$:

$$(N \setminus \mathsf{p})(\mathsf{q}) \triangleq \begin{cases} \mathbf{0} & \text{if } \mathsf{q} = \mathsf{p} \\ N(\mathsf{q}) & \text{otherwise} \end{cases}.$$

Removal is left-associative: $N \setminus \mathsf{p} \setminus \mathsf{q} = (N \setminus \mathsf{p}) \setminus \mathsf{q}$. Further, we give $\setminus$ a higher priority than $\mid$, in the sense that

$$N \setminus \mathsf{p} \mid M = (N \setminus \mathsf{p}) \mid M$$

for all N, M, and p.

Example 3.11 Let N be the network from (3.1):

$$N \triangleq \mathsf{Client}[\mathsf{Gateway!}; \mathbf{0}] \mid \mathsf{Gateway}[\mathsf{Client?}; \mathsf{Server!}; \mathbf{0}] \mid \mathsf{Server}[\mathsf{Gateway?}; \mathbf{0}].$$

Then,

$$N \setminus \mathsf{Client} = \mathsf{Gateway}[\mathsf{Client?}; \mathsf{Server!}; \mathbf{0}] \mid \mathsf{Server}[\mathsf{Gateway?}; \mathbf{0}]$$
$$N \setminus \mathsf{Client} \setminus \mathsf{Gateway} = \mathsf{Server}[\mathsf{Gateway?}; \mathbf{0}]$$
$$N \setminus \mathsf{Gateway} \setminus \mathsf{Server} = \mathsf{Client}[\mathsf{Gateway!}; \mathbf{0}]$$
$$N \setminus \mathsf{Client} \setminus \mathsf{Gateway} \setminus \mathsf{Server} = \mathbf{0}.$$

Removing a process that is not running does not alter a network.

Proposition 3.8 For all N and p, $\mathsf{p} \notin \mathrm{supp}(N)$ implies $N \setminus \mathsf{p} = N$.

Exercise 3.6   Prove Proposition 3.8.

The order in which processes are removed from a network is irrelevant.

Proposition 3.9   For all N, p, and q, $N \setminus p \setminus q = N \setminus q \setminus p$.

We can now prove that a transition needs only the processes mentioned in its label in order to be performed.

Lemma 3.10   For all N, μ, N', and r, if $N \xrightarrow{\mu} N'$ and $r \notin pn(\mu)$, then $N \setminus r \xrightarrow{\mu} N' \setminus r$.

Proof   Let $\mathcal{D}$ be the derivation of $N \xrightarrow{\mu} N'$. We proceed by induction on the structure of $\mathcal{D}$.

Case 1 $\mathcal{D}$ ends with an application of rule COM:

$$\mathcal{D} = \overline{p[q!; P] \mid q[p?; Q] \xrightarrow{p \to q} p[P] \mid q[Q]} \;\text{COM}$$

for some p, q, P, and Q. Since $\mu = p \to q$, we know from the hypothesis $r \notin pn(\mu)$ that $r \notin \{p, q\}$.

We further observe that $supp(N) = \{p, q\}$ and that $supp(N') \subseteq \{p, q\}$ (P and Q might be $\mathbf{0}$, so p and q might not be running in N'). Consequently, $r \notin supp(N)$ and $r \notin supp(N')$. Now, by Proposition 3.8, $N \setminus r = N$ and $N' \setminus r = N'$. The thesis follows directly from the derivation $\mathcal{D}$.

Case 2 $\mathcal{D}$ ends with an application of rule PAR:

$$\mathcal{D} = \frac{\begin{array}{c}\mathcal{D}' \\ M_1 \xrightarrow{\mu} M_1'\end{array}}{M_1 \mid M_2 \xrightarrow{\mu} M_1' \mid M_2} \;\text{PAR}$$

for some $\mathcal{D}'$, M_1, M_2, and M_1'. We have three subcases: r is running in M_1, M_2, or neither of them.

Case 2.1   If $r \in supp(M_1)$, then $N \setminus r = M_1 \setminus r \mid M_2$ and $N' \setminus r = M_1' \setminus r \mid M_2$. By induction hypothesis on $\mathcal{D}'$, there exists a derivation $\mathcal{E} :: M_1 \setminus r \xrightarrow{\mu} M_1' \setminus r$. We conclude by rule PAR:

$$\frac{\begin{array}{c}\mathcal{E} \\ M_1 \setminus r \xrightarrow{\mu} M_1' \setminus r\end{array}}{M_1 \setminus r \mid M_2 \xrightarrow{\mu} M_1' \setminus r \mid M_2} \;\text{PAR}\;.$$

Case 2.2   If $r \in supp(M_2)$, then $N \setminus r = M_1 \mid M_2 \setminus r$ and $N' \setminus r = M_1' \mid M_2 \setminus r$. We conclude by rule PAR:

$$\frac{\begin{array}{c}\mathcal{D}' \\ M_1 \xrightarrow{\mu} M_1'\end{array}}{M_1 \mid M_2 \setminus r \xrightarrow{\mu} M_1' \mid M_2 \setminus r} \;\text{PAR}\;.$$

Case 2.3 If $r \notin \text{supp}(M_1)$ and $r \notin \text{supp}(M_2)$, then by Proposition 3.8 $N \setminus r = (M_1 \mid M_2) \setminus r = (M_1 \mid M_2)$. Further, by Proposition 3.7, $(M'_1 \mid M_2)(r) = (M_1 \mid M_2)(r) = \mathbf{0}$ and thus $N' \setminus r = (M'_1 \mid M_2) \setminus r = M'_1 \mid M_2$. Consequently, the thesis follows from the derivation $\mathcal{D}$. $\qquad \square$

The notation for removing processes is generalised to sequences of process names in the expected way. For any process name p and sequence of process names $\vec{p}$, we write $p, \vec{q}$ for the sequence that has p as first element and then proceeds as $\vec{q}$. We write $N \setminus \vec{p}$ for the network obtained by updating N to map all processes in $\vec{p}$ to $\mathbf{0}$, as defined by the following two equations.

$$N \setminus p, \vec{q} \triangleq (N \setminus p) \setminus \vec{q}$$
$$N \setminus \epsilon \triangleq N$$

Removing all running processes gives the terminated network: for all networks N, $N \setminus \text{supp}(N) = \mathbf{0}$. Also, thanks to Proposition 3.9, the ordering of $\vec{p}$ in $N \setminus \vec{p}$ does not matter.

Proposition 3.11 For all N, $\vec{p}$, and $\vec{q}$, if $\vec{q}$ is a permutation of $\vec{p}$, then $N \setminus \vec{p} = N \setminus \vec{q}$.

By iterating applications of Lemma 3.10, we can generalise the result to the removal of multiple processes.

Lemma 3.12 For all N, μ, N', and $\vec{r}$, if $N \xrightarrow{\mu} N'$ and $\{\vec{r}\} \, \# \, \text{pn}(\mu)$, then $N \setminus \vec{r} \xrightarrow{\mu} N' \setminus \vec{r}$.

Exercise 3.7 ($\hookrightarrow$) Prove Lemma 3.12. (Hint: Lemma 3.10 can be useful.)

3.4.3 Transitions and Network Restriction

The opposite operation of removing processes from a network is to extract the subnetwork that consists exactly of them. We obtain this by using a notion akin to restricting a function. Formally, let N be a network and $\{p_1, \ldots, p_n\}$ be a set of process names. The *restriction* of N to $\{p_1, \ldots, p_n\}$, written $N \restriction_{\{p_1, \ldots, p_n\}}$, is defined as:

$$N \restriction_{\{p_1, \ldots, p_n\}} \triangleq p_1[N(p_1)] \mid \cdots \mid p_n[N(p_n)].$$

We shall write $N \restriction_{p_1, \ldots, p_n}$ as abbreviation for $N \restriction_{\{p_1, \ldots, p_n\}}$, since the laws of commutativity and associativity for parallel composition make the ordering of $p_1, \ldots, p_n$ irrelevant.[2]

Example 3.12 Consider again the network from (3.1):

$$N \triangleq \text{Client}[\text{Gateway}!; \mathbf{0}] \mid \text{Gateway}[\text{Client}?; \text{Server}!; \mathbf{0}] \mid \text{Server}[\text{Gateway}?; \mathbf{0}].$$

---

[2] Our notion of restriction for networks works almost in the same way as the standard notion of function restriction. In the literature, the restriction of a function typically gives a function whose domain is the set that it has been restricted to. In our case, restricting a network gives a network whose domain is still the entire set **PName**, but in which all processes that are not considered in the restriction are mapped to $\mathbf{0}$.

Then,

$$N\upharpoonright_{\text{Client}} = \text{Client}[\text{Gateway}!; \mathbf{0}]$$

$$N\upharpoonright_{\text{Client,Gateway}} = \text{Client}[\text{Gateway}!; \mathbf{0}] \mid \text{Gateway}[\text{Client}?; \text{Server}!; \mathbf{0}]$$

$$N\upharpoonright_{\text{Gateway,Server}} = \text{Gateway}[\text{Client}?; \text{Server}!; \mathbf{0}] \mid \text{Server}[\text{Gateway}?; \mathbf{0}].$$

As for \, we give $\upharpoonright$ higher priority than $|$:

$$N\upharpoonright_{\vec{p}} \mid M = (N\upharpoonright_{\vec{p}}) \mid M$$

for all N, M, and $\vec{p}$.

Restricting a network to its own support yields the same network.

Proposition 3.13   For all N, $N\upharpoonright_{\text{supp}(N)} = N$.

Furthermore, restriction distributes over parallel composition.

Proposition 3.14   For all N, M, and $\vec{p}$, $(N \mid M)\upharpoonright_{\vec{p}} = N\upharpoonright_{\vec{p}} \mid M\upharpoonright_{\vec{p}}$.

Restriction and removal are in harmony, in the sense that removing some processes and then adding them back as they originally were by means of parallel composition yields the initial network.

Proposition 3.15   For any N and $\vec{p}$, $N = (N \setminus \vec{p}) \mid N\upharpoonright_{\vec{p}}$.

We end our discussion of restriction by proving a semantic property similar to Lemma 3.10: if a network can perform a transition, then the subnetwork that consists only of the processes mentioned in the label is sufficient to perform the same transition.

Lemma 3.16   If $N\backslash N'$, then $N\upharpoonright_{\text{pn}(\mu)} \xrightarrow{\mu} N'\upharpoonright_{\text{pn}(\mu)}$.

Proof   Let $\mathcal{D}$ be the derivation of $N \xrightarrow{\mu} N'$. We proceed by structural induction on $\mathcal{D}$.

Case 1 $\mathcal{D}$ ends with an application of rule COM:

$$\mathcal{D} = \dfrac{}{\text{p}[\text{q}!; P] \mid \text{q}[\text{p}?; Q] \xrightarrow{\text{p}\to\text{q}} \text{p}[P] \mid \text{q}[Q]} \text{ COM}$$

for some p, q, P, and Q. In this case, $N\upharpoonright_{\text{pn}(\mu)} = N\upharpoonright_{\{\text{p,q}\}} = N$ and $N'\upharpoonright_{\text{pn}(\mu)} = N'\upharpoonright_{\{\text{p,q}\}} = N'$, so the thesis follows by $\mathcal{D}$.

Case 2 $\mathcal{D}$ ends with an application of rule PAR:

$$\mathcal{D} = \dfrac{\begin{array}{c}\mathcal{D}'\\ M_1 \xrightarrow{\mu} M'_1\end{array}}{M_1 \mid M_2 \xrightarrow{\mu} M'_1 \mid M_2} \text{ PAR}$$

for some $\mathcal{D}'$, M_1, M_2, and M'_1.

By induction hypothesis on $\mathcal{D}'$, there exists $\mathcal{E} :: M_1\upharpoonright_{\text{pn}(\mu)} \xrightarrow{\mu} M'_1\upharpoonright_{\text{pn}(\mu)}$. By distributivity of restriction (Proposition 3.14), we get:

$$(M_1 \mid M_2)\upharpoonright_{\text{pn}(\mu)} = M_1\upharpoonright_{\text{pn}(\mu)} \mid M_2\upharpoonright_{\text{pn}(\mu)}$$

$$(M'_1 \mid M_2)\upharpoonright_{\text{pn}(\mu)} = M_1\upharpoonright_{\text{pn}(\mu)} \mid M_2\upharpoonright_{\text{pn}(\mu)}.$$

We conclude by the following derivation.

$$\frac{\mathcal{E} \\ M_1\!\upharpoonright_{\mathrm{pn}(\mu)} \xrightarrow{\mu} M_1'\!\upharpoonright_{\mathrm{pn}(\mu)}}{M_1\!\upharpoonright_{\mathrm{pn}(\mu)} \mid M_2\!\upharpoonright_{\mathrm{pn}(\mu)} \xrightarrow{\mu} M_1'\!\upharpoonright_{\mathrm{pn}(\mu)} \mid M_2\!\upharpoonright_{\mathrm{pn}(\mu)}}\ \text{PAR} \qquad \square$$

3.5 Parallelism, Communication Safety, and Starvation-Freedom

Simple Processes is a very minimalistic theory: it does not include features that one would normally expect in programming models, like process memory and the capability of choosing between alternative behaviours. These features will be introduced in later chapters. Nevertheless, the theory is already expressive enough to discuss some key aspects of concurrent and distributed programming. In this section, we discuss the following three.

Parallelism The capability of executing independent communications in any order. This is similar to out-of-order execution in Simple Choreographies, but it is technically obtained differently: parallelism arises in Simple Processes because of how parallel composition works.

Communication Safety The property that processes never attempt to interact by performing incompatible actions.

Starvation-Freedom The property that every running process eventually gets to act in a transition.

3.5.1 Parallelism

Recall the choreography in (2.1), where two buyers communicate with their respective sellers:

$$\mathsf{Buyer}_1 \to \mathsf{Seller}_1; \mathsf{Buyer}_2 \to \mathsf{Seller}_2; \mathbf{0}.$$

The following network implements the same scenario.

$$\begin{aligned} &\mathsf{Buyer}_1[\mathsf{Seller}_1\,!;\mathbf{0}] \mid \mathsf{Seller}_1[\mathsf{Buyer}_1\,?;\mathbf{0}] \\ &\mid \mathsf{Buyer}_2[\mathsf{Seller}_2\,!;\mathbf{0}] \mid \mathsf{Seller}_2[\mathsf{Buyer}_2\,?;\mathbf{0}] \end{aligned} \tag{3.6}$$

Because of commutativity of parallel composition and rule PAR, an execution of this network might start with the communication from Buyer_1 to Seller_1 or with the communication from Buyer_2 to Seller_2, as shown by the following two derivations:

$$\frac{\dfrac{\begin{array}{l}\mathsf{Buyer}_1[\mathsf{Seller}_1\,!;\mathbf{0}] \\ \mid \mathsf{Seller}_1[\mathsf{Buyer}_1\,?;\mathbf{0}]\end{array} \xrightarrow{\mathsf{Buyer}_1 \to \mathsf{Seller}_1} \mathbf{0}}{\begin{array}{l}\mathsf{Buyer}_1[\mathsf{Seller}_1\,!;\mathbf{0}] \\ \mid \mathsf{Seller}_1[\mathsf{Buyer}_1\,?;\mathbf{0}] \\ \mid \mathsf{Buyer}_2[\mathsf{Seller}_2\,!;\mathbf{0}] \\ \mid \mathsf{Seller}_2[\mathsf{Buyer}_2\,?;\mathbf{0}]\end{array} \xrightarrow{\mathsf{Buyer}_1 \to \mathsf{Seller}_1} \begin{array}{l}\mathsf{Buyer}_2[\mathsf{Seller}_2\,!;\mathbf{0}] \\ \mid \mathsf{Seller}_2[\mathsf{Buyer}_2\,?;\mathbf{0}]\end{array}}}{}\ \text{COM / PAR}$$

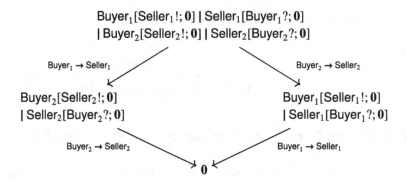

Figure 3.3 Graphical representation of the lts generated by the network in (3.6).

and

$$
\frac{\overline{\begin{matrix} \text{Buyer}_2[\text{Seller}_2!;\mathbf{0}] & \xrightarrow{\text{Buyer}_2 \to \text{Seller}_2} \mathbf{0} \\ |\ \text{Seller}_2[\text{Buyer}_2?;\mathbf{0}] \end{matrix}}\ \text{COM}}{\begin{matrix} \text{Buyer}_1[\text{Seller}_1!;\mathbf{0}] \\ |\ \text{Seller}_1[\text{Buyer}_1?;\mathbf{0}] & \xrightarrow{\text{Buyer}_2 \to \text{Seller}_2} & \text{Buyer}_1[\text{Seller}_1!;\mathbf{0}] \\ |\ \text{Buyer}_2[\text{Seller}_2!;\mathbf{0}] & & |\ \text{Seller}_1[\text{Buyer}_1?;\mathbf{0}] \\ |\ \text{Seller}_2[\text{Buyer}_2?;\mathbf{0}] \end{matrix}}\ \text{PAR}
$$

This is an instance of parallelism: the two transitions are completely independent because they involve separate parts of the network. In other words, the two communications $\text{Buyer}_1 \to \text{Seller}_1$ and $\text{Buyer}_2 \to \text{Seller}_2$ are independent of each other.

We can see the independence of the two communications clearly from the graphical representation of the lts generated by the network in (3.6), which is given in Figure 3.3. The graphical representation reveals also that choosing one transition before the other does not really matter: the processes not affected by the first transition have an opportunity to perform their communication in a later transition. Generalising this observation leads us to the following property about the semantics of Simple Processes: if a network can perform transitions that respectively involve distinct processes, then performing one transition does not prevent performing the other later and we can observe them in any order.

Proposition 3.17 Let N be a network and μ and μ' be transition labels. If $N \xrightarrow{\mu}$, $N \xrightarrow{\mu'}$, and $\text{pn}(\mu) \,\#\, \text{pn}(\mu')$, then $N \xrightarrow{\mu,\mu'}$.

Proof Since $\text{pn}(\mu) \,\#\, \text{pn}(\mu')$, we can rewrite N as the composition of three networks: the subnetwork of N consisting of the processes mentioned in μ, the subnetwork of N consisting of the processes mentioned in μ', and the rest of N.

$$N = N\!\restriction_{\text{pn}(\mu)} \ |\ N\!\restriction_{\text{pn}(\mu')} \ |\ N\!\restriction_{\text{supp}(N)\setminus\text{pn}(\mu)\setminus\text{pn}(\mu')}$$

From the hypotheses $N \xrightarrow{\mu}$ and $N \xrightarrow{\mu'}$, we know that there exist N_1 and N_2 such that $N \xrightarrow{\mu} N_1$ and $N \xrightarrow{\mu'} N_2$. By Lemma 3.16, we get $N\!\restriction_{\text{pn}(\mu)} \xrightarrow{\mu} N_1\!\restriction_{\text{pn}(\mu)}$ and $N\!\restriction_{\text{pn}(\mu')} \xrightarrow{\mu} N_2\!\restriction_{\text{pn}(\mu')}$.

We now prove that N has the following execution.

$$N = N\!\upharpoonright_{\mathrm{pn}(\mu)} \mid N\!\upharpoonright_{\mathrm{pn}(\mu')} \mid N\!\upharpoonright_{\mathrm{supp}(N)\backslash\mathrm{pn}(\mu)\backslash\mathrm{pn}(\mu')}$$

$$\xrightarrow{\mu} N_1\!\upharpoonright_{\mathrm{pn}(\mu)} \mid N\!\upharpoonright_{\mathrm{pn}(\mu')} \mid N\!\upharpoonright_{\mathrm{supp}(N)\backslash\mathrm{pn}(\mu)\backslash\mathrm{pn}(\mu')} \qquad\qquad \text{by rule PAR}$$

$$\xrightarrow{\mu'} N_1\!\upharpoonright_{\mathrm{pn}(\mu)} \mid N_2\!\upharpoonright_{\mathrm{pn}(\mu')} \mid N\!\upharpoonright_{\mathrm{supp}(N)\backslash\mathrm{pn}(\mu)\backslash\mathrm{pn}(\mu')} \qquad\qquad \text{by rule PAR}$$

This is the derivation for the first transition:

$$\frac{N\!\upharpoonright_{\mathrm{pn}(\mu)} \xrightarrow{\mu} N_1\!\upharpoonright_{\mathrm{pn}(\mu)}}{N\!\upharpoonright_{\mathrm{pn}(\mu)} \mid N\!\upharpoonright_{\mathrm{pn}(\mu')} \mid N\!\upharpoonright_{\mathrm{supp}(N)\backslash\mathrm{pn}(\mu)\backslash\mathrm{pn}(\mu')} \xrightarrow{\mu} N_1\!\upharpoonright_{\mathrm{pn}(\mu)} \mid N\!\upharpoonright_{\mathrm{pn}(\mu')} \mid N\!\upharpoonright_{\mathrm{supp}(N)\backslash\mathrm{pn}(\mu)\backslash\mathrm{pn}(\mu')}} \;\text{PAR} \;.$$

And this is the derivation of the second transition:

$$\frac{N\!\upharpoonright_{\mathrm{pn}(\mu')} \xrightarrow{\mu} N_2\!\upharpoonright_{\mathrm{pn}(\mu')}}{N_1\!\upharpoonright_{\mathrm{pn}(\mu)} \mid N\!\upharpoonright_{\mathrm{pn}(\mu')} \mid N\!\upharpoonright_{\mathrm{supp}(N)\backslash\mathrm{pn}(\mu)\backslash\mathrm{pn}(\mu')} \xrightarrow{\mu} N_1\!\upharpoonright_{\mathrm{pn}(\mu)} \mid N_2\!\upharpoonright_{\mathrm{pn}(\mu')} \mid N\!\upharpoonright_{\mathrm{supp}(N)\backslash\mathrm{pn}(\mu)\backslash\mathrm{pn}(\mu')}} \;\text{PAR} \;\square \;.$$

Exercise 3.8 Draw the graphical representations of the labelled transition systems generated by the following networks. (While the purpose of this exercise is mainly to get acquainted with the technicalities of the semantics of Simple Processes, we provide some intuition as to what the following networks might represent in practice.)

1. $o_1[c_1!; 0] \mid o_2[c_2!; 0] \mid c_1[o_1?; a!; 0] \mid c_2[o_2?; a!; 0] \mid a[c_1?; c_2?; 0]$. This network abstracts a system at a factory, where two ordering processes o_1 and o_2 ask the construction processes c_1 and c_2 to build some parts, which are then sent to process a for assembly. Observe how the system initially exhibits parallelism, but then the collection of parts happens in sequence following the order specified in process a.

2. $c[s_1!; s_2!; 0] \mid s_1[c?; l_1!; 0] \mid s_2[c?; l_2!; 0] \mid l_1[s_1?; 0] \mid l_2[s_2?; 0]$. This network abstracts a scenario where a client c sends a command to two independent servers s_1 and s_2, which then log the received command in their respective logging processes, l_1 and l_2. The network exhibits parallelism after the initial interaction between c and s_1.

3.5.2 Communication Safety

A common mistake in distributed programming is to implement processes that end up trying to execute incompatible communication actions [Leesatapornwongsa et al. 2016]. An example in Simple Processes is the network

$$\text{Alice}[\text{Bob}?; 0] \mid \text{Bob}[\text{Alice}?; 0], \tag{3.7}$$

where both Alice and Bob are trying to receive from each other. The network is stuck forever as a result, in the sense that it cannot perform any transitions. Another example of communication mismatch is the following network, where both Alice and Bob try to send to each other.

$$\text{Alice}[\text{Bob}!; 0] \mid \text{Bob}[\text{Alice}!; 0] \tag{3.8}$$

The networks in (3.7) and (3.8) are stuck in Simple Processes because communication actions are matched and executed together by rule COM. This is called a *synchronous communication* semantics: the sender and the receiver synchronise the executions of their respective actions. We formalise the property of having mismatched communications in Simple Processes in the following definition.

Definition 3.18 (Communication Error) A network N has a *communication error* if there are p and q such that one of the following conditions holds.

1. $N(p) = q!; P$ and $N(q) = p!; Q$ for some P and Q.
2. $N(p) = q?; P$ and $N(q) = p?; Q$ for some P and Q.

In the networks in (3.7) and (3.8), communication errors are immediately evident. In general, however, a network that does not show a communication error immediately might encounter one during its execution. As an example, consider the following network, where Alice communicates a message to Bob and then both Alice and Bob wait to receive a message from each other.

$$\text{Alice[Bob!; Bob?; 0] | Bob[Alice?; Alice?; 0]} \tag{3.9}$$

The network in (3.9) does not have a communication error. However, by rule COM, it can perform a transition to a network that has an error:

$$\text{Alice[Bob!; Bob?; 0] | Bob[Alice?; Alice?; 0]} \xrightarrow{\text{Bob→Alice}} \text{Alice[Bob?; 0] | Bob[Alice?; 0]}.$$

This exemplifies that not having an immediately visible communication error does not mean that we are 'safe' from them. To ensure that a network never encounters communication errors, we need to look at all its multi-step derivatives. We say that a network has the *communication safety* property if all its multi-step derivatives do not have communication errors.

Definition 3.19 (Communication Safety) A network N is *communication safe* if all its multi-step derivatives do not have communication errors.

Remark 3.20 Another interesting way of modelling communication is by an *asynchronous communication* semantics. In asynchronous communication, a send action can be executed independently of the state of the receiver and the message is received later when the receiver is ready. This allows senders to proceed even while the intended receivers are busy and cannot process the message yet. We are going to explore asynchronous communication in Chapter 11.

3.5.3 Starvation-Freedom

Networks without communication errors can still have other kinds of problems. A very important one is *starvation*. A process is starving if it is never allowed by the rest of the network to proceed.

In Simple Processes, the presence of a communication error is a sufficient condition for starvation. For example, in the network in (3.7), the process Alice starves because it will never be able to execute its receive action, and Bob starves as well for the same reason. However, the absence of communication errors does not guarantee lack of starvation. For example, in the network Alice[Bob?; 0], the process Alice starves simply because Bob is not running.

We say that a network is *starvation-free* if all its (multi-step) derivatives allow all running processes to eventually participate in a transition.

Definition 3.21 (Starvation-Freedom) A network N is starvation-free if, for all its multi-step derivatives N' and for all $p \in \text{supp}(N')$, there exist $\vec{\mu}, \mu$, and N'' such that $p \in \text{pn}(\mu)$ and $N' \xrightarrow{\vec{\mu}} \xrightarrow{\mu} N''$.

Remark 3.22 In Simple Processes, the multi-step derivatives of a network cannot have more running processes than the initial network. We could therefore give a simpler definition of starvation-freedom based on the processes mentioned by the initial network, rather than all the processes that any multi-step derivative of the initial network can mention. However, this would yield an atypical formulation of starvation-freedom that makes sense only for this particular framework. The formulation given in Definition 3.21 is more standard.

Remark 3.23 Starvation-freedom is a *liveness* property. Liveness properties deal with guaranteeing that some form of progress can be made. Starvation-freedom is one of the strongest forms of progress because progress is guaranteed for each individual process. Another liveness property commonly studied in concurrency is *deadlock-freedom*. Deadlock-freedom states that there is always some process in the network that can eventually progress. It is thus weaker than starvation-freedom, which requires that all processes must eventually make progress [Kobayashi 2002]. (Starvation-freedom implies deadlock-freedom.) We shall come back to deadlock-freedom in Section 8.5.2.

In the next chapter (Section 4.4 in particular), we are going to see that choreographies can be very helpful in achieving communication safety and starvation-freedom.

Exercise 3.9 Let p, q, and r be process names. Prove the following statements.
1. $p[q!; 0] \xrightarrow{\mu}\!\!\!\!/\;$ for any μ.
2. $p[q!; 0] \mid q[p!; 0] \xrightarrow{\mu}\!\!\!\!/\;$ for any μ.
3. There is no $\vec{\mu}$ such that

$$p[q?; r!; q?; 0] \mid q[p!; p!; 0] \mid r[q?; p?; 0] \xrightarrow{\vec{\mu}} 0.$$

---

4 Endpoint Projection

In Chapter 2, we have defined a language for expressing choreographies. Then, in Chapter 3, we have explored how implementations of choreographies can be expressed in terms of compositions of processes called networks. In this chapter, we introduce *endpoint projection (EPP)*: a mechanical translation of choreographies into networks. The name of EPP comes from the fact that an interaction $p \to q$ is implemented by two communication endpoints: the processes p and q, which should execute the appropriate actions that will give rise to the interaction [Qiu et al. 2007; Lanese et al. 2008; Carbone et al. 2012].

Endpoint projection is a cornerstone of both theory and practice of choreographies. It provides the foundation to build compilers from choreographies to specifications or executable programs that define the behaviours of the involved participants, and its exploration led to the discovery of a good portion of what we know about choreographies today. As we are going to see, even for minimalistic languages such as Simple Choreographies and Simple Processes, endpoint projection requires careful formulation and a nontrivial proof to demonstrate its correctness. Correctness, in this setting, is going to be a formalisation of the notion of choreography compliance that we have mentioned in the Preface: each transition performed by a choreography is matched by its endpoint projection, and vice versa. An illustration of the idea of EPP is given in Figure 4.1.

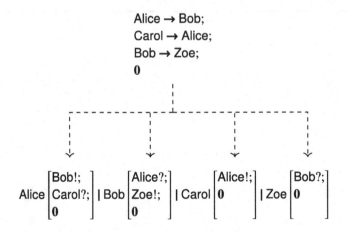

Figure 4.1 An illustration of the idea of endpoint projection (represented by the dashed arrow): a choreography is translated into a compliant network by generating a correct process term for each process mentioned in the choreography.

4.1 Definition of Endpoint Projection

To gain some intuition on how we can define a mapping from choreographies to networks, let us revisit our online bookstore protocol. In Example 2.2, we formalised the protocol with the following choreography.

$$\text{Buyer} \rightarrow \text{Seller}; \text{Seller} \rightarrow \text{Buyer}; \mathbf{0} \qquad (4.1)$$

Then, in Example 3.4, we defined a network that implements the choreography:

$$\text{Buyer}[\text{Seller}!; \text{Seller}?; \mathbf{0}] \mid \text{Seller}[\text{Buyer}?; \text{Buyer}!; \mathbf{0}]. \qquad (4.2)$$

We can observe that for each communication in the choreography, there is a corresponding send action in the program of the sender and a corresponding receive action in the program of the receiver. Specifically, for the first communication, Buyer→Seller, we have the send action Seller! at Buyer and the receive action Buyer? at Seller, and for the second communication, Seller → Buyer, we have the send action Buyer! at Seller and the receive action Seller? at Buyer.

Formalising this principle leads us to the definition of *process projection*, written $[\![]\!]$, which is the core notion of EPP. Process projection is a function from choreographies and process names to process terms:

$$[\![]\!] : \textbf{SimpleChor} \times \textbf{PName} \longrightarrow \textbf{SimpleProc}.$$

Given a choreography C and a process name p, we write $[\![C]\!]_p$ for $[\![]\!](C, p)$. This notation will make presenting equations regarding projection easier in our exposition. Intuitively, $[\![C]\!]_p$ returns the process term that defines the actions that p should execute in order to play its part in the implementation of C. We also call $[\![C]\!]_p$ the 'projection of C on p'.

The definition of process projection is given by recursion on the structure of choreographies.

Definition 4.1 (Process projection) Let C be a choreography and p a process name. The projection of C on p, written $[\![C]\!]_p$, is defined by Equations (4.3) and (4.4).

Process projection for Simple Choreographies

$$[\![p \rightarrow q; C]\!]_r \triangleq \begin{cases} q!; [\![C]\!]_r & \text{if } r = p \\ p?; [\![C]\!]_r & \text{if } r = q \\ [\![C]\!]_r & \text{otherwise} \end{cases} \qquad (4.3)$$

$$[\![\mathbf{0}]\!]_r \triangleq \mathbf{0} \qquad (4.4)$$

Equation (4.3) handles the case in which, for any p, q, and C, the input choreography is an interaction – that is, it has the form $p \rightarrow q; C$. We have three subcases:

- If the input process name r is equal to the name of the sender p, then the result of projection is a send action towards the receiver q, with the projection of C on r as continuation.
- Conversely, if the input process name r is equal to the name of the receiver q, then the result of projection is a receive action from the sender p, with the projection of C on r as continuation.

- If the input process name r is neither p nor q, then we skip the interaction entirely because it does not involve r. We return the projection of the continuation C on r.

The other equation, (4.4), handles the terminated choreography $\mathbf{0}$. Since nothing needs to be done by any process, the returned process term is just $\mathbf{0}$.

Example 4.1   Consider again the choreography in (4.1):

$$\text{Buyer} \to \text{Seller}; \text{Seller} \to \text{Buyer}; \mathbf{0}.$$

The projection of the choreography on Buyer is:

$$
\begin{aligned}
[\![\text{Buyer} \to \text{Seller}; \text{Seller} \to \text{Buyer}; \mathbf{0}]\!]_{\text{Buyer}} &= \text{Seller!}; [\![\text{Seller} \to \text{Buyer}; \mathbf{0}]\!]_{\text{Buyer}} &&\text{by (4.3)} \\
&= \text{Seller!}; \text{Seller?}; [\![\mathbf{0}]\!]_{\text{Buyer}} &&\text{by (4.3)} \\
&= \text{Seller!}; \text{Seller?}; \mathbf{0} &&\text{by (4.4).}
\end{aligned}
$$

The projection on Seller, instead, is:

$$
\begin{aligned}
[\![\text{Buyer} \to \text{Seller}; \text{Seller} \to \text{Buyer}; \mathbf{0}]\!]_{\text{Seller}} &= \text{Buyer?}; [\![\text{Seller} \to \text{Buyer}; \mathbf{0}]\!]_{\text{Seller}} &&\text{by (4.3)} \\
&= \text{Buyer?}; \text{Buyer!}; [\![\mathbf{0}]\!]_{\text{Seller}} &&\text{by (4.3)} \\
&= \text{Buyer?}; \text{Buyer!}; \mathbf{0} &&\text{by (4.4)}
\end{aligned}
$$

Building on process projection, we define endpoint projection (EPP) as a function from choreographies to networks:

$$[\![\,]\!] : \textbf{SimpleChor} \longrightarrow \textbf{SimpleNet}.$$

Notice that we overload the notation $[\![\,]\!]$, which sometimes refers to process projection and sometimes to EPP. This does not cause ambiguity because the two functions have different domains. Given a choreography C, we write $[\![C]\!]$ for $[\![\,]\!](C)$. We call $[\![C]\!]$ 'the EPP of C'.

Definition 4.2 (EndPoint Projection (EPP))   Let C be a choreography. The endpoint projection (EPP) of C, written $[\![C]\!]$, is the network defined as follows, for all $p \in$ **PName**,

$$[\![C]\!](p) \triangleq [\![C]\!]_p.$$

Example 4.2   By Definition 4.2, the EPP of the choreography in (4.1) is as follows.

$$[\![\text{Buyer} \to \text{Seller}; \text{Seller} \to \text{Buyer}; \mathbf{0}]\!](\text{Buyer}) =$$
$$[\![\text{Buyer} \to \text{Seller}; \text{Seller} \to \text{Buyer}; \mathbf{0}]\!]_{\text{Buyer}}$$

$$[\![\text{Buyer} \to \text{Seller}; \text{Seller} \to \text{Buyer}; \mathbf{0}]\!](\text{Seller}) =$$
$$[\![\text{Buyer} \to \text{Seller}; \text{Seller} \to \text{Buyer}; \mathbf{0}]\!]_{\text{Seller}}$$

$$[\![\text{Buyer} \to \text{Seller}; \text{Seller} \to \text{Buyer}; \mathbf{0}]\!](p) = \mathbf{0} \quad \text{for all } p \notin \{\text{Buyer}, \text{Seller}\}$$

More succinctly:

$$[\![\mathsf{Buyer} \to \mathsf{Seller}; \mathsf{Seller} \to \mathsf{Buyer}; \mathbf{0}]\!] =$$
$$\mathsf{Buyer}[[\![\mathsf{Buyer} \to \mathsf{Seller}; \mathsf{Seller} \to \mathsf{Buyer}; \mathbf{0}]\!]_{\mathsf{Buyer}}]$$
$$\mid \mathsf{Seller}[[\![\mathsf{Buyer} \to \mathsf{Seller}; \mathsf{Seller} \to \mathsf{Buyer}; \mathbf{0}]\!]_{\mathsf{Seller}}].$$

From Example 4.1, we know that:

$$[\![\mathsf{Buyer} \to \mathsf{Seller}; \mathsf{Seller} \to \mathsf{Buyer}; \mathbf{0}]\!]_{\mathsf{Buyer}} = \mathsf{Seller}!; \mathsf{Seller}?; \mathbf{0}$$
$$[\![\mathsf{Buyer} \to \mathsf{Seller}; \mathsf{Seller} \to \mathsf{Buyer}; \mathbf{0}]\!]_{\mathsf{Seller}} = \mathsf{Buyer}?; \mathsf{Buyer}!; \mathbf{0}.$$

Hence, the result returned by the EPP of the choreography in (4.1) is:

$$[\![\mathsf{Buyer} \to \mathsf{Seller}; \mathsf{Seller} \to \mathsf{Buyer}; \mathbf{0}]\!] =$$
$$\mathsf{Buyer}[\mathsf{Seller}!; \mathsf{Seller}?; \mathbf{0}] \mid \mathsf{Seller}[\mathsf{Buyer}?; \mathsf{Buyer}!; \mathbf{0}].$$

Example 4.3 Consider the following choreography, in which a postman (called p) delivers a message to three different recipients (called r_1, r_2, and r_3).

$$\mathsf{p} \to r_1; \mathsf{p} \to r_2; \mathsf{p} \to r_3; \mathbf{0}$$

The process projection on p participates in all communications:

$$[\![\mathsf{p} \to r_1; \mathsf{p} \to r_2; \mathsf{p} \to r_3; \mathbf{0}]\!]_{\mathsf{p}} = r_1!; [\![\mathsf{p} \to r_2; \mathsf{p} \to r_3; \mathbf{0}]\!]_{\mathsf{p}}$$
$$= r_1!; r_2!; [\![\mathsf{p} \to r_3; \mathbf{0}]\!]_{\mathsf{p}}$$
$$= r_1!; r_2!; r_3!; [\![\mathbf{0}]\!]_{\mathsf{p}}$$
$$= r_1!; r_2!; r_3!; \mathbf{0}.$$

Instead, the projection on each recipient has only one action, corresponding to the communication in which it is involved.

$$[\![\mathsf{p} \to r_1; \mathsf{p} \to r_2; \mathsf{p} \to r_3; \mathbf{0}]\!]_{r_1} = \mathsf{p}?; [\![\mathsf{p} \to r_2; \mathsf{p} \to r_3; \mathbf{0}]\!]_{r_1}$$
$$= \mathsf{p}?; [\![\mathsf{p} \to r_3; \mathbf{0}]\!]_{r_1}$$
$$= \mathsf{p}?; [\![\mathbf{0}]\!]_{r_1}$$
$$= \mathsf{p}?; \mathbf{0}$$

$$[\![\mathsf{p} \to r_1; \mathsf{p} \to r_2; \mathsf{p} \to r_3; \mathbf{0}]\!]_{r_2} = [\![\mathsf{p} \to r_2; \mathsf{p} \to r_3; \mathbf{0}]\!]_{r_2}$$
$$= \mathsf{p}?; [\![\mathsf{p} \to r_3; \mathbf{0}]\!]_{r_2}$$
$$= \mathsf{p}?; [\![\mathbf{0}]\!]_{r_2}$$
$$= \mathsf{p}?; \mathbf{0}$$

$$[\![\mathsf{p} \to r_1; \mathsf{p} \to r_2; \mathsf{p} \to r_3; \mathbf{0}]\!]_{r_3} = [\![\mathsf{p} \to r_2; \mathsf{p} \to r_3; \mathbf{0}]\!]_{r_3}$$
$$= [\![\mathsf{p} \to r_3; \mathbf{0}]\!]_{r_3}$$
$$= \mathsf{p}?; [\![\mathbf{0}]\!]_{r_3}$$
$$= \mathsf{p}?; \mathbf{0}$$

Hence, the EPP of the choreography is as follows.

$$[\![\mathsf{p} \to r_1; \mathsf{p} \to r_2; \mathsf{p} \to r_3; \mathbf{0}]\!] = \mathsf{p}[r_1!; r_2!; r_3!; \mathbf{0}] \mid r_1[\mathsf{p}?; \mathbf{0}] \mid r_2[\mathsf{p}?; \mathbf{0}] \mid r_3[\mathsf{p}?; \mathbf{0}]$$

Exercise 4.1 Let p, q, r, and s be process names. Write the EPPs of the following choreography.

$$p \to q; r \to q; r \to s; q \to p; 0$$

4.2   Finite Representability of Endpoint Projections

The image of EPP enjoys finite representability. That is, all networks returned by EPP can be finitely represented, specifically by using the notation that we defined in Section 3.2.2.

To prove that EPPs are finitely representable, we show that every EPP of a choreography has finite support, and then invoke the property that all networks with finite support are finitely representable (Proposition 3.6).

As starting point, recall that for every choreography C, the support of $[\![C]\!]$ is defined as

$$\mathrm{supp}([\![C]\!]) = \{p \mid [\![C]\!](p) \neq 0\}.$$

Since $[\![C]\!](p) = [\![C]\!]_p$, we can rewrite the equation as

$$\mathrm{supp}([\![C]\!]) = \{p \mid [\![C]\!]_p \neq 0\}.$$

Is the set $\{p \mid [\![C]\!]_p \neq 0\}$ finite? Intuitively it should because every choreography is finite and can thus only mention a finite number of processes.

Let us make precise the notion of 'processes mentioned in a choreography'. We build a function, pn (for process names), that maps each choreography to the set of process names that it mentions. The function is defined by recursion on the structure of the input choreography, as follows.

$$\mathrm{pn}(0) \triangleq \emptyset$$
$$\mathrm{pn}(p \to q; C) \triangleq \{p, q\} \cup \mathrm{pn}(C)$$

Example 4.4 For example, the choreography in Example 4.3 mentions the names p, r_1, r_2, and r_3.

$$\begin{aligned}
\mathrm{pn}(p \to r_1; p \to r_2; p \to r_3; 0) &= \{p, r_1\} \cup \mathrm{pn}(p \to r_2; p \to r_3; 0) \\
&= \{p, r_1, r_2\} \cup \mathrm{pn}(p \to r_3; 0) \\
&= \{p, r_1, r_2, r_3\} \cup \mathrm{pn}(0) \\
&= \{p, r_1, r_2, r_3\}
\end{aligned}$$

Notice that pn can now refer to either the function just given or the one presented in Section 3.4.1 for computing the set of processes mentioned in a transition label. There is no ambiguity since their domains are disjoint.

For every choreography C, the set $\text{pn}(C)$ is finite because at each recursive step in the definition of pn we are returning the union of finite sets (the base case is the $\emptyset$ for the choreography $\mathbf{0}$). Proving this might be considered overzealous, but it is also a nice opportunity to showcase how the induction principle can be used to reason about a recursive function.

Proposition 4.3   For every C, $\text{pn}(C)$ is a finite set.

Proof   By structural induction on C.

Case 1 $C = \mathbf{0}$. In this case, $\text{pn}(\mathbf{0}) = \emptyset$, which is a finite set.

Case 2 $C = \mathsf{p} \to \mathsf{q}; C'$ for some p, q, and C'. By induction hypothesis, we know that $\text{pn}(C')$ is a finite set. By definition of pn, $\text{pn}(C) = \{\mathsf{p}, \mathsf{q}\} \cup \text{pn}(C')$. Hence, $\text{pn}(C)$ is the union of two finite sets, and it is therefore itself a finite set. $\square$

We now prove that $\text{supp}(\llbracket C \rrbracket) = \text{pn}(C)$ for every choreography C by showing that any process name appears in $\text{supp}(\llbracket C \rrbracket)$ if and only if it appears in $\text{pn}(C)$. Since $\text{pn}(C)$ is finite for all C, this will imply that $\text{supp}(\llbracket C \rrbracket)$ is finite as well.

Proposition 4.4   For every C and r, $\text{supp}(\llbracket C \rrbracket) = \text{pn}(C)$.

Proof   By structural induction on C.

Case 1 $C = \mathbf{0}$. In this case, $\text{supp}(\llbracket C \rrbracket) = \text{supp}(\mathbf{0}) = \emptyset = \text{pn}(\mathbf{0}) = \text{pn}(C)$.

Case 2 $C = \mathsf{p} \to \mathsf{q}; C'$ for some p, q, and C'. By definition of EPP, in particular (4.3), $\llbracket C \rrbracket_\mathsf{p} = \mathsf{q}!; \llbracket C' \rrbracket_\mathsf{p}$ and $\llbracket C \rrbracket_\mathsf{q} = \mathsf{p}?; \llbracket C' \rrbracket_\mathsf{q}$. Therefore, $\llbracket C \rrbracket(\mathsf{p}) \neq \mathbf{0}$ and $\llbracket C \rrbracket(\mathsf{q}) \neq \mathbf{0}$. For all other processes $\mathsf{r} \neq \mathsf{p}, \mathsf{q}$, $\llbracket C \rrbracket_\mathsf{r} = \llbracket C' \rrbracket_\mathsf{r}$. Hence, $\text{supp}(\llbracket C \rrbracket) = \{\mathsf{p}, \mathsf{q}\} \cup \text{supp}(\llbracket C' \rrbracket)$.

By definition of pn, $\text{pn}(C) = \{\mathsf{p}, \mathsf{q}\} \cup \text{pn}(C')$. By induction hypothesis, we have that $\text{supp}(\llbracket C' \rrbracket) = \text{pn}(C')$. Thus,

$$\text{supp}(\llbracket C \rrbracket) = \{\mathsf{p}, \mathsf{q}\} \cup \text{supp}(\llbracket C' \rrbracket) = \{\mathsf{p}, \mathsf{q}\} \cup \text{pn}(C') = \text{pn}(C). \qquad \square$$

Combining Proposition 4.3 and 4.4 gives us the property that every result of EPP has finite support.

Corollary 4.5   For every C, $\text{supp}(\llbracket C \rrbracket)$ is finite.

By combining Corollary 4.5 and Proposition 3.6, we finally obtain the result that we set out to prove in this section: all endpoint projections are representable.

Corollary 4.6   For every C, $\llbracket C \rrbracket$ has a finite representation.

4.3   Correctness of Endpoint Projection

Next in our order of business is to prove that EPP is correct, in the sense that the implementations that it returns actually comply with the choreographies given as input.

Labelled transition systems give us an elegant way of formalising compliance: we can say that a network implements a choreography if it mimics all and only the transitions that the choreography can perform.

$$p \to r_1; p \to r_2; p \to r_3; 0 \dashrightarrow p[r_1!; r_2!; r_3!; 0] \mid r_1[p?; 0] \mid r_2[p?; 0] \mid r_3[p?; 0]$$

$$\Big\downarrow p \to r_1 \qquad\qquad\qquad\qquad\qquad\qquad \Big\downarrow p \to r_1$$

$$p \to r_2; p \to r_3; 0 \dashrightarrow p[r_2!; r_3!; 0] \mid r_2[p?; 0] \mid r_3[p?; 0]$$

$$\Big\downarrow p \to r_2 \qquad\qquad\qquad\qquad\qquad\qquad \Big\downarrow p \to r_2$$

$$p \to r_3; 0 \dashrightarrow p[r_3!; 0] \mid r_3[p?; 0]$$

$$\Big\downarrow p \to r_3 \qquad\qquad\qquad\qquad\qquad\qquad \Big\downarrow p \to r_3$$

$$0 \dashrightarrow 0$$

Figure 4.2 Labelled transition systems generated by the choreography in Example 4.3 (on the left) and its endpoint projection (on the right). A dashed arrow from a choreography to a network denotes that the latter is the result of applying endpoint projection to the former.

Let us build some intuition first. Recall the choreography from Example 4.3,

$$p \to r_1; p \to r_2; p \to r_3; 0,$$

and its EPP,

$$[\![p \to r_1; p \to r_2; p \to r_3; 0]\!] = p[r_1!; r_2!; r_3!; 0] \mid r_1[p?; 0] \mid r_2[p?; 0] \mid r_3[p?; 0].$$

Looking at the labelled transition systems respectively generated by the choreography and its EPP, displayed in Figure 4.2, we can see that they are isomorphic. In particular, each transition in one is matched by a corresponding transition in the other. Furthermore, notice that each node in the graph on the right is the projection of a corresponding node in the graph on the left. That is, all the multi-step derivatives of the initial choreography are still related by EPP to the multi-step derivatives of the EPP of the initial choreography.

As an example that the observations we made so far still hold in the presence of parallelism, consider the following choreography, where p_1 communicates with q_1 and p_2 communicates with q_2:

$$p_1 \to q_1; p_2 \to q_2; 0. \tag{4.5}$$

The EPP of this choreography is:

$$[\![p_1 \to q_1; p_2 \to q_2; 0]\!] = p_1[q_1!; 0] \mid q_1[p_1?; 0] \mid p_2[q_2!; 0] \mid q_2[p_2?; 0].$$

The graphical representations of the labelled transition systems generated by the choreography and its EPP, given in Figure 4.3, match as expected.

Generalising the observations that we have made so far, we reach the following formulation for the correctness of EPP.

Theorem 4.7 (Correctness of EPP for Simple Choreographies)   The following statements hold for every choreography C.

Completeness For any μ and C', $C \xrightarrow{\mu} C'$ implies $[\![C]\!] \xrightarrow{\mu} [\![C']\!]$.

Soundness For any μ and N, $[\![C]\!] \xrightarrow{\mu} N$ implies $C \xrightarrow{\mu} C'$ for some C' such that $N = [\![C']\!]$.

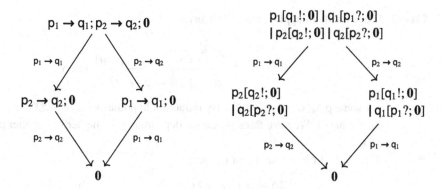

Figure 4.3 Labelled transition systems generated by the choreography in (4.5) (on the left) and its endpoint projection (on the right).

The completeness part of Theorem 4.7 states that EPP returns networks that can mimic all transitions of their originating choreographies: whenever a choreography has a μ-derivative, the EPP of the choreography has itself the EPP of such μ-derivative as μ-derivative. In other words, all networks returned by EPP are *complete* implementations of their originating choreographies.

Conversely, the soundness part of Theorem 4.7 states that EPP returns networks that can only perform transitions prescribed by their originating choreographies: whenever the EPP of a choreography has a μ-derivative – that is the EPP of a μ-derivative of the choreography. In other words, all networks returned by EPP are *sound* implementations, in the sense that they never perform actions not prescribed by the choreography.

Completeness and soundness together tell us that the EPP of a choreography does exactly what the choreography defines. Hence, what happens in the implementation (the network) is what we want to happen (defined in the choreography), so to speak. We prove the two results of Theorem 4.7 as separate lemmas, respectively Lemma 4.9 and Lemma 4.10, in the next two subsections. In the proofs, we extensively use the results that we have proved about networks in Sections 3.2 and 3.4. We point out explicitly which results are used in the key steps of the proofs. Sometimes, we apply the equality laws of parallel composition implicitly to present networks in forms that match better the text in the proofs.

4.3.1 Completeness

We start with an auxiliary lemma: process projection remains invariant under transitions that do not involve the projected process.

Lemma 4.8 For all C, μ, and C', if $C \xrightarrow{\mu} C'$, then $[\![C]\!]_r = [\![C']\!]_r$ for all $r \notin pn(\mu)$.

Proof Let $\mathcal{D}$ be the derivation of $C \xrightarrow{\mu} C'$. We proceed by induction on $\mathcal{D}$.

Case 1 $\mathcal{D}$ ends with an application of rule com:

$$\mathcal{D} = \frac{}{p \to q; C' \xrightarrow{p \to q} C'} \text{ COM}$$

for some p, q, and C'. The thesis follows by definition of process projection, since $[\![p \to q; C']\!]_r = [\![C']\!]_r$ for all $r \notin \{p, q\}$.

Case 2 $\mathcal{D}$ ends with an application of rule DELAY:

$$\mathcal{D} = \dfrac{\overset{\mathcal{D}'}{\overline{C_1 \xrightarrow{\mu} C_2}} \quad \{\mathsf{p}, \mathsf{q}\} \,\#\, pn(\mu)}{\mathsf{p} \to \mathsf{q}; C_1 \xrightarrow{\mu} \mathsf{p} \to \mathsf{q}; C_2} \; \text{DELAY}$$

for some $\mathsf{p}, \mathsf{q}, C_1, C_2$, and $\mathcal{D}'$. By induction hypothesis (i.h.) on $\mathcal{D}'$, $[\![C_1]\!]_\mathsf{r} = [\![C_2]\!]_\mathsf{r}$ for all $\mathsf{r} \notin pn(\mu)$. We have three subcases, depending on whether r is neither p nor q, r is p, or r is q.

Case 2.1 If r is neither p nor q, then:

$$\begin{aligned}
[\![\mathsf{p} \to \mathsf{q}; C_1]\!]_\mathsf{r} &= [\![C_1]\!]_\mathsf{r} && \text{by (4.3)}\\
&= [\![C_2]\!]_\mathsf{r} && \text{by i.h. and } \mathsf{r} \notin pn(\mu)\\
&= [\![\mathsf{p} \to \mathsf{q}; C_2]\!]_\mathsf{r} && \text{by (4.3).}
\end{aligned}$$

Case 2.2 If $\mathsf{r} = \mathsf{p}$, then:

$$\begin{aligned}
[\![\mathsf{p} \to \mathsf{q}; C_1]\!]_\mathsf{r} &= \mathsf{q}!; [\![C_1]\!]_\mathsf{r} && \text{by (4.3)}\\
&= \mathsf{q}!; [\![C_2]\!]_\mathsf{r} && \text{by i.h. and } \mathsf{r} \notin pn(\mu)\\
&= [\![\mathsf{p} \to \mathsf{q}; C_2]\!]_\mathsf{r} && \text{by (4.3).}
\end{aligned}$$

Case 2.3 If $\mathsf{r} = \mathsf{q}$, then:

$$\begin{aligned}
[\![\mathsf{p} \to \mathsf{q}; C_1]\!]_\mathsf{r} &= \mathsf{p}?; [\![C_1]\!]_\mathsf{r} && \text{by (4.3)}\\
&= \mathsf{p}?; [\![C_2]\!]_\mathsf{r} && \text{by i.h. and } \mathsf{r} \notin pn(\mu)\\
&= [\![\mathsf{p} \to \mathsf{q}; C_2]\!]_\mathsf{r} && \text{by (4.3).} \qquad \square
\end{aligned}$$

We now have all the necessary ingredients to prove the completeness part of the correctness of EPP.

Lemma 4.9 For every C, μ, and C', $C \xrightarrow{\mu} C'$ implies $[\![C]\!] \xrightarrow{\mu} [\![C']\!]$.

Proof Let $\mathcal{D}$ be the derivation of $C \xrightarrow{\mu} C'$. We proceed by structural induction on $\mathcal{D}$.

Case 1 $\mathcal{D}$ ends with an application of rule COM:

$$\mathcal{D} = \dfrac{}{\mathsf{p} \to \mathsf{q}; C' \xrightarrow{\mathsf{p} \to \mathsf{q}} C'} \; \text{COM}$$

for some p, q, and C'. We have the following equalities for $[\![C]\!]$.

$$[\![C]\!] = [\![C]\!] \setminus \mathsf{p}, \mathsf{q} \mid \mathsf{p}[\mathsf{q}!; [\![C']\!]_\mathsf{p}] \mid \mathsf{q}[\mathsf{p}?; [\![C']\!]_\mathsf{q}]$$
$$\text{by Proposition 3.15 and (4.3)}$$
$$= [\![C']\!] \setminus \mathsf{p}, \mathsf{q} \mid \mathsf{p}[\mathsf{q}!; [\![C']\!]_\mathsf{p}] \mid \mathsf{q}[\mathsf{p}?; [\![C']\!]_\mathsf{q}] \qquad \text{by Lemma 4.8}$$

By rules PAR and COM for networks, $[\![C]\!]$ can mimic the choreographic transition:

$$\dfrac{\dfrac{}{\mathsf{p}[\mathsf{q}!; [\![C']\!]_\mathsf{p}] \mid \mathsf{q}[\mathsf{p}?; [\![C']\!]_\mathsf{q}] \xrightarrow{\mathsf{p} \to \mathsf{q}} \mathsf{p}[[\![C']\!]_\mathsf{p}] \mid \mathsf{q}[[\![C']\!]_\mathsf{q}]} \; \text{COM}}{\begin{aligned} [\![C']\!] \setminus \mathsf{p}, \mathsf{q} \mid \mathsf{p}[\mathsf{q}!; [\![C']\!]_\mathsf{p}] \mid \mathsf{q}[\mathsf{p}?; [\![C']\!]_\mathsf{q}] \\ \xrightarrow{\mathsf{p} \to \mathsf{q}} [\![C']\!] \setminus \mathsf{p}, \mathsf{q} \mid \mathsf{p}[[\![C']\!]_\mathsf{p}] \mid \mathsf{q}[[\![C']\!]_\mathsf{q}] \end{aligned}} \; \text{PAR} \qquad (4.6)$$

By Proposition 3.15,

$$\llbracket C' \rrbracket \setminus \mathsf{p}, \mathsf{q} \mid \mathsf{p}[\llbracket C' \rrbracket_\mathsf{p}] \mid \mathsf{q}[\llbracket C' \rrbracket_\mathsf{q}] = \llbracket C' \rrbracket.$$

This concludes the case. To recap:

$$\llbracket C \rrbracket = \llbracket C \rrbracket \setminus \mathsf{p}, \mathsf{q} \mid \mathsf{p}[\mathsf{q}!; \llbracket C' \rrbracket_\mathsf{p}] \mid \mathsf{q}[\mathsf{p}?; \llbracket C' \rrbracket_\mathsf{q}]$$

by Proposition 3.15 and (4.3)

$$= \llbracket C' \rrbracket \setminus \mathsf{p}, \mathsf{q} \mid \mathsf{p}[\mathsf{q}!; \llbracket C' \rrbracket_\mathsf{p}] \mid \mathsf{q}[\mathsf{p}?; \llbracket C' \rrbracket_\mathsf{q}] \qquad \text{by Lemma 4.8}$$

$$\xrightarrow{\mathsf{p} \to \mathsf{q}} \llbracket C' \rrbracket \setminus \mathsf{p}, \mathsf{q} \mid \mathsf{p}[\llbracket C' \rrbracket_\mathsf{p}] \mid \mathsf{q}[\llbracket C' \rrbracket_\mathsf{q}]$$

by rules PAR and COM, see (4.6)

$$= \llbracket C' \rrbracket \qquad \qquad \text{by Proposition 3.15.}$$

Case 2 $\mathcal{D}$ ends with an application of rule DELAY:

$$\mathcal{D} = \frac{\overset{\mathcal{D}'}{C_1 \xrightarrow{\mu} C_2} \quad \{\mathsf{p}, \mathsf{q}\} \# \mathrm{pn}(\mu)}{\mathsf{p} \to \mathsf{q}; C_1 \xrightarrow{\mu} \mathsf{p} \to \mathsf{q}; C_2} \; \text{DELAY}$$

for some p, q, C_1, C_2, and $\mathcal{D}'$.

By (4.3) and Proposition 3.15,

$$\llbracket C \rrbracket = \llbracket C_1 \rrbracket \setminus \mathsf{p}, \mathsf{q} \mid \mathsf{p}[\mathsf{q}!; \llbracket C_1 \rrbracket_\mathsf{p}] \mid \mathsf{q}[\mathsf{p}?; \llbracket C_1 \rrbracket_\mathsf{q}].$$

By induction hypothesis on $\mathcal{D}'$, there exists $\mathcal{E} :: \llbracket C_1 \rrbracket \xrightarrow{\mu} \llbracket C_2 \rrbracket$. Since p and q do not appear in μ (by $\mathcal{D}$), we can invoke Lemma 3.10 and obtain that $\llbracket C_1 \rrbracket \setminus \mathsf{p}, \mathsf{q} \xrightarrow{\mu} \llbracket C_2 \rrbracket \setminus \mathsf{p}, \mathsf{q}$. We use this to make the following derivation:

$$\frac{\overset{\mathcal{E}}{\llbracket C_1 \rrbracket \setminus \mathsf{p}, \mathsf{q} \xrightarrow{\mu} \llbracket C_2 \rrbracket \setminus \mathsf{p}, \mathsf{q}}}{\llbracket C_1 \rrbracket \setminus \mathsf{p}, \mathsf{q} \mid \mathsf{p}[\mathsf{q}!; \llbracket C_1 \rrbracket_\mathsf{p}] \mid \mathsf{q}[\mathsf{p}?; \llbracket C_1 \rrbracket_\mathsf{q}]} \; \text{PAR} \qquad (4.7)$$
$$\xrightarrow{\mu} \llbracket C_2 \rrbracket \setminus \mathsf{p}, \mathsf{q} \mid \mathsf{p}[\mathsf{q}!; \llbracket C_1 \rrbracket_\mathsf{p}] \mid \mathsf{q}[\mathsf{p}?; \llbracket C_1 \rrbracket_\mathsf{q}]$$

Again, since p and q do not appear in μ, by Proposition 3.7 we obtain that $\llbracket C_1 \rrbracket_\mathsf{p} = \llbracket C_2 \rrbracket_\mathsf{p}$ and $\llbracket C_1 \rrbracket_\mathsf{q} = \llbracket C_2 \rrbracket_\mathsf{q}$. Therefore the derivative we obtained with rule PAR is equal to $\llbracket \mathsf{p} \to \mathsf{q}; C_2 \rrbracket$, and the thesis follows. We summarise the reasoning for this case:

$$\llbracket C \rrbracket = \llbracket C_1 \rrbracket \setminus \mathsf{p}, \mathsf{q} \mid \mathsf{p}[\mathsf{q}!; \llbracket C_1 \rrbracket_\mathsf{p}] \mid \mathsf{q}[\mathsf{p}?; \llbracket C_1 \rrbracket_\mathsf{q}]$$

by Proposition 3.15 and (4.3)

$$\xrightarrow{\mu} \llbracket C_2 \rrbracket \setminus \mathsf{p}, \mathsf{q} \mid \mathsf{p}[\mathsf{q}!; \llbracket C_1 \rrbracket_\mathsf{p}] \mid \mathsf{q}[\mathsf{p}?; \llbracket C_1 \rrbracket_\mathsf{q}] \qquad \text{by (4.7)}$$

$$= \llbracket C_2 \rrbracket \setminus \mathsf{p}, \mathsf{q} \mid \mathsf{p}[\mathsf{q}!; \llbracket C_2 \rrbracket_\mathsf{p}] \mid \mathsf{q}[\mathsf{p}?; \llbracket C_2 \rrbracket_\mathsf{q}] \qquad \text{by Lemma 4.8}$$

$$= \llbracket C_2 \rrbracket \setminus \mathsf{p}, \mathsf{q} \mid \mathsf{p}[\llbracket \mathsf{p} \to \mathsf{q}; C_2 \rrbracket_\mathsf{p}] \mid \mathsf{q}[\llbracket \mathsf{p} \to \mathsf{q}; C_2 \rrbracket_\mathsf{q}] \qquad \text{by (4.3)}$$

$$= \llbracket \mathsf{p} \to \mathsf{q}; C_2 \rrbracket \qquad \qquad \text{by Definition 4.2.} \qquad \square$$

4.3.2   Soundness

We now move to proving the soundness result for EPP.

Lemma 4.10 (Soundness of EPP)   For all C, μ, and N, $[\![C]\!] \xrightarrow{\mu} N$ implies $C \xrightarrow{\mu} C'$ for some C' such that $N = [\![C']\!]$.

Proof   By structural induction on C.

Case 1 $C = \mathbf{0}$. In this case, $[\![C]\!] = \mathbf{0}$ so there are no transitions to consider.

Case 2 $C = \mathsf{p} \to \mathsf{q}; C_1$ for some C_1. By definition of EPP and Proposition 3.15,

$$[\![C]\!] = [\![C_1]\!] \setminus \mathsf{p}, \mathsf{q} \mid \mathsf{p}[\mathsf{q}!; [\![C_1]\!]_\mathsf{p}] \mid \mathsf{q}[\mathsf{p}?; [\![C_1]\!]_\mathsf{q}]. \tag{4.8}$$

For all μ and N such that $[\![C]\!] \xrightarrow{\mu} N$, given the structures of the process terms for p and q in (4.8), we have two cases: the transition is either the interaction between p and q ($\mu = \mathsf{p} \to \mathsf{q}$), or it is not ($\{\mathsf{p}, \mathsf{q}\} \# \mathrm{pn}(\mu)$).

Case 2.1 If $\mu = \mathsf{p} \to \mathsf{q}$, then we are synchronising the send and receive actions at p and q. By Proposition 3.7, the rest of the network remains the same and we thus obtain that N is $[\![C_1]\!]$:

$$N = [\![C_1]\!] \setminus \mathsf{p}, \mathsf{q} \mid \mathsf{p}[[\![C_1]\!]_\mathsf{p}] \mid \mathsf{q}[[\![C_1]\!]_\mathsf{q}] = [\![C_1]\!].$$

The thesis now follows by rule com, for $C' \triangleq C_1$:

$$C = \mathsf{p} \to \mathsf{q}; C_1 \xrightarrow{\mathsf{p} \to \mathsf{q}} C_1.$$

Case 2.2 If $\{\mathsf{p}, \mathsf{q}\} \# \mathrm{pn}(\mu)$, then by (4.8), $[\![C]\!] \xrightarrow{\mu} N$, and Lemma 3.12 we get:

$$[\![C_1]\!] \setminus \mathsf{p}, \mathsf{q} \xrightarrow{\mu} N \setminus \mathsf{p}, \mathsf{q}. \tag{4.9}$$

The EPP of C_1 can mimic the transition:

$$
\begin{aligned}
[\![C_1]\!] &= [\![C_1]\!] \setminus \mathsf{p}, \mathsf{q} \mid \mathsf{p}[[\![C_1]\!]_\mathsf{p}] \mid \mathsf{q}[[\![C_1]\!]_\mathsf{q}] && \text{by Proposition 3.15}\\
&\xrightarrow{\mu} N \setminus \mathsf{p}, \mathsf{q} \mid \mathsf{p}[[\![C_1]\!]_\mathsf{p}] \mid \mathsf{q}[[\![C_1]\!]_\mathsf{q}] && \text{by (4.9) and rule par.}
\end{aligned}
$$

Since $[\![C_1]\!]$ can perform a transition, by induction hypothesis there is $\mathcal{E} :: C_1 \xrightarrow{\mu} C_2$ for some C_2 such that

$$[\![C_2]\!] = N \setminus \mathsf{p}, \mathsf{q} \mid \mathsf{p}[[\![C_1]\!]_\mathsf{p}] \mid \mathsf{q}[[\![C_1]\!]_\mathsf{q}]. \tag{4.10}$$

By definition of EPP,

$$[\![C_2]\!] = [\![C_2]\!] \setminus \mathsf{p}, \mathsf{q} \mid \mathsf{p}[[\![C_2]\!]_\mathsf{p}] \mid \mathsf{q}[[\![C_2]\!]_\mathsf{q}]. \tag{4.11}$$

The system formed by the equations in (4.10) and (4.12) gives us:

$$N \setminus \mathsf{p}, \mathsf{q} = [\![C_2]\!] \setminus \mathsf{p}, \mathsf{q} \tag{4.12}$$

$$[\![C_1]\!]_\mathsf{p} = [\![C_2]\!]_\mathsf{p} \tag{4.13}$$

$$[\![C_1]\!]_\mathsf{q} = [\![C_2]\!]_\mathsf{q}. \tag{4.14}$$

By rule DELAY, we obtain the following transition for C.

$$\frac{\mathcal{E} \atop C_1 \xrightarrow{\mu} C_2 \quad \{\mathsf{p}, \mathsf{q}\} \,\#\, \mathrm{pn}(\mu)}{\mathsf{p} \to \mathsf{q}; C_1 \xrightarrow{\mu} \mathsf{p} \to \mathsf{q}; C_2} \; \text{DELAY}$$

We now prove the thesis for $C' \triangleq \mathsf{p} \to \mathsf{q}; C_2$, by showing that $N = [\![C']\!]$. In the second equation that follows, the equality is justified by the definition of EPP and Proposition 3.7, since $\{\mathsf{p}, \mathsf{q}\} \,\#\, \mathrm{pn}(\mu)$ and $[\![C]\!] \xrightarrow{\mu} N$.

$$
\begin{aligned}
N &= N \setminus \mathsf{p}, \mathsf{q} \mid \mathsf{p}[N(\mathsf{p})] \mid \mathsf{q}[N(\mathsf{q})] && \text{by Proposition 3.15} \\
&= N \setminus \mathsf{p}, \mathsf{q} \mid \mathsf{p}[[\![C]\!]_\mathsf{p}] \mid \mathsf{q}[[\![C]\!]_\mathsf{q}] && \text{by Proposition 3.7} \\
&= N \setminus \mathsf{p}, \mathsf{q} \mid \mathsf{p}[\mathsf{q}!; [\![C_1]\!]_\mathsf{p}] \mid \mathsf{q}[\mathsf{p}?; [\![C_1]\!]_\mathsf{q}] && \text{by } C = \mathsf{p} \to \mathsf{q}; C_1 \\
&= [\![C_2]\!] \setminus \mathsf{p}, \mathsf{q} \mid \mathsf{p}[\mathsf{q}!; [\![C_1]\!]_\mathsf{p}] \mid \mathsf{q}[\mathsf{p}?; [\![C_1]\!]_\mathsf{q}] && \text{by (4.12)} \\
&= [\![C_2]\!] \setminus \mathsf{p}, \mathsf{q} \mid \mathsf{p}[\mathsf{q}!; [\![C_2]\!]_\mathsf{p}] \mid \mathsf{q}[\mathsf{p}?; [\![C_2]\!]_\mathsf{q}] && \text{by (4.13) and (4.14)} \\
&= [\![\mathsf{p} \to \mathsf{q}; C_2]\!] && \text{by Definition 4.2} \\
&= [\![C']\!] && \text{by } C' = \mathsf{p} \to \mathsf{q}; C_2 \qquad \square
\end{aligned}
$$

Theorem 4.7 now follows immediately from Lemmas 4.9 and 4.10.

4.4 Consequences of the Correctness of Endpoint Projection

The correctness of EPP has important consequences: all networks produced by EPP are both communication safe and starvation-free. We discuss these results in the following two subsections. Their proofs rely on the following property, in which we generalise the correctness of EPP from a single transition to many.

Theorem 4.11 The following statements hold for every choreography C.

Completeness of Executions For any $\vec{\mu}$ and C', $C \xrightarrow{\vec{\mu}}{}^* C'$ implies $[\![C]\!] \xrightarrow{\vec{\mu}}{}^* [\![C']\!]$.

Soundness of Executions For any $\vec{\mu}$ and N, if $[\![C]\!] \xrightarrow{\vec{\mu}}{}^* N$, then $C \xrightarrow{\vec{\mu}}{}^* C'$ for some C' such that $N = [\![C']\!]$.

Exercise 4.2 ($\hookrightarrow$) Prove Theorem 4.11. (Hint: prove the two results separately, proceeding for each by structural induction on the derivation of its respective hypothesis.)

4.4.1 Communication Safety for Endpoint Projection

We can now prove that all endpoint projections are communication safe.

Theorem 4.12 For every C, $[\![C]\!]$ is communication safe.

Proof We need to prove that, for every N and $\vec{\mu}$ such that $[\![C]\!] \xrightarrow{\vec{\mu}} N$, N does not have communication errors. For every such N, by Theorem 4.11 there exists C' such that $C \xrightarrow{\vec{\mu}} C'$ and $N = [\![C']\!]$.

We proceed to showing that $[\![C']\!]$ does not have communication errors, by induction on the structure of C'.

Case 1 $C' = \mathbf{0}$. Trivial, because in this case $[\![C']\!] = \mathbf{0}$.

Case 2 $C' = \mathsf{p} \to \mathsf{q}; C''$ for some p, q, and C''. By induction hypothesis, $[\![C'']\!]$ does not have communication errors. Thus, the only way for $[\![\mathsf{p} \to \mathsf{q}; C'']\!]$ to have a communication error is that the process projections of p and q start with incompatible communication actions. However, by Definition 4.1, this cannot be the case.   □

4.4.2 Starvation-Freedom for Endpoint Projection

Moving to liveness, we first observe that all choreographies eventually allow processes to participate in a transition, by design of the semantics of Simple Choreographies.

Lemma 4.13 For every C and process r, $\mathsf{r} \in \mathrm{pn}(C)$ implies that there exist $\vec{\mu}$, μ, and C' such that $C \xrightarrow{\vec{\mu}} \xrightarrow{\mu} C'$ and $\mathsf{r} \in \mathrm{pn}(\mu)$.

Proof By induction on the structure of C.

Case 1 $C = \mathbf{0}$. Trivial, since $\mathrm{pn}(C) = \emptyset$.

Case 2 $C = \mathsf{p} \to \mathsf{q}; C''$ for some p, q, and C''. By rule COM, we get $C \xrightarrow{\mathsf{p} \to \mathsf{q}} C''$. We have two cases: r is p or q, or r is some other process in $\mathrm{pn}(C'')$.

Case 2.1 If r is either p or q, the thesis follows by rules REFL and STEP-R, for $\vec{\mu} \triangleq \epsilon$, $\mu \triangleq \mathsf{p} \to \mathsf{q}$, and $C' \triangleq C''$.

Case 2.2 If $\mathsf{r} \in \mathrm{pn}(C'') \setminus \{\mathsf{p}, \mathsf{q}\}$, then we observe that, by induction hypothesis, we get that there exist $\vec{\mu}'$, μ', and C''' such that $C'' \xrightarrow{\vec{\mu}'} \xrightarrow{\mu'} C'''$ and $\mathsf{r} \in \mathrm{pn}(\mu')$. The thesis follows by rule STEP-L for $\vec{\mu} \triangleq \mathsf{p} \to \mathsf{q}, \vec{\mu}', \mu \triangleq \mu'$, and $C' \triangleq C'''$.   □

The combination of Lemma 4.13 and Theorem 4.11 gives us that all endpoint projections are starvation-free.

Theorem 4.14 For every C, $[\![C]\!]$ is starvation-free.

Proof Let N' be a multi-step derivative of $[\![C]\!]$. According to the definition of starvation-freedom (Definition 3.21) we have to prove that, for every $\mathsf{p} \in \mathrm{supp}(N')$, there exist $\vec{\mu}$, μ, and N'' such that $N' \xrightarrow{\vec{\mu}} \xrightarrow{\mu} N''$ and $\mathsf{p} \in \mathrm{pn}(\mu)$.

We know from Theorem 4.11 that there exists a choreography C' such that $N' = [\![C']\!]$. Proposition 4.4 tells us that $\mathrm{supp}([\![C']\!]) = \mathrm{pn}(C')$. By this equation and Lemma 4.13, for every $\mathsf{p} \in \mathrm{supp}([\![C']\!])$, there exist $\vec{\mu}'$, μ', and C'' such that $C' \xrightarrow{\vec{\mu}'} \xrightarrow{\mu'} C''$ and $\mathsf{p} \in \mathrm{pn}(C')$. By Theorem 4.11, $[\![C']\!]$ can mimic these transitions. Hence, the thesis follows for $\vec{\mu} \triangleq \vec{\mu}', \mu \triangleq \mu'$, and $N'' \triangleq [\![C'']\!]$.   □

Exercise 4.3 (!) Following a similar strategy to the one for proving starvation-freedom, it is possible to show that the EPP of a choreography in Simple Choreographies always *terminates*: for any choreography C and network N, if N is a multi-step derivative of $[\![C]\!]$, then there exists $\vec{\mu}$ such that $N \xrightarrow{\vec{\mu}} \mathbf{0}$. Prove this property.

  (Hint: prove first a lemma stating that, for any choreography C and C', if C' is a multi-step derivative of C then there exists $\vec{\mu}$ such that $C \xrightarrow{\vec{\mu}} \mathbf{0}$.)

Part II

Computation

Introduction to Part II

Part I was propaedeutic: we leveraged the minimalism of Simple Choreographies to get acquainted with the essential elements of choreography theory. Minimalism, however, came at the cost of expressivity. Simple Choreographies can only express finite sequences of interactions and does not even capture what data are communicated from one process to another.

In this part, we study how the theory of Part I can be extended to capture standard features from the world of computation. In fact, the choreographies that we are going to see here can be seen as programs that define in detail the expected behaviour of a system. The act of programming with choreographies is known as *choreographic programming* and the associated choreographic languages are called *choreographic programming languages* [Montesi 2013]. Choreographic programming languages typically come with a method for translating choreographies into executable implementations, following the principles of EPP. A simplification of the languages presented in this part yields choreographic languages that are typically used in *multiparty session types*, a line of research where choreographies and EPP are leveraged for code verification. More details on how the theory presented here relates to both choreographic programming and multiparty session types will be given in Chapter 12.

In Chapter 5, we equip processes with local memories for storing values and the capability to evaluate expressions that can access such memories. This will allow choreographies to capture what data are transmitted in communications and how processes manipulate such data.

In Chapter 6, we introduce the capability of expressing choices in choreographies: a process might evaluate a boolean expression and, depending on the outcome of the evaluation, choose between alternative choreographies that the system should then follow. The capability of performing choices motivates the study of how endpoint projection can make sure that processes will agree on what they should do, and in particular that they do so in a decentralised way.

In Chapter 7, we study a theory of parametric choreographic procedures that allows for general recursion. From a practical viewpoint, recursion enables the writing of protocols that permit 'multiple attempts' and parametric procedures will bring the additional benefit of choreographies that can be reused in different contexts (by using procedure calls). From a theoretical perspective, general recursion makes it possible to write choreographies with infinite executions. (Therefore termination, as in Exercise 4.3, does not hold anymore in this setting.)

In each chapter, we are going to change some technical definitions about choreographies, networks, or endpoint projection. This means that some of the results shown in Part I need to be reformulated or proven again. We report the most salient issues brought by each extension right after its presentation, but postpone a proof of correctness of EPP until Chapter 8. The proof will address the language presented in Chapter 7, which includes all features presented in this part. Therefore, the proofs of correctness of EPP in all the other chapters in this part are simpler cases.

It is known that adding the features studied in this part to a choreographic language makes the language computationally complete (Turing complete), thus greatly enhancing its expressivity [Cruz-Filipe & Montesi 2020]. Notwithstanding, in Chapter 8, we are going to see that the framework of choreographies and EPP can guarantee strong correctness properties even in this more general setting.

5 Memory and Local Computation

In this chapter, we equip processes with the capabilities of storing values and performing local computation. This will enable us more faithfully to capture our online bookstore scenario from Example 2.1: we will be able to define the content of the messages exchanged by Buyer and Seller. Expressing how data are computed is also necessary for writing some security protocols, where defining precisely how data are encrypted and decrypted is essential. We are going to see an example with the protocol for cryptographic key exchange by Diffie and Hellman [1976].

We begin in Section 5.1 by designing Stateful Choreographies: an extension of the language of Simple Choreographies with expressions and memory stores. These elements are then added to the language of Simple Processes as well, in Section 5.2, leveraging the fact that the relevant definitions for memory stores can be shared between the two languages. Accordingly, we call the resulting language Stateful Processes. We end the chapter by presenting how endpoint projection can be adjusted to these new languages in Section 5.3.

5.1 Stateful Choreographies

Stateful Choreographies brings two new key elements in play: *values*, which represent data, and *variables*, which are names for memory locations.

Formally, let **Var** be an infinite set of variables ranged over by x, y, z. These represent the usual variable identifiers found in programming languages. Furthermore, let **Val** be an infinite set of values ranged over by v, u. The set **Val** is purposefully left underspecified: we just assume that it contains all data that we might be interested in modelling, including integers, strings, (texts), tuples, and lists. We identify string values by delimiting them with double quotation marks in examples.

5.1.1 Syntax

The syntax of Stateful Choreographies is given in Figure 5.1. In the syntax, I stands for *instruction*. A choreography is either a term $I; C$, read 'do I and then C', or the terminated choreography **0**. An instruction I can be:

- A *communication* p.$e \rightarrow$ q.x, where process p evaluates the *expression* e locally (according to its process store) and communicates the resulting value to process q, which stores it in its local variable x. Expressions are introduced right after this list.
- A *local assignment* p.$x := e$, where p evaluates expression e and stores the resulting value in its variable x.

$$C ::= I; C \mid 0$$
$$I ::= \mathsf{p}.e \to \mathsf{q}.x \mid \mathsf{p}.x := e$$
$$e ::= v \mid x \mid f(\vec{e})$$

Figure 5.1 Syntax of Stateful Choreographies.

An expression e can take three forms:

- A constant value v.
- A variable x.
- A *function call* $f(\vec{e})$, where f is a *function* name and $\vec{e}$ ranges over sequences of expressions $e_1, \ldots, e_n$. We call $\vec{e}$ the *arguments* of f.

A function name f is a reference to a function that maps value tuples to values. The idea is that these functions can be evaluated locally, in the sense that processes compute their results without communicating with other processes. For this reason, we call functions ranged over by f also *local functions*. We write **StatefulChor** for the set of all Stateful Choreographies.

Example 5.1   We can finally give a precise choreography for our online bookstore scenario from Example 2.1, including computation and message contents. Recall the informal description of the example:

1. Buyer communicates the title of a book that they wish to buy to Seller.
2. Seller replies to Buyer with the price of the book.

A corresponding choreography that defines this behaviour is

$$\mathsf{Buyer}.title \to \mathsf{Seller}.x; \mathsf{Seller}.cat(x) \to \mathsf{Buyer}.price; 0$$

where:

- *title* is a variable.
- *cat* is the name of a function that, given a book title, returns the price for it (*cat* stands for catalogue, if you like).
- *price* is a variable.

From here onwards, any choreography is essentially a list of instructions $I_1; \ldots; I_n; 0$ for some instructions $I_1, \ldots, I_n$. For conciseness, we will usually omit trailing 0s in examples, thus abbreviating $I_1; \ldots; I_n; 0$ to $I_1; \ldots; I_n$. For example, the choreography in Example 5.1 can be abbreviated as follows.

$$\mathsf{Buyer}.title \to \mathsf{Seller}.x; \mathsf{Seller}.cat(x) \to \mathsf{Buyer}.price$$

We use this convention in the following example and in the rest of the book, with the exception of formal definitions and proofs.

Example 5.2   The key exchange protocol by Diffie and Hellman [1976] is a famous protocol for establishing a shared secret key between two participants, called Alice and Bob, over a public (insecure) channel. The idea is that Alice and Bob compute the shared key by exchanging the results of computations based on secret data in their respective memories; the computations are defined such that it is practically unfeasible for a malicious observer to compute the original secret data or the shared key without using quantum computation.

The protocol assumes that, before execution, the participants (in our case, processes) agree on two numbers, p and g, where p is a prime number and g is a primitive root modulo p. These numbers need not be secret. The processes Alice and Bob also possess a secret number each, respectively called a and b, which they wish to keep secret. The protocol proceeds as follows.

1. Alice communicates the result of g^a mod p ('g^a modulo p') to Bob, who stores it as x.
2. Bob communicates g^b mod p to Alice, who stores it as y.
3. Alice computes the shared key $s = y^a$ mod p.
4. Bob computes the shared key $s = x^b$ mod p.

The shared key s computed by the two processes is the same:

$$y^a \bmod p = (g^b \bmod p)^a \bmod p = g^{ba} \bmod p = g^{ab} \bmod p = (g^a \bmod p)^b \bmod p = x^b \bmod p.$$

Let *modPow* be the name of a function that computes modular exponentiation – that is, *modPow* (*base*, *exp*, *m*) computes $base^{exp}$ mod m. Then we can express the protocol in Stateful Choreographies as follows.

$$\begin{aligned}
&\text{Alice}.modPow(g, a, p) \rightarrow \text{Bob}.x; \\
&\text{Bob}.modPow(g, b, p) \rightarrow \text{Alice}.y; \\
&\text{Alice}.s := modPow(y, a, p); \\
&\text{Bob}.s := modPow(x, b, p)
\end{aligned} \tag{5.1}$$

Observe that the choreography in (5.1) is very near to what could be implemented in a real programming language. Function *modPow* is even offered in the Java standard library (for class BigInteger). Thus the choreography can be used as reference for implementing the protocol correctly. We will see how to produce (abstractions of) correct implementations automatically when we will extend endpoint projection in Section 5.3.

We will sometimes abuse the notation of expressions and adopt infix notation for standard operators. For example, we will write: $1 + 2$ (the sum of 1 and 2) as an abbreviation of the function invocation $add(1, 2)$, where add is the function that returns the sum of its arguments. Likewise, the choreography in (5.1) could be presented as follows.

$$\begin{aligned}
&\text{Alice}.(g^a \bmod p) \rightarrow \text{Bob}.x; \\
&\text{Bob}.(g^b \bmod p) \rightarrow \text{Alice}.y; \\
&\text{Alice}.s := y^a \bmod p; \\
&\text{Bob}.s := x^b \bmod p
\end{aligned}$$

We update the definition of pn for choreographies, extending its domain to instructions as well.

$$\text{pn}(0) \triangleq \emptyset \qquad\qquad \text{pn}(I; C) \triangleq \text{pn}(I) \cup \text{pn}(C)$$

$$\text{pn}(\text{p}.e \rightarrow \text{q}.x) \triangleq \{\text{p}, \text{q}\} \qquad\qquad \text{pn}(\text{p}.x := e) \triangleq \{\text{p}\}$$

5.1.2   Semantics

To formulate a semantics for Stateful Choreographies, we first have to define (memory) stores and the meaning of expressions. We will then use these elements to define a labelled transition system for choreographies.

Stores and Expression Evaluation

A *process store* σ models the memory of a process, mapping variables to values. Formally, a process store is a function from variables to values:

$$\sigma \colon \mathbf{Var} \longrightarrow \mathbf{Val}.$$

We write **PStore** for the set of all process stores. It will often be necessary to update the content of a store, so we define a notation for that purpose. Namely, we write $\sigma[x \mapsto v]$ for the update of store σ with the new mapping $x \mapsto v$:

$$\sigma[y \mapsto v](x) = \begin{cases} v & \text{if } x = y \\ \sigma(x) & \text{otherwise.} \end{cases}$$

A *choreographic store* Σ models the memory state of an entire system: it maps process names to their respective process stores. Formally,

$$\Sigma \colon \mathbf{PName} \longrightarrow \mathbf{PStore}.$$

We shall write $\Sigma[\mathsf{p}.x \mapsto v]$ for the update of store Σ such that the local variable x of process p is now mapped to v:

$$\Sigma[\mathsf{q}.x \mapsto v](\mathsf{p}) = \begin{cases} \Sigma(\mathsf{p})[x \mapsto v] & \text{if } \mathsf{p} = \mathsf{q} \\ \Sigma(\mathsf{p}) & \text{otherwise.} \end{cases}$$

Store updates are left associative – that is:

$$\sigma[x \mapsto v][y \mapsto u] = (\sigma[x \mapsto v])[y \mapsto u]$$
$$\Sigma[\mathsf{p}.x \mapsto v][\mathsf{q}.y \mapsto u] = (\Sigma[\mathsf{p}.x \mapsto v])[\mathsf{q}.y \mapsto u].$$

As for networks, we adopt extensional equality for both process and choreographic stores: two process stores are deemed equal if they return the same value for each variable, and two choreographic stores are deemed equal if they return equal process stores for each process.

Proposition 5.1   Store updates support the following laws, for all Σ, σ, x, y, v, u, p, and q.

$$\sigma[x \mapsto v][x \mapsto u] = \sigma[x \mapsto u] \tag{5.2}$$
$$\sigma[x \mapsto v][y \mapsto u] = \sigma[y \mapsto u][x \mapsto v] \qquad \text{if } x \neq y \tag{5.3}$$
$$\Sigma[\mathsf{p}.x \mapsto v][\mathsf{p}.x \mapsto u] = \sigma[\mathsf{p}.x \mapsto u] \tag{5.4}$$
$$\Sigma[\mathsf{p}.x \mapsto v][\mathsf{q}.y \mapsto u] = \Sigma[\mathsf{q}.y \mapsto u][\mathsf{p}.x \mapsto v] \qquad \text{if } \mathsf{p} \neq \mathsf{q} \text{ or } x \neq y \tag{5.5}$$

Exercise 5.1   Prove Proposition 5.1.

$$\frac{}{\sigma \vdash v \downarrow v} \text{ VAL} \qquad \frac{}{\sigma \vdash x \downarrow \sigma(x)} \text{ VAR} \qquad \frac{\sigma \vdash e_1 \downarrow v_1 \cdots \sigma \vdash e_n \downarrow v_n \quad \vdash f(v_1, \dots, v_n) \downarrow v}{\sigma \vdash f(e_1, \dots, e_n) \downarrow v} \text{ CALL}$$

Figure 5.2 Expression evaluation.

Using stores, we can define a simple inference system for evaluating expressions. We write the proposition $\sigma \vdash e \downarrow v$ for 'e is evaluated to the value v under the process store σ'. The idea is that we might need to read the process store in order to compute an expression, since expressions can contain variables whose values are defined in the store.

The inference system for expression evaluation is displayed in Figure 5.2. The axiom VAL states that a constant value v is always evaluated to itself: $\sigma \vdash v \downarrow v$. The other axiom, VAR, evaluates a variable x to the value that it is mapped to in the process store, $\sigma(x)$. Finally, rule CALL evaluates a function call.

In rule CALL, $\sigma \vdash e_1 \downarrow v_1 \cdots \sigma \vdash e_n \downarrow v_n$ means that there is a premise for each argument e_i in $\vec{e}$. Therefore, the number of premises of this rule depends on the number of arguments in the function call. Each premise $\sigma \vdash e_i \downarrow v_i$, for $1 \le i \le n$, evaluates an expression that is passed as argument in the function call in the conclusion. Then, the proposition in the right-most premise, $\vdash f(\vec{v}) \downarrow v$, reads 'invoking function f with arguments $\vec{v}$ evaluates to the value v'. Value v is thus also the value that we assign to the entire evaluation in the conclusion.[1]

We do not specify a system for deriving propositions of the kind $\vdash f(\vec{v}) \downarrow v$, since it is not important for our development: this system would depend on how functions are defined, which we choose to abstract from. Instead, we will just assume that such a system exists, and that for any f and $\vec{v}$, it is always possible to derive $\vdash f(\vec{v}) \downarrow v$ for some v.

Example 5.3 Let σ be a process store such that $\sigma(x) = 2$, and let *add* be the name of a function that computes the sum of two numbers. Then, $\sigma \vdash add(x, 2) \downarrow 4$, as shown by the following derivation.

$$\frac{\dfrac{}{\sigma \vdash x \downarrow 2} \text{ VAR} \qquad \dfrac{}{\sigma \vdash 2 \downarrow 2} \text{ VAL} \qquad \vdash add(2, 2) \downarrow 4}{\sigma \vdash add(x, 2) \downarrow 4} \text{ CALL}$$

Using our notation $e + e'$ for $add(e, e')$, we get that $\sigma \vdash x + 2 \downarrow 4$.

Remark 5.2 In this chapter, we assume that all functions referred to by function names are total. In other words, we are assuming that, for every f used in a choreography and every sequence of values $\vec{v}$, there exists exactly one v such that $\vdash f(\vec{v}) \downarrow v$. In practice, many programming languages use the term 'functions' to refer to procedures that might not return a value or whose evaluation might not terminate (e.g., due to an infinite loop). This is not a problem for the applicability of our

---

[1] Rule CALL evaluates the expressions passed as arguments in a function call before evaluating the function invocation. This strategy is also called *eager evaluation*, since all arguments are evaluated regardless of whether the function that we are invoking will actually use them. Eager evaluation is used widely in mainstream programming languages, including C, Java, JavaScript, and Python. Some programming languages, like Haskell, can apply another strategy to function invocations: *lazy evaluation*, whereby expressions are passed as they are in function invocations and can then be evaluated later when their results are needed. Lazy evaluation requires that the set of values, **Val**, includes expressions.

$$\frac{\Sigma(\mathsf{p}) \vdash e \downarrow v}{\langle \mathsf{p}.x := e; C, \Sigma \rangle \xrightarrow{\tau @\mathsf{p}} \langle C, \Sigma[\mathsf{p}.x \mapsto v] \rangle} \text{ LOCAL}$$

$$\frac{\Sigma(\mathsf{p}) \vdash e \downarrow v}{\langle \mathsf{p}.e \to \mathsf{q}.x; C, \Sigma \rangle \xrightarrow{\mathsf{p}.v \to \mathsf{q}} \langle C, \Sigma[\mathsf{q}.x \mapsto v] \rangle} \text{ COM} \qquad \frac{\langle C, \Sigma \rangle \xrightarrow{\mu} \langle C', \Sigma' \rangle \quad \text{pn}(I) \# \text{pn}(\mu)}{\langle I; C, \Sigma \rangle \xrightarrow{\mu} \langle I; C', \Sigma' \rangle} \text{ DELAY}$$

Figure 5.3 Semantics of Stateful Choreographies.

theory: an implementation could enforce a timeout on evaluations, such that a special 'failure' value is returned if the timeout is reached before the evaluation terminates.

Another important concern is that evaluating a function invocation might have typing constraints. For example, *plus* might be invocable only by passing numbers as arguments. What if we pass two strings instead? Again, we can assume that a special failure value is returned in these cases too (e.g., an 'absurd' value $\perp$). Cruz-Filipe and Montesi [2017c] showed that choreographies can be modularly combined with typing disciplines for expressions and local functions that prevent this kind of errors. The reader interested in type systems for expressions is referred to Pierce [2002].

Transition System

We formulate a semantics for Stateful Choreographies by generalising the labelled transition system of Simple Choreographies to pairs that consist of a choreography and a choreographic store.

Formally, the semantics of Stateful Choreographies is defined by the rules given in Figure 5.3. States in this transition system are pairs of the form $\langle C, \Sigma \rangle$, which we call *choreographic configurations*. Transitions thus now have the form $\langle C, \Sigma \rangle \xrightarrow{\mu} \langle C', \Sigma' \rangle$, read 'the choreography C equipped with store Σ has a transition with label μ to the choreography C' with store Σ''.

Rule LOCAL executes a local assignment. The premise $\Sigma(\mathsf{p}) \vdash e \downarrow v$ states that evaluating the expression e under the store of the evaluating process p yields the result v. In the derivative, we update the store of process p to map the destination variable x to v. The (new) label $\tau @\mathsf{p}$ indicates that process p has performed an *internal action*.[2]

Rule COM is similar to the rule with the same name presented for Simple Choreographies, but it is updated to consider that messages now contain values. The premise $\Sigma(\mathsf{p}) \vdash e \downarrow v$ determines the value v that we get from evaluating the expression e at the sender p. In the derivative, the store of the receiver process q is updated to map the variable x, in which q wishes to store the value from p, to v. The label of the transition is $\mathsf{p}.v \to \mathsf{q}$, read '$\mathsf{p}$ communicates v to q'. The label models what is commonly observable over network communications in practice, where the content of the message is visible, but not the internal details of how it has been produced (the expression e) and what the receiver will do with it (store it in variable x).

---

[2] Using τ as symbol for internal actions comes from the tradition of concurrency theory [Milner 1980]. However, in other concurrency models, this label usually does not carry process names and it is used for communication transitions as well. In our case, carrying process names and making communications visible are convenient design choices for making the correctness of EPP more informative: it allows us to know that the EPP of a choreography performs local actions at and communications among the expected processes just by looking at transition labels.

Finally, rule DELAY captures out-of-order execution. In the rule, the continuation C in a choreography $I; C$ is allowed to perform a transition with label μ if μ does not involve any of the processes in the instruction I. For this system, the function $\text{pn}(\mu)$ is defined as follows.

$$\text{pn}(\mathsf{p}.v \to \mathsf{q}) \triangleq \{\mathsf{p}, \mathsf{q}\} \qquad\qquad \text{pn}(\tau \, @\mathsf{p}) \triangleq \{\mathsf{p}\}$$

Example 5.4 Recall the choreography from Example 5.1:

$$\mathsf{Buyer}.title \to \mathsf{Seller}.x; \mathsf{Seller}.cat(x) \to \mathsf{Buyer}.price. \tag{5.6}$$

Let Σ be a choreographic store such that $\Sigma(\mathsf{Buyer})(title) = $ "My Choreographies" and cat be a function name such that $\vdash cat(\text{"My Choreographies"}) \downarrow 100$, where "My Choreographies" is a string and 100 a natural number (we abstract from the currency of the price of the book). We can derive the transition:

$$\cfrac{\cfrac{\Sigma(\mathsf{Buyer}) \vdash title \downarrow \text{"My Choreographies"}}{\langle \mathsf{Buyer}.title \to \mathsf{Seller}.x; \mathsf{Seller}.cat(x) \to \mathsf{Buyer}.price, \Sigma \rangle} \text{ VAR}}{\quad\xrightarrow{\mathsf{Buyer}.\text{"My Choreographies"} \to \mathsf{Seller}}\; \langle \mathsf{Seller}.cat(x) \to \mathsf{Buyer}.price, \Sigma' \rangle} \text{ COM}$$

where Σ' is defined as

$$\Sigma' \triangleq \Sigma[\mathsf{Seller}.x \mapsto \text{"My Choreographies"}]. \tag{5.7}$$

More in general, we have the following execution:

$$\langle \mathsf{Buyer}.title \to \mathsf{Seller}.x; \mathsf{Seller}.cat(x) \to \mathsf{Buyer}.price, \Sigma \rangle$$

$$\xrightarrow{\mathsf{Buyer}.\text{"My Choreographies"} \to \mathsf{Seller}} \langle \mathsf{Seller}.cat(x) \to \mathsf{Buyer}.price, \Sigma' \rangle \qquad \text{by rule COM}$$

$$\xrightarrow{\mathsf{Seller}.100 \to \mathsf{Buyer}} \langle \mathbf{0}, \Sigma'' \rangle \qquad \text{by rule COM,}$$

where Σ' is the one in (5.7) and $\Sigma'' \triangleq \Sigma'[\mathsf{Buyer}.price \mapsto 100]$.

Example 5.5 Assignments and interactions at distinct processes can be executed in any order, thanks to rule DELAY. Consider the following choreography for some distinct process names p, q, and r and some variables x and y.

$$\mathsf{p}.5 \to \mathsf{q}.x; \mathsf{r}.y := 4$$

For any store Σ, both of the following derivations are valid. That is, both the first and the second instructions can be executed first.

$$\cfrac{\cfrac{\Sigma(\mathsf{p}) \vdash 5 \downarrow 5}{} \text{ VAL}}{\langle \mathsf{p}.5 \to \mathsf{q}.x; \mathsf{r}.y := 4, \Sigma \rangle \xrightarrow{\mathsf{p}.5 \to \mathsf{q}} \langle \mathsf{r}.y := 4, \Sigma[\mathsf{q}.x \mapsto 5] \rangle} \text{ COM}$$

$$\cfrac{\cfrac{\cfrac{\Sigma(\mathsf{r}) \vdash 4 \downarrow 4}{} \text{ VAL}}{\langle \mathsf{r}.y := 4, \Sigma \rangle \xrightarrow{\tau \, @\mathsf{r}} \langle \mathbf{0}, \Sigma[\mathsf{r}.y \mapsto 4] \rangle} \text{ LOCAL}}{\langle \mathsf{p}.5 \to \mathsf{q}.x; \mathsf{r}.y := 4, \Sigma \rangle \xrightarrow{\tau \, @\mathsf{r}} \langle \mathsf{p}.5 \to \mathsf{q}.x, \Sigma[\mathsf{r}.y \mapsto 4] \rangle} \text{ DELAY}$$

$$P, Q, R ::= I; P \mid \mathbf{0}$$
$$I ::= \mathsf{p}!e \mid \mathsf{p}?x \mid x := e$$
$$e ::= v \mid x \mid f(\vec{e})$$

Figure 5.4 Stateful Processes, syntax.

Exercise 5.2   Let C be the choreography for secure key exchange in (5.1) and Σ be a store such that:

$$\Sigma(\text{Alice})(g) = \Sigma(\text{Bob})(g) = 5$$
$$\Sigma(\text{Alice})(p) = \Sigma(\text{Bob})(p) = 23$$
$$\Sigma(\text{Alice})(a) = 4$$
$$\Sigma(\text{Bob})(b) = 3.$$

Draw the graphical representation of the lts generated by the configuration $\langle C, \Sigma \rangle$. Do Alice and Bob have the same secret key s in their respective memories after all instructions are executed?

5.2   Stateful Processes

In this section, we update the language of processes to handle stores, in accordance to what we have done for choreographies. We call the resulting language Stateful Processes.

5.2.1   Syntax

The syntax of Stateful Processes is given in Figure 5.4.

We use the same symbol I as in Stateful Choreographies to range over instructions, but in this context the syntax is different: instructions in Stateful Processes are local actions performed by a process. A process term P can be either a term $I; P$ ('do I and then P'), or the terminated process **0**. An instruction I can be:

- A *send action* $\mathsf{p}!e$, read 'send the result of evaluating expression e to p'. The syntax of expressions is the same as the one given for Stateful Choreographies in Figure 5.1.
- A *receive action* $\mathsf{p}?x$, read 'receive a value from process p and store it in variable x'.
- An *assignment* $x := e$, read 'store the value obtained by evaluating expression e in variable x'.

We write **StatefulProc** for the set of all stateful processes. The notion of networks is updated accordingly – that is, every network N is a total function from process names to terms in **StatefulProc**:

$$N: \textbf{PName} \longrightarrow \textbf{StatefulProc}.$$

The set of networks in this language is denoted **StatefulNet**.

As for choreographies, we omit trailing **0**s in examples.

$$\frac{\Sigma(\mathsf{p}) \vdash e \downarrow v}{\langle \mathsf{p}[x := e; P], \Sigma \rangle \xrightarrow{\tau@\mathsf{p}} \langle \mathsf{p}[P], \Sigma[\mathsf{p}.x \mapsto v] \rangle} \text{ LOCAL}$$

$$\frac{\Sigma(\mathsf{p}) \vdash e \downarrow v}{\langle \mathsf{p}[\mathsf{q}!e; P] \mid \mathsf{q}[\mathsf{p}?x; Q], \Sigma \rangle \xrightarrow{\mathsf{p}.v \to \mathsf{q}} \langle \mathsf{p}[P] \mid \mathsf{q}[Q], \Sigma[\mathsf{q}.x \mapsto v] \rangle} \text{ COM} \qquad \frac{\langle N, \Sigma \rangle \xrightarrow{\mu} \langle N', \Sigma' \rangle}{\langle N \mid M, \Sigma \rangle \xrightarrow{\mu} \langle N' \mid M, \Sigma' \rangle} \text{ PAR}$$

Figure 5.5 Semantics of Stateful Processes.

Example 5.6 The choreography in Example 5.4 is implemented by the following network.

$$\mathsf{Buyer}[\mathsf{Seller}!title; \mathsf{Seller}?price] \mid \mathsf{Seller}[\mathsf{Buyer}?x; \mathsf{Buyer}!cat(x)]$$

Example 5.7 The following network implements the choreography for secure key exchange from Example 5.2.

$$\mathsf{Alice}[\mathsf{Bob}!modPow(g, a, p); \mathsf{Bob}?y; s := modPow(y, a, p)]$$
$$\mid \mathsf{Bob}[\mathsf{Alice}?x; \mathsf{Alice}!modPow(g, b, p); s := modPow(x, b, p)]$$

5.2.2 Semantics

The semantics of Stateful Processes is an extension of the semantics of Simple Processes, which recalls the development of the semantics of Stateful Choreographies from that of Simple Choreographies. In particular, we extend networks to *network configurations* of the form $\langle N, \Sigma \rangle$, similarly to what we did for Stateful Choreographies. The rules for transitions are given in Figure 5.5.

Rule LOCAL executes an assignment. In the premise, the expression e is evaluated to v under the state of the process of interest p. In the derivative in the conclusion, we update the store of p accordingly.

Rule COM matches a send action from a process p to a process q with a compatible receive action by process q. Compared to the homonymous rule in Simple Processes, here we also update the state of the receiver q in the derivative, which now stores in its local variable the value sent by p.

Rule PAR states that if part of a network in a network configuration can perform a transition, then a configuration with a larger network can do the same.

The meaning of the labels has already been described in the discussion of the semantics of Stateful Choreographies (the labels are the same).

Example 5.8 Under the same assumptions for Σ and *cat* as in Example 5.4, the configuration formed by the network in Example 5.6 and Σ has the following execution.

$$\langle \mathsf{Buyer}[\mathsf{Seller}!title; \mathsf{Seller}?price] \mid \mathsf{Seller}[\mathsf{Buyer}?x; \mathsf{Buyer}!cat(x)], \Sigma \rangle$$

$$\xrightarrow{\mathsf{Buyer}.\text{"My Choreographies"} \to \mathsf{Seller}.x} \langle \mathsf{Buyer}[\mathsf{Seller}?price] \mid \mathsf{Seller}[\mathsf{Buyer}!cat(x)], \Sigma'' \rangle$$

$$\xrightarrow{\mathsf{Seller}.100 \to \mathsf{Buyer}} \langle \mathbf{0}, \Sigma'' \rangle$$

Both of these transitions follow by rule COM. The stores Σ' and Σ'' are defined as in Example 5.4 – that is,

$$\Sigma' \triangleq \Sigma[\text{Seller}.x \mapsto \text{"My Choreographies"}] \qquad \Sigma'' \triangleq \Sigma'[\text{Buyer}.price \mapsto 100].$$

Exercise 5.3 Let N be the network defined in Example 5.7, and let Σ be as described in Exercise 5.2. Draw the graphical representation of the lts generated by the configuration $\langle N, \Sigma \rangle$.

5.3   Endpoint Projection

We update the definition of EPP to deal with the new languages of Stateful Choreographies and Stateful Processes.

The general principle of distributing code over process terms remains the same: we just need to update the definition of process projection to handle our new primitives. The projection of a stateful choreography C for process p, written $[\![C]\!]_p$, is defined by Equations (5.8) to (5.10).

Process projection for Stateful Choreographies

$$[\![\text{p}.e \to \text{q}.x; C]\!]_r \triangleq \begin{cases} \text{q}!e; [\![C]\!]_r & \text{if } r = p \\ \text{p}?x; [\![C]\!]_r & \text{if } r = q \\ [\![C]\!]_r & \text{otherwise} \end{cases} \qquad (5.8)$$

$$[\![\text{p}.x := e; C]\!]_r \triangleq \begin{cases} x := e; [\![C]\!]_r & \text{if } r = p \\ [\![C]\!]_r & \text{otherwise} \end{cases} \qquad (5.9)$$

$$[\![\mathbf{0}]\!]_r \triangleq \mathbf{0} \qquad (5.10)$$

The definition of EPP remains the same (Definition 4.2), modulo the usage of our updated process projection. We recall it for convenience: for all $p \in \mathbf{PName}$, $[\![C]\!](p) \triangleq [\![C]\!]_p$.

Example 5.9 The EPP of the choreography in Example 5.2 is the network given in Example 5.7.

To state the correctness of EPP for Stateful Choreographies, we need to take stores into consideration: the EPP of a choreography should comply with the choreography under all possible stores. More precisely, we formulate that any choreographic configuration $\langle C, \Sigma \rangle$ mimics and is mimicked by the network configuration $\langle [\![C]\!], \Sigma \rangle$.

Theorem 5.3 (Correctness of EPP for Stateful Choreographies)   The following statements hold for every configuration $\langle C, \Sigma \rangle$.

Completeness For any μ and $\langle C', \Sigma' \rangle$, $\langle C, \Sigma \rangle \xrightarrow{\mu} \langle C', \Sigma' \rangle$ implies $\langle [\![C]\!], \Sigma \rangle \xrightarrow{\mu} \langle [\![C']\!], \Sigma' \rangle$.

Soundness For any μ and $\langle N, \Sigma' \rangle$, $\langle [\![C]\!], \Sigma \rangle \xrightarrow{\mu} \langle N, \Sigma' \rangle$ implies $\langle C, \Sigma \rangle \xrightarrow{\mu} \langle C', \Sigma' \rangle$ for some C' such that $N = [\![C']\!]$.

The proof of this result follows the same strategy as that of Theorem 4.7 (correctness of EPP for Simple Choreographies). Some of the auxiliary results used in that proof need to be reformulated as well. In particular, we need to update the statements of Proposition 3.7 and Lemma 4.8 to deal with stores.

Proposition 5.4   For all $\langle N, \Sigma \rangle$, μ, $\langle N', \Sigma' \rangle$, and r, if $\langle N, \Sigma \rangle \xrightarrow{\mu} \langle N', \Sigma' \rangle$ and r $\notin$ pn(μ), then $N(r) = N'(r)$.

Lemma 5.5   For every $\langle C, \Sigma \rangle$, μ, and $\langle C', \Sigma' \rangle$, if $\langle C, \Sigma \rangle \xrightarrow{\mu} \langle C', \Sigma' \rangle$, then $[\![C]\!]_r = [\![C']\!]_r$ for all r $\notin$ pn(μ).

Exercise 5.4   Prove Proposition 5.4. (Hint: follow the strategy of the proof of Proposition 3.7.)

Exercise 5.5   Prove Lemma 5.5. (Hint: follow the strategy of the proof of Lemma 4.8.)

Exercise 5.6   Prove Theorem 5.3.

---

6 Conditionals and Knowledge of Choice

The choreographic languages that we have presented so far can only express sequences of instructions. What if we wanted to express a choice between alternative behaviours? For instance, it would be plausible to extend our online book store choreography with Buyer and Seller from Example 5.1, such that Buyer would decide whether to purchase the book depending on the price communicated by Seller. In this chapter, we extend our framework with *conditionals*: instructions that allow a process to evaluate a condition to choose between alternative ways in which the choreography might proceed.

As we are going to see, the syntax and semantics of conditionals are straightforward adaptations of what is commonly found in mainstream programming languages – the 'if-then-else' statement. However, the introduction of conditionals has deep ramifications for the theory of projection: conditionals make it possible to write choreographies where processes might not have enough information to know what they are supposed to do, a problem known in the world of choreographies as *knowledge of choice* [Castagna et al. 2012]. Fortunately, it is possible to extend projection to check for knowledge of choice for each process, and we can even provide linguistic primitives in choreographies that make it easier to write choreographies for which this is guaranteed.

6.1 Conditionals

In this section, we extend the languages of Stateful Choreographies and Stateful Processes with conditionals. The resulting extended languages are called Conditional Choreographies and Conditional Processes, respectively.

6.1.1 Conditional Choreographies

Syntax
The syntax of Conditional Choreographies brings only one addition compared to the syntax of Stateful Choreographies from the previous chapter: an instruction I can now be a *conditional*, written if p.e then C_1 else C_2. The rest of the syntax is the same. The full syntax of Conditional Choreographies is given in Figure 6.1, where we <u>underline</u> the new construct for better visibility. The underlining is not part of the syntax; it is just a visual aid that we use here and in the remainder to identify extensions. From now on, like here, we are going to extend our choreographic and process languages instead of redefining them from scratch.

A conditional if p.e then C_1 else C_2 reads 'process p evaluates expression e, and then the choreography proceeds as C_1 if the result of the evaluation is the value *true*, or as C_2 otherwise'. Thus,

$$C ::= I; C \mid 0$$
$$I ::= \text{p}.e \to \text{q}.x \mid \text{p}.x := e \mid \underline{\text{if p}.e \text{ then } C_1 \text{ else } C_2}$$
$$e ::= v \mid x \mid f(\vec{e})$$

Figure 6.1 Syntax of Conditional Choreographies.

we now assume that the set of possible values contains the Boolean value *true*. (We sometimes also use the other Boolean value *false* in examples.) Given a conditional if p.e then C_1 else C_2: e is called the *condition*, or *guard* of the conditional; and the two choreographies C_1 and C_2 are called the *branches* of the conditional or, more precisely, C_1 is the *then-branch* and C_2 is the *else-branch*.

We write **ConditionalChor** for the set of all Conditional Choreographies.

In the presentation of choreographies, we often omit trailing **0**s (as in the previous chapter) and sometimes use round parentheses to facilitate reading. For example, consider the following choreography, where p is a process, e is an expression, and x and y are variables.

$$\text{if p}.e \text{ then } \mathbf{0} \text{ else p}.x := x + 1; \mathbf{0}; \text{p}.y := x; \mathbf{0}$$

Even if there is only one correct way of reading it, we can make it obvious by writing

$$(\text{if p}.e \text{ then } \mathbf{0} \text{ else p}.x := true; \mathbf{0}); \text{p}.y := x; \mathbf{0},$$

which separates clearly the conditional from its continuation. This is particularly important when trailing **0**s are omitted: without parentheses, the following choreography would have a different reading.

$$(\text{if p}.e \text{ then } \mathbf{0} \text{ else p}.x := true); \text{p}.y := x$$

Example 6.1   Alice is responsible for distributing some news to Bob and Carol, and she needs to decide who between them should receive the news first. She uses a local expression *bobFirst* (*news*) that evaluates to *true* if the news is more relevant for Bob. In that case, she sends the news to Bob first and to Carol later. Otherwise, vice versa, she sends the news to Carol first and to Bob later. The following choreography captures this scenario.

> if Alice.*bobFirst*(*news*) then
>   Alice.*news* → Bob.*x*; Alice.*news* → Carol.*y*
> else
>   Alice.*news* → Carol.*y*; Alice.*news* → Bob.*x*

Extending function pn to the new syntax requires adding a case for conditionals. In that case, we return the set containing the process evaluating the guard and all the processes involved in the two branches of the conditional. The new equation is underlined; the others are unchanged with respect to Stateful Choreographies.

$$\frac{\Sigma(\mathsf{p}) \vdash e \downarrow v}{\langle \mathsf{p}.x := e; C, \Sigma \rangle \xrightarrow{\tau @ \mathsf{p}} \langle C, \Sigma[\mathsf{p}.x \mapsto v] \rangle} \quad \text{LOCAL}$$

$$\frac{\Sigma(\mathsf{p}) \vdash e \downarrow v}{\langle \mathsf{p}.e \to \mathsf{q}.x; C, \Sigma \rangle \xrightarrow{\mathsf{p}.v \to \mathsf{q}} \langle C, \Sigma[\mathsf{q}.x \mapsto v] \rangle} \quad \text{COM}$$

$$\frac{\Sigma(\mathsf{p}) \vdash e \downarrow \mathit{true}}{\langle \text{if } \mathsf{p}.e \text{ then } C_1 \text{ else } C_2; C, \Sigma \rangle \xrightarrow{\tau @ \mathsf{p}} \langle C_1 \,\fatsemi\, C, \Sigma \rangle} \quad \text{COND-THEN}$$

$$\frac{\Sigma(\mathsf{p}) \vdash e \downarrow v \quad v \neq \mathit{true}}{\langle \text{if } \mathsf{p}.e \text{ then } C_1 \text{ else } C_2; C, \Sigma \rangle \xrightarrow{\tau @ \mathsf{p}} \langle C_2 \,\fatsemi\, C, \Sigma \rangle} \quad \text{COND-ELSE}$$

$$\frac{\langle C, \Sigma \rangle \xrightarrow{\mu} \langle C', \Sigma' \rangle \quad \mathrm{pn}(I) \,\#\, \mathrm{pn}(\mu)}{\langle I; C, \Sigma \rangle \xrightarrow{\mu} \langle I; C', \Sigma' \rangle} \quad \text{DELAY}$$

$$\frac{\langle C_1, \Sigma \rangle \xrightarrow{\mu} \langle C_1', \Sigma' \rangle \quad \langle C_2, \Sigma \rangle \xrightarrow{\mu} \langle C_2', \Sigma' \rangle \quad \mathsf{p} \notin \mathrm{pn}(\mu)}{\langle \text{if } \mathsf{p}.e \text{ then } C_1 \text{ else } C_2; C, \Sigma \rangle \xrightarrow{\mu} \langle \text{if } \mathsf{p}.e \text{ then } C_1' \text{ else } C_2'; C, \Sigma' \rangle} \quad \text{DELAY-COND}$$

Figure 6.2 Semantics of Conditional Choreographies.

$$\mathrm{pn}(\mathbf{0}) \triangleq \emptyset \qquad\qquad\qquad \mathrm{pn}(I; C) \triangleq \mathrm{pn}(I) \cup \mathrm{pn}(C)$$

$$\mathrm{pn}(\mathsf{p}.e \to \mathsf{q}.x) \triangleq \{\mathsf{p}, \mathsf{q}\} \qquad\qquad \mathrm{pn}(\mathsf{p}.x := e) \triangleq \{\mathsf{p}\}$$

$$\mathrm{pn}(\text{if } \mathsf{p}.e \text{ then } C_1 \text{ else } C_2) \triangleq \{\mathsf{p}\} \cup \mathrm{pn}(C_1) \cup \mathrm{pn}(C_2)$$

Semantics

The semantics of Conditional Choreographies is defined by the rules displayed in Figure 6.2. This is an extension of the inference system presented for Stateful Choreographies in Section 5.1.2: there are three new rules whose names are underlined for visibility. These rules use a new binary operator for choreographies, the *sequential composition operator* $\fatsemi$, which we discuss next.

Conditional Execution

The rules COND-THEN and COND-ELSE model conditional execution, respectively the cases in which a conditional should transition to its then- or else-branch.

In the premise of COND-THEN, the guard e of a conditional at process p is evaluated to the value *true*. The rule then concludes that the conditional should continue by executing its then-branch. The label $\tau @ \mathsf{p}$ denotes that the transition is an internal action at process p. In the derivative, the choreography $C_1 \,\fatsemi\, C$ reads as 'C_1 and then C'. The operator $\fatsemi$ is not part of the syntax of choreographies: $C_1 \,\fatsemi\, C$ is not a term, but rather the choreography returned by applying the operator $\fatsemi$ to the arguments C_1 and C.

Before giving the formal definition of $\fatsemi$, let us see an example of why it is necessary. Consider the choreography:

$$(\text{if } \mathsf{Alice}.\mathit{true} \text{ then } \mathbf{0} \text{ else } \mathbf{0}); \mathbf{0}.$$

$$0 \, ; \, C \triangleq C \qquad\qquad (I; C) \, ; \, C' \triangleq I; (C \, ; \, C')$$

Figure 6.3 Definition of the $;$ operator for choreographies.

This choreography illustrates a potential bureaucratic issue between the syntax and semantics of Conditional Choreographies: if we wrote the semicolon ; instead of the fat semicolon $;$ in the conclusion of rule COND-THEN, the choreography would perform a transition to $0; 0$, which is not a valid term in our syntax. In other words, the syntax does not allow for writing redundant 0s in choreographies, as in $0; 0$. The $;$ operator avoids this problem: given two choreographies, it returns a choreography that is valid in our syntax and behaves as the sequential composition of the provided arguments. In this example, $;$ is defined such that $0 \, ; \, 0 = 0$.[1]

Formally, $;$ is defined by the equations given in Figure 6.3. For all C and C', when we write $C \, ; \, C'$, we mean the choreography C'' such that $C \, ; \, C' = C''$. That is, the choreography obtained by recursively applying the equations that define $;$. Notice that this is a terminating procedure: $;$ is defined by structural recursion on its first argument (which diminishes in size) and all cases are covered.

Rule COND-ELSE is the counterpart of rule COND-THEN: it states that whenever the guard of a conditional can be evaluated to a value v that is not *true* (given by the premise $\Sigma(\mathsf{p}) \vdash e \downarrow v$ and the side condition $v \neq true$), then the conditional continues as its else-branch.

Example 6.2 Let Σ be a choreographic store and C be the choreography presented in Example 6.1:

$$C \triangleq \begin{array}{l} \text{if Alice.}bobFirst(news)\,\text{then} \\ \quad \text{Alice.}news \rightarrow \text{Bob.}x; \text{Alice.}news \rightarrow \text{Carol.}y \\ \text{else} \\ \quad \text{Alice.}news \rightarrow \text{Carol.}y; \text{Alice.}news \rightarrow \text{Bob.}x. \end{array} \qquad (6.1)$$

Suppose that $\Sigma(\text{Alice}) \vdash bobFirst(news) \downarrow true$. Then, the conditional in C can proceed to its then-branch by rule COND-THEN.

$$\frac{\Sigma(\text{Alice}) \vdash bobFirst(news) \downarrow true}{\langle C, \Sigma \rangle \xrightarrow{\tau @ \mathsf{p}} \langle \text{Alice.}news \rightarrow \text{Bob.}x; \text{Alice.}news \rightarrow \text{Carol.}y, \Sigma \rangle} \text{ COND-THEN}$$

Otherwise, under the assumption that $\Sigma(\text{Alice}) \vdash bobFirst(news) \downarrow false$, the conditional in C can proceed to its else-branch by rule COND-ELSE.

$$\frac{\Sigma(\text{Alice}) \vdash bobFirst(news) \downarrow false}{\langle C, \Sigma \rangle \xrightarrow{\tau @ \mathsf{p}} \langle \text{Alice.}news \rightarrow \text{Carol.}y; \text{Alice.}news \rightarrow \text{Bob.}x, \Sigma \rangle} \text{ COND-ELSE}$$

Sequential composition respects the following laws.

---

[1] An alternative to the usage of $;$ would be to extend our syntax to general sequential composition of choreographies, whereby for any choreographies C and C', it is possible to write and execute $C; C'$ (C and then C'). However, this would make it necessary to deal with choreographies of the form $0; C$, which can complicate the semantics of choreographies and processes [Lanese et al. 2008].

Proposition 6.1 The set of Conditional Choreographies equipped with the sequential composition operator $\, \fatsemi\,$ is a *monoid* with $\mathbf{0}$ as identity element.

Identity Element For all C, $C \fatsemi \mathbf{0} = C$ and $\mathbf{0} \fatsemi C = C$.
Associativity For all C_1, C_2, and C_3, $C_1 \fatsemi (C_2 \fatsemi C_3) = (C_1 \fatsemi C_2) \fatsemi C_3$.

Exercise 6.1 ($\hookrightarrow$) Prove Proposition 6.1.

Out-of-Order Execution for Conditionals

The other new rule in our semantics, rule DELAY-COND, models the concurrent execution of instructions that are independent of a conditional. Consider the following choreography, where p and q are some processes, and x and y are variables.

$$
\begin{aligned}
&\text{if p}.(x < 10)\,\text{then} \\
&\qquad \text{q}.y := \mathit{true};\, \text{p}.x := x + 1 \\
&\text{else} \\
&\qquad \text{q}.y := \mathit{true}
\end{aligned}
\tag{6.2}
$$

Regardless of which branch p chooses by evaluating the guard of the conditional, the local assignment performed by q is the same: q.$y := \mathit{true}$. Thus, since p and q are (the names of) independent processes, we can anticipate the execution of the local assignment to before that of the conditional.

Rule DELAY-COND captures this kind of situation by allowing for transitions from the branches of a conditional, whenever these do not depend on evaluating the guard. Formally, the rule states that if (i) both branches of a conditional can perform the same transition (μ) ending up in the same state Σ' and (ii) the transition does not involve the process evaluating the conditional (p), then the execution of the conditional can be delayed and we can immediately observe the transition.

Example 6.3 Let C be the choreography in (6.2), Σ be a choreographic store and $\Sigma' \triangleq \Sigma[\text{q}.y \mapsto \mathit{true}]$. Then we can use rule DELAY-COND to derive a transition for $\langle C, \Sigma \rangle$ as follows. (For space reasons, we omit the side condition p $\notin$ {q} in the application of the rule.)

$$
\dfrac{\dfrac{\overline{\Sigma(\text{q}) \vdash \mathit{true} \downarrow \mathit{true}}\ \text{VAL}}{\langle \text{q}.y := \mathit{true};\, \text{p}.x := x + 1, \Sigma \rangle \xrightarrow{\ \tau @ \text{q}\ } \langle \text{p}.x := x + 1, \Sigma' \rangle}\ \text{LOCAL} \qquad \dfrac{\dfrac{\overline{\Sigma(\text{q}) \vdash \mathit{true} \downarrow \mathit{true}}\ \text{VAL}}{\langle \text{q}.y := \mathit{true}, \Sigma \rangle \xrightarrow{\ \tau @ \text{q}\ } \langle \mathbf{0}, \Sigma' \rangle}\ \text{LOCAL}}{\langle C, \Sigma \rangle \xrightarrow{\ \tau @ \text{q}\ } \langle \text{if p}.(x < 10)\,\text{then p}.x := x + 1\,\text{else}\,\mathbf{0}, \Sigma' \rangle}\ \text{DELAY-COND}
$$

Exercise 6.2 Let Σ be a choreographic store such that $\Sigma(\mathsf{p}) \vdash x < 10 \downarrow true$, and let C be the following choreography, where p, q, and r are process names and x, y, and z are variables.

$$\left(\begin{array}{l} \text{if } \mathsf{p}.(x < 10) \text{ then} \\ \quad \mathsf{p}.x := x + 1; \mathsf{q}.y := true \\ \text{else} \\ \quad \mathsf{q}.y := true \end{array} \right) ; \mathsf{q}.y \to \mathsf{r}.z \tag{6.3}$$

Draw the graphical representation of the lts generated by the configuration $\langle C, \Sigma \rangle$.

6.1.2 Nondeterminism

We relax our assumption on local functions to allow for *nondeterminism*. That is, for every function name f used in a choreography and for every sequence of values $\vec{v}$, we now require that there exists at least one v such that $\vdash f(\vec{v}) \downarrow v$ (instead of exactly one such v, as in Stateful Choreographies). Consequently, some function calls might now be evaluated to several different values: for some function names f, sequences of values $\vec{v}$, and distinct values v and v', it is possible that $\vdash f(\vec{v}) \downarrow v$ and $\vdash f(\vec{v}) \downarrow v'$.[2]

We say that a local function f is *deterministic* if for every sequence of values $\vec{v}$ there exists exactly one v such that $\vdash f(\vec{v}) \downarrow v$. Otherwise, we say that f is *nondeterministic*. In all examples in the remainder, local functions are deterministic unless we explicitly state otherwise.

Local nondeterminism is not essential to our development of Conditional Choreographies, but it contributes to the expressivity of choreographies in an interesting way: some communications that share processes can be nondeterministically reordered at runtime. This is different from out-of-order execution, formalised by the DELAY-rules, which can be used to observe communications in different orders only if the involved processes are distinct. We illustrate this feature in the next two examples.

Example 6.4 A process can use a nondeterministic local function to choose in which order it will communicate messages to some recipients.

Let *flipCoin* be a function name such that $\vdash flipCoin() \downarrow true$ and $\vdash flipCoin() \downarrow false$ (but no other evaluations are possible), and consider the following modification of the choreography from (6.1).

$$C \triangleq \begin{array}{l} \text{if } Alice.flipCoin() \text{ then} \\ \quad Alice.news \to Bob.x; Alice.news \to Carol.y \\ \text{else} \\ \quad Alice.news \to Carol.y; Alice.news \to Bob.x \end{array}$$

In C, Alice flips a coin to decide whether she should send her news to Bob or to Carol first.

---

[2] In a strict mathematical sense, this means that function names actually refer to something more general than standard mathematical functions, since the outputs of the latter are entirely determined by their inputs. We keep calling them function names anyway, which is in line with the nomenclature adopted in some mainstream programming languages. This is also done in mathematics sometimes, for example with the concept of 'random function'.

For any Σ and v such that $\Sigma(\text{Alice}) \vdash news \downarrow v$, the lts generated by the configuration $\langle C, \Sigma \rangle$ can be graphically represented as follows.

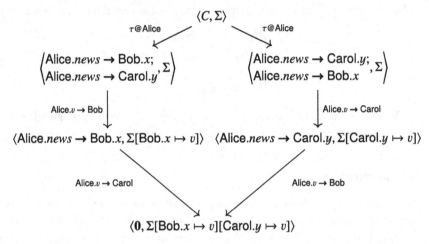

Observe, in particular, that the choreography can execute the two communications in any order. Constructing this kind of transition systems with Conditional Choreographies would not be possible without local nondeterminism, since the condition checked by Alice would always evaluate to the same value (*true* or otherwise) under the same choreographic store.

Example 6.5 Using function $flipCoin$ from Example 6.4, we can also write a choreography where a process chooses nondeterministically the order in which it will receive messages from other processes. In the following choreography, Bob and Carol communicate some news to Alice. Alice flips a coin to decide whether it wants to receive some news from Alice or Bob first.

$$
\begin{aligned}
&\text{if Alice}.flipCoin() \text{ then} \\
&\quad\quad \text{Bob}.news \rightarrow \text{Alice}.x; \text{Carol}.news \rightarrow \text{Alice}.y \\
&\text{else} \\
&\quad\quad \text{Carol}.news \rightarrow \text{Alice}.y; \text{Bob}.news \rightarrow \text{Alice}.x
\end{aligned}
\tag{6.4}
$$

Exercise 6.3 Let C be the choreography in (6.4) and Σ be a choreographic store such that $\Sigma(\text{Bob}) \vdash news \downarrow v$ and $\Sigma(\text{Carol}) \vdash news \downarrow v'$ for some v and v'. Draw the graphical representation of the lts generated by the configuration $\langle C, \Sigma \rangle$.

6.1.3 Conditional Processes

We now move to presenting the language of Conditional Processes, which is obtained by extending the language of Stateful Processes from Section 5.2.

$$P, Q, R ::= I; P \mid \mathbf{0}$$
$$I ::= \mathsf{p}!e \mid \mathsf{p}?x \mid x := e \mid \underline{\text{if } e \text{ then } P \text{ else } Q}$$
$$e ::= v \mid x \mid f(\vec{e})$$

Figure 6.4 Syntax of Conditional Processes.

Syntax

The syntax of Conditional Processes is given in Figure 6.4. The novelty (underlined) is that instructions can now be *conditionals* of the form if e then P else Q, read 'evaluate the expression e, and then proceed as P if the result is *true*, or proceed as Q otherwise'.

We write **ConditionalProc** for the set of all terms generated by the grammar of Conditional Processes and update the definition of networks accordingly. That is, a network N in Conditional Processes is a function from process names to terms in **ConditionalProc**:

$$N: \mathbf{PName} \longrightarrow \mathbf{ConditionalProc}.$$

The set of all such networks is denoted by **ConditionalNet**.

Example 6.6   The following network implements the choreography from Example 6.1.

$$\mathsf{Alice}\begin{bmatrix} \text{if } bobFirst(news) \text{ then} \\ \quad \mathsf{Bob}!news; \mathsf{Carol}!news \\ \text{else} \\ \quad \mathsf{Carol}!news; \mathsf{Bob}!news \end{bmatrix} \mid \mathsf{Bob}[\mathsf{Alice}?x] \mid \mathsf{Carol}[\mathsf{Alice}?y] \qquad (6.5)$$

Observe that the process terms of Bob and Carol are unaware of the fact that Alice makes an internal choice to decide on who will first receive the news: from their points of view, this aspect of the choreography is hidden. This is a typical feature of decentralised control.

Example 6.7   The following network implements the choreography in (6.3).

$$\mathsf{p}[\text{if } x < 10 \text{ then } x := x + 1 \text{ else}] \mid \mathsf{q}[y := true; \mathsf{r}!y] \mid \mathsf{r}[\mathsf{q}?z]$$

Semantics

The inference system that defines the semantics of Conditional Processes, displayed in Figure 6.5, is obtained by adding rules for conditionals (underlined): COND-THEN and COND-ELSE.

The rules are similar to their counterparts in Conditional Choreographies. Rule COND-THEN selects the then-branch of a conditional if the guard e evaluates to *true* under the store of the running process. Rule COND-ELSE instead selects the else-branch in case that the guard of the conditional does not evaluate to *true*.

Both COND-THEN and COND-ELSE make use of the sequential composition operator $\mathring{,}$, which we define for processes as we did for choreographies. The equations defining $\mathring{,}$ are given in Figure 6.6.

$$\frac{\Sigma(\mathsf{p}) \vdash e \downarrow v}{\langle \mathsf{p}[x := e; P], \Sigma \rangle \xrightarrow{\tau@\mathsf{p}} \langle \mathsf{p}[P], \Sigma[\mathsf{p}.x \mapsto v] \rangle} \text{ LOCAL}$$

$$\frac{\Sigma(\mathsf{p}) \vdash e \downarrow v}{\langle \mathsf{p}[\mathsf{q}!e; P] \mid \mathsf{q}[\mathsf{p}?x; Q], \Sigma \rangle \xrightarrow{\mathsf{p}.v \to \mathsf{q}} \langle \mathsf{p}[P] \mid \mathsf{q}[Q], \Sigma[\mathsf{q}.x \mapsto v] \rangle} \text{ COM}$$

$$\frac{\Sigma(\mathsf{p}) \vdash e \downarrow \mathit{true}}{\langle \mathsf{p}[\text{if } e \text{ then } P_1 \text{ else } P_2; Q], \Sigma \rangle \xrightarrow{\tau@\mathsf{p}} \langle \mathsf{p}[P_1 \,\fatsemi\, Q], \Sigma \rangle} \text{ COND-THEN}$$

$$\frac{\Sigma(\mathsf{p}) \vdash e \downarrow v \quad v \neq \mathit{true}}{\langle \mathsf{p}[\text{if } e \text{ then } P_1 \text{ else } P_2; Q], \Sigma \rangle \xrightarrow{\tau@\mathsf{p}} \langle \mathsf{p}[P_2 \,\fatsemi\, Q], \Sigma \rangle} \text{ COND-ELSE}$$

$$\frac{\langle N, \Sigma \rangle \xrightarrow{\mu} \langle N', \Sigma' \rangle}{\langle N \mid M, \Sigma \rangle \xrightarrow{\mu} \langle N' \mid M, \Sigma' \rangle} \text{ PAR}$$

Figure 6.5 Semantics of Conditional Processes.

Example 6.8 Let N be the network in (6.5) and Σ be a choreographic store such that Alice $\vdash$ *bobFirst*(*news*) $\downarrow$ *true*. Then we obtain a transition for the configuration $\langle N, \Sigma \rangle$ as follows.

$$\frac{\mathsf{Alice} \vdash \mathit{bobFirst}(\mathit{news}) \downarrow \mathit{true}}{\left\langle \mathsf{Alice}\begin{bmatrix} \text{if } \mathit{bobFirst}(\mathit{news}) \text{ then} \\ \quad \mathsf{Bob}!\mathit{news}; \mathsf{Carol}!\mathit{news} \\ \text{else} \\ \quad \mathsf{Carol}!\mathit{news}; \mathsf{Bob}!\mathit{news} \end{bmatrix}, \Sigma \right\rangle \xrightarrow{\tau\,@\mathsf{Alice}} \left\langle \mathsf{Alice}\begin{bmatrix} \mathsf{Bob}!\mathit{news}; \\ \mathsf{Carol}!\mathit{news} \end{bmatrix}, \Sigma \right\rangle} \text{ COND-THEN}$$

$$\frac{}{\langle N, \Sigma \rangle \xrightarrow{\tau\,@\mathsf{Alice}} \langle \mathsf{Alice}[\mathsf{Bob}!\mathit{news}; \mathsf{Carol}!\mathit{news}] \mid \mathsf{Bob}[\mathsf{Alice}?x] \mid \mathsf{Carol}[\mathsf{Alice}?y], \Sigma \rangle} \text{ PAR}$$

Exercise 6.4 Let N be the network in (6.5) and Σ be a store such that $\Sigma(\mathsf{Alice}) \vdash \mathit{bobFirst}$ (*news*) $\downarrow$ *false*. Draw the graphical representation of the lts of the configuration $\langle N, \Sigma \rangle$.

Exercise 6.5 Let N be the network in Example 6.7 and Σ be a store such that $\Sigma(\mathsf{p}) \vdash x \downarrow 5$. Draw the graphical representation of the lts of the configuration $\langle N, \Sigma \rangle$.

The $\fatsemi$ operator for Conditional Processes supports the same equality laws that we have seen for Conditional Choreographies.

$$\mathbf{0} \,\fatsemi\, P \triangleq P \qquad\qquad\qquad (I; P) \,\fatsemi\, Q \triangleq I; (P \,\fatsemi\, Q)$$

Figure 6.6 Definition of the $\fatsemi$ operator for processes.

Proposition 6.2 The set of Conditional Processes equipped with the sequential composition operator $\,\fatsemi\,$ is a monoid with **0** as identity element.

Identity Element For all P, $P \fatsemi 0 = P$ and $0 \fatsemi P = P$.
Associativity For all P, Q, and R, $P \fatsemi (Q \fatsemi R) = (P \fatsemi Q) \fatsemi R$.

The reader can check that Proposition 6.2 can be proven by following the same strategy used in the proof of Proposition 6.1.

6.1.4 Endpoint Projection

Since we added conditionals to the syntax of choreographies, we need to understand how the theory of EPP can be extended to translate choreographic conditionals into process implementations. In this regard, adding conditionals to choreographies has intriguing consequences. We introduce the issue – called *knowledge of choice* – with an example before getting to formalities.

The Problem of Knowledge of Choice
Consider the following choreography, C.

$$C \triangleq \text{if p.}e \text{ then p.}true \rightarrow \text{q.}x \text{ else } 0 \tag{6.6}$$

If p chooses the then-branch of the conditional, then it sends the value *true* to q. Otherwise, the choreography terminates.

What should the EPP of C look like? Following our usual strategy, we should obtain a network where p and q implement the necessary actions to participate in the choreography according to their respective process projections:

$$[\![C]\!] = \text{p}[[\![C]\!]_\text{p}] \mid \text{q}[[\![C]\!]_\text{q}]. \tag{6.7}$$

The question is now how to define the projection of the conditional in (6.6) on the processes p and q.

In the projection on p, the straightforward choice is to output a conditional with the same guard and then proceed by projecting the then-branch and the else-branch (for which we can reuse the rules from the previous chapter since those branches do not contain conditionals). We obtain:

$$[\![C]\!]_\text{p} = \text{if } e \text{ then q!}true \text{ else } 0.$$

By contrast, when we move to the projection on q, we run into a novel issue. Process q is not the process evaluating the conditional (p is), so its implementation should just 'ignore' it. Indeed, the only piece of code in the choreography that mentions q is p.*true* $\rightarrow$ q.*x*, which appears in the then-branch. Given that, the question is: what is a correct implementation of q? We have two possibilities.

1. We could say that the projection on q should implement the communication that might happen if p chooses the then-branch: $[\![C]\!]_\text{q} = \text{p?}x$. Hence we would obtain the following EPP for C.

$$[\![C]\!] = \text{p}[\text{if } e \text{ then q!}true \text{ else } 0] \mid \text{q}[\text{p?}x]$$

Unfortunately, this implementation makes it possible for q to starve. For example, consider a store Σ such that $\Sigma(\text{p}) \vdash e \downarrow false$. Then,

$$\langle [\![C]\!], \Sigma \rangle \xrightarrow{\tau @ p} \langle p[0] \mid q[p?x], \Sigma \rangle.$$

In the derivative, there is no opportunity for q to execute its receive action.

2. Alternatively, we could say that the projection on q should implement what might happen if p chooses the else-branch. In the else-branch, q does not do anything, so that gives us $[\![C]\!]_q = \mathbf{0}$. If we went down this path, the EPP of C would be as follows.

$$[\![C]\!] = p[\text{if } e \text{ then } q!true \text{ else } 0] \mid q[0]$$

Alas, this implementation is obviously incorrect as well. For a store Σ such that $\Sigma(p) \vdash e \downarrow$ *true*, we obtain a transition that makes p starve and the derivative has no chance to implement the communication between p and q prescribed by the choreography:

$$\langle [\![C]\!], \Sigma \rangle \xrightarrow{\tau @ p} \langle p[q!true] \mid q[0], \Sigma \rangle.$$

Neither of these two possibilities gives us a correct notion of EPP. Intuitively, this is because the choreography states that p and q have to behave differently depending on the branch chosen by the conditional. For p, this is not a problem because p is the process making the choice and thus gets to know whether we should run the then- or the else-branch. On the other hand, q does not have any information that it can use to determine which branch has been chosen: should q wait for a message from p (to implement the then-branch) or simply terminate (to implement the else-branch)? We say that q does not have *knowledge of choice* [Castagna et al. 2012]. In other words, the problem is that the choreography does not specify a sufficient flow of information that propagates the necessary knowledge of the local choices performed by processes.

Process projection for Conditional Choreographies

$$[\![p.e \rightarrow q.x; C]\!]_r \triangleq \begin{cases} q!e; [\![C]\!]_r & \text{if } r = p \\ p?x; [\![C]\!]_r & \text{if } r = q \\ [\![C]\!]_r & \text{otherwise} \end{cases} \tag{6.8}$$

$$[\![p.x := e; C]\!]_r \triangleq \begin{cases} x := e; [\![C]\!]_r & \text{if } r = p \\ [\![C]\!]_r & \text{otherwise} \end{cases} \tag{6.9}$$

$$[\![\text{if } p.e \text{ then } C_1 \text{ else } C_2; C]\!]_r \triangleq \begin{cases} (\text{if } e \text{ then} [\![C_1]\!]_r \text{ else} [\![C_2]\!]_r) ; [\![C]\!]_r & \text{if } r = p \\ [\![C_1]\!]_r \,\mathring{,}\, [\![C]\!]_r & \text{if } r \neq p \text{ and} \\ & \quad [\![C_1]\!]_r = [\![C_2]\!]_r \\ \text{undefined} & \text{otherwise} \end{cases} \tag{6.10}$$

$$[\![0]\!]_r \triangleq 0 \tag{6.11}$$

To address knowledge of choice, we shall make process projection a partial function. More precisely, projection will be defined only for choreographies where all processes get sufficient knowledge of choice.

Definition of Endpoint Projection

We start by updating the definition of process projection for Conditional Choreographies, which is now typed as follows.

$$[\![\,]\!] : \textbf{ConditionalChor} \times \textbf{PName} \rightharpoonup \textbf{ConditionalProc}$$

Notice that process projection is now a partial function ($\rightharpoonup$). In particular, it is going to be undefined whenever we cannot guarantee knowledge of choice.

Process projection is given by Equations (6.8) to (6.11). The projection of a conditional if $p.e$ then C_1 else C_2 is defined in (6.10) (the other equations are unchanged). We have three cases.

1. If we are projecting on the process that evaluates the guard ($r = p$), then we just proceed homomorphically, meaning we follow the structure of the choreography and return a corresponding conditional with the same structure where the two respective branches are given by process projection again.
2. If we are projecting on some other process ($r \neq p$), we need to consider that this process will not know which branch of the conditional p will choose to execute between C_1 and C_2. We ensure that this lack of knowledge at this point does not matter by requiring that the behaviour of this 'uninformed' process is the same in both branches of the conditional: $[\![C_1]\!]_r = [\![C_2]\!]_r$. The returned choreography is then the sequential composition $[\![C_1]\!]_r \,\fatsemi\, [\![C]\!]_r$ (which is equal to $[\![C_2]\!]_r \,\fatsemi\, [\![C]\!]_r$).
3. Otherwise, in the third case, we are projecting on a process that is not evaluating the guard and whose behaviour differs in the two branches of the conditional (because the condition $[\![C_1]\!]_r = [\![C_2]\!]_r$ of the second case is not respected). In this case, process projection is undefined.

Example 6.9 The projection of the problematic choreography in (6.6) on process p is defined. (For the sake of precision, we write all trailing 0s in this example.)

$$[\![(\text{if } p.e \text{ then } p.\textit{true} \rightarrow q.x; 0 \text{ else } 0); 0]\!]_p = (\text{if } e \text{ then}$$

$$[\![p.\textit{true} \rightarrow q.x; 0]\!]_p$$

$$\text{else}$$

$$[\![0]\!]_p);$$

$$[\![0]\!]_p$$

$$= (\text{if } e \text{ then } q!\textit{true}; [\![0]\!]_p \text{ else } 0); 0$$

$$= (\text{if } e \text{ then } q!\textit{true}; 0 \text{ else } 0); 0$$

By contrast, the projection of the same choreography on process q is undefined. The choreography is handled by Eq. (6.10), and since $q \neq p$ we need to satisfy the requirement that the projections of the two branches of the conditional on q are the same. That is, the following equation needs to hold.

$$[\![p.\textit{true} \rightarrow q.x; 0]\!]_q = [\![0]\!]_q$$

However, this is not the case, since $[\![p.\textit{true} \rightarrow q.x; 0]\!]_q = p?x; 0$ and $[\![0]\!]_q = 0$.

We set process projection to be undefined if any of the recursive calls to projection for the subterms of the input choreography is undefined.

Example 6.10   Consider the following choreography, where q performs a local assignment and then the system proceeds as the problematic choreography from (6.6).

$$\text{q.}y := 1; (\text{if p.}e \text{ then p.}true \to \text{q.}x; 0 \text{ else } 0); 0$$

The process projection of the choreography on q is undefined. We can initially expand the definition of process projection for the first instruction:

$$[\![\text{q.}y := 1; (\text{if p.}e \text{ then p.}true \to \text{q.}x; 0 \text{ else } 0); 0]\!]_q =$$

$$y := 1; [\![(\text{if p.}e \text{ then p.}true \to \text{q.}x; 0 \text{ else } 0); 0]\!]_q.$$

However, we now get stuck because $[\![(\text{if p.}e \text{ then p.}true \to \text{q.}x; 0 \text{ else } 0); 0]\!]_q$ is undefined. Hence, projection on q is not defined for this choreography.

We say that a choreography is *projectable* if it can be projected on all processes. Conversely, we say that it is *unprojectable* if it is not projectable.

Definition 6.3 (Projectability)   Let C be a choreography. We say that C is projectable if, for all p, $[\![C]\!]_p$ is defined.

Example 6.11   The choreographies in (6.6) and Example 6.10 are unprojectable.

Endpoint projection is defined as usual for Conditional Choreographies.

Definition 6.4 (EndPoint Projection (EPP))   Let C be a choreography. The endpoint projection (EPP) of C, written $[\![C]\!]$, is the network such that, for all p $\in$ **PName**,

$$[\![C]\!](\text{p}) \triangleq [\![C]\!]_\text{p}.$$

Differently from previous definitions of EPP, here EPP is a partial function (because process projection is partial in this context):

$$[\![]\!] : \textbf{ConditionalChor} \rightharpoonup \textbf{ConditionalNet}.$$

In other words, EPP is defined exactly for those choreographies that are projectable.

Exercise 6.6   Check that the following statements hold by writing the intermediate expansions of process projection on each process mentioned in the respective choreographies according to Equations (6.8) to (6.11) on page 118.
- The EPP of the choreography in Example 6.1 is the network in (6.5).
- The EPP of the choreography in (6.3) is the network in Example 6.7.

6.1.5 Limitations of Projectability

Let us take a pause from technical development and reflect on the implications of making projection a partial function.

Up until this chapter, anything that we could write as a choreography could be projected to an implementation. Therefore, when presented with an informal protocol that we wished to formalise, we just asked ourselves, 'Can we write it as a choreography?', backed by the reassurance that EPP would be able to provide an implementation.

Now that projection is partial, not all choreographies are equally useful: EPP produces implementations only for some choreographies. Given a scenario for which we wish to obtain an implementation, the question is not any more 'Can we write it as a choreography?', but rather 'Can we write it as a *projectable* choreography?'.

EPP is partial because of our equality requirement for projecting conditionals on the processes that do not evaluate the guard. We have already seen some choreographies that respect this requirement. For example, the choreography in (6.3),

$$\left(\begin{array}{l} \text{if p.}(x < 10) \text{ then} \\ \quad \text{p.}x := x + 1; \text{q.}y := true \\ \text{else} \\ \quad \text{q.}y := true \end{array} \right); \text{q.}y \to \text{r.}z, \tag{6.12}$$

is projectable, which is not surprising: the local choice performed by p is completely irrelevant for the rest of the system. The observation is even more evident if we rewrite the choreography as follows.

$$\left(\begin{array}{l} \text{if p.}(x < 10) \text{ then} \\ \quad \text{p.}x := x + 1 \\ \text{else} \\ \quad \mathbf{0} \end{array} \right); \text{q.}y := true; \text{q.}y \to \text{r.}z \tag{6.13}$$

The two choreographies mean the same thing: the labelled transition systems generated by them are identical (checking this is given as an exercise at the end of this subsection).

A more interesting projectable choreography is the one from Example 6.1:

> if Alice.*bobFirst*(*news*) then
>   Alice.*news* → Bob.*x*; Alice.*news* → Carol.*y*
> else
>   Alice.*news* → Carol.*y*; Alice.*news* → Bob.*x*.

Here, we cannot rewrite the choreography to bring instructions in the then- and the else-branches out of the conditional since they are different. This makes sense because the choice performed by Alice is not relevant only to herself: it also influences the order in which Bob and Carol will receive their news.

Unfortunately, there are interesting choreographies that are not projectable either. Consider an extension of our online bookstore choreography from Example 5.1: after the initial exchange of the book price between Buyer and Seller, Buyer now checks the price to choose whether to go ahead with the purchase. If so, Buyer sends their address to Seller and Seller replies with an expected delivery date. The choreography follows.

$$\text{Buyer}.\textit{title} \rightarrow \text{Seller}.x; \text{Seller}.\textit{cat}(x) \rightarrow \text{Buyer}.\textit{price};$$

if Buyer.*check(price)* then

    Buyer.*address* → Seller.*y*; Seller.*getDate(y)* → Buyer.*date*   (6.14)

else

    0

The choreography in (6.14) is unprojectable because Seller does not have knowledge of the local choice performed by Buyer. However, we can repair it by having Buyer send an empty address value *None* to Seller, which Seller could check for to decide whether it should actually schedule a delivery (in this case, it will send back a date) or not (in this case, it will send back *None* as well), as follows.

Buyer.*title* → Seller.*x*; Seller.*cat(x)* → Buyer.*price*;

if Buyer.*check(price)* then

    Buyer.*address* → Seller.*y*;

    if Seller.(*y = None*) then

        Seller.*None* → Buyer.*date*

    else

        Seller.*getDate(y)* → Buyer.*date*   (6.15)

else

    Buyer.*None* → Seller.*y*;

    if Seller.(*y = None*) then

        Seller.*None* → Buyer.*date*

    else

        Seller.*getDate(y)* → Buyer.*date*

The choreography in (6.15) is projectable. In particular, it is projectable on Seller, which was not the case before, because now Seller runs the same code regardless of the choice performed by Buyer. The following two equations show that the projections on Seller of the then-branch and the else-branch of the conditional executed by Buyer are the same.

$$
\left[
\begin{array}{l}
\text{Buyer}.\textit{address} \rightarrow \text{Seller}.y; \\
\text{if Seller}.(y = \textit{None}) \text{ then} \\
\quad \text{Seller}.\textit{None} \rightarrow \text{Buyer}.\textit{date} \\
\text{else} \\
\quad \text{Seller}.\textit{getDate}(y) \rightarrow \text{Buyer}.\textit{date}
\end{array}
\right]_{\text{Seller}}
=
\begin{array}{l}
\text{Buyer?}y; \\
(\text{if } y = \textit{None} \text{ then} \\
\quad \text{Buyer!}\textit{None} \\
\text{else} \\
\quad \text{Buyer!}\textit{getDate}(y))
\end{array}
$$

$$
\left[
\begin{array}{l}
\text{Buyer}.\textit{None} \rightarrow \text{Seller}.y; \\
\text{if Seller}.(y = \textit{None}) \text{ then} \\
\quad \text{Seller}.\textit{None} \rightarrow \text{Buyer}.\textit{date} \\
\text{else} \\
\quad \text{Seller}.\textit{getDate}(y) \rightarrow \text{Buyer}.\textit{date}
\end{array}
\right]_{\text{Seller}}
=
\begin{array}{l}
\text{Buyer?}y; \\
\text{if } y = \textit{None} \text{ then} \\
\quad \text{Buyer!}\textit{None} \\
\text{else} \\
\quad \text{Buyer!}\textit{getDate}(y)
\end{array}
$$

In essence, we went from the unprojectable choreography in (6.14) to the projectable choreography in (6.15) by adding the communication of a special value (the 'empty address' *None*) that Seller can then compare against in a local conditional of its own to determine what to do. However, this technique carries two issues:

$$C ::= I; C \mid 0$$
$$I ::= p.e \rightarrow q.x \mid \underline{p \rightarrow q[L]} \mid p.x := e \mid \text{if } p.e \text{ then } C_1 \text{ else } C_2$$
$$e ::= v \mid x \mid f(\tilde{e})$$

Figure 6.7 Syntax of Selective Choreographies.

- The resulting choreography is repetitive. In (6.15), the same conditional evaluated by Seller appears in both branches of the outer conditional evaluated by Buyer. This issue makes reading and writing the choreography tedious and error-prone.
- All possible executions have the same number of communications. In (6.15), the Seller needs to send a delivery date (possibly *None*) back to Buyer even when the Buyer decided not to proceed with an order. If we did not write so, then the choreography would have been unprojectable on Buyer (Buyer needs to behave in the same way in both branches of the inner conditional evaluated by Seller). This issue makes choreographies suboptimal: the interaction Seller.*None* → Buyer.*date* is useless since Buyer already knows that there will not be a delivery.

In the next section, we extend our theory with *selections*: communications of constants that can be used to propagate knowledge of choice. As we will see, selections avoid the issues that we have just described and can be used to achieve projectable choreographies that are nearly as concise as the one that we started from in (6.14).

Exercise 6.7 Check that the labelled transition systems generated by the choreographies in (6.12) and (6.13) are identical.

Exercise 6.8 Write the EPP of the choreography in (6.15).

6.2   Selections

In this section, we explore the theory of *selections*: communications of constants that receiving processes can use to react correctly to choices performed by other processes. We do this by extending the languages of Conditional Choreographies and Conditional Processes with primitives for such communications. We call these extensions, respectively, Selective Choreographies and Selective Processes.

6.2.1   Selective Choreographies

Syntax
Let **SLabel** be an infinite set of *selection labels* ranged over by L. The syntax of Selective Choreographies is given in Figure 6.7. The new kind of instructions (underlined), the *selection* p→q[L], reads 'process p communicates to process q the selection of label L'. We write **SelectiveChor** for the set of all Selective Choreographies.

We extend function pn to the new syntax by adding a case for selections, as follows.

$$pn(p \rightarrow q[L]) = \{p, q\}$$

The key idea behind the introduction of label selections is that we will allow for processes to behave differently based on the labels that they receive.

Example 6.12 Recall the choreography from (6.14):

> Buyer.*title* $\rightarrow$ Seller.*x*; Seller.*cat*(*x*) $\rightarrow$ Buyer.*price*;
> if Buyer.*check*(*price*) then
>   Buyer.*address* $\rightarrow$ Seller.*y*; Seller.*getDate*(*y*) $\rightarrow$ Buyer.*date*
> else
>   **0**.

The choreography is unprojectable because Seller does not know whether Buyer chose the then- or the else-branch of the conditional. We repair the choreography by adding the communication of this information via selections:

> Buyer.*title* $\rightarrow$ Seller.*x*; Seller.*cat*(*x*) $\rightarrow$ Buyer.*price*;
> if Buyer.*check*(*price*) then
>   Buyer $\rightarrow$ Seller[ok];
>   Buyer.*address* $\rightarrow$ Seller.*y*; Seller.*getDate*(*y*) $\rightarrow$ Buyer.*date*
> else
>   Buyer $\rightarrow$ Seller[ko],

(6.16)

where ok and ko are selection labels (ok, ko $\in$ **SLabel**). The fact that Seller has to implement different behaviours in the two branches of the conditional is not a problem anymore: if Seller needs to implement the then-branch of the conditional, then it will first receive the selection of label ok from Buyer (which knows the branch that it has chosen); conversely, if Seller needs to behave according to the else-branch, then it will first receive the selection of a different label (ko). Since Seller is guaranteed to receive an informative label before it needs to behave differently, we can exploit this information in its implementation to react correctly to the choice performed by Buyer. We will generalise and formalise this concept in the presentations of our updated process language and EPP, for which the choreography in (6.16) will be projectable.

Example 6.13 We model part of a simple *single sign-on* scenario in which a client (c) can gain access to a service (s) by getting its (user's) credentials checked by a third-party central authentication service (cas) [OpenID 2021; Neuman & Ts'o 1994]. Single sign-on enables the client's user to use a single account (at the central authentication service) for accessing multiple services (like s), without sharing credentials with these services (e.g., username and password).

More concretely, in the following choreography, we model the case in which the client c has to use its credentials in order to establish an authenticated session with s. The choreography begins with the client c communicating its credentials to the central authentication service cas. Then cas checks if the credentials are valid:

- If so, cas informs s that authentication is successful and in turn s informs the client c that it will receive an access token (generated by a nondeterministic function called *newToken*)

$$\frac{}{\langle p \rightarrow q[L]; C, \Sigma \rangle \xrightarrow{p \rightarrow q[L]} \langle C, \Sigma \rangle} \text{ SEL}$$

Figure 6.8 Semantics of Selective Choreographies, rule for selections.

that the client can use to further interact with the service in the future (e.g., this could be a web cookie).

- Otherwise, cas informs s that authentication failed and in turn s informs c that it will not receive a token.

$$c.creds \rightarrow cas.x;$$
$$\text{if } cas.valid(x) \text{ then}$$
$$\quad cas \rightarrow s[\text{OK}]; s \rightarrow c[\text{TOKEN}];$$
$$\quad s.newToken() \rightarrow c.t$$
$$\text{else}$$
$$\quad cas \rightarrow s[\text{KO}]; s \rightarrow c[\text{ERROR}]$$

Observe that c does not receive information on the branch chosen by cas directly from cas, but rather from another process (s) that has been previously informed by cas. That is to say, knowledge of choice can be transitively propagated by selections.

Semantics

The inference system that defines the semantics of Selective Choreographies consists of all the rules for Conditional Choreographies (Figure 6.2) and a new rule to deal with selections, which is displayed in Figure 6.8.

The new rule, SEL, is an axiom: a selection can always be executed. The label of the transition has the same form of selections, $p \rightarrow q[L]$, and reads the same. Executing a selection does not alter the store.

The function pn for transition labels is updated by adding the following case, like we did for the syntax of choreographies.

$$\text{pn}(p \rightarrow q[L]) \triangleq \{p, q\}$$

Example 6.14 Let C be the choreography in (6.16) and Σ be a choreographic store. Assume that

$$\Sigma(\text{Buyer}) \vdash title \downarrow \text{"My Choreographies"}$$
$$\Sigma(\text{Buyer}) \vdash address \downarrow \text{"Internet Street"}$$
$$\vdash cat(\text{"My Choreographies"}) \downarrow 100.$$

Then, C has the execution (we omit the intermediate states):

$$\langle C, \Sigma \rangle \xrightarrow{\text{Buyer.}\text{"My Choreographies"} \rightarrow \text{Seller}} \xrightarrow{\text{Seller.}100 \rightarrow \text{Buyer}}$$

$$\xrightarrow{\tau @\text{Buyer}} \xrightarrow{\text{Buyer} \rightarrow \text{Seller}[\text{OK}]} \xrightarrow{\text{Buyer.}\text{"Internet Street"} \rightarrow \text{Seller}} \xrightarrow{\text{Seller.}\text{"2055-03-08"} \rightarrow \text{Buyer}} \langle 0, \Sigma' \rangle$$

where Σ' is defined as

$$\Sigma' \triangleq \Sigma[\text{Seller}.x \mapsto \text{"My Choreographies"}]$$
$$[\text{Buyer}.price \mapsto 100]$$
$$[\text{Seller}.y \mapsto \text{"Internet Street"}]$$
$$[\text{Buyer}.date \mapsto \text{"2055-03-08"}].$$

$$P, Q, R ::= I; P \mid 0$$
$$I ::= \mathsf{p}!e \mid \mathsf{p}?x \mid \underline{\mathsf{p} \oplus \mathsf{L}} \mid \underline{\mathsf{p} \,\&\, \{\mathsf{L}_i : P_i\}_{i \in I}} \mid x := e \mid \text{if } e \text{ then } P \text{ else } Q$$
$$e ::= v \mid x \mid f(\tilde{e})$$

Figure 6.9 Syntax of Selective Processes.

6.2.2   Selective Processes

Syntax

The syntax of the process language that corresponds to Selective Choreographies, called Selective Processes, is given in Figure 6.9. The syntax has two new constructs (underlined), which respectively enable the sending and receiving of selections:

- *Selection actions* of the form $\mathsf{p} \oplus \mathsf{L}$, read 'send to p the choice of label L'.
- *Branching terms* of the form $\mathsf{p} \,\&\, \{\mathsf{L}_i : P_i\}_{i \in I}$, read 'receive from p a label L_j for some j in the (finite) set of indices I and then proceed as P_j'.

In a branching term, the component $\{\mathsf{L}_i : P_i\}_{i \in I}$ is a set. The order in which elements are specified is therefore irrelevant – for example, $\{\text{LEFT}: P, \text{RIGHT}: Q\} = \{\text{RIGHT}: Q, \text{LEFT}: P\}$ for all P and Q. We assume these sets to represent mappings of labels to processes, whereby each L_i is mapped to its respective process P_i. Hence, labels cannot be repeated: $\{\text{LEFT}: P, \text{RIGHT}: Q\}$ is valid, but $\{\text{LEFT}: P, \text{LEFT}: Q\}$ is not. We write **SelectiveProc** for the set of all Selective Processes.

The reading of branching terms is similar to that of conditionals, but instead of having an expression as guard we have labels. For example, we can read the term $\mathsf{p} \,\&\, \{\text{LEFT}: P, \text{RIGHT}: Q\}$ as 'receive a label from p, and proceed as P if the label is LEFT or as Q if the label is RIGHT'.

A selection action is used to send a choice (represented by the sent label) made by a process. For this reason, it is also called *internal choice*. Dually, branching offers a set of possible behaviours that an external process can choose from (through a selection action). It is therefore also called *external choice*.

Example 6.15   Using branching terms, we can define processes that react correctly to choices performed by other processes. The following network uses this principle to implement the choreography in Example 6.13.

$$c\left[cas!creds; s \& \begin{Bmatrix} \text{TOKEN}: s?t, \\ \text{ERROR}: \mathbf{0} \end{Bmatrix}\right] \mid s\left[cas \& \begin{Bmatrix} \text{OK}: c \oplus \text{TOKEN}; c!newToken(), \\ \text{KO}: c \oplus \text{ERROR} \end{Bmatrix}\right]$$
$$\mid cas[c?x; \text{if } valid(x) \text{ then } s \oplus \text{OK else } s \oplus \text{KO}]$$

The system starts with the communication of credentials from c to cas. Observe how the local choice made later by cas in its conditional is then propagated through a selection to s, which gets to know whether it should proceed by sending a token to c or not. Right afterwards, s communicates to c whether it will receive a token by selecting different labels, and c can thus react correctly (respectively by receiving the token or by terminating).

$$\frac{j \in I}{\langle p[q \oplus L_j; P] \mid q[p \& \{L_i : P_i\}_{i \in I}; Q], \Sigma \rangle \xrightarrow{p \to q[L_j]} \langle p[P] \mid q[P_j \, ; Q], \Sigma \rangle} \text{ SEL}$$

Figure 6.10 Semantics of Selective Processes, rule for selections.

Semantics

The semantics of Selective Processes is given by the system that consists of the rules in Figure 6.5 (for Conditional Processes) and the rule given in Figure 6.10.

Rule SEL matches a selection action at a process p towards a process q with a compatible branching term at process q coded to receive from p. The side condition $j \in I$ ensures that the label L_j sent by p is among those offered by the branching term at q. In the derivative, q proceeds by running the process P_j associated with the received label L_j.

Example 6.16 Consider a process q that offers to another process p a choice among three possible labels with respective continuations P, Q, and R:

$$q[p \& \{\text{YES}: P, \text{NO}: Q, \text{MAYBE}: R\}].$$

For any store Σ, we have the following derivations.

$$\frac{}{\langle p[q \oplus \text{YES}] \mid q[p \& \{\text{YES}: P, \text{NO}: Q, \text{MAYBE}: R\}], \Sigma \rangle \xrightarrow{p \to q[\text{YES}]} \langle q[P], \Sigma \rangle} \text{ SEL}$$

$$\frac{}{\langle p[q \oplus \text{NO}] \mid q[p \& \{\text{YES}: P, \text{NO}: Q, \text{MAYBE}: R\}], \Sigma \rangle \xrightarrow{p \to q[\text{NO}]} \langle q[Q], \Sigma \rangle} \text{ SEL}$$

$$\frac{}{\langle p[q \oplus \text{MAYBE}] \mid q[p \& \{\text{YES}: P, \text{NO}: Q, \text{MAYBE}: R\}], \Sigma \rangle \xrightarrow{p \to q[\text{MAYBE}]} \langle q[R], \Sigma \rangle} \text{ SEL}$$

Example 6.17 Let N be the network in Example 6.15, $\vdash newToken() \downarrow stoken$ (*stoken* is some random secure token value), v be a value such that $\vdash valid(v) \downarrow true$, and Σ be a store such that $\Sigma(c) \vdash creds \downarrow v$. Then, the configuration $\langle N, \Sigma \rangle$ has the following execution (we omit the intermediate states).

$$\langle N, \Sigma \rangle \xrightarrow{c.v \rightarrow cas} \xrightarrow{\tau @ cas} \xrightarrow{cas \rightarrow s[OK]} \xrightarrow{s \rightarrow c[TOKEN]} \xrightarrow{s.stoken \rightarrow c} \langle 0, \Sigma[cas.x \mapsto v][c.t \mapsto stoken] \rangle$$

Process projection for Selective Choreographies

$$[\![p.e \rightarrow q.x; C]\!]_r \triangleq \begin{cases} q!e; [\![C]\!]_r & \text{if } r = p \\ p?x; [\![C]\!]_r & \text{if } r = q \\ [\![C]\!]_r & \text{otherwise} \end{cases} \tag{6.17}$$

$$[\![p \rightarrow q[L]; C]\!]_r \triangleq \begin{cases} q \oplus L; [\![C]\!]_r & \text{if } r = p \\ p \,\&\, \{L: [\![C]\!]_r\}; 0 & \text{if } r = q \\ [\![C]\!]_r & \text{otherwise} \end{cases} \tag{6.18}$$

$$[\![p.x := e; C]\!]_r \triangleq \begin{cases} x := e; [\![C]\!]_r & \text{if } r = p \\ [\![C]\!]_r & \text{otherwise} \end{cases} \tag{6.19}$$

$$[\![\text{if } p.e \text{ then } C_1 \text{ else } C_2; C]\!]_r \triangleq \begin{cases} (\text{if } e \text{ then} [\![C_1]\!]_r \text{ else} [\![C_2]\!]_r) ; [\![C]\!]_r & \text{if } r = p \\ ([\![C_1]\!]_r \sqcup [\![C_2]\!]_r) \,\mathring{,}\, [\![C]\!]_r & \text{otherwise} \end{cases} \tag{6.20}$$

$$[\![0]\!]_r \triangleq 0 \tag{6.21}$$

Exercise 6.9   Show the derivations of all transitions in the execution given in Example 6.17.

6.2.3   Endpoint Projection

We are ready to design a more powerful notion of EPP than the problematic one presented in Section 6.1.4 by leveraging selections. The key idea follows the intuition that we discussed in Example 6.15: we update the definition of process projection such that it can mechanically produce branching terms that can react correctly to choices performed by other processes.

As a minimalistic example of what we wish to achieve, consider the choreography if $p.e$ then $p \rightarrow q[\text{THEN}]; C_1$ else $p \rightarrow q[\text{ELSE}]; C_2$, for some p, q, C_1, and C_2. The process q gets to know which branch has been chosen from the selection communicated by p. Hence, we wish the projection of this choreography on q to be a branching term that can react to the two possible labels that p could send, as follows.

$$[\![\text{if } p.e \text{ then } p \rightarrow q[\text{THEN}]; C_1 \text{ else } p \rightarrow q[\text{ELSE}]; C_2]\!]_q = p \,\&\, \{\text{THEN}: [\![C_1]\!]_q, \text{ELSE}: [\![C_2]\!]_q\}$$

The new definition of process projection is given by Equations (6.17) to (6.21). There are two differences with respect to the definition given for Conditional Choreographies in Section 6.1.4:

there is a new equation, (6.18), for projecting selections, and the equation for projecting conditionals, (6.20), is updated.

The projection of a selection $\mathsf{p} \to \mathsf{q}[\mathsf{L}]$ is simple: on the sender, p, we get an action that sends the selection of label L to the receiver, q; on the receiver, we obtain a branching term that waits

---

Merging operator ($\sqcup$) for Selective Processes

$$0 \sqcup 0 \triangleq 0 \tag{6.22}$$

$$(I; P) \sqcup (I; P') \triangleq I; (P \sqcup P') \qquad (*) \tag{6.23}$$

$$\frac{(\text{if } e \text{ then } P \text{ else } Q; R) \sqcup}{(\text{if } e \text{ then } P' \text{ else } Q'; R')} \triangleq \text{if } e \text{ then}(P \sqcup P') \text{ else}(Q \sqcup Q'); (R \sqcup R') \tag{6.24}$$

$$(\mathsf{p} \,\&\, \{\mathsf{L}_i : P_i\}_{i \in I}; Q) \sqcup (\mathsf{p} \,\&\, \{\mathsf{L}_j : P'_j\}_{j \in J}; Q') = \mathsf{p} \,\&\, \begin{pmatrix} \{\mathsf{L}_k : (P_k \sqcup P'_k)\}_{k \in I \cap J} \\ \cup \{\mathsf{L}_i : P_i\}_{i \in I \setminus J} \\ \cup \{\mathsf{L}_j : P'_j\}_{j \in J \setminus I} \end{pmatrix}; (Q \sqcup Q') \tag{6.25}$$

$(*)$: I is not a conditional or a branching.

---

to receive the same label from p. Both terms then proceed with the projection of the continuation of the choreography.

In the projection of a conditional if $\mathsf{p}.e$ then C_1 else C_2, on the process evaluating the guard (p) we get a conditional as before. The projection on a process that does not evaluate the guard is more interesting, in that we do not require equality of the projections of the then- and the else-branches anymore. Instead, we return the result of applying the *merging operator* $\sqcup$ to the projections of the two branches of the conditional, C_1 and C_2. Merging is the new ingredient to the theory of projection, which deals with the generation of branching terms that can react correctly to choices performed by other processes. We describe merging in detail in the following.

Merging
Merging is a partial binary operator on process terms:

$$\sqcup: \textbf{SelectiveProc} \times \textbf{SelectiveProc} \rightharpoonup \textbf{SelectiveProc}.$$

It is defined as the smallest operator that satisfies Equations (6.22) to (6.25). In every case, the two process terms that are being merged are required to have the same shape. We discuss each equation in the following.

Equation (6.22) Merging the terminated process 0 with itself returns 0.

Equation (6.23) Any term $I; P$, where I is not a conditional or a branching (condition $*$), can be merged with any other term that starts with the same I and has a continuation P'. The result is the process $I; (P \sqcup P')$ – that is, a process that starts with I and then continues with the process term that results from merging the continuations P and P'. Notice that if $P \sqcup P'$ is undefined, then the merging of $I; P$ and $I; P'$ is undefined as well.

Equation (6.24) Any process starting with a conditional, if e then P else $Q; R$, can be merged with any other process starting with a conditional with the same guard, if e then P' else $Q'; R'$. The result is a process starting with a conditional where the branches and the continuation are obtained by merging the respective branches and continuations of the two input processes, if e then$(P \sqcup P')$ else$(Q \sqcup Q')$; $(R \sqcup R')$. If the two conditionals in the two input processes do not have the same guard e, then merging is undefined for this case. Likewise, if any of $P \sqcup P'$, $Q \sqcup Q'$, or $R \sqcup R'$ is undefined, then merging is undefined for this case as well.

Equation (6.25) This is the most interesting and important equation. The merging of two branching terms is a branching term such that:

- It contains the union of all the labels of the two input branching terms.
- Each label that appears in both input branching terms, L_k for $k \in I \cap J$, is associated to the term obtained by merging the two respective processes for the same label in the input terms, $P_k \sqcup P'_k$.
- Each label that appears in the first input term but not the second, L_i for $i \in I \setminus J$, is associated to the process for the same label in the first input term.
- Each label that appears in the second input term but not the first, L_j for $j \in J \setminus I$, is associated to the process for the same label in the second input term.

For all cases not covered by these equations, merging is undefined.

Example 6.18 We give a few examples of (pairs of) terms for which merging is defined ($\checkmark$, in which case we show the result) and is undefined ($\times$, in which case we explain why).

$\checkmark$ $p?x; 0 \sqcup p?x; 0 = p?x; 0$ for all p and x.

$\times$ $p?x; 0 \sqcup q?x; 0$ is undefined for all p, q, and x such that p $\neq$ q. Equation (6.23) requires the receive actions to be exactly the same.

$\times$ $p?x; 0 \sqcup p?y; 0$ is undefined for all p, x, and y such that $x \neq y$. Equation (6.23) requires the receive actions to be exactly the same.

$\times$ $p?x; p!x; 0 \sqcup p?x; 0$ is undefined for all p and x. Equation (6.23) requires the continuations $p!x; 0$ and 0 to be mergeable, but this is not the case.

$\checkmark$ $p \& \{\text{OK}: P\} \sqcup p \& \{\text{KO}: Q\} = p \& \{\text{OK}: P, \text{KO}: Q\}$ for all p, P, and Q. Since the labels OK and KO are distinct, according to (6.23) there is no need to merge P and Q and they are just reported as they are in the result.

$\times$ $p \& \{\text{OK}: P\} \sqcup q \& \{\text{KO}: Q\}$ is undefined for all p, q, P, and Q such that p $\neq$ q. Equation (6.25) requires the process names mentioned in the input branching terms to be the same.

$\checkmark$ $p\&\{\text{YES}: p?x; 0, \text{MAYBE}: q?x; 0\} \sqcup p\&\{\text{NO}: 0, \text{MAYBE}: q?x; 0\} = p\&\{\text{YES}: p?x; 0, \text{NO}: 0, \text{MAYBE}: q?x; 0\}$. Here the two input terms share the label MAYBE, but the processes associated to it are mergeable.

$\checkmark$ $p \& \{\text{YES}: p?x; 0, \text{MAYBE}: q \& \{\text{OK}: 0\}; 0\} \sqcup p \& \{\text{NO}: 0, \text{MAYBE}: q \& \{\text{KO}: 0\}; 0\} = p \& \{\text{YES}: p?x; 0, \text{NO}: 0, \text{MAYBE}: q\&\{\text{OK}: 0, \text{KO}: 0\}; 0\}$. A variation of the previous example, where the two processes share the label MAYBE and the associated processes are mergeable. In this case, the latter are themselves branches that can be merged because they have distinct labels.

$\times$ if e then P else $Q \sqcup$ if e' then P' else Q' is undefined for all e, P, Q, e', P', and Q' such that $e \neq e'$. Equation (6.24) requires the two guards to be the same.

$\checkmark$ if e then $p \& \{\text{OK}: P\}$ else $0 \sqcup$ if e then $p \& \{\text{KO}: Q\}$ else $0 =$ if e then $p \& \{\text{OK}: P, \text{KO}: Q\}$ else 0 for all e, P, and Q. Equation (6.24) requires the respective branches of the conditionals to be mergeable, and in this case they are because $p \& \{\text{OK} : P\} \sqcup p \& \{\text{KO} : Q\} = p \& \{\text{OK} : P, \text{KO} : Q\}$.

Examples of Projection

The addition of merging gives us a more powerful theory of EPP. To gain some intuition about what this means, we present a few examples of projectable choreographies and what their projections look like.

Example 6.19 Consider the following toy choreography, where p decides whether another process q should communicate a message to it.

$$\text{if } p.e \text{ then } p \to q[\text{THEN}]; q.x \to p.y \text{ else } p \to q[\text{ELSE}]; \mathbf{0} \qquad (6.26)$$

The projection on p is straightforward:

$[\![\text{if } p.e \text{ then } p \to q[\text{THEN}]; q.x \to p.y \text{ else } p \to q[\text{ELSE}]; \mathbf{0}]\!]_p$

$= \text{if } e \text{ then} [\![p \to q[\text{THEN}]; q.x \to p.y]\!]_p \text{ else} [\![p \to q[\text{ELSE}]; \mathbf{0}]\!]_p$

$= \text{if } e \text{ then } q \oplus \text{THEN}; [\![q.x \to p.y]\!]_p \text{ else } q \oplus \text{ELSE}; [\![\mathbf{0}]\!]_p$

$= \text{if } e \text{ then } q \oplus \text{THEN}; q?y \text{ else } q \oplus \text{ELSE}; \mathbf{0}.$

The projection on q is more involved because it requires merging.

$[\![\text{if } p.e \text{ then } p \to q[\text{THEN}]; q.x \to p.y \text{ else } p \to q[\text{ELSE}]; \mathbf{0}]\!]_q$

$= [\![p \to q[\text{THEN}]; q.x \to p.y]\!]_q \sqcup [\![p \to q[\text{ELSE}]; \mathbf{0}]\!]_q$

$= p \& \{\text{THEN}: [\![q.x \to p.y]\!]_q\} \sqcup p \& \{\text{ELSE}: [\![\mathbf{0}]\!]_q\}$

$= p \& \{\text{THEN}: p!x\} \sqcup p \& \{\text{ELSE}: \mathbf{0}\}$

$= p \& \{\text{THEN}: p!x, \text{ELSE}: \mathbf{0}\}$

Notice that before we could resolve merging we had to resolve the inner applications of projection.

Therefore, the EPP of the choreography in (6.26) is the following network.

$$p[\text{if } e \text{ then}(q \oplus \text{THEN}; q?y) \text{ else}(q \oplus \text{ELSE}; \mathbf{0})] \mid q[p \& \{\text{THEN}: p!x, \text{ELSE}: \mathbf{0}\}]$$

Example 6.20 The following network is the EPP of the choreography in (6.16).

$$\text{Buyer} \begin{bmatrix} \text{Seller}!title; \text{Seller}?price; \\ \text{if } check(price) \text{ then} \\ \quad \text{Seller} \oplus \text{OK}; \\ \quad \text{Seller}!address; \\ \quad \text{Seller}?date \\ \text{else} \\ \quad \text{Seller} \oplus \text{KO} \end{bmatrix} \mid \text{Seller} \begin{bmatrix} \text{Buyer}?x; \text{Buyer}!cat(x); \\ \text{Buyer} \& \begin{cases} \text{OK}: \text{Buyer}?y; \\ \quad \text{Buyer}!getDate(y), \\ \text{KO}: \mathbf{0} \end{cases} \end{bmatrix}$$

Example 6.21   The EPP of the choreography in Example 6.13 is the network in Example 6.15.

Example 6.22   We extend the authentication choreography from Example 6.13, such that the central authentication service communicates the outcome of the authentication attempt to a logging process l, which keeps counters of how many attempts succeeded (*succs*) and how many failed (*fails*). The modifications are underlined.

$$
\begin{aligned}
&\text{c.}creds \rightarrow \text{cas.}x; \\
&(\text{if cas.}valid(x)\,\text{then} \\
&\qquad \text{cas} \rightarrow \text{s}[\text{OK}]; \text{s} \rightarrow \text{c}[\text{TOKEN}]; \\
&\qquad \text{s.}newToken() \rightarrow \text{c.}t; \underline{\text{cas.}true \rightarrow \text{l.}r} \\
&\text{else} \\
&\qquad \text{cas} \rightarrow \text{s}[\text{KO}]; \text{s} \rightarrow \text{c}[\text{ERROR}]; \\
&\qquad \underline{\text{cas.}false \rightarrow \text{l.}r}); \\
&\underline{\text{if l.}r\,\text{then l.}succs := succs + 1\,\text{else l.}fails := fails + 1}
\end{aligned}
$$

The projections on c and s remain unaltered since the modifications do not concern them. On cas, we obtain the following projection (modifications are underlined):

$$\text{cas}[\text{c}?x; \text{if }valid(x)\,\text{then s} \oplus \text{OK}; \underline{\text{l!}true}\,\text{else s} \oplus \text{KO}; \underline{\text{l!}false}].$$

The projection on the new process, l, is interesting and showcases the flexibility of merging: since l performs the same actions regardless of which branch of the conditional evaluated by cas is chosen, merging boils down to equality and does not require any selections. We show how projection on l is obtained step by step.

$$
\left[\!\!\left[
\begin{aligned}
&\text{c.}creds \rightarrow \text{cas.}x; \\
&(\text{if cas.}valid(x)\,\text{then} \\
&\quad \text{cas} \rightarrow \text{s}[\text{OK}]; \text{s} \rightarrow \text{c}[\text{TOKEN}]; \\
&\quad \text{s.}newToken() \rightarrow \text{c.}t; \\
&\quad \text{cas.}true \rightarrow \text{l.}r \\
&\text{else} \\
&\quad \text{cas} \rightarrow \text{s}[\text{KO}]; \text{s} \rightarrow \text{c}[\text{ERROR}]; \\
&\quad \text{cas.}false \rightarrow \text{l.}r); \\
&\text{if l.}r\,\text{then} \\
&\quad \text{l.}succs := succs + 1 \\
&\text{else} \\
&\quad \text{l.}fails := fails + 1
\end{aligned}
\right]\!\!\right]_{l}
=
\left[\!\!\left[
\begin{aligned}
&(\text{if cas.}valid(x)\,\text{then} \\
&\quad \text{cas} \rightarrow \text{s}[\text{OK}]; \text{s} \rightarrow \text{c}[\text{TOKEN}]; \\
&\quad \text{s.}newToken() \rightarrow \text{c.}t; \\
&\quad \text{cas.}true \rightarrow \text{l.}r \\
&\text{else} \\
&\quad \text{cas} \rightarrow \text{s}[\text{KO}]; \text{s} \rightarrow \text{c}[\text{ERROR}]; \\
&\quad \text{cas.}false \rightarrow \text{l.}r); \\
&\text{if l.}r\,\text{then} \\
&\quad \text{l.}succs := succs + 1 \\
&\text{else} \\
&\quad \text{l.}fails := fails + 1
\end{aligned}
\right]\!\!\right]_{l}
$$

$$
=
\left(
\left(
\left[\!\!\left[
\begin{aligned}
&\text{cas} \rightarrow \text{s}[\text{OK}]; \text{s} \rightarrow \text{c}[\text{TOKEN}]; \\
&\text{s.}newToken() \rightarrow \text{c.}t; \\
&\text{cas.}true \rightarrow \text{l.}r
\end{aligned}
\right]\!\!\right]_{l}
\sqcup
\left[\!\!\left[
\begin{aligned}
&\text{cas} \rightarrow \text{s}[\text{KO}]; \text{s} \rightarrow \text{c}[\text{ERROR}]; \\
&\text{cas.}false \rightarrow \text{l.}r)
\end{aligned}
\right]\!\!\right]_{l}
\right)_{9}^{\circ}
\right.
$$
$$
\left[\!\!\left[
\begin{aligned}
&\text{if l.}r\,\text{then} \\
&\quad \text{l.}succs := succs + 1 \\
&\text{else} \\
&\quad \text{l.}fails := fails + 1
\end{aligned}
\right]\!\!\right]_{l}
\right)
$$

$= (\dots \text{skipping all instructions that do not mention } l \dots)$

$$= (\llbracket \mathsf{cas}.true \to l.r \rrbracket_l \sqcup \llbracket \mathsf{cas}.false \to l.r \rrbracket_l) \mathbin{;} \begin{bmatrix} \text{if } l.r \text{ then} \\ \quad l.succs := succs + 1 \\ \text{else} \\ \quad l.fails := fails + 1 \end{bmatrix}_l$$

$= (\mathsf{cas}?r \sqcup \mathsf{cas}?r) \mathbin{;} \text{if } r \text{ then} \llbracket l.succs := succs + 1 \rrbracket_l \text{ else} \llbracket l.fails := fails + 1 \rrbracket_l$

$= \mathsf{cas}?r \mathbin{;} \text{if } r \text{ then } succs := succs + 1 \text{ else } fails := fails + 1$

$= \mathsf{cas}?r; \text{if } r \text{ then } succs := succs + 1 \text{ else } fails := fails + 1$

Example 6.23 We give a few further examples of conditionals that are projectable ($\checkmark$) or unprojectable ($\times$).

$\checkmark$ (if $p.e$ then $p.1 \to q.x$ else $p.2 \to q.x$); $q.f(x) \to r.y$. Even if there are no selections, no process other than p needs to know the result of the conditional.

$\times$ if $p.e$ then $q.2 \to r.x$ else $q.(1+1) \to r.x$ is unprojectable. The process q needs to be informed about p's choice to know if it should communicate the number 2 or the result of the expression $1 + 1$ to r.

$\times$ if $p.e$ then $p \to q[\mathsf{OK}]$ else $\mathbf{0}$ is unprojectable. The process q does not know whether it should wait to receive a selection (then-branch) or do nothing (else-branch).

$\checkmark$ if $p.e$ then $p \to q[\mathsf{OK}]$ else $p \to q[\mathsf{KO}]$ is projectable. However, the selections from p to q are arguably useless, since q behaves in the same way in both branches of the conditional.

$\checkmark$ if $p.e$ then $(p \to q[\mathsf{OK}]; p \to r[\mathsf{KO}]; r.1 \to q.x)$ else $(p \to q[\mathsf{KO}]; p \to r[\mathsf{OK}]; q.1 \to r.x)$ is projectable. Notice that q and r behave differently depending on the choice made by p, so the selections are needed. The example is purposefully a little intricate: the labels communicated from p to q and r are switched in the two branches. Nevertheless, the choreography is projectable because both q and r can figure out what they should do based on the received label.

Remark 6.5 The second choreography in Example 6.23 might trigger some curiosity. We cannot project it on q because the terms $r!2$ and $r!(1 + 1)$ are not mergeable. However, the expression $1 + 1$ always evaluates to 2, so it would be safe to say that the projection of the choreography on q is $r!2$. This suggests that a more permissive notion of projectability might be obtained by allowing for some simplification of the expressions in a choreography. For example, by simplifying $1 + 1$ to 2, we could rewrite the choreography as if $p.e$ then $q.2 \to r.x$ else $q.2 \to r.x$, which is projectable.

Transformations like these are commonly known as compile-time optimisations (here we are optimising $1 + 1$ to 2). The reader interested in an introduction to the topic of compilation and related techniques can consult Appel and Palsberg [2002] and Cooper and Torczon [2011].

Exercise 6.10 Write the endpoint projections of the projectable choreographies in Example 6.23.

Example 6.24   We exemplify the usage of nested conditionals in projectable choreographies. Consider a scenario in which a process p checks whether:

- It is owed money by another process q (represented by the condition e in the choreography below), in which case q should send some money to p.
- It owes some money to q (represented by the condition e' in the choreography that follows), in which case p sends some money to q.
- No money needs to be transferred, in which case nothing happens.

The choreography follows.

$$\text{if p}.e \text{ then}$$
$$\quad \text{p} \rightarrow \text{q}[\text{PAY}]; \text{q}.money \rightarrow \text{p}.m$$
$$\text{else}$$
$$\quad \text{if p}.e' \text{ then}$$
$$\qquad \text{p} \rightarrow \text{q}[\text{REIMBURSE}]; \text{p}.money \rightarrow \text{q}.m$$
$$\quad \text{else}$$
$$\qquad \text{p} \rightarrow \text{q}[\text{NO}]$$

Exercise 6.11   Write the EPP of the choreography in Example 6.24.

Relating Choreographies to their Endpoint Projections

The introduction of merging makes stating the correctness of EPP more challenging. Up until now, EPP was enough to relate choreographies and networks in configurations under transitions (see, e.g., the statement of Theorem 5.3). This simple formulation does not work anymore. As an example, let C be the following choreography, where p and q are some processes and e is an expression.

$$C \triangleq \text{if p}.e \text{ then p} \rightarrow \text{q}[\text{THEN}] \text{ else p} \rightarrow \text{q}[\text{ELSE}] \tag{6.27}$$

Let Σ be a choreographic store such that $\Sigma(\text{p}) \vdash e \downarrow true$. We show that the configuration $\langle C, \Sigma \rangle$ has a derivative whose choreography is not related by EPP to the corresponding derivative of its implementation.

By rule COND-THEN for choreographies, we can execute the conditional at p:

$$\langle \text{if p}.e \text{ then p} \rightarrow \text{q}[\text{THEN}] \text{ else p} \rightarrow \text{q}[\text{ELSE}], \Sigma \rangle \xrightarrow{\tau @ \text{p}} \langle \text{p} \rightarrow \text{q}[\text{THEN}], \Sigma \rangle.$$

The EPP of the choreography $\text{p} \rightarrow \text{q}[\text{THEN}]$ in the derivative is the network:

$$N \triangleq \text{p}[\text{q} \oplus \text{THEN}] \mid \text{q}[\text{p} \& \{\text{THEN} : \mathbf{0}\}]. \tag{6.28}$$

Unfortunately, the configuration $\langle N, \Sigma \rangle$ is *not* a derivative of $\langle C, \Sigma \rangle$. Specifically, the EPP of the initial choreography is defined as

$[\![$ if $p.e$ then $p \rightarrow q[\text{THEN}]$ else $p \rightarrow q[\text{ELSE}]]\!] =$

$$p[\text{if } e \text{ then } q \oplus \text{THEN else } q \oplus \text{ELSE}] \mid q[p \& \{\text{THEN} : \mathbf{0}, \text{ELSE} : \mathbf{0}\}],$$

and by rule COND-THEN for processes we have the following transition.

$$\langle p[\text{if } e \text{ then } q \oplus \text{THEN else } q \oplus \text{ELSE}] \mid q[p \& \{\text{THEN}: \mathbf{0}, \text{ELSE}: \mathbf{0}\}], \Sigma \rangle$$

$$\xrightarrow{\tau @p} \langle p[q \oplus \text{THEN}] \mid q[p \& \{\text{THEN}: \mathbf{0}, \text{ELSE}: \mathbf{0}\}], \Sigma \rangle \quad (6.29)$$

Comparing N with the network in the derivative in (6.29) reveals that the latter is 'bigger': there is an extra branch (ELSE: $\mathbf{0}$) in the branching term at process q. This difference is not a problem since the extra branch remains unused. However, this means that Lemma 5.5 does not hold for Selective Choreographies.

The issue that we have just exemplified happens because executing a conditional in a choreography can cut off code that involves multiple processes (the branch that was not chosen), whereas executing a conditional in a network cuts off only code at a single process: the other processes need to wait for appropriate selections before they become aware of what branches they can discard. In Chapter 8, we will obtain a correct formulation of the correctness of EPP by generalising this observation.

7 Recursion

In this chapter, we enhance choreographies with the capability of general recursion (technically procedure calls with continuations). Recursion opens the door to communication structures that repeat themselves, which is useful in different contexts. For example, we can design protocols for the communication of data streams of unbounded lengths, or protocols where participants continuously signal each other of their presence ad infinitum. Recursion is also typically found in choreographies that allow for retries. For instance, we might extend the authentication protocol from Example 6.13 such that the client can perform multiple attempts at providing valid credentials.

7.1 Choreographies

7.1.1 Syntax

Our starting point is the language of Selective Choreographies. We extend the language with *procedures* whose names are ranged over by X. The syntax of the resulting language, called Recursive Choreographies and denoted **RecursiveChor**, is displayed in Figure 7.1. The new terms are underlined.

In Recursive Choreographies, a choreography is executed in the context of a set of *procedure definitions* ranged over by $\mathscr{C}$. A set of procedure definitions is a (possibly empty) set of equations of the form $X(\vec{p}) = C$, read 'procedure X has parameters $\vec{p}$ and body C', where all procedure names are distinct. We call the parameters $\vec{p}$ of a procedure definition the *formal parameters* of the procedure.

We also add a new kind of instruction, namely the *procedure call* $X(\vec{p})$, read 'run procedure X with the processes $\vec{p}$'. We call the processes $\vec{p}$ the *arguments* of the procedure call. Another common name for procedure call is procedure invocation.

We update the definition of pn to deal with the new syntax. There is only one new case, for procedure calls.

$$\mathrm{pn}(\mathbf{0}) \triangleq \emptyset \qquad\qquad \mathrm{pn}(I; C) \triangleq \mathrm{pn}(I) \cup \mathrm{pn}(C)$$

$$\mathrm{pn}(\mathsf{p}.e \to \mathsf{q}.x) \triangleq \{\mathsf{p}, \mathsf{q}\} \qquad\qquad \mathrm{pn}(\mathsf{p}.x := e) \triangleq \{\mathsf{p}\}$$

$$\mathrm{pn}(\mathsf{p} \to \mathsf{q}[\mathsf{L}]) \triangleq \{\mathsf{p}, \mathsf{q}\} \qquad\qquad \underline{\mathrm{pn}(X(\vec{\mathsf{p}})) \triangleq \{\vec{\mathsf{p}}\}}$$

$$\mathrm{pn}(\mathsf{if}\ \mathsf{p}.e\ \mathsf{then}\ C_1\ \mathsf{else}\ C_2) \triangleq \{\mathsf{p}\} \cup \mathrm{pn}(C_1) \cup \mathrm{pn}(C_2)$$

$$\mathscr{C} ::= \{X_i(\vec{\mathsf{p}}_i) = C_i\}_{i \in I}$$

$$C ::= I; C \mid 0$$

$$I ::= \mathsf{p}.e \to \mathsf{q}.x \mid \mathsf{p} \to \mathsf{q}[\mathsf{L}] \mid \mathsf{p}.x := e \mid \text{if } \mathsf{p}.e \text{ then } C_1 \text{ else } C_2 \mid \underline{X(\vec{\mathsf{p}})}$$

$$e ::= v \mid x \mid f(\vec{e})$$

Figure 7.1 Recursive Choreographies, syntax.

7.1.2 Expressivity of Recursive Choreographies

Parametric procedures enhance significantly the expressivity of a choreographic language. We discuss a few demonstrative examples before continuing with the formal presentation of Recursive Choreographies.

We start with a couple of toy examples on choreographies that can have infinite executions, and then move to more practical examples on data streams, reattempts, and parallel computing.

Example 7.1   The following equation defines a procedure *Ping*, where a process p repeatedly communicates a signal (represented by the label SIG) to another process q.

$$Ping(\mathsf{p}, \mathsf{q}) = \mathsf{p} \to \mathsf{q}[\text{SIG}]; Ping(\mathsf{p}, \mathsf{q}) \tag{7.1}$$

Let C be a choreography that invokes the procedure *Ping* by passing Alice and Bob as arguments:

$$C \triangleq Ping(\text{Alice}, \text{Bob}).$$

Intuitively, the semantics of C is determined by the body of *Ping*, where all occurrences of p are replaced by occurrences of Alice and all occurrences of q are replaced by occurrences of Bob. In the context of a set of procedure definitions that includes (7.1), we can roughly think of C as the following infinite sequence of communications.

$$\text{Alice} \to \text{Bob}[\text{SIG}]; \text{Alice} \to \text{Bob}[\text{SIG}]; \text{Alice} \to \text{Bob}[\text{SIG}]; \cdots$$

We will formalise these concepts in the next section, when we will present the semantics of Recursive Choreographies. As we will see, C has an infinite execution.

Example 7.2   With the addition of parametric procedures, processes might now play different parts of a choreography at different times.

Consider the following definition of a 'ping-pong' procedure, *PP*.

$$PP(\mathsf{p}, \mathsf{q}) = \mathsf{p} \to \mathsf{q}[\text{SIG}]; PP(\mathsf{q}, \mathsf{p})$$

The procedure starts with p signalling q. It then proceeds by recursively invoking *PP*, but notice that p and q are passed in reverse order.

To understand the meaning of *PP*, let us consider the invocation *PP*(Alice, Bob). This invocation should run the body of *PP* by replacing p with Alice and q with Bob, which is the choreography:

$$\text{Alice} \to \text{Bob}[\text{SIG}]; PP(\text{Bob}, \text{Alice}).$$

Expanding the choreography further, we get that $PP(\text{Bob}, \text{Alice})$ runs the body of PP by replacing p with Bob and q with Alice:

$$\text{Alice} \rightarrow \text{Bob}[\text{SIG}]; \text{Bob} \rightarrow \text{Alice}[\text{SIG}]; PP(\text{Alice}, \text{Bob}).$$

Essentially, we can think of an invocation to $PP(\text{Alice}, \text{Bob})$ as a choreography that will run the following infinite series of communications, where Alice and Bob switch roles at each step.

$$\text{Alice} \rightarrow \text{Bob}[\text{SIG}]; \text{Bob} \rightarrow \text{Alice}[\text{SIG}]; \text{Alice} \rightarrow \text{Bob}[\text{SIG}]; \text{Bob} \rightarrow \text{Alice}[\text{SIG}]; \cdots$$

Example 7.3   A common technique for transmitting a large file over a network is to split the file into multiple parts (also called chunks or packets), which are then reassembled at the destination. We write a choreography that follows this idea.

First, we define a procedure S that streams a series of packets from a server, called s, to a client, called c. In the procedure, s keeps a counter n of how many packets have been communicated so far.

$$
\begin{aligned}
S(\text{c}, \text{s}) = \text{if s.} & (n \leq \mathit{packets}(\mathit{file})) \text{ then} \\
& \text{s} \rightarrow \text{c}[\text{NEXT}]; \\
& \text{s.}\mathit{mkPacket}(\mathit{file}, n) \rightarrow \text{c.}\mathit{packet}; \\
& \text{c.}\mathit{file} := \mathit{append}(\mathit{file}, \mathit{packet}); \\
& \text{s.}n := n + 1; \\
& S(\text{c}, \text{s}) \\
\text{else} & \\
& \text{s} \rightarrow \text{c}[\text{END}]
\end{aligned}
\tag{7.2}
$$

Procedure S starts with a conditional, where s checks that (the value of) its variable n is less than the number of packets that need to be communicated in order to transmit its local *file* fully. If so, s informs the client c that it will receive a packet, through the selection of label NEXT. We assume the expression $mkPacket(file, n)$ to return the n-th packet that should be communicated from s, which c stores in its local variable *packet*. The c appends the received packet to its local file (where it is aggregating the received packets) and s increments its local counter of sent packets n by 1. Finally, we recursively invoke S to communicate the remaining packets. When s has sent all packets ($n \leq packets(file)$), it sends the label END to c to inform it that the transfer is complete.

Using S, we can write a choreography where a **downloader** tool downloads a large file from some remote **storage**:

$$
\begin{aligned}
& \text{downloader.}\mathit{filename} \rightarrow \text{storage.}\mathit{filename}; \\
& \text{storage.}\mathit{file} := \mathit{readFile}(\mathit{filename}); \\
& \text{downloader.}\mathit{file} := \mathit{emptyFile}(); \\
& \text{storage.}n := 1; \\
& S(\text{downloader}, \text{storage}); \\
& \text{storage.}\mathit{crc}(\mathit{file}) \rightarrow \text{downloader.}\mathit{crc}_{\mathit{orig}}; \\
& \text{downloader.}\mathit{ok} := \mathit{equals}(\mathit{crc}(\mathit{file}), \mathit{crc}_{\mathit{orig}}).
\end{aligned}
\tag{7.3}
$$

In this choreography, **downloader** communicates the *filename* of the file it wishes to download from **storage**, which is then used by **storage** to read the content of the file from its local filesystem (using the local function *readFile*). Right afterwards, **downloader** initialises its own variable *file* (for storing the received packets) with an empty file, storage initialises the packet counter n to 1, and procedure S is invoked to stream the file.

In the last two lines, we implement a check for data corruption in transmission. Process storage sends to downloader a cyclic redundancy check (CRC): a short, fixed-length code computed from its local *file* [Peterson & Brown 1961]. Finally, downloader generates its own CRC based on the file that it received and checks whether this is equal to the CRC received by the storage.

Example 7.4   We rework the single sign-on choreography in Example 6.13 to allow for reattempts. That is, when the client provides invalid credentials, it is offered the possibility of attempting authentication again. The protocol is defined by the following procedure, *Auth*.

$$Auth(\text{c}, \text{s}, \text{cas}) = \text{c}.creds() \rightarrow \text{cas}.x;$$

$$\text{if cas}.valid(x) \text{ then}$$
$$\qquad \text{cas} \rightarrow \text{c}[\text{TOKEN}];$$
$$\qquad \text{cas} \rightarrow \text{s}[\text{TOKEN}];$$
$$\qquad \text{s}.newToken() \rightarrow \text{c}.t$$
$$\text{else}$$
$$\qquad \text{cas} \rightarrow \text{c}[\text{INVALID}];$$
$$\qquad \text{if c}.again() \text{ then}$$
$$\qquad\qquad \text{c} \rightarrow \text{cas}[\text{RETRY}];$$
$$\qquad\qquad \text{cas} \rightarrow \text{s}[\text{RETRY}];$$
$$\qquad\qquad Auth(\text{c}, \text{s}, \text{cas})$$
$$\qquad \text{else}$$
$$\qquad\qquad \text{c} \rightarrow \text{cas}[\text{ERROR}];$$
$$\qquad\qquad \text{cas} \rightarrow \text{s}[\text{ERROR}]$$

In procedure *Auth*, the client c communicates some credentials (obtained by evaluating the local expression *creds*()) to the central authentication service cas. Process cas then checks whether the received credentials are valid. If so, a token for c is issued by the service s as in Example 6.13.

If the credentials provided by c are invalid, cas informs c (selection of label INVALID). If the client then decides that it wishes to try again (conditional evaluated by c), it informs cas (selection of label RETRY), which in turn informs s, and the procedure recurs by invoking itself. Otherwise, the procedure terminates (with appropriate selections to implement knowledge of choice).

Example 7.5   A common pattern in parallel computing is splitting a task into subtasks that are then performed by separate processes. The results of these processes are then combined in order to compute the result for the original task.

We exemplify this in the following procedure definition, in which a manager process (m) splits a *task* into a pair of two *tasks* that are then respectively assigned to two worker processes (w_1 and w_2).

$$
\begin{aligned}
SplitAndCombine(\mathsf{m}, \mathsf{w}_1, \mathsf{w}_2) = \ &\mathsf{m}.tasks := split(task); \\
&\mathsf{m}.first(tasks) \to \mathsf{w}_1.ptask; \\
&\mathsf{m}.second(tasks) \to \mathsf{w}_2.ptask; \\
&\mathsf{w}_1.presult := do(ptask); \\
&\mathsf{w}_2.presult := do(ptask); \\
&\mathsf{w}_1.presult \to \mathsf{m}.presult_1; \\
&\mathsf{w}_2.presult \to \mathsf{m}.presult_2; \\
&\mathsf{m}.result := combine(presult_1, presult_2)
\end{aligned}
\tag{7.4}
$$

Using procedure *SplitAndCombine* in (7.4), we can write a choreography in which a client c delegates a task to be performed in parallel to a manager m:

$$
\mathsf{c}.task \to \mathsf{m}.task; SplitAndCombine(\mathsf{m}, \mathsf{w}_1, \mathsf{w}_2); \mathsf{m}.result \to \mathsf{c}.result.
\tag{7.5}
$$

Or we could invoke *SplitAndCombine* directly by saying that the client is the manager:

$$
SplitAndCombine(\mathsf{c}, \mathsf{w}_1, \mathsf{w}_2).
\tag{7.6}
$$

The key difference between the two solutions is that the choreography in (7.5) keeps the client oblivious to how the computation is actually performed, whereas in (7.6) the client needs to participate in *SplitAndCombine*.

7.1.3   Well-Formedness

In Section 2.1, we introduced the requirement that communications written in choreographies are always between different processes. Here, we add a few conditions regarding the definition and usage of procedures. We postpone a formal discussion of how a choreography can be mechanically checked to respect our conditions to Chapter 8, where we will discuss the properties of Recursive Choreographies.

We say that a choreography that respects the conditions described in this subsection is *well-formed*. In the remainder of this chapter, we assume that choreographies are well-formed.

For all procedure definitions, of the form $X(\vec{\mathsf{p}}) = C$, we impose the following conditions.

- All formal parameters are distinct. That is, the sequence $\vec{\mathsf{p}}$ does not include any process name more than once.
- The procedure can only mention the processes that appear in its formal parameters: $pn(C) \subseteq \{\vec{\mathsf{p}}\}$.
- There are least two formal parameters: $\vec{\mathsf{p}}$ is a sequence of at least two processes.

While the first two conditions are typical for parameters in general (think of, e.g., functions), the last one is merely a convenience for the definition of the semantics of Recursive Choreographies (since we will not have to deal with the case of procedures that involve a single process).

We define a few conditions also for all procedure calls found in choreographies, of the form $X(\vec{\mathsf{p}})$.

- All process names used as arguments are distinct. That is, $\vec{\mathsf{p}}$ does not include any process name more than once. This is important to avoid invocations that might break our other assumptions, e.g., for $X(\mathsf{p}, \mathsf{q}) = \mathsf{p} \to \mathsf{q}[\mathsf{L}]$, the invocation $X(\mathsf{p}, \mathsf{p})$ would lead to the ill-formed choreography $\mathsf{p} \to \mathsf{p}[\mathsf{L}]$.

- In the context of a set of procedure definitions $\mathscr{C}$:
  - Procedure X is defined in $\mathscr{C}$, that is, $X(\vec{q}) = C \in \mathscr{C}$ for some $\vec{q}$ and C. (Otherwise, we will not be able to resolve the call to X.)
  - The lengths of $\vec{p}$ and $\vec{q}$ are the same (every procedure invocation provides the right number of arguments).

Example 7.6   For each condition just explained, we give a respective example of its violation (✗), following the same order in which we presented the conditions.

✗   The procedure definition $X(p, p) = C$ is not well-formed for any C because its parameters are not distinct.

✗   The procedure definition $X(p, q) = p \rightarrow r[\text{HELLO}]$ is not well-formed because the process r that appears in the body of the procedure is not a formal parameter of the definition.

✗   The procedure definition $X(p) = C$ is not well-formed for any C because its list of parameters does not have at least two elements.

✗   The procedure call $X(\text{Alice}, \text{Alice})$ is not well-formed because its arguments are not distinct.

In the context of the set of procedure definitions $\{Hello(p, q) = p \rightarrow q[\text{HELLO}]\}$:

✗   The procedure call $Hey(\text{Alice}, \text{Bob})$ is not well-formed because the procedure Hey is not defined.

✗   The procedure call $Hello(\text{Alice}, \text{Bob}, \text{Carol})$ is not well-formed because of the mismatch between the arities of the call and the procedure definition (three arguments are passed, but the procedure definition has only two formal parameters).

7.1.4   Semantics

Substitution

The essential characteristic of Recursive Choreographies is the capability of performing a procedure call, written $X(\vec{p})$, where X is the name of procedure being called and $\vec{p}$ are the arguments with which the formal parameters of the procedure should be replaced. We make the notion of replacing process names precise by introducing the operation of *name substitution*.

Name substitution is an operation that traverses the structure of a choreography to replace process names with others. We write $C[r/s]$ for the choreography obtained by substituting every occurrence of s with r, read 'C where r replaces s'.

To define name substitution, we start from the basic case of checking whether an occurrence of a process name, say p, should be replaced under a substitution $[r/s]$. If $p = s$, then p should be replaced with r. Otherwise, p should not be substituted. This is formalised by the equation:

$$p[r/s] \triangleq \begin{cases} r & \text{if } p = s \\ p & \text{otherwise.} \end{cases}$$

Name substitution is generalised to sequences of process names, written $\vec{p}[r/s]$, by propagation to each name in $\vec{p}$:

$$(p_1, \ldots, p_n)[r/s] \triangleq p_1[r/s], \ldots, p_n[r/s].$$

We can now define name substitution for choreographies by propagating its application to all subterms, as specified by the following equations.

$$\mathbf{0}[r/s] \triangleq \mathbf{0}$$

$$(I; C)[r/s] \triangleq (I[r/s]); (C[r/s])$$

$$(p.e \rightarrow q.x)[r/s] \triangleq (p[r/s]).e \rightarrow (q[r/s]).x$$

$$(p \rightarrow q[\text{L}])[r/s] \triangleq (p[r/s]) \rightarrow (q[r/s])[\text{L}]$$

$$(p.x := e)[r/s] = (p[r/s]).x := e$$

$$(\text{if } p.e \text{ then } C_1 \text{ else } C_2) \triangleq \text{if } (p[r/s]).e \text{ then}(C_1[r/s]) \text{ else}(C_2[r/s])$$

$$(X(\vec{p})[r/s]) \triangleq X(\vec{p}[r/s])$$

Finally, building on the substitution of a single name, we define a shorthand for substituting many names at once. We write $C[\vec{r}/\vec{s}]$ for the substitution of each name in $\vec{s}$ with the respective name in $\vec{r}$ ($\vec{r}$ and $\vec{s}$ must have the same length):

$$C[r_1, \ldots, r_n/s_1, \ldots, s_n] \triangleq C[r_1/s_1] \cdots [r_n/s_n].$$

Example 7.7   Let C be the body of the procedure *Ping* from Example 7.1:

$$C \triangleq p \rightarrow q[\text{SIG}]; Ping(p, q).$$

Then, $C[\text{Alice}, \text{Bob}/p, q]$ is as follows.

$$
\begin{aligned}
C[\text{Alice}, \text{Bob}/p, q] &= C[\text{Alice}/p][\text{Bob}/q] \\
&= (p \rightarrow q[\text{SIG}]; Ping(p, q))[\text{Alice}/p])[\text{Bob}/q] \\
&= ((p \rightarrow q[\text{SIG}])[\text{Alice}/p]; (Ping(p, q))[\text{Alice}/p])[\text{Bob}/q] \\
&= (\text{Alice} \rightarrow q[\text{SIG}]; Ping(\text{Alice}, q))[\text{Bob}/q] \\
&= (\text{Alice} \rightarrow q[\text{SIG}])[\text{Bob}/q]; (Ping(\text{Alice}, q))[\text{Bob}/q] \\
&= \text{Alice} \rightarrow \text{Bob}[\text{SIG}]; Ping(\text{Alice}, \text{Bob})
\end{aligned}
$$

Transitions

With substitution in place, we are ready to formulate transitions for Recursive Choreographies. The semantics of a procedure call depends on the definition of the invoked procedure. Therefore we extend the semantics of choreographies to consider also the set of procedure definitions used during execution. This gives us configurations of the form $\langle C, \Sigma, \mathscr{C} \rangle$ (a triple) and transitions of the form $\langle C, \Sigma, \mathscr{C} \rangle \xrightarrow{\mu} \langle C', \Sigma', \mathscr{C} \rangle$. (The new ingredient being $\mathscr{C}$.)

Before delving into the inference rules that define the transition relation, it is instructive to explore their design. A typical and simple approach to the modelling of procedure calls in programming languages is to unfold a procedure call to the body of the procedure, substituting parameters with arguments appropriately. The following rule exemplifies this method.

$$\frac{X(\vec{q}) = C \in \mathscr{C}}{\langle X(\vec{p}); C', \Sigma, \mathscr{C} \rangle \xrightarrow{\tau @ \vec{p}} \langle C[\vec{p}/\vec{q}] \, ; C', \Sigma, \mathscr{C} \rangle} \text{ UNFOLD}$$

The rule candidate UNFOLD states that a call to procedure X with arguments $\vec{p}$ and continuation C' transitions to the sequential composition of the body of X, where its parameters are replaced by the arguments of the call ($C[\vec{p}/\vec{q}]$), and C'. The transition label $\tau@\vec{p}$ denotes that all processes mentioned in the arguments are participating in the transition, since they are all 'entering' X. While the rule is pleasantly simple, the fact that we have a single transition with a label that involves multiple processes ($\tau@\vec{p}$) is suspicious: all processes are entering the procedure at the same time, as if coordinated centrally by some underlying mechanism. Such coordination violates the principle that processes run independently of one another. By contrast, in practice we would observe that each process would begin the execution of (its part of) the procedure independently. This means that we should be able to observe a transition for each process entering the procedure, and that these transitions should be able to take place in any order.

To capture the fact that each process begins the execution of a procedure call independently, we use an auxiliary syntactic term, or *runtime term*. The purpose of a runtime term is to represent an intermediate state in the execution of a choreography: they are not to be used in the writing of choreographies, but they are rather a technical aid for the definition of transitions. Specifically, we extend the syntax of choreographic instructions as follows.

$$I ::= \cdots \mid \vec{q} : X(\vec{p}).C$$

The new term $\vec{q} : X(\vec{p}).C$ is a runtime term denoting that the processes $\vec{q}$ still have to begin execution of the procedure invocation $X(\vec{p})$; the component $X(\vec{p}).C$ in the runtime term is an annotation in the sense that it will not influence our semantics. The reason for such annotations is technical and regards only the definition of endpoint projection, which we shall discuss later. For now, it is fine to ignore them: as far as the semantics of choreographies is concerned, these annotations are immaterial. (Were we not interested in formulating EPP, they would not be present.)

We update the definition of pn to deal with runtime terms as follows.

$$\text{pn}(\vec{q} : X(\vec{p}).C) \triangleq \{\vec{q}\}$$

Using runtime terms, we can finally define the semantics of Recursive Choreographies. The inference rules for transitions are displayed in Figure 7.2. The three new rules, underlined, are CALL-FIRST, CALL-ENTER, and CALL-LAST. The other rules are straightforward extensions of the rules already seen for Selective Choreographies in order to accommodate for sets of procedures definitions.

Rule CALL-FIRST states that any process passed as argument in a procedure call ($r \in \vec{p}$) may start executing the procedure first. In the derivative, we use the runtime term that we have recently introduced. We write $\vec{p} \setminus r$ for the sequence obtained by removing r (the process that started executing the procedure) from $\vec{p}$ (the processes involved in the call), denoting that all process arguments but r have not executed the procedure call yet: from the point of view of these processes, the choreography is still formed by the procedure call followed by the original continuation C' – this will be relevant for the definition of projection, as we have already hinted. The continuation of the runtime term is the body of the called procedure C (coming from the first premise, which checks the definition of X), where the passed arguments replace the parameters ([$\vec{p}/\vec{q}$]), followed by the continuation of the procedure call (C').

Rule CALL-ENTER allows any process r that should begin executing a procedure ($r \in \vec{q}$) to enter it, assuming that other processes remain that should enter the procedure later ($\vec{q} \setminus r$ nonempty).

$$\frac{\Sigma(\mathsf{p}) \vdash e \downarrow v}{\langle \mathsf{p}.x := e; C, \Sigma, \mathscr{C}\rangle \xrightarrow{\tau@\mathsf{p}} \langle C, \Sigma[\mathsf{p}.x \mapsto v], \mathscr{C}\rangle} \; \text{LOCAL}$$

$$\frac{\Sigma(\mathsf{p}) \vdash e \downarrow v}{\langle \mathsf{p}.e \to \mathsf{q}.x; C, \Sigma, \mathscr{C}\rangle \xrightarrow{\mathsf{p}.v \to \mathsf{q}} \langle C, \Sigma[\mathsf{q}.x \mapsto v], \mathscr{C}\rangle} \; \text{COM} \qquad \frac{}{\langle \mathsf{p} \to \mathsf{q}[\mathsf{L}]; C, \Sigma, \mathscr{C}\rangle \xrightarrow{\mathsf{p}\to\mathsf{q}[\mathsf{L}]} \langle C, \Sigma, \mathscr{C}\rangle} \; \text{SEL}$$

$$\frac{\Sigma(\mathsf{p}) \vdash e \downarrow true}{\langle \text{if } \mathsf{p}.e \text{ then } C_1 \text{ else } C_2; C, \Sigma, \mathscr{C}\rangle \xrightarrow{\tau@\mathsf{p}} \langle C_1 \,\mathring{,}\, C, \Sigma, \mathscr{C}\rangle} \; \text{COND-THEN}$$

$$\frac{\Sigma(\mathsf{p}) \vdash e \downarrow v \quad v \neq true}{\langle \text{if } \mathsf{p}.e \text{ then } C_1 \text{ else } C_2; C, \Sigma, \mathscr{C}\rangle \xrightarrow{\tau@\mathsf{p}} \langle C_2 \,\mathring{,}\, C, \Sigma, \mathscr{C}\rangle} \; \text{COND-ELSE}$$

$$\frac{X(\vec{\mathsf{q}}) = C \in \mathscr{C} \quad r \in \vec{\mathsf{p}}}{\langle X(\vec{\mathsf{p}}); C', \Sigma, \mathscr{C}\rangle \xrightarrow{\tau@r} \langle \vec{\mathsf{p}} \setminus r: X(\vec{\mathsf{p}}).C'; C[\vec{\mathsf{p}}/\vec{\mathsf{q}}] \,\mathring{,}\, C', \Sigma, \mathscr{C}\rangle} \; \text{CALL-FIRST}$$

$$\frac{r \in \vec{\mathsf{q}} \quad \vec{\mathsf{q}} \setminus r \text{ nonempty}}{\langle \vec{\mathsf{q}}: X(\vec{\mathsf{p}}).C'; C, \Sigma, \mathscr{C}\rangle \xrightarrow{\tau@r} \langle \vec{\mathsf{q}} \setminus r: X(\vec{\mathsf{p}}).C'; C, \Sigma, \mathscr{C}\rangle} \; \text{CALL-ENTER}$$

$$\frac{}{\langle \mathsf{q}: X(\vec{\mathsf{p}}).C'; C, \Sigma, \mathscr{C}\rangle \xrightarrow{\tau@\mathsf{q}} \langle C, \Sigma, \mathscr{C}\rangle} \; \text{CALL-LAST} \qquad \frac{\langle C, \Sigma, \mathscr{C}\rangle \xrightarrow{\mu} \langle C', \Sigma', \mathscr{C}\rangle \quad \text{pn}(I) \# \text{pn}(\mu)}{\langle I; C, \Sigma, \mathscr{C}\rangle \xrightarrow{\mu} \langle I; C', \Sigma', \mathscr{C}\rangle} \; \text{DELAY}$$

$$\frac{\langle C_1, \Sigma, \mathscr{C}\rangle \xrightarrow{\mu} \langle C_1', \Sigma', \mathscr{C}\rangle \quad \langle C_2, \Sigma, \mathscr{C}\rangle \xrightarrow{\mu} \langle C_2', \Sigma', \mathscr{C}\rangle \quad \mathsf{p} \notin \text{pn}(\mu)}{\langle \text{if } \mathsf{p}.e \text{ then } C_1 \text{ else } C_2; C, \Sigma, \mathscr{C}\rangle \xrightarrow{\mu} \langle \text{if } \mathsf{p}.e \text{ then } C_1' \text{ else } C_2'; C, \Sigma', \mathscr{C}\rangle} \; \text{DELAY-COND}$$

Figure 7.2 Recursive Choreographies, semantics.

The runtime term is thus kept, with the only difference that the entering process r is removed from it ($\vec{\mathsf{q}} \setminus r$ in the derivative).

Finally, rule CALL-LAST deals with the case where we have exactly one process left that should enter the procedure. The process is let in and the runtime term is removed.

In the rest of this subsection, we exemplify and discuss a few interesting aspects of the semantics of Recursive Choreographies.

Example 7.8 Let $\mathscr{C}$ be a set consisting exactly of the ping-pong procedure definition from Example 7.2, and let C be a choreography that calls that procedure:

$$\mathscr{C} \triangleq \{PP(\mathsf{p}, \mathsf{q}) = \mathsf{p} \to \mathsf{q}[\text{SIG}]; PP(\mathsf{q}, \mathsf{p})\}$$
$$C \triangleq PP(\text{Alice}, \text{Bob})$$

By rule CALL-FIRST, both Alice or Bob can be the first process entering the procedure. To be more precise, both of the following two transitions are valid for any choreographic store Σ.

$$\langle C, \Sigma, \mathscr{C} \rangle \xrightarrow{\tau @ \text{Alice}} \langle \text{Bob}: PP(\text{Alice}, \text{Bob}).\mathbf{0}; \text{Alice} \to \text{Bob}[\text{SIG}]; PP(\text{Bob}, \text{Alice}), \Sigma, \mathscr{C} \rangle \quad (7.7)$$

$$\langle C, \Sigma, \mathscr{C} \rangle \xrightarrow{\tau @ \text{Bob}} \langle \text{Alice}: PP(\text{Alice}, \text{Bob}).\mathbf{0}; \text{Alice} \to \text{Bob}[\text{SIG}]; PP(\text{Bob}, \text{Alice}), \Sigma, \mathscr{C} \rangle \quad (7.8)$$

Let us consider the derivative of the first transition, in (7.7). By rule CALL-LAST, we have that

$$\langle \text{Bob}: PP(\text{Alice}, \text{Bob}).\mathbf{0}; \text{Alice} \to \text{Bob}[\text{SIG}]; PP(\text{Bob}, \text{Alice}), \Sigma, \mathscr{C} \rangle$$
$$\xrightarrow{\tau @ \text{Bob}} \langle \text{Alice} \to \text{Bob}[\text{SIG}]; PP(\text{Bob}, \text{Alice}), \Sigma, \mathscr{C} \rangle$$

We can now execute the selection by rule SEL:

$$\langle \text{Alice} \to \text{Bob}[\text{SIG}]; PP(\text{Bob}, \text{Alice}), \Sigma, \mathscr{C} \rangle \xrightarrow{\text{Alice} \to \text{Bob}[\text{SIG}]} \langle PP(\text{Bob}, \text{Alice}), \Sigma, \mathscr{C} \rangle.$$

Thus, we have reached a choreography that is similar to the initial one (C), the difference being that PP is invoked with arguments in reverse order. By rule CALL-ENTER, we can see that the consequence is that Bob is going to signal Alice.

$$\langle PP(\text{Bob}, \text{Alice}), \Sigma, \mathscr{C} \rangle$$
$$\xrightarrow{\tau @ \text{Bob}} \langle \text{Alice}: PP(\text{Bob}, \text{Alice}).\mathbf{0}; \text{Bob} \to \text{Alice}[\text{SIG}]; PP(\text{Alice}, \text{Bob}), \Sigma, \mathscr{C} \rangle$$

By rules CALL-LAST and SEL, we get the following multi-step derivative,

$$\langle \text{Alice}: PP(\text{Bob}, \text{Alice}).\mathbf{0}; \text{Bob} \to \text{Alice}[\text{SIG}]; PP(\text{Alice}, \text{Bob}), \Sigma, \mathscr{C} \rangle$$
$$\xrightarrow{\tau @ \text{Alice}} \xrightarrow{\text{Bob} \to \text{Alice}[\text{SIG}]} \langle PP(\text{Alice}, \text{Bob}), \Sigma, \mathscr{C} \rangle,$$

which brings us back to our initial choreography C. Executing the choreography continues indefinitely as shown earlier, alternating signals from Alice to Bob and vice versa.

Example 7.9 Example 7.8 shows that the graphical representation of the lts generated by a configuration in Recursive Choreographies might have loops. We illustrate this aspect with a simpler choreography. Consider the following set of procedure definitions and choreography, where we use the procedure from Example 7.1.

$$\mathscr{C} \triangleq \{Ping(\mathsf{p}, \mathsf{q}) = \mathsf{p} \to \mathsf{q}[\text{SIG}]; Ping(\mathsf{p}, \mathsf{q})\}$$
$$C \triangleq Ping(\text{Alice}, \text{Bob})$$

For any choreographic store Σ, the graphical representation of the lts generated by the configuration $\langle C, \Sigma, \mathscr{C} \rangle$ is as follows. In particular, the initial configuration is a multi-step derivative of itself.

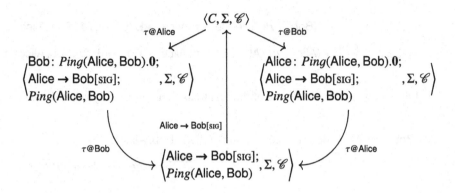

Exercise 7.1   Derive all the transitions shown in the graph in Example 7.9.

- $\langle C, \Sigma, \mathscr{C} \rangle$
  $\xrightarrow{\tau @ \text{Alice}}$ $\langle \text{Bob}: Ping(\text{Alice}, \text{Bob}).\mathbf{0}; \text{Alice} \rightarrow \text{Bob}[\text{SIG}]; Ping(\text{Alice}, \text{Bob}), \Sigma, \mathscr{C} \rangle.$

- $\langle C, \Sigma, \mathscr{C} \rangle$
  $\xrightarrow{\tau @ \text{Bob}}$ $\langle \text{Alice}: Ping(\text{Alice}, \text{Bob}).\mathbf{0}; \text{Alice} \rightarrow \text{Bob}[\text{SIG}]; Ping(\text{Alice}, \text{Bob}), \Sigma, \mathscr{C} \rangle.$

- $\langle \text{Bob}: Ping(\text{Alice}, \text{Bob}).\mathbf{0}; \text{Alice} \rightarrow \text{Bob}[\text{SIG}]; Ping(\text{Alice}, \text{Bob}), \Sigma, \mathscr{C} \rangle$
  $\xrightarrow{\tau @ \text{Bob}}$ $\langle \text{Alice} \rightarrow \text{Bob}[\text{SIG}]; Ping(\text{Alice}, \text{Bob}), \Sigma, \mathscr{C} \rangle.$

- $\langle \text{Alice}: Ping(\text{Alice}, \text{Bob}).\mathbf{0}; \text{Alice} \rightarrow \text{Bob}[\text{SIG}]; Ping(\text{Alice}, \text{Bob}), \Sigma, \mathscr{C} \rangle$
  $\xrightarrow{\tau @ \text{Alice}}$ $\langle \text{Alice} \rightarrow \text{Bob}[\text{SIG}]; Ping(\text{Alice}, \text{Bob}), \Sigma, \mathscr{C} \rangle.$

- $\langle \text{Alice} \rightarrow \text{Bob}[\text{SIG}]; Ping(\text{Alice}, \text{Bob}), \Sigma, \mathscr{C} \rangle$ $\xrightarrow{\text{Alice} \rightarrow \text{Bob}[\text{SIG}]}$ $\langle C, \Sigma, \mathscr{C} \rangle.$

Example 7.10   Let us consider an example in which remembering the continuation of a procedure call is important (because it is not the trivial $\mathbf{0}$).

Let Σ be a choreographic store and C_S be the body of procedure S in (7.2). Also, let $\mathscr{C}$ be a set of procedure definitions that consists of the definition in (7.2) and C be the choreography consisting of the last three lines in (7.3):

$$\mathscr{C} \triangleq \{ S(\text{c}, \text{s}) = C_S \}$$

$$C \triangleq S(\text{downloader}, \text{storage}); C'$$

$$C' \triangleq \text{storage}.crc(\text{file}) \rightarrow \text{downloader}.crc_{orig}$$
$$\text{downloader}.ok := equals(crc(\text{file}), crc_{orig}).$$

By rule CALL-FIRST,

$$\langle C, \Sigma, \mathscr{C} \rangle \xrightarrow{\tau @ \text{downloader}} \left\langle \begin{array}{l} \text{storage}: S(\text{downloader}, \text{storage}).C'; \\ C_S[\text{downloader}, \text{storage}/\text{c}, \text{s}]; \\ C' \end{array}, \Sigma, \mathscr{C} \right\rangle.$$

Example 7.11 In Recursive Choreographies, the lts generated by a configuration might have an infinite number of states. Consider the scenario in which a process p streams the natural numbers to another process q, which we model with the following set of procedure definitions and choreography.

$$\mathscr{C} \triangleq \{X(\mathsf{s},\mathsf{r}) = \mathsf{s}.x \rightarrow \mathsf{r}.y; \mathsf{s}.x := x + 1; X(\mathsf{s},\mathsf{r})\}$$
$$C \triangleq \mathsf{p}.x := 0; X(\mathsf{p},\mathsf{q})$$

For any state Σ, we have the following execution.

$$\langle C, \Sigma, \mathscr{C} \rangle \xrightarrow{\tau@\mathsf{p}} \xrightarrow{\tau@\mathsf{p}} \xrightarrow{\tau@\mathsf{q}} \xrightarrow{\mathsf{p}.0\rightarrow\mathsf{q}} \xrightarrow{\tau@\mathsf{p}} \langle X(\mathsf{p},\mathsf{q}), \Sigma[\mathsf{p}.x \mapsto 1][\mathsf{q}.y \mapsto 0], \mathscr{C} \rangle$$

From the derivative, we can reach the configuration $\langle X(\mathsf{p},\mathsf{q}), \Sigma[\mathsf{p}.x \mapsto 2][\mathsf{q}.y \mapsto 1], \mathscr{C} \rangle$, from which we can reach the configuration $\langle X(\mathsf{p},\mathsf{q}), \Sigma[\mathsf{p}.x \mapsto 3][\mathsf{q}.y \mapsto 2], \mathscr{C} \rangle$, and so on. More in general, the configuration $\langle X(\mathsf{p},\mathsf{q}), \Sigma[\mathsf{p}.x \mapsto n + 1][\mathsf{q}.y \mapsto n], \mathscr{C} \rangle$ is a multi-step derivative of $\langle C, \Sigma, \mathscr{C} \rangle$ for any natural number n, and the lts generated by the initial configuration has an infinite number of states.

Exercise 7.2 Let C and $\mathscr{C}$ be defined as in Example 7.11, Σ be a choreographic store, and n be a natural number. Prove that the following execution holds.

$$\langle X(\mathsf{p},\mathsf{q}), \Sigma[\mathsf{p}.x \mapsto n + 1][\mathsf{q}.y \mapsto n], \mathscr{C} \rangle$$
$$\xrightarrow{\tau@\mathsf{p}} \xrightarrow{\tau@\mathsf{p}} \xrightarrow{\tau@\mathsf{q}} \xrightarrow{\mathsf{p}.n\rightarrow\mathsf{q}} \xrightarrow{\tau@\mathsf{p}} \langle X(\mathsf{p},\mathsf{q}), \Sigma[\mathsf{p}.x \mapsto n + 2][\mathsf{q}.y \mapsto n + 1], \mathscr{C} \rangle$$

Exercise 7.3 Let C and $\mathscr{C}$ be defined as in Example 7.8, and let Σ be a choreographic store. Draw the graphical representation of the lts of the configuration $\langle C, \Sigma, \mathscr{C} \rangle$.

Recall the rule candidate that we discarded in our design of transition rules:

$$\frac{X(\vec{\mathsf{q}}) = C \in \mathscr{C}}{\langle X(\vec{\mathsf{p}}); C', \Sigma, \mathscr{C} \rangle \xrightarrow{\tau@\vec{\mathsf{p}}} \langle C[\vec{\mathsf{p}}/\vec{\mathsf{q}}] \, \mathring{,} \, C', \Sigma, \mathscr{C} \rangle} \text{ UNFOLD}$$

A similar rule that reaches the same result in multiple steps can be derived, as in the following proposition.

Proposition 7.1 The following rule is derivable in the system in Figure 7.2.

$$\frac{X(\vec{\mathsf{q}}) = C \in \mathscr{C} \qquad \vec{\mathsf{p}} = \mathsf{p}_1, \ldots, \mathsf{p}_n}{\langle X(\vec{\mathsf{p}}); C', \Sigma, \mathscr{C} \rangle \xrightarrow{\tau@\mathsf{p}_1, \ldots, \tau@\mathsf{p}_n} \langle C[\vec{\mathsf{p}}/\vec{\mathsf{q}}] \, \mathring{,} \, C', \Sigma, \mathscr{C} \rangle} \text{ CALL}$$

Exercise 7.4 Prove Proposition 7.1. (Hint: use rule STEP-L from Section 2.3.5 to compose transitions obtained by rules CALL-FIRST, CALL-ENTER, and CALL-LAST.)

Example 7.12 We exemplify the interplay between procedure calls and out-of-order execution.

Consider the following procedure, where a signal (label SIG) is repeatedly propagated among three processes (p, q, and r) by following a ring architecture: from p to q, from q to r, from r to p, and again from the start.

$$Ring3(p, q, r) = p \rightarrow q[\text{SIG}]; q \rightarrow r[\text{SIG}]; r \rightarrow p[\text{SIG}]; Ring3(p, q, r) \tag{7.9}$$

Let $\mathscr{C}$ be a set consisting exactly of the procedure definition in (7.9), Σ be a choreographic store, and $C \triangleq Ring3(p_1, p_2, p_3)$ for some distinct p_1, p_2, and p_3. The configuration consisting of these three components has the following execution.

$$\langle C, \Sigma, \mathscr{C} \rangle \xrightarrow{\tau @p_1} \xrightarrow{\tau @p_2} \left\langle \begin{matrix} p_3 : Ring3(p_1, p_2, p_3).0; \\ p_1 \rightarrow p_2[\text{SIG}]; p_2 \rightarrow p_3[\text{SIG}]; p_3 \rightarrow p_1[\text{SIG}];, \Sigma, \mathscr{C} \\ Ring3(p_1, p_2, p_3) \end{matrix} \right\rangle$$

Let C' be the choreography in the aforementioned multi-step derivative (the configuration on the right-hand side). A possible transition is that p_3 enters the procedure as well, by rule CALL-LAST. However, by rule DELAY, another possibility is that p_1 communicates the signal to p_2 before that happens, as shown by the following derivation.

$$
\dfrac{
\dfrac{
\left\langle \begin{matrix} p_1 \rightarrow p_2[\text{SIG}]; \\ p_2 \rightarrow p_3[\text{SIG}]; \\ p_3 \rightarrow p_1[\text{SIG}]; \\ Ring3(p_1, p_2, p_3) \end{matrix} , \Sigma, \mathscr{C} \right\rangle \xrightarrow{p_1 \rightarrow p_2[\text{SIG}]} \left\langle \begin{matrix} p_2 \rightarrow p_3[\text{SIG}]; \\ p_3 \rightarrow p_1[\text{SIG}]; , \Sigma, \mathscr{C} \\ Ring3(p_1, p_2, p_3) \end{matrix} \right\rangle \qquad \{p_3\} \# \{p_1, p_2\}
}{
}\text{SEL}
}{
\left\langle \begin{matrix} p_3 : Ring3(p_1, p_2, p_3).0; \\ p_1 \rightarrow p_2[\text{SIG}]; \\ p_2 \rightarrow p_3[\text{SIG}]; \\ p_3 \rightarrow p_1[\text{SIG}]; \\ Ring3(p_1, p_2, p_3) \end{matrix} , \Sigma, \mathscr{C} \right\rangle \xrightarrow{p_1 \rightarrow p_2[\text{SIG}]} \left\langle \begin{matrix} p_3 : Ring3(p_1, p_2, p_3).0; \\ p_2 \rightarrow p_3[\text{SIG}]; \\ p_3 \rightarrow p_1[\text{SIG}]; \\ Ring3(p_1, p_2, p_3) \end{matrix} , \Sigma, \mathscr{C} \right\rangle
}\text{DELAY}
$$

The concluded transition is an example of how the processes that enter a procedure before others can proceed freely, provided that they do not need to interact with the processes that are still waiting to enter.

Exercise 7.5 The following are alternative formulations of the ping-pong procedure and choreography from Example 7.2.

$$\mathscr{C}_{alt} \triangleq \left\{ \begin{matrix} Ping(p, q) = p \rightarrow q[\text{SIG}]; Pong(p, q), \\ Pong(p, q) = q \rightarrow p[\text{SIG}]; Ping(p, q) \end{matrix} \right\}$$

$$C_{alt} \triangleq Ping(\text{Alice}, \text{Bob})$$

Let $\mathscr{C}$ and C be defined as in Example 7.2, and let Σ be a choreographic store. Draw the graphical representations of the labelled transition systems generated by the configurations $\langle C, \Sigma, \mathscr{C} \rangle$ and $\langle C_{alt}, \Sigma, \mathscr{C}_{alt} \rangle$. Are they isomorphic?

Remark 7.2   A transition never changes the set of procedure definitions ($\mathscr{C}$). This is different from choreographies (C) and stores (Σ), which can be updated by transitions. Indeed, in most programming systems, procedure definitions are fixed and never change during execution.

There are, however, examples of choreographic programming models where the code of procedures might change at runtime. This is useful, for example, when a system needs to adapt its code to a set of conditions that become clear only during execution. A model where the definitions of choreographies can evolve dynamically was presented by Dalla Preda et al. [2017].

Exercise 7.6   Prove the equivalent of Proposition 2.5 for Recursive Choreographies. That is, show that for any natural number $n > 0$, the rule

$$\frac{\langle C, \Sigma, \mathscr{C} \rangle \xrightarrow{\mu} \langle C', \Sigma', \mathscr{C} \rangle \quad (\mathrm{pn}(I_1) \cup \cdots \cup \mathrm{pn}(I_n)) \# \mathrm{pn}(\mu)}{\langle I_1; \cdots I_n; C, \Sigma, \mathscr{C} \rangle \xrightarrow{\mu} \langle I_1; \cdots I_n; C', \Sigma', \mathscr{C} \rangle} \text{ DELAY-}n$$

is derivable.

Exercise 7.7   Prove that the following rule is derivable.

$$\frac{\langle C, \Sigma, \mathscr{C} \rangle \xrightarrow{\vec{\mu}} \langle C', \Sigma', \mathscr{C} \rangle \quad \mathrm{pn}(I) \# \mathrm{pn}(\vec{\mu})}{\langle I; C, \Sigma, \mathscr{C} \rangle \xrightarrow{\vec{\mu}} \langle I; C', \Sigma', \mathscr{C} \rangle} \text{ DELAY-MULTI}$$

7.2   Processes

To model implementations of recursive choreographies, we extend our process language with procedures as well. The resulting process language is called Recursive Processes and denoted **RecursiveProc**.

7.2.1   Syntax

The syntax of Recursive Processes is given in Figure 7.3. The new additions, underlined, recall those made to obtain Recursive Choreographies. Specifically, processes can now invoke procedures with the instruction $X(\vec{p})$, read 'run procedure X with the arguments $\vec{p}$'. Procedures are defined in sets of procedure definitions, ranged over by $\mathscr{P}$, which consist of equations of the form $X(\vec{p}) = P$, read 'procedure X has parameters $\vec{p}$ and body P'.

$$\mathscr{P} ::= \{X_i(\vec{p_i}) = P_i\}_{i \in I}$$

$$P, Q, R ::= I; P \mid \mathbf{0}$$

$$I ::= \mathsf{p}!e \mid \mathsf{p}?x \mid \mathsf{p} \oplus \mathsf{L} \mid \mathsf{p} \,\&\, \{\mathsf{L}_i : P_i\}_{i \in I} \mid x := e \mid \text{if } e \text{ then } P \text{ else } Q \mid X(\vec{\mathsf{p}})$$

$$e ::= v \mid x \mid f(\vec{e})$$

Figure 7.3 Recursive Processes, syntax.

Example 7.13   Consider again a set $\mathscr{C}$ that consists of the ping-pong procedure definition in Example 7.2 and a choreography C that invokes the procedure:

$$\mathscr{C} \triangleq \{PP(\mathsf{p}, \mathsf{q}) = \mathsf{p} \to \mathsf{q}[\text{SIG}]; PP(\mathsf{q}, \mathsf{p})\}$$

$$C \triangleq PP(\mathsf{Alice}, \mathsf{Bob}).$$

To implement the choreography C in the context of $\mathscr{C}$ in the language of Recursive Processes, we construct a network consisting of two processes – Alice and Bob. In the choreography, Alice and Bob enter the choreographic procedure PP, which defines a choreography for its two parameters p and q. What Alice and Bob should do in the procedure is determined by the order in which they are passed as arguments: Alice is passed as the first argument, so its behaviour will be that of process p in the body of the procedure; Bob is passed as the second argument, so its behaviour will be that of process q in the procedure. This means that, at the level of the process language, we should have two procedures: one that implements the behaviour of the first parameter in PP, and one that implements the behaviour of the second parameter in PP. We call these two procedures PP_1 and PP_2, respectively, using the subscript notation to remind ourselves that they stand for 'PP from the point of view of the first parameter' and 'PP from the point of view of the second parameter'. We obtain the following set of procedure definitions and network.

$$\mathscr{P} \triangleq \begin{cases} PP_1(\mathsf{q}) = \mathsf{q} \oplus \text{SIG}; PP_2(\mathsf{q}), \\ PP_2(\mathsf{p}) = \mathsf{p} \,\&\, \{\text{SIG} : PP_1(\mathsf{p})\} \end{cases}$$

$$N \triangleq \mathsf{Alice}[PP_1(\mathsf{Bob})] \mid \mathsf{Bob}[PP_2(\mathsf{Alice})].$$

In the network N, Alice invokes procedure PP_1 passing Bob as argument, and Bob invokes procedure PP_2 passing Alice as argument. Therefore, Alice will send the selection of label SIG to Bob since the parameter q is replaced by the argument Bob. Symmetrically, Bob offers the choice of label SIG to Alice since the parameter p is replaced by the argument Alice.

After the first interaction, Alice will proceed by invoking procedure PP_2, and conversely Bob will invoke PP_1: this reflects the swapping of roles between the two processes performed in the choreography, where the processes in procedure PP alternate each other as the sender and receiver of the signal. We will check this formally after presenting the semantics of Recursive Processes, in the next subsection.

7.2.2 Semantics

Name Substitution

As for Recursive Choreographies, we define a notion of name substitution for Recursive Processes. We write $P[r/s]$ for the process obtained by substituting every occurrence of s with r, read 'P where r replaces s'. This notation is extended to multiple processes: $P[\vec{r}/\vec{s}]$ denotes the substitution of each name in $\vec{s}$ with the respective name in $\vec{r}$ ($\vec{r}$ and $\vec{s}$ must have the same length). Name substitution in this context is defined by the following equations. The equations cover the same development of name substitution explained for Recursive Choreographies, but adapted to the syntax of Recursive Processes.

$$p[r/s] \triangleq \begin{cases} r & \text{if } p = s \\ p & \text{otherwise} \end{cases}$$

$$(p_1, \ldots, p_n)[r/s] \triangleq p_1[r/s], \ldots, p_n[r/s]$$

$$0[r/s] \triangleq 0$$

$$(I; P)[r/s] \triangleq (I[r/s]); (P[r/s])$$

$$(p!e)[r/s] \triangleq (p[r/s])!e$$

$$(p?x)[r/s] \triangleq (p[r/s])?x$$

$$(x := e)[r/s] \triangleq x := e$$

$$(\text{if } e \text{ then } P \text{ else } Q) \triangleq \text{if } e \text{ then}(P[r/s]) \text{ else}(Q[r/s])$$

$$(X(\vec{p})) \triangleq X(\vec{p}[r/s])$$

$$P[r_1, \ldots, r_n/s_1, \ldots, s_n] \triangleq P[r_1/s_1] \cdots [r_n/s_n]$$

Example 7.14 Let P_1 and P_2 be the bodies of the procedures PP_1 and PP_2 from Example 7.13, respectively:

$$P_1 \triangleq q \oplus \text{SIG}; PP_2(q)$$
$$P_2 \triangleq p \& \{\text{SIG} : PP_1(p)\}.$$

Then, the following equations indicate the code that the processes Alice and Bob are going to run with their respective procedure invocations in the same example:

$$P_1[\text{Bob}/q] = \text{Bob} \oplus \text{SIG}; PP_2(\text{Bob})$$
$$P_2[\text{Alice}/p] = \text{Alice} \& \{\text{SIG} : PP_1(\text{Alice})\}.$$

Transitions

Configurations in Recursive Processes have the form $\langle N, \Sigma, \mathscr{P} \rangle$, extending those of Selective Processes to sets of procedure definitions. The inference rules for transitions are displayed in Figure 7.4. Compared to Selective Processes, the only new rule is rule CALL (underlined), which deals with procedure invocations. All other rules have been adapted to the new form of configurations, in order to take sets of procedure definitions into account. The adaptation is simple

$$\frac{\Sigma(\mathsf{p}) \vdash e \downarrow v}{\langle \mathsf{p}[x := e; P], \Sigma, \mathscr{P} \rangle \xrightarrow{\tau @ \mathsf{p}} \langle \mathsf{p}[P], \Sigma[\mathsf{p}.x \mapsto v], \mathscr{P} \rangle} \text{ LOCAL}$$

$$\frac{\Sigma(\mathsf{p}) \vdash e \downarrow v}{\langle \mathsf{p}[\mathsf{q}!e; P] \mid \mathsf{q}[\mathsf{p}?x; Q], \Sigma, \mathscr{P} \rangle \xrightarrow{\mathsf{p}.v \to \mathsf{q}} \langle \mathsf{p}[P] \mid \mathsf{q}[Q], \Sigma[\mathsf{q}.x \mapsto v], \mathscr{P} \rangle} \text{ COM}$$

$$\frac{j \in I}{\langle \mathsf{p}[\mathsf{q} \oplus \mathsf{L}_j; P] \mid \mathsf{q}[\mathsf{p} \, \& \, \{\mathsf{L}_i : P_i\}_{i \in I}; Q], \Sigma, \mathscr{P} \rangle \xrightarrow{\mathsf{p} \to \mathsf{q}[\mathsf{L}_j]} \langle \mathsf{p}[P] \mid \mathsf{q}[P_j \, \mathring{,} \, Q], \Sigma, \mathscr{P} \rangle} \text{ SEL}$$

$$\frac{\Sigma(\mathsf{p}) \vdash e \downarrow \textit{true}}{\langle \mathsf{p}[\text{if } e \text{ then } P_1 \text{ else } P_2; Q], \Sigma, \mathscr{P} \rangle \xrightarrow{\tau @ \mathsf{p}} \langle \mathsf{p}[P_1 \, \mathring{,} \, Q], \Sigma, \mathscr{P} \rangle} \text{ COND-THEN}$$

$$\frac{\Sigma(\mathsf{p}) \vdash e \downarrow v \quad v \neq \textit{true}}{\langle \mathsf{p}[\text{if } e \text{ then } P_1 \text{ else } P_2; Q], \Sigma, \mathscr{P} \rangle \xrightarrow{\tau @ \mathsf{p}} \langle \mathsf{p}[P_2 \, \mathring{,} \, Q], \Sigma, \mathscr{P} \rangle} \text{ COND-ELSE}$$

$$\frac{X(\vec{r}) = Q \in \mathscr{P}}{\langle \mathsf{p}[X(\vec{q}); P], \Sigma, \mathscr{P} \rangle \xrightarrow{\tau @ \mathsf{p}} \langle \mathsf{p}[Q[\vec{q}/\vec{r}] \, \mathring{,} \, P], \Sigma, \mathscr{P} \rangle} \text{ CALL} \qquad \frac{\langle N, \Sigma, \mathscr{P} \rangle \xrightarrow{\mu} \langle N', \Sigma', \mathscr{P} \rangle}{\langle N \mid M, \Sigma, \mathscr{P} \rangle \xrightarrow{\mu} \langle N' \mid M, \Sigma', \mathscr{P} \rangle} \text{ PAR}$$

Figure 7.4 Recursive Processes, semantics.

because procedure definitions are immaterial to these rules: the transitions in the conclusions of these rules apply to any $\mathscr{P}$, which is left unchanged in the derivative.

The new rule, CALL, is the only one that requires something of the set of procedure definitions in a configuration. Namely, in the premise of the rule, we require that procedure X has parameters $\vec{r}$ and body Q in the set of procedure definitions $\mathscr{P}$. Then, in the conclusion, an invocation of X with arguments $\vec{q}$ is replaced by the body Q in a transition with label $\tau @\mathsf{p}$ (denoting an internal action). In the body Q in the derivative, the parameters $\vec{r}$ are replaced by the arguments $\vec{q}$.

Compared to Recursive Choreographies, the treatment of procedure calls is simpler because every procedure call is local to one process (the caller).

Example 7.15 Let Σ be a choreographic store. Further, let $\mathscr{P}$ and N be as in Example 7.13:

$$\mathscr{P} \triangleq \begin{cases} PP_1(\mathsf{q}) = \mathsf{q} \oplus \text{SIG}; PP_2(\mathsf{q}), \\ PP_2(\mathsf{p}) = \mathsf{p} \, \& \, \{\text{SIG} : PP_1(\mathsf{p})\} \end{cases}$$

$$N \triangleq \text{Alice}[PP_1(\text{Bob})] \mid \text{Bob}[PP_2(\text{Alice})].$$

By rules PAR and CALL, we have the following execution.

$$\langle N, \Sigma, \mathscr{P} \rangle \xrightarrow{\tau @ \text{Alice}} \langle \text{Alice}[\text{Bob} \oplus \text{SIG}; PP_2(\text{Bob})] \mid \text{Bob}[PP_2(\text{Alice})], \Sigma, \mathscr{P} \rangle$$

$$\xrightarrow{\tau @ \text{Bob}} \langle \text{Alice}[\text{Bob} \oplus \text{SIG}; PP_2(\text{Bob})] \mid \text{Bob}[\text{Alice} \, \& \, \{\text{SIG} : PP_1(\text{Alice})\}], \Sigma, \mathscr{P} \rangle$$

Observe that Alice and Bob are independent in entering their procedures: Bob could perform the first transition, as in the following execution.

$$\langle N, \Sigma, \mathscr{P} \rangle \xrightarrow{\ \tau\,@\text{Bob}\ } \langle \text{Alice}[PP_1(\text{Bob})] \mid \text{Bob}[\text{Alice} \,\&\, \{\text{SIG} : PP_1(\text{Alice})\}], \Sigma, \mathscr{P} \rangle$$

$$\xrightarrow{\ \tau\,@\text{Alice}\ } \langle \text{Alice}[\text{Bob} \oplus \text{SIG}; PP_2(\text{Bob})] \mid \text{Bob}[\text{Alice} \,\&\, \{\text{SIG} : PP_1(\text{Alice})\}], \Sigma, \mathscr{P} \rangle$$

Example 7.16 Recall from Example 7.1 the choreography and procedure where Alice repeatedly communicates a signal to Bob, given next.

$$\mathscr{C} \triangleq \{Ping(\mathsf{p}, \mathsf{q}) = \mathsf{p} \to \mathsf{q}[\text{SIG}]; Ping(\mathsf{p}, \mathsf{q})\}$$
$$C \triangleq Ping(\text{Alice}, \text{Bob})$$

We can implement this choreography in Recursive Processes with the following procedures and network.

$$\mathscr{P} \triangleq \begin{cases} Ping_1(\mathsf{q}) = \mathsf{q} \oplus \text{SIG}; Ping_1(\mathsf{q}), \\ Ping_2(\mathsf{p}) = \mathsf{p} \,\&\, \{\text{SIG} : Ping_2(\mathsf{p})\} \end{cases}$$
$$N \triangleq \text{Alice}[Ping_1(\text{Bob})] \mid \text{Bob}[Ping_2(\text{Alice})]$$

Exercise 7.8 Let N and $\mathscr{P}$ be as in Example 7.16. Draw the graphical representation of the lts generated by the configuration $\langle N, \Sigma, \mathscr{P} \rangle$, where Σ is a choreographic store (its concrete definition is immaterial for this exercise). (Hint: the graph should be isomorphic to the graphical representation of the configuration $\langle C, \Sigma, \mathscr{C} \rangle$, which was shown in Example 7.9.)

The semantics of Recursive Processes supports a reformulation of Proposition 3.7 (from Simple Processes), which is going to be useful in proofs later.

Proposition 7.3 For all $\langle N, \Sigma, \mathscr{P} \rangle$, μ, and $\langle N', \Sigma', \mathscr{P} \rangle$, if $\langle N, \Sigma, \mathscr{P} \rangle \xrightarrow{\mu} \langle N', \Sigma', \mathscr{P} \rangle$ and $\mathsf{r} \notin$ pn(μ), then $N(\mathsf{r}) = N'(\mathsf{r})$.

Exercise 7.9 Prove Proposition 7.3.

7.3 Endpoint Projection

To design an EPP for Recursive Choreographies, we need to:

- Establish a translation from sets of procedure definitions in Recursive Choreographies to sets of procedure definitions in Recursive Processes.
- Expand process projection to project the new terms for procedure invocations.

The key principle for translating sets of procedure definitions has already been illustrated in Example 7.13. In that example, we had to implement a choreographic procedure (*PP*) that involves two processes (abstracted by the parameters p and q), so we wrote two procedures in Recursive Processes: one that implements the behaviour of the first process, and the other that implements the behaviour of the second process. In general, given a choreographic procedure with n process parameters, we have to generate n procedures, each one defining the behaviour of one of the processes. We write $[\![\mathscr{C}]\!]$ for the EPP of $\mathscr{C}$, overloading the meaning of $[\![\,]\!]$.

Definition 7.4   The EPP of a set of choreographic procedure definitions $\mathscr{C}$, written $[\![\mathscr{C}]\!]$, is the set of process procedure definitions defined by the following equation.

$$[\![\mathscr{C}]\!] \triangleq \left\{ X_i(\vec{\mathsf{p}} \setminus \mathsf{p}_i) = [\![C]\!]_{\mathsf{p}_i} \;\middle|\; \begin{array}{l} X(\vec{\mathsf{p}}) = C \in \mathscr{C} \text{ and} \\ \vec{\mathsf{p}} = \mathsf{p}_1, \ldots, \mathsf{p}_n \text{ and } 1 \leq i \leq n \end{array} \right\}$$

The process projection $[\![C]\!]_{\mathsf{p}}$ is fully defined in Definition 7.5.

Definition 7.4 is given in set-builder notation. It states that the EPP of a set of choreographic procedure definitions $\mathscr{C}$ is the set of procedure definitions $\mathscr{P}$ that respects the following conditions.

- For each procedure definition $X(\vec{\mathsf{p}}) = C \in \mathscr{C}$ and process p_i in $\vec{\mathsf{p}}$, there is a procedure X_i defined in $\mathscr{P}$ such that:

  - The parameter list of X_i is the list obtained by removing p_i from $\vec{\mathsf{p}}$.

  - The body of X_i is the projection of C on p_i.

- $\mathscr{P}$ contains no other procedures.

Observe that since process projection is a partial function, the EPP of a set of procedure definitions can be undefined. In the remainder, we say that a set of procedure definitions $\mathscr{C}$ is *projectable* if $[\![\mathscr{C}]\!]$ is defined.

Next, we extend the definition of process projection from Selective Choreographies to include cases for the new terms that regard procedure invocations: $X(\vec{\mathsf{p}})$ and $\vec{\mathsf{q}}: X(\vec{\mathsf{p}}).C$. Process projection for Recursive Choreographies is defined by Equations (7.10) to (7.16), the new ones being Equations (7.14) and (7.15).

In (7.14), the projection of a procedure invocation $X(\vec{\mathsf{p}})$ on a process r depends on whether r is one of the arguments of the call. If it is (first case), then r appears in position i in $\vec{\mathsf{p}}$, for some i such that $1 \leq i \leq n$ and n such that $\vec{\mathsf{p}} = \mathsf{p}_1, \ldots, \mathsf{p}_n$; thus, we project the procedure call to an invocation of procedure X_i ('X from the point of view of the i-th argument'), followed by the projection of the continuation C. Notice that r itself is removed from the list of arguments in the result: since processes do not self-communicate, passing r as an argument in its procedure invocation would be useless. If r is not one of the arguments (second case), then we just return the projection of the continuation C.

Process projection for Recursive Choreographies

$$[\![p.e \to q.x; C]\!]_r \triangleq \begin{cases} q!e; [\![C]\!]_r & \text{if } r = p \\ p?x; [\![C]\!]_r & \text{if } r = q \\ [\![C]\!]_r & \text{otherwise} \end{cases} \tag{7.10}$$

$$[\![p \to q[L]; C]\!]_r \triangleq \begin{cases} q \oplus L; [\![C]\!]_r & \text{if } r = p \\ p \ \& \ \{L: [\![C]\!]_r\}; 0 & \text{if } r = q \\ [\![C]\!]_r & \text{otherwise} \end{cases} \tag{7.11}$$

$$[\![p.x := e; C]\!]_r \triangleq \begin{cases} x := e; [\![C]\!]_r & \text{if } r = p \\ [\![C]\!]_r & \text{otherwise} \end{cases} \tag{7.12}$$

$$[\![\text{if } p.e \text{ then } C_1 \text{ else } C_2; C]\!]_r \triangleq \begin{cases} (\text{if } e \text{ then} [\![C_1]\!]_r \text{ else} [\![C_2]\!]_r); [\![C]\!]_r & \text{if } r = p \\ ([\![C_1]\!]_r \sqcup [\![C_2]\!]_r) \, \text{\scriptsize\textbf{9}} \, [\![C]\!]_r & \text{otherwise} \end{cases} \tag{7.13}$$

$$[\![X(\vec{p}); C]\!]_r \triangleq \begin{cases} X_i(\vec{p} \setminus r); [\![C]\!]_r & \text{if } r = p_i \text{ for } \vec{p} = p_1, \dots, p_n \\ & \text{and } 1 \leq i \leq n \\ [\![C]\!]_r & \text{otherwise} \end{cases} \tag{7.14}$$

$$[\![\vec{q}: X(\vec{p}).C'; C]\!]_r \triangleq \begin{cases} X_i(\vec{p} \setminus r); [\![C']\!]_r & \text{if } r \in \vec{q} \text{ and } r = p_i \text{ for } \\ & \qquad \vec{p} = p_1, \dots, p_n \text{ and } \\ & \qquad \quad 1 \leq i \leq n \\ [\![C]\!]_r & \text{otherwise} \end{cases} \tag{7.15}$$

$$[\![0]\!]_r \triangleq 0 \tag{7.16}$$

Equation (7.15) handles the projection of any runtime term for a procedure invocation, of the form $\vec{q}: X(\vec{p}).C'; C$, on any process r. The result depends on whether r is one of the processes that have yet to enter procedure X, checked by the condition $r \in \vec{q}$. If so (first case), we return an invocation of procedure X_i, followed by the projection of C'. The reason for using the projection of C' as continuation for r is that this process has not entered X yet, and therefore its code should not include the unfolding of the body of X inside of C (yet). Process r is removed from the arguments, as in the case of procedure calls. If r is not one of the processes that have yet to enter X (second case), then we return the projection of the continuation C since the runtime term does not concern r at all.

Definition 7.5 (Process Projection for Recursive Choreographies)   Let C be a choreography in the language of Recursive Choreographies and p a process name. The projection of C on p, written $[\![C]\!]_p$, is defined by Equations (7.10) to (7.16).

The definition of EPP for Recursive Choreographies retains the same structure as for the previous languages, but uses the updated definition of process projection. We state it again for later reference in proofs about Recursive Choreographies.

Definition 7.6 (EPP for Recursive Choreographies)   The endpoint projection (EPP) of a choreography C, written $[\![C]\!]$, is the network such that, for any process name p,

$$[\![C]\!](\mathsf{p}) \triangleq [\![C]\!]_\mathsf{p}.$$

Example 7.17   Recall the set of procedures and choreography for a simple ping-pong scenario, $\mathscr{C}$ and C, from Example 7.2:

$$\mathscr{C} \triangleq \{PP(\mathsf{p},\mathsf{q}) = \mathsf{p} \to \mathsf{q}[\mathrm{SIG}]; PP(\mathsf{q},\mathsf{p})\}$$

$$C \triangleq PP(\mathsf{Alice},\mathsf{Bob}).$$

The EPP of $\mathscr{C}$ is the set of procedure definitions $\mathscr{P}$ given in Example 7.13. We use round parentheses to clarify which list of processes a removal operation applies to, for example, $(\mathsf{p},\mathsf{q}) \setminus \mathsf{q}$ reads 'the list obtained by removing q from p, q'.

$$[\![\mathscr{C}]\!] = \begin{cases} PP_1((\mathsf{p},\mathsf{q}) \setminus \mathsf{p}) = [\![\mathsf{p} \to \mathsf{q}[\mathrm{SIG}]; PP(\mathsf{q},\mathsf{p})]\!]_\mathsf{p}, \\ PP_2((\mathsf{p},\mathsf{q}) \setminus \mathsf{q}) = [\![\mathsf{p} \to \mathsf{q}[\mathrm{SIG}]; PP(\mathsf{q},\mathsf{p})]\!]_\mathsf{q} \end{cases}$$

$$= \begin{cases} PP_1(\mathsf{q}) = [\![\mathsf{p} \to \mathsf{q}[\mathrm{SIG}]; PP(\mathsf{q},\mathsf{p})]\!]_\mathsf{p}, \\ PP_2(\mathsf{p}) = [\![\mathsf{p} \to \mathsf{q}[\mathrm{SIG}]; PP(\mathsf{q},\mathsf{p})]\!]_\mathsf{q} \end{cases}$$

$$= \begin{cases} PP_1(\mathsf{q}) = \mathsf{q} \oplus \mathrm{SIG}; [\![PP(\mathsf{q},\mathsf{p})]\!]_\mathsf{p}, \\ PP_2(\mathsf{p}) = \mathsf{p} \,\&\, \{\mathrm{SIG} : [\![PP(\mathsf{q},\mathsf{p})]\!]_\mathsf{q}\} \end{cases}$$

$$= \begin{cases} PP_1(\mathsf{q}) = \mathsf{q} \oplus \mathrm{SIG}; PP_2(\mathsf{q}), \\ PP_2(\mathsf{p}) = \mathsf{p} \,\&\, \{\mathrm{SIG} : PP_1(\mathsf{p})\} \end{cases}$$

Likewise, the EPP of C is the network N given in Example 7.13.

$$[\![C]\!] = \mathsf{Alice}[[\![PP(\mathsf{Alice},\mathsf{Bob})]\!]_\mathsf{Alice}] \mid \mathsf{Bob}[[\![PP(\mathsf{Alice},\mathsf{Bob})]\!]_\mathsf{Bob}]$$

$$= \mathsf{Alice}[PP_1((\mathsf{Alice},\mathsf{Bob}) \setminus \mathsf{Alice})] \mid \mathsf{Bob}[PP_2((\mathsf{Alice},\mathsf{Bob}) \setminus \mathsf{Bob})]$$

$$= \mathsf{Alice}[PP_1(\mathsf{Bob})] \mid \mathsf{Bob}[PP_2(\mathsf{Alice})]$$

Exercise 7.10   Let C be the body of the authentication procedure $Auth$ from Example 7.4, and let $\mathscr{C} \triangleq \{Auth(\mathsf{c},\mathsf{s},\mathsf{cas}) = C\}$. The EPP of $\mathscr{C}$ is defined as:

$$[\![\mathscr{C}]\!] = \begin{cases} Auth_1(\mathsf{s},\mathsf{cas}) = [\![C]\!]_\mathsf{c}, \\ Auth_2(\mathsf{c},\mathsf{cas}) = [\![C]\!]_\mathsf{s}, \\ Auth_3(\mathsf{c},\mathsf{s}) = [\![C]\!]_\mathsf{cas} \end{cases}.$$

Finish writing the EPP of $\mathscr{C}$, by unfolding $[\![C]\!]_\mathsf{c}$, $[\![C]\!]_\mathsf{s}$, and $[\![C]\!]_\mathsf{cas}$.

Exercise 7.11   Write the EPP of the set consisting of the procedure definition in Eq. (7.2).

Exercise 7.12 Let $\mathscr{C}$ and C be defined as in Example 7.12:

$$\mathscr{C} \triangleq \{Ring3(\mathsf{p,q,r}) = \mathsf{p} \to \mathsf{q}[\text{SIG}]; \mathsf{q} \to \mathsf{r}[\text{SIG}]; \mathsf{q} \to \mathsf{r}[\text{SIG}]; Ring3(\mathsf{p,q,r})\}$$
$$C \triangleq Ring3(\mathsf{p_1,p_2,p_3}).$$

Write the EPP of $\mathscr{C}$ and the EPP of C.

Exercise 7.13 Consider again the formulations of the ping-pong scenario from Example 7.2 and Exercise 7.5, respectively given by $\mathscr{C}$ and C for the former and $\mathscr{C}_{alt}$ and C_{alt} for the latter.

$$\mathscr{C} \triangleq \{PP(\mathsf{p,q}) = \mathsf{p} \to \mathsf{q}[\text{SIG}]; PP(\mathsf{q,p})\}$$
$$C \triangleq PP(\text{Alice, Bob})$$
$$\mathscr{C}_{alt} \triangleq \begin{cases} Ping(\mathsf{p,q}) = \mathsf{p} \to \mathsf{q}[\text{SIG}]; Pong(\mathsf{p,q}), \\ Pong(\mathsf{p,q}) = \mathsf{q} \to \mathsf{p}[\text{SIG}]; Ping(\mathsf{p,q}) \end{cases}$$
$$C_{alt} \triangleq Ping(\text{Alice, Bob})$$

1.. Write the EPPs of $\mathscr{C}$, C, $\mathscr{C}_{alt}$, and C_{alt}.
2.. Let Σ be a choreographic store (its definition is irrelevant for this exercise). Draw the graphical representations of the labelled transition systems generated by the configurations $\langle [\![C]\!], \Sigma, [\![\mathscr{C}]\!]\rangle$ and $\langle [\![C_{alt}]\!], \Sigma, [\![\mathscr{C}_{alt}]\!]\rangle$. Are they isomorphic? Do they differ from the graphs drawn in Exercise 7.5?

8 Properties of Choreographies and Endpoint Projection

In the previous chapters of this part of the book, we have augmented our framework with several features (like conditionals and procedures). In this chapter, we investigate some of their interesting properties. Our study will build up to proving the correctness of EPP for the language that includes all of these features: Recursive Choreographies.

In particular, compared to the study of EPP for Simple Choreographies in Chapter 4, we have to deal with two important issues:

1. EPP is substantially more sophisticated. In particular, reasoning about the semantics of choreographies and their projections now requires paying attention to how terms are manipulated by the merging operator $\sqcup$ (in process projection) and the sequential composition operator $\mathbin{\mathring{,}}$ (in process projection and the semantics of choreographies and processes). We shall see that these operators respect useful laws that we can avail to reason about the interaction between them and with process projection.

2. The notion of well-formedness for Recursive Choreographies has been introduced only informally in Chapter 7. Well-formedness is important for proving that EPP is correct, so we shall define it formally by means of an inference system in order to be precise.

8.1 Basic Properties of Process Projection

Process projection is in harmony with the syntactic presence of process names in choreographies.

First, we observe that whether the projection of a choreography C on a process p is $\mathbf{0}$ is characterised by the absence of p in C.

Proposition 8.1 $[\![C]\!]_{\mathsf{p}} = \mathbf{0}$ if and only if $\mathsf{p} \notin \mathrm{pn}(C)$.

For any p, either $\mathsf{p} \in \mathrm{pn}(C)$ or $\mathsf{p} \notin \mathrm{pn}(C)$. Hence, Proposition 8.1 implies that $[\![C]\!]_{\mathsf{p}} \neq \mathbf{0}$ if and only if $\mathsf{p} \in \mathrm{pn}(C)$.

Another basic harmony property between process projection and presence of process names is that projection skips instructions that do not involve a process.

Proposition 8.2 If $\mathsf{p} \notin \mathrm{pn}(I)$, then $[\![I; C]\!]_{\mathsf{p}} = [\![C]\!]_{\mathsf{p}}$.

Exercise 8.1 Prove Proposition 8.2.

8.2   Properties of Merging and Sequential Composition

The merging operator ($\sqcup$) and the sequential composition operator ($\mathbin{\raise.1ex\hbox{$\scriptscriptstyle\circ$}}\kern-.15em_{\scriptscriptstyle 9}$) satisfy algebraic properties that are essential for reasoning about endpoint projection. Sometimes these properties are about the interplay between these two operators, so we study them together in this section.

8.2.1   Fundamental Properties of Merging

When we merge two processes P and Q, we obtain a 'bigger' process in terms of branchings: $P \sqcup Q$ behaves like P and Q with the exception of when branchings are offered to other processes, which now can access the combination of all the branches offered by P and Q. This intuition on how we can compare processes suggests a connection between merging and order theory.

Formally, borrowing terminology for lattices, $\sqcup$ behaves as a *join operator*. The reader interested in learning more about lattice theory can consult Davey and Priestley [2002], but this is not necessary to proceed: we are going to state explicitly all relevant properties as we go forward.

The language of Recursive Processes and the merging operator respect algebraic laws for a partial semilattice.[1] That is, the laws stated in the following proposition hold.

Proposition 8.3   The set **RecursiveProc** equipped with merging, (**RecursiveProc**, $\sqcup$), forms a *partial semilattice*. That is, it respects the following laws.

Idempotency   For all P, $P \sqcup P = P$.
Commutativity   For all P and Q, $P \sqcup Q = Q \sqcup P$.
Associativity   For all P, Q, and R, $P \sqcup (Q \sqcup R) = (P \sqcup Q) \sqcup R$.

Exercise 8.2 (!)   Prove Proposition 8.3.

Another fundamental property of merging is that it always mimics the structure of its arguments. For example, if $P \sqcup Q = \mathbf{0}$, then it is easy to see from the definition of merging that both P and Q are necessarily $\mathbf{0}$. This observation holds in general for all process constructs: if the result of merging two processes starts by sending a message, then so do the merged processes, and so forth. This means that looking at the structure of the result of merging reveals the structures of the processes that have been merged as well.

8.2.2   Ordering Processes by Branchings

The observation that $\sqcup$ is a join operator allows us to tap into a cornerstone result of lattice theory: there exists an ordering of processes based on $\sqcup$. Specifically, we shall write $P \sqsupseteq Q$ when P has at least as many branches in branchings as Q.

Definition 8.4   Relation $\sqsupseteq$ on processes is the binary relation such that, for all processes P and Q, $P \sqsupseteq Q$ if and only if $P \sqcup Q = P$.

---

[1]   We call this semilattice 'partial' because merging is not defined for all pairs of processes (merging is a partial operator).

It is well known that this way of defining a relation ($\sqsupseteq$) based on a join operator ($\sqcup$) guarantees that the relation is a partial order [Davey and Priestley 2002]. That is, it respects the properties stated in the following proposition.

Proposition 8.5 Relation $\sqsupseteq$ on processes is a *partial order*. That is, it has the following properties.

Reflexivity For all P, $P \sqsupseteq P$.
Antisymmetry For all P and Q, if $P \sqsupseteq Q$ and $Q \sqsupseteq P$, then $P = Q$.
Transitivity For all P, Q, and R, if $P \sqsupseteq Q$ and $Q \sqsupseteq R$, then $P \sqsupseteq R$.

We call $\sqsupseteq$ the *branching order*, because it compares processes based on their branching terms. The reader unfamiliar with lattice theory is invited to prove that Proposition 8.5 holds, as proposed in the following exercise.

Exercise 8.3 (!, $\hookrightarrow$) Prove Proposition 8.5.

The join of two processes is their least upper bound according to $\sqsupseteq$.

Lemma 8.6 For all P, Q, and R:

- $P \sqcup Q \sqsupseteq P$ and $P \sqcup Q \sqsupseteq Q$.
- If $P \sqsupseteq Q$ and $P \sqsupseteq R$, then $P \sqsupseteq Q \sqcup R$.

Exercise 8.4 ($\hookrightarrow$) Prove Lemma 8.6.

The branching order is preserved by adding instructions to processes.

Lemma 8.7 For all P, Q, and I, $P \sqsupseteq Q$ implies $I; P \sqsupseteq I; Q$.

Proof By definition of $\sqsupseteq$, we need to prove that

$$I; P \sqcup I; Q = I; P.$$

By definition and idempotency of $\sqcup$, $I; P \sqcup I; Q = I;(P \sqcup Q)$. Since $P \sqcup Q = P$ by hypothesis, we obtain the thesis. $\square$

Similarly, if the process projections of two choreographies are related by $\sqsupseteq$, then this relation is preserved under additional choreographic instructions.

Lemma 8.8 For all C, C', r, and I, if $[\![C]\!]_r \sqsupseteq [\![C']\!]_r$, then $[\![I; C]\!]_r \sqsupseteq [\![I; C']\!]_r$.

Proof We proceed by cases on I.

Case 1 $I = \mathsf{p}.x := e$ for some p, x, and e. If $\mathsf{r} = \mathsf{p}$, then the thesis follows by definition of projection and Lemma 8.7. Otherwise, if $\mathsf{r} \neq \mathsf{p}$, then by definition of projection we have that $[\![I;C]\!]_\mathsf{r} = [\![C]\!]_\mathsf{r}$ and $[\![I;C']\!]_\mathsf{r} = [\![C']\!]_\mathsf{r}$. The thesis follows from the hypothesis $[\![C]\!]_\mathsf{r} \sqsupseteq [\![C']\!]_\mathsf{r}$.

Case 2 $I = \mathsf{p}.e \to \mathsf{q}.x$ or $I = \mathsf{p} \to \mathsf{q}[\mathsf{L}]$, for some p, e, q, x, and L. The reasoning for this case is similar to that for the previous one, where the possibilities to distinguish are $\mathsf{r} = \mathsf{p}$, $\mathsf{r} = \mathsf{q}$, and $\mathsf{r} \notin \{\mathsf{p}, \mathsf{q}\}$.

Case 3 $I = \mathsf{if}\, \mathsf{p}.e \,\mathsf{then}\, C_1 \,\mathsf{else}\, C_2$ for some p, e, C_1, and C_2. If $\mathsf{r} = \mathsf{p}$, then the thesis follows by definition of projection and Lemma 8.7. If $\mathsf{r} \neq \mathsf{p}$, then

$$[\![I;C]\!]_\mathsf{r} = ([\![C_1]\!]_\mathsf{r} \sqcup [\![C_2]\!]_\mathsf{r}) \,\fatsemi\, [\![C]\!]_\mathsf{r}$$
$$[\![I;C']\!]_\mathsf{r} = ([\![C_1]\!]_\mathsf{r} \sqcup [\![C_2]\!]_\mathsf{r}) \,\fatsemi\, [\![C']\!]_\mathsf{r}.$$

The thesis follows by Lemma 8.15.   □

We overload the notation $\sqsupseteq$ to denote a similar relation on networks. Namely, we write $N \sqsupseteq M$ when all processes in N have at least as many branches in branching terms as in M.

Definition 8.9 Relation $\sqsupseteq$ on networks is the binary relation such that, for all networks N and M, $N \sqsupseteq M$ if and only if $N(\mathsf{p}) \sqsupseteq M(\mathsf{p})$ for all p.

Since $\sqsupseteq$ on networks applies $\sqsupseteq$ on processes pointwise, it inherits the laws of the latter from Proposition 8.5.

Proposition 8.10 Relation $\sqsupseteq$ on networks is a partial order. That is, it has the following properties.

Reflexivity For all N, $N \sqsupseteq N$.

Antisymmetry For all N and M, if $N \sqsupseteq M$ and $M \sqsupseteq N$, then $N = M$.

Transitivity For all N_1, N_2, and N_3, if $N_1 \sqsupseteq N_2$ and $N_2 \sqsupseteq N_3$, then $N_1 \sqsupseteq N_3$.

Networks related by $\sqsupseteq$ have the same set of running processes.

Proposition 8.11 For all N and M, if $N \sqsupseteq M$, then $\mathrm{supp}(N) = \mathrm{supp}(M)$.

Exercise 8.5 Prove Proposition 8.11. (Hint: observe that, for all P, $P \sqcup 0$ implies $P = 0$.)

Finally, relation $\sqsupseteq$ distributes over parallel composition.

Proposition 8.12 Let N and M be two networks with disjoint supports: $\mathrm{supp}(N) \,\#\, \mathrm{supp}(M)$. Then, for all N' and M', $N \mid M \sqsupseteq N' \mid M'$ if and only if $N \sqsupseteq N'$ and $M \sqsupseteq M'$.

Exercise 8.6 Prove Proposition 8.12.

8.2.3 Sequential Composition

Just as we have seen for the languages of Conditional Choreographies and Conditional Processes, $\mathring{,}$ in Recursive Choreographies and Recursive Processes yields monoids: for both languages, $\mathring{,}$ has **0** as identity element and it is associative. The proofs of these results follow the same strategy as seen for Propositions 6.1 and 6.2.

Sequential composition is in harmony with the syntactic operator ; found in the languages of choreographies and processes, in the sense of the following propositions.

Proposition 8.13 Let $I; C$ be a choreography. Then, $I; C = (I; \mathbf{0}) \mathring{,} C$.

Proposition 8.14 Let $I; P$ be a process. Then, $I; P = (I; \mathbf{0}) \mathring{,} P$.

Using $\mathring{,}$ to compose a process with continuations related by $\sqsupseteq$ yields processes that are still related by the branching order.

Lemma 8.15 For all P, Q, and R, $P \sqsupseteq Q$ implies $R \mathring{,} P \sqsupseteq R \mathring{,} Q$.

Proof By induction on the structure of R.

Case 1 $R = \mathbf{0}$. In this case, $R \mathring{,} P = P$ and $R \mathring{,} Q = Q$, so the thesis follows immediately by the hypothesis $P \sqsupseteq Q$.

Case 2 $R = I; R'$. In this case, by definition of $\mathring{,}$,

$$R \mathring{,} P = I; (R' \mathring{,} P)$$
$$R \mathring{,} Q = I; (R' \mathring{,} Q).$$

By induction hypothesis, $R' \mathring{,} P \sqsupseteq R' \mathring{,} Q$. The thesis follows by Lemma 8.7. □

The result in Lemma 8.15 can be generalised as follows.

Lemma 8.16 For all P, Q, R, and S, if $P \sqsupseteq R$ and $Q \sqsupseteq S$, then $P \mathring{,} Q \sqsupseteq R \mathring{,} S$.

Exercise 8.7 (!, $\hookrightarrow$) Prove Lemma 8.16.

Projection distributes over sequential composition, in the following sense.

Lemma 8.17 For all C, C', and r, $[\![C \mathring{,} C']\!]_r = [\![C]\!]_r \mathring{,} [\![C']\!]_r$.

Exercise 8.8 ($\hookrightarrow$) Prove Lemma 8.17. (Hint: proceed by induction on C.)

8.2.4 Merging and Transitions

Merging has strong interplays with the semantics of choreographies and processes.

For any two networks related by $\sqsupseteq$, their μ-derivatives are still related.

Lemma 8.18 For any $\langle N, \Sigma, \mathscr{P} \rangle$, μ, and $\langle M, \Sigma, \mathscr{P} \rangle$ such that $N \sqsupseteq M$, if $\langle N, \Sigma, \mathscr{P} \rangle \xrightarrow{\mu} \langle N', \Sigma', \mathscr{P} \rangle$ and $\langle M, \Sigma, \mathscr{P} \rangle \xrightarrow{\mu} \langle M', \Sigma', \mathscr{P} \rangle$, then $N' \sqsupseteq M'$.

Exercise 8.9 (!)   Prove Lemma 8.18.

In fact, for any two networks N and M such that $N \sqsupseteq M$, if the 'smaller' network M can perform a transition, then so can N. In other words, merging does not impede transitions.

Lemma 8.19   For any $\langle N, \Sigma, \mathscr{P} \rangle$, μ, and $\langle M, \Sigma, \mathscr{P} \rangle$ such that $N \sqsupseteq M$, if $\langle M, \Sigma, \mathscr{P} \rangle \xrightarrow{\mu} \langle M', \Sigma', \mathscr{P} \rangle$, then $\langle N, \Sigma, \mathscr{P} \rangle \xrightarrow{\mu} \langle N', \Sigma, \mathscr{P} \rangle$ for some N' such that $N' \sqsupseteq M'$.

Exercise 8.10   Prove Lemma 8.19. (Hint: proceed by induction on the derivation of the transition $\langle M, \Sigma, \mathscr{P} \rangle \xrightarrow{\mu} \langle M', \Sigma', \mathscr{P} \rangle$; in each case, once N' is obtained, $N' \sqsupseteq M'$ follows by Lemma 8.18.)

Recall that, at the end of Section 6.2.3, we observed that Lemma 5.5 does not hold once we introduce merging and selections: if a choreography performs a transition, this might affect its projections on processes even for those processes that are not involved in the transition. Thanks to $\sqsupseteq$, we can recover a weaker property that is going to be sufficient for proving the correctness of EPP.

Lemma 8.20   For any $\langle C, \Sigma, \mathscr{C} \rangle$, μ, and $\langle C', \Sigma', \mathscr{C} \rangle$, if C is projectable and $\langle C, \Sigma, \mathscr{C} \rangle \xrightarrow{\mu} \langle C', \Sigma', \mathscr{C} \rangle$, then C' is projectable and $[\![C]\!]_r \sqsupseteq [\![C']\!]_r$ for all $r \notin \mathrm{pn}(\mu)$.

Exercise 8.11 (!)   Prove Lemma 8.20. (Hint: proceed by structural induction on the derivation of the transition, using the properties of merging and sequential composition to deal with the interesting cases about conditionals, recursion, and delayed actions.)

8.3   Well-Formedness

The assumptions that fall under the umbrella of well-formedness (from Section 7.1.3) are aimed at excluding erroneous choreographies. They concern in particular the usage of procedures and the processes that a procedure can involve. For example, for any procedure definition of the form $X(\vec{p}) = C$, we assume that C mentions only processes in $\vec{p}$. Furthermore, we observe that whether a choreography is well-formed can depend on the accompanying set of procedure definitions: in the context of a set of procedure definitions $\mathscr{C}$, an invocation to a procedure X is wrong if X is not defined in $\mathscr{C}$. Indeed, we would not be able to derive any transitions for such a choreography.

We introduce the notation $\langle \mathscr{C}, \{\vec{p}\}, C \rangle \checkmark$ as a short-hand for 'the choreography C is well-formed in the context of the set of procedure definitions $\mathscr{C}$ and may involve the processes in the set $\{\vec{p}\}$'. Checking which processes may participate in a choreography is going to be important for checks related to procedures. In order to determine mechanically whether a proposition $\langle \mathscr{C}, \{\vec{p}\}, C \rangle \checkmark$ is valid, we define the inference system in Figure 8.1.

$$\dfrac{\mathsf{p} \neq \mathsf{q} \quad \mathsf{p},\mathsf{q} \in \{\vec{r}\} \quad \langle \mathscr{C}, \{\vec{r}\}, C\rangle \checkmark}{\langle \mathscr{C}, \{\vec{r}\}, \mathsf{p}.e \to \mathsf{q}.x; C\rangle \checkmark} \text{ WF-COM} \qquad \dfrac{\mathsf{p} \neq \mathsf{q} \quad \mathsf{p},\mathsf{q} \in \{\vec{r}\} \quad \langle \mathscr{C}, \{\vec{r}\}, C\rangle \checkmark}{\langle \mathscr{C}, \{\vec{r}\}, \mathsf{p} \to \mathsf{q}[L]; C\rangle \checkmark} \text{ WF-SEL}$$

$$\dfrac{\mathsf{p} \in \{\vec{r}\} \quad \langle \mathscr{C}, \{\vec{r}\}, C\rangle \checkmark}{\langle \mathscr{C}, \{\vec{r}\}, \mathsf{p}.x := e; C\rangle \checkmark} \text{ WF-LOCAL} \qquad \dfrac{}{\langle \mathscr{C}, \{\vec{r}\}, \mathbf{0}\rangle \checkmark} \text{ WF-END}$$

$$\dfrac{\mathsf{p} \in \{\vec{r}\} \quad \langle \mathscr{C}, \{\vec{r}\}, C_1\rangle \checkmark \quad \langle \mathscr{C}, \{\vec{r}\}, C_2\rangle \checkmark \quad \langle \mathscr{C}, \{\vec{r}\}, C\rangle \checkmark}{\langle \mathscr{C}, \{\vec{r}\}, \text{if } \mathsf{p}.e \text{ then } C_1 \text{ else } C_2; C\rangle \checkmark} \text{ WF-COND}$$

$$\dfrac{\text{distinct}(\vec{\mathsf{p}}) \quad \{\vec{\mathsf{p}}\} \subseteq \{\vec{r}\} \quad X(\vec{\mathsf{q}}) = C' \in \mathscr{C} \quad |\vec{\mathsf{p}}| = |\vec{\mathsf{q}}| \quad \langle \mathscr{C}, \{\vec{r}\}, C\rangle \checkmark}{\langle \mathscr{C}, \{\vec{r}\}, X(\vec{\mathsf{p}}); C\rangle \checkmark} \text{ WF-CALL}$$

$$\dfrac{\text{distinct}(\vec{\mathsf{p}}) \quad \text{distinct}(\vec{\mathsf{q}}) \quad \{\vec{\mathsf{q}}\} \subseteq \{\vec{r}\} \quad \{\vec{\mathsf{q}}\} \subset \{\vec{\mathsf{p}}\} \quad X(\vec{\mathsf{s}}) = C'' \in \mathscr{C}}{|\vec{\mathsf{p}}| = |\vec{\mathsf{s}}| \quad \langle \mathscr{C}, \{\vec{r}\}, C\rangle \checkmark \quad \langle \mathscr{C}, \{\vec{r}\}, C'\rangle \checkmark \quad \forall \mathsf{q} \in \vec{\mathsf{q}}.[\![C''[\vec{\mathsf{p}}/\vec{\mathsf{s}}] \mathbin{\mathaccent\cdot{9} } C]\!]_\mathsf{q} \sqsupseteq [\![C']\!]_\mathsf{q}} \atop {\langle \mathscr{C}, \{\vec{r}\}, \vec{\mathsf{q}}: X(\vec{\mathsf{p}}).C; C'\rangle \checkmark} \text{ WF-RT-CALL}$$

Figure 8.1 Well-formedness for Recursive Choreographies.

Rule WF-COM checks that a choreography of the form $\mathsf{p}.e \to \mathsf{q}.x; C$ is well-formed: the process names p and q need to be distinct (first premise, $\mathsf{p} \neq \mathsf{q}$); p and q need to be among the processes that can be involved in the choreography (second premise, $\mathsf{p},\mathsf{q} \in \{\vec{r}\}$); and the continuation C needs to be well-formed (third premise). The first requirement has actually been an assumption since the introduction of Simple Choreographies (Chapter 2), not just from Recursive Choreographies: we take the opportunity to formalise it here for the sake of comprehensiveness. Rule WF-SEL checks choreographies that start with a selection and has the same premises of rule WF-COM.

Rule WF-LOCAL, for local assignments, is even simpler: we just check that the process performing the assignment is among those that can be used (first premise) and that the continuation is well-formed (second premise). Similarly, WF-COND states that a conditional is well-formed if the process evaluating the guard is among those that can be used (first premise), the branches of the conditional are all well-formed (second and third premise), and the continuation of the conditional is well-formed (fourth premise).

Rule WF-END states that the terminated choreography $\mathbf{0}$ is always well-formed – there is nothing to check.

Rule WF-CALL checks procedure calls. Specifically, a choreography of the form $X(\vec{\mathsf{p}}); C$ is well-formed if: all the process names in $\vec{\mathsf{p}}$ are distinct, which we note by writing $\text{distinct}(\vec{\mathsf{p}})$ (first premise); all processes involved in the call are among those that can be used (second premise); the invoked procedure is actually defined (third premise); the number of passed arguments matches the number of expected parameters (fourth premise); and the continuation is well-formed as well (fifth premise).

The last rule, WF-RT-CALL, examines runtime terms for procedure invocations and is the most involved one. It checks that: the arguments passed in the call are distinct (first premise); the processes that still have to enter the procedure are distinct (second premise) and form a strict subset of the passed arguments (fourth premise); all processes involved in the runtime term can be used (third premise); the invoked procedure is defined (fifth premise); the number of passed arguments matches the number of expected parameters (sixth premise, or the first of the second row); the continuation for the processes that still have to enter the procedure is well-formed (seventh premise); the continuation of the choreography is well-formed (eight premise); and, finally, for each (∀) process q that still has to enter the call (q ∈ q⃗), the continuation of the invocation (C′) does not prescribe more actions that involve q than the body of the invoked procedure C″ (followed by the continuation for q, C). The last condition guarantees that the continuation of a runtime term is consistent with the definition of its procedure for all processes that still have to enter. Ensuring this property requires looking at what the choreography prescribes only for each process of interest, for which projection is a convenient technical means.

The following definition states accurately what we mean when we say that a choreography is well-formed in the context of a set of procedure definitions.

Definition 8.21 (Well-Formedness of Choreographies)   Let C be a choreography and $\mathscr{C}$ be a set of choreographic procedure definitions. We say that C is *well-formed in the context of* $\mathscr{C}$ if there exists $\vec{p}$ such that $\langle \mathscr{C}, \{\vec{p}\}, C \rangle \checkmark$ is derivable.

Dually to well-formedness, we say that a choreography C is *ill-formed* in the context of a set $\mathscr{C}$ if its well-formedness is underivable – that is, there is no $\vec{p}$ such that $\langle \mathscr{C}, \{\vec{p}\}, C \rangle \checkmark$ is derivable. When $\mathscr{C}$ is clear from the context, we simply say that 'C is well-formed' as a shorthand for 'C is well-formed in the context of $\mathscr{C}$'.

We define a notion of well-formedness for sets of choreographic procedures, as well.

Definition 8.22 (Well-Formedness of Choreographic Procedures)   Let $\mathscr{C}$ be a set of choreographic procedure definitions. We say that $\mathscr{C}$ is *well-formed* if, for all $X(\vec{p}) = C$ in $\mathscr{C}$, all process names in $\vec{p}$ are distinct and $\langle \mathscr{C}, \{\vec{p}\}, C \rangle \checkmark$ is derivable.

Finally, we introduce a notion of well-formedness for configurations. This is convenient when stating properties about the semantics of choreographies or of their endpoint projections.

Definition 8.23 (Well-Formedness of Choreographic Configurations)   A configuration $\langle C, \Sigma, \mathscr{C} \rangle$ is *well-formed* if C is well-formed in the context of $\mathscr{C}$ and $\mathscr{C}$ is well-formed.

8.3.1 Properties of Well-Formed Choreographies

All premises of the rules for well-formedness still hold if the set of processes that can be used is made larger, which leads to Lemma 8.24.

Lemma 8.24   For any $\mathscr{C}$, $\vec{p}$, C, and $\vec{q}$, if $\langle \mathscr{C}, \{\vec{p}\}, C \rangle \checkmark$ and $\{\vec{q}\} \supseteq \{\vec{p}\}$, then $\langle \mathscr{C}, \{\vec{q}\}, C \rangle \checkmark$.

Proof   By structural induction on the derivation of $\langle \mathscr{C}, \{\vec{p}\}, C \rangle \checkmark$.   □

Furthermore, since each rule for well-formedness performs checks only on the processes that syntactically appear in a choreography, we have that:

Proposition 8.25   For any $\mathscr{C}$, $\vec{p}$, and C, $\langle \mathscr{C}, \{\vec{p}\}, C \rangle \checkmark$ implies $\langle \mathscr{C}, \mathrm{pn}(C), C \rangle \checkmark$ and $\{\vec{p}\} \supseteq \mathrm{pn}(C)$.

Proof   By structural induction on the derivation of $\langle \mathscr{C}, \{\vec{p}\}, C \rangle \checkmark$. The choreography checked in the premise of a rule might have fewer processes than the choreography in the conclusion, but this is addressed by Lemma 8.24.   □

By contraposition on Proposition 8.25:

Proposition 8.26   For any $\mathscr{C}$, $\vec{p}$, and C, if $\{\vec{p}\} \not\supseteq \mathrm{pn}(C)$, then $\langle \mathscr{C}, \{\vec{p}\}, C \rangle \checkmark$ is not derivable.

From Propositions 8.25 and 8.26 we obtain a characterisation as a corollary: for any choreography C, $\mathrm{pn}(C)$ is the minimal and representative set of process names for establishing whether C is well-formed. This means that, when trying to determine whether a choreography is well-formed, we can just refer to the set of processes returned by pn.

Corollary 8.27   For any $\mathscr{C}$, $\vec{p}$, and C:

- $\langle \mathscr{C}, \{\vec{p}\}, C \rangle \checkmark$ only if $\langle \mathscr{C}, \mathrm{pn}(C), C \rangle \checkmark$.
- If $\{\vec{p}\} \supseteq \mathrm{pn}(C)$ and $\langle \mathscr{C}, \mathrm{pn}(C), C \rangle \checkmark$, then $\langle \mathscr{C}, \{\vec{p}\}, C \rangle \checkmark$.

Well-formedness guarantees that the set of processes mentioned by a choreography does not increase under transitions.

Proposition 8.28   Let $\langle C, \Sigma, \mathscr{C} \rangle$ be a well-formed configuration. If $\langle C, \Sigma, \mathscr{C} \rangle \xrightarrow{\mu} \langle C', \Sigma', \mathscr{C} \rangle$, then $\mathrm{pn}(C) \supseteq \mathrm{pn}(C')$.

Exercise 8.12   Without its premise regarding well-formedness, Proposition 8.28 would be false. Provide a counterexample that proves this. (Hint: procedure calls in ill-formed choreographies might introduce new process names.)

Exercise 8.13   Prove Proposition 8.28.

Finally well-formedness is preserved by the semantics of choreographies: if a configuration is well-formed, then all of its derivatives are as well.

Theorem 8.29   Let $\langle C, \Sigma, \mathscr{C} \rangle$ be a well-formed configuration. If $\langle C, \Sigma, \mathscr{C} \rangle \xrightarrow{\mu} \langle C', \Sigma', \mathscr{C} \rangle$, then $\langle C', \Sigma', \mathscr{C} \rangle$ is well-formed.

Proof   By induction on the derivation of the transition $\langle C, \Sigma, \mathscr{C} \rangle \xrightarrow{\mu} \langle C', \Sigma', \mathscr{C} \rangle$. The interesting cases are those that deal with procedure invocations and their runtime terms, which are supported by Lemma 8.20.   □

8.4   Correctness of EPP for Recursive Choreographies

We now move to proving that EPP is correct for the case of Recursive Choreographies, which is formalised by the following theorem.

Theorem 8.30 (Correctness of EPP for Recursive Choreographies)   The following statements hold for every well-formed configuration $\langle C, \Sigma, \mathscr{C} \rangle$.

Completeness   For any μ and $\langle C', \Sigma', \mathscr{C} \rangle$, $\langle C, \Sigma, \mathscr{C} \rangle \xrightarrow{\mu} \langle C', \Sigma', \mathscr{C} \rangle$ implies $\langle [\![C]\!], \Sigma, [\![\mathscr{C}]\!] \rangle \xrightarrow{\mu}$
    $\langle N, \Sigma', [\![\mathscr{C}]\!] \rangle$ for some N such that $N \sqsupseteq [\![C']\!]$.

Soundness For any N, μ, N', and Σ' such that $N \sqsupseteq [\![C]\!]$, $\langle N, \Sigma, [\![\mathscr{C}]\!] \rangle \xrightarrow{\mu} \langle N', \Sigma', [\![\mathscr{C}]\!] \rangle$ implies $\langle C, \Sigma, \mathscr{C} \rangle \xrightarrow{\mu} \langle C', \Sigma', \mathscr{C} \rangle$ for some C' such that $N' \sqsupseteq [\![C']\!]$.

The hypothesis $N \sqsupseteq [\![C]\!]$ in the soundness part is designed to make it easier to generalise the theorem to executions of arbitrary length, which we will do in Section 8.5.

We prove the two parts of Theorem 8.30 as separate lemmas, like we did for the case of Simple Choreographies in Section 4.3. In the proofs, we use often Proposition 3.15, which is still valid for Recursive Processes.

Lemma 8.31 (Completeness of EPP) For any $\langle C, \Sigma, \mathscr{C} \rangle$, μ, and $\langle C', \Sigma', \mathscr{C} \rangle$ such that $\langle C, \Sigma, \mathscr{C} \rangle$ is well-formed, $\langle C, \Sigma, \mathscr{C} \rangle \xrightarrow{\mu} \langle C', \Sigma', \mathscr{C} \rangle$ implies $\langle [\![C]\!], \Sigma, [\![\mathscr{C}]\!] \rangle \xrightarrow{\mu} \langle N, \Sigma', [\![\mathscr{C}]\!] \rangle$ for some N such that $N \sqsupseteq [\![C']\!]$.

Proof Let $\mathcal{D}$ be the derivation of the transition $\langle C, \Sigma, \mathscr{C} \rangle \xrightarrow{\mu} \langle C', \Sigma', \mathscr{C} \rangle$. We proceed by induction on the structure of $\mathcal{D}$.

Case 1 $\mathcal{D}$ ends with an application of rule LOCAL:

$$\mathcal{D} = \frac{\Sigma(\mathsf{p}) \vdash e \downarrow v}{\langle \mathsf{p}.x := e; C', \Sigma, \mathscr{C} \rangle \xrightarrow{\tau @ \mathsf{p}} \langle C', \Sigma[\mathsf{p}.x \mapsto v], \mathscr{C} \rangle} \text{ LOCAL}$$

for some p, x, e, and v. We have that

$$
\begin{aligned}
[\![C]\!] &= [\![C]\!] \setminus \mathsf{p} \mid \mathsf{p}[x := e; [\![C']\!]_\mathsf{p}] && \text{by (7.12) and Proposition 3.15} \\
&= [\![C']\!] \setminus \mathsf{p} \mid \mathsf{p}[x := e; [\![C']\!]_\mathsf{p}] && \text{by Proposition 8.2.}
\end{aligned}
$$

We conclude with the following transition.

$$
\begin{aligned}
&\langle [\![C']\!] \setminus \mathsf{p} \mid \mathsf{p}[x := e; [\![C']\!]_\mathsf{p}], \Sigma, [\![\mathscr{C}]\!] \rangle \\
&\xrightarrow{\tau @ \mathsf{p}} \langle [\![C']\!] \setminus \mathsf{p} \mid \mathsf{p}[[\![C']\!]_\mathsf{p}], \Sigma[\mathsf{p}.x \mapsto v], [\![\mathscr{C}]\!] \rangle && \text{by rules PAR and LOCAL} \\
&= \langle [\![C']\!], \Sigma[\mathsf{p}.x \mapsto v], [\![\mathscr{C}]\!] \rangle && \text{by Proposition 3.15}
\end{aligned}
$$

Case 2 $\mathcal{D}$ ends with an application of rule COM:

$$\mathcal{D} = \frac{\Sigma(\mathsf{p}) \vdash e \downarrow v}{\langle \mathsf{p}.e \to \mathsf{q}.x; C', \Sigma, \mathscr{C} \rangle \xrightarrow{\mathsf{p}.v \to \mathsf{q}} \langle C', \Sigma[\mathsf{q}.x \mapsto v], \mathscr{C} \rangle} \text{ COM}$$

for some p, e, q, e, and v. We have that

$$
\begin{aligned}
[\![C]\!] &= [\![C]\!] \setminus \mathsf{p}, \mathsf{q} \mid \mathsf{p}[\mathsf{q}!e; [\![C']\!]_\mathsf{p}] \mid \mathsf{q}[\mathsf{p}?x; [\![C']\!]_\mathsf{q}] \\
&\qquad\qquad\qquad\qquad\qquad\qquad\qquad \text{by (7.10) and Proposition 3.15} \\
&= [\![C']\!] \setminus \mathsf{p}, \mathsf{q} \mid \mathsf{p}[\mathsf{q}!e; [\![C']\!]_\mathsf{p}] \mid \mathsf{q}[\mathsf{p}?x; [\![C']\!]_\mathsf{q}] \quad \text{by Proposition 8.2}
\end{aligned}
$$

We conclude with the following transition.

$$
\begin{aligned}
&\langle [\![C']\!] \setminus \mathsf{p}, \mathsf{q} \mid \mathsf{p}[\mathsf{q}!e; [\![C']\!]_\mathsf{p}] \mid \mathsf{q}[\mathsf{p}?x; [\![C']\!]_\mathsf{q}], \Sigma, [\![\mathscr{C}]\!] \rangle \\
&\xrightarrow{\mathsf{p}.v \to \mathsf{q}} \langle [\![C']\!] \setminus \mathsf{p}, \mathsf{q} \mid \mathsf{p}[[\![C']\!]_\mathsf{p}] \mid \mathsf{q}[[\![C']\!]_\mathsf{q}], \Sigma[\mathsf{q}.x \mapsto v], [\![\mathscr{C}]\!] \rangle \\
&\qquad\qquad\qquad\qquad\qquad\qquad\qquad\qquad\quad \text{by rules PAR and COM} \\
&= \langle [\![C']\!], \Sigma[\mathsf{q}.x \mapsto v], [\![\mathscr{C}]\!] \rangle \qquad\qquad \text{by Proposition 3.15}
\end{aligned}
$$

Case 3 $\mathcal{D}$ ends with an application of rule SEL. Similar to Case 2.

Case 4 $\mathcal{D}$ ends with an application of rule COND-THEN:

$$\mathcal{D} = \cfrac{\Sigma(p) \vdash e \downarrow \textit{true}}{\langle \text{if } p.e \text{ then } C_1 \text{ else } C_2; C'', \Sigma, \mathscr{C}\rangle \xrightarrow{\tau @p} \langle C_1 \, \mathbin{\raisebox{0.2ex}{\scriptsize$\,^\circ_\circ\,$}} \, C'', \Sigma, \mathscr{C}\rangle} \text{ COND-THEN}$$

for some p, e, C_1, C_2, and C''. By (7.13), Proposition 3.15, and Lemma 8.20,

$$[\![C]\!] \sqsupseteq [\![C_1 \, \mathbin{\raisebox{0.2ex}{\scriptsize$\,^\circ_\circ\,$}} \, C'']\!] \setminus p \mid p[\text{if } e \text{ then}[\![C_1]\!]_p \text{ else}[\![C_2]\!]_p; [\![C'']\!]_p]. \tag{8.1}$$

By (8.1) and rules COND-THEN and PAR for Recursive Processes,

$$\langle [\![C_1 \, \mathbin{\raisebox{0.2ex}{\scriptsize$\,^\circ_\circ\,$}} \, C'']\!] \setminus p \mid p[\text{if } e \text{ then}[\![C_1]\!]_p \text{ else}[\![C_2]\!]_p; [\![C'']\!]_p], \Sigma, [\![\mathscr{C}]\!]\rangle$$

$$\xrightarrow{\tau @p} \langle [\![C_1 \, \mathbin{\raisebox{0.2ex}{\scriptsize$\,^\circ_\circ\,$}} \, C'']\!] \setminus p \mid p[[\![C_1]\!]_p \, \mathbin{\raisebox{0.2ex}{\scriptsize$\,^\circ_\circ\,$}} \, [\![C'']\!]_p], \Sigma, [\![\mathscr{C}]\!]\rangle.$$

We conclude by Lemma 8.19.

Case 5 $\mathcal{D}$ ends with an application of rule COND-ELSE. Similar to Case 4.

Case 6 $\mathcal{D}$ ends with an application of rule CALL-FIRST:

$$\mathcal{D} = \cfrac{X(\vec{q}) = C''' \in \mathscr{C} \quad r \in \vec{p}}{\langle X(\vec{p}); C'', \Sigma, \mathscr{C}\rangle \xrightarrow{\tau @r} \langle \vec{p} \setminus r\colon X(\vec{p}).C'''; C'''[\vec{p}/\vec{q}] \, \mathbin{\raisebox{0.2ex}{\scriptsize$\,^\circ_\circ\,$}} \, C'', \Sigma, \mathscr{C}\rangle} \text{ CALL-FIRST}$$

for some X, C'', C''', $\vec{p}$, $\vec{q}$, and r. Thus, in this case,

$$C' = \vec{p} \setminus r\colon X(\vec{p}).C''; C'''[\vec{p}/\vec{q}] \, \mathbin{\raisebox{0.2ex}{\scriptsize$\,^\circ_\circ\,$}} \, C''.$$

Say that r appears at position i in $\vec{p}$. Also, let $\vec{p}' = \vec{p} \setminus r$. We have that

$$[\![C]\!] = [\![C]\!] \setminus r \mid r[X_i(\vec{p}'); [\![C'']\!]_r] \qquad \text{by (7.14) and Proposition 3.15}$$

$$= [\![C']\!] \setminus r \mid r[X_i(\vec{p}'); [\![C'']\!]_r] \qquad \text{by Lemma 8.20.}$$

From the last network in the comparisons, we have the following transition and equalities, where $\vec{q}' = \vec{q} \setminus r$.

$$\langle [\![C']\!] \setminus r \mid r[X_i(\vec{p}'); [\![C'']\!]_r], \Sigma, [\![\mathscr{C}]\!]\rangle$$

$$\xrightarrow{\tau @r} \langle [\![C']\!] \setminus r \mid r[Q[\vec{p}'/\vec{q}'] \, \mathbin{\raisebox{0.2ex}{\scriptsize$\,^\circ_\circ\,$}} \, [\![C'']\!]_r], \Sigma, [\![\mathscr{C}]\!]\rangle$$

$$\qquad\qquad\qquad\qquad\text{by rules CALL and PAR, for } X_i(\vec{p}') = Q \in [\![\mathscr{C}]\!]$$

$$= \langle [\![C']\!] \setminus r \mid r[[\![C''']\!]_r[\vec{p}'/\vec{q}'] \, \mathbin{\raisebox{0.2ex}{\scriptsize$\,^\circ_\circ\,$}} \, [\![C'']\!]_r], \Sigma, [\![\mathscr{C}]\!]\rangle \quad \text{by Definition 7.4}$$

$$= \langle [\![C']\!] \setminus r \mid r[[\![C'''[\vec{p}'/\vec{q}'] \, \mathbin{\raisebox{0.2ex}{\scriptsize$\,^\circ_\circ\,$}} \, C'']\!]_r], \Sigma, [\![\mathscr{C}]\!]\rangle \quad \text{by Lemma 8.17}$$

$$= \langle [\![C']\!], \Sigma, [\![\mathscr{C}]\!]\rangle \qquad\qquad\qquad\qquad\qquad \text{by (7.15)}$$

$$\qquad\qquad\qquad\qquad\qquad\qquad\qquad\qquad\qquad\text{and Proposition 3.15}$$

We conclude by Lemma 8.19.

Case 7 $\mathcal{D}$ ends with an application of rule CALL-LAST:

$$\mathcal{D} = \cfrac{}{\langle r\colon X(\vec{p}).C''; C', \Sigma, \mathscr{C}\rangle \xrightarrow{\tau @r} \langle C', \Sigma, \mathscr{C}\rangle} \text{ CALL-LAST}$$

for some X, r, $\vec{p}$, and C''. Say that r appears at position i in $\vec{p}$, and let $\vec{p}' = \vec{p} \setminus r$. By (7.15), Proposition 3.15, and Proposition 8.2, we have that:

$$[\![C]\!] = [\![C']\!] \setminus r \mid r[X_i(\vec{p}'); [\![C'']\!]_r]. \tag{8.2}$$

From the network on the right-hand side in (8.2) we proceed as follows, where $\vec{q}' = \vec{q} \setminus r$.

$\langle [\![C']\!] \setminus r \mid r[X_i(\vec{p}'); [\![C'']\!]_r], \Sigma, [\![\mathscr{C}]\!] \rangle$

$\xrightarrow{\tau @ r} \langle [\![C']\!] \setminus r \mid r[Q[\vec{p}'/\vec{q}'] \, \mathring{,} \, [\![C'']\!]_r], \Sigma, [\![\mathscr{C}]\!] \rangle$

> by rules CALL and PAR, for $X_i(\vec{p}') = Q \in [\![\mathscr{C}]\!]$

$= \langle [\![C']\!] \setminus r \mid r[[\![C''']\!]_r[\vec{p}'/\vec{q}'] \, \mathring{,} \, [\![C'']\!]_r], \Sigma, [\![\mathscr{C}]\!] \rangle$

> by Definition 7.4, for $X(\vec{p}) = C''' \in \mathscr{C}$

$\sqsupseteq \langle [\![C']\!] \setminus r \mid r[[\![C']\!]_r], \Sigma, [\![\mathscr{C}]\!] \rangle$ by well-formedness of C

$= \langle [\![C']\!], \Sigma, [\![\mathscr{C}]\!] \rangle$ by Definition 7.6 and Proposition 3.15

More specifically, in the step that invokes well-formedness of C, we mean that: C is well-formed, and due to its shape this can be derived only by means of rule WF-RT-CALL; therefore, the premises of that rule hold. We conclude by Lemma 8.19.

Case 8 $\mathcal{D}$ ends with an application of rule CALL-ENTER. Similar to Case 7.

Case 9 $\mathcal{D}$ ends with an application of rule DELAY:

$$\mathcal{D} = \frac{\overset{\mathcal{D}'}{\langle C_1, \Sigma, \mathscr{C} \rangle \xrightarrow{\mu} \langle C_1', \Sigma', \mathscr{C} \rangle} \quad \mathrm{pn}(I) \,\#\, \mathrm{pn}(\mu)}{\langle I; C_1, \Sigma, \mathscr{C} \rangle \xrightarrow{\mu} \langle I; C_1', \Sigma', \mathscr{C} \rangle} \text{ DELAY}$$

for some I, C_1, C_1', and $\mathcal{D}'$.

By induction hypothesis on $\mathcal{D}'$, there exists M such that

$$\langle [\![C_1]\!], \Sigma, [\![\mathscr{C}]\!] \rangle \xrightarrow{\mu} \langle M, \Sigma', [\![\mathscr{C}]\!] \rangle \tag{8.3}$$

and $M \sqsupseteq [\![C_1']\!]$.

Let $\mathrm{pn}(I) = \{\vec{p}\}$. Since $\vec{p}$ do not appear in μ, we have that

$\langle [\![C_1]\!] \setminus \vec{p}, \Sigma, [\![\mathscr{C}]\!] \rangle \xrightarrow{\mu} \langle M \setminus \vec{p}, \Sigma', [\![\mathscr{C}]\!] \rangle$ by (8.3) and Proposition 3.15

and

$[\![C_1]\!] \setminus \vec{p} = [\![I; C_1]\!] \setminus \vec{p}$ by Proposition 8.2.

Therefore, by rule PAR,

$$\langle [\![I; C_1]\!] \setminus \vec{p} \mid [\![I; C_1]\!]{\restriction}_{\vec{p}}, \Sigma, [\![\mathscr{C}]\!] \rangle \xrightarrow{\mu} \langle M \setminus \vec{p} \mid [\![I; C_1]\!]{\restriction}_{\vec{p}}, \Sigma', [\![\mathscr{C}]\!] \rangle,$$

which we can rewrite into

$$\langle [\![C]\!], \Sigma, [\![\mathscr{C}]\!] \rangle \xrightarrow{\mu} \langle M \setminus \vec{p} \mid [\![I; C_1]\!]{\restriction}_{\vec{p}}, \Sigma', [\![\mathscr{C}]\!] \rangle.$$

We conclude by Lemma 8.20, which gives us $[\![I; C_1]\!]{\restriction}_{\vec{p}} \sqsupseteq [\![I; C_1']\!]{\restriction}_{\vec{p}}$.

Case 10 $\mathcal{D}$ ends with an application of rule DELAY-COND:

$$\mathcal{D} = \frac{\overset{\mathcal{D}_1}{\langle C_1, \Sigma, \mathscr{C} \rangle \overset{\mu}{\to} \langle C_1', \Sigma', \mathscr{C} \rangle} \quad \overset{\mathcal{D}_2}{\langle C_2, \Sigma, \mathscr{C} \rangle \overset{\mu}{\to} \langle C_2', \Sigma', \mathscr{C} \rangle}}{\langle \text{if p}.e \text{ then } C_1 \text{ else } C_2; C'', \Sigma, \mathscr{C} \rangle} \quad \text{DELAY-COND}$$
$$\overset{\mu}{\to} \langle \text{if p}.e \text{ then } C_1' \text{ else } C_2'; C'', \Sigma', \mathscr{C} \rangle$$

for some p such that $\text{p} \notin \text{pn}(\mu)$ (we report this side-condition here for space reasons), e, $C_1, C_2, C'', C_1', C_2', \mathcal{D}_1$, and $\mathcal{D}_2$.

By induction hypothesis on $\mathcal{D}_1$, there exists M_1 such that

$$\langle [\![C_1]\!], \Sigma, [\![\mathscr{C}]\!] \rangle \overset{\mu}{\to} \langle M_1, \Sigma', [\![\mathscr{C}]\!] \rangle \tag{8.4}$$

and $M_1 \sqsupseteq [\![C_1']\!]$. Likewise, by induction hypothesis on $\mathcal{D}_2$, there exists M_2 such that

$$\langle [\![C_2]\!], \Sigma, [\![\mathscr{C}]\!] \rangle \overset{\mu}{\to} \langle M_2, \Sigma', [\![\mathscr{C}]\!] \rangle \tag{8.5}$$

and $M_2 \sqsupseteq [\![C_2']\!]$.

The EPP of C is as follows.

$$[\![C]\!](r) = \begin{cases} \text{if } e \text{ then} [\![C_1]\!]_r \text{ else} [\![C_2]\!]_r; [\![C'']\!]_r & \text{if } r = p \\ ([\![C_1]\!]_r \sqcup [\![C_2]\!]_r) \,\fatsemi\, [\![C'']\!]_r & \text{otherwise} \end{cases}$$

By (8.4), (8.5), Lemma 8.20, and the properties of merging and sequential composition (in particular Lemma 8.19, Lemma 8.6, and Lemma 8.15), we obtain $\langle [\![C]\!], \Sigma, [\![\mathscr{C}]\!] \rangle \overset{\mu}{\to} \langle N, \Sigma', [\![\mathscr{C}]\!] \rangle$, for some $N \sqsupseteq [\![C']\!]$, as needed. $\square$

Exercise 8.14 Write the developments for the cases of rules SEL and CALL-ENTER in the proof of Lemma 8.31.

Lemma 8.32 (Soundness of EPP) For any $\langle C, \Sigma, \mathscr{C} \rangle$, N, μ, N', and Σ' such that $\langle C, \Sigma, \mathscr{C} \rangle$ is well-formed and $N \sqsupseteq [\![C]\!]$, $\langle N, \Sigma, [\![\mathscr{C}]\!] \rangle \overset{\mu}{\to} \langle N', \Sigma', [\![\mathscr{C}]\!] \rangle$ implies $\langle C, \Sigma, \mathscr{C} \rangle \overset{\mu}{\to} \langle C', \Sigma', \mathscr{C} \rangle$ for some C' such that $N' \sqsupseteq [\![C']\!]$.

Proof By structural induction on C. By the grammar of Recursive Choreographies, C can either (i) be the terminated choreography $\mathbf{0}$ or (ii) start with an instruction, that is, C is of the form $I; C''$ for some I and C''. If C starts with an instruction, we have several cases depending on what kind of instruction it is (an assignment, a communication, etc.). Most of these cases have very similar developments; we report the full development for a representative one. The important exception is the case that deals with conditionals, so we describe how it differs.

Case 1 $C = \mathbf{0}$. In this case, the configuration $\langle N, \Sigma, [\![\mathscr{C}]\!] \rangle$ has no derivatives, so the thesis holds vacuously.

Case 2 $C = \text{p}.x := e; C''$, for some p, x, e, and C''. By (7.12), Proposition 3.15, the definition of merging, and Lemma 8.7:

$$N = N \setminus \text{p} \mid \text{p}[x := e; P] \text{ for some } P \text{ such that } P \sqsupseteq [\![C'']\!]_\text{p}.$$

Observe now that p can either be involved in μ, $p \in pn(\mu)$, or not, $p \notin pn(\mu)$. We deal with these subcases separately.

Case 2.1 If $p \in pn(\mu)$, then by the semantics of networks, μ, N', and Σ' are determined by rule LOCAL:

$$\mu = \tau \,@\, p \qquad \Sigma' = \Sigma[p.x \mapsto v] \qquad N' = N \setminus p \,|\, p[P]$$

for v such that $\Sigma(p) \vdash e \downarrow v$. A consequence is that $N' \setminus p = N \setminus p$, which will be useful soon. By rule LOCAL for choreographies, we obtain:

$$\langle p.x := e; C'', \Sigma, \mathscr{C} \rangle \xrightarrow{\tau \,@\, p} \langle C'', \Sigma', \mathscr{C} \rangle.$$

Let us set $C' \triangleq C''$. We need to prove that $N' \sqsupseteq [\![C'']\!]$. By Proposition 8.2, $[\![C]\!] \setminus p = [\![C'']\!] \setminus p$. Therefore, by hypothesis and definition of $\sqsupseteq$, $N' \setminus p = N \setminus p \sqsupseteq [\![C]\!] \setminus p$. The thesis follows from this fact and $P \sqsupseteq [\![C'']\!]_p$.

Case 2.2 If $p \notin pn(\mu)$, then the transition must originate from the subnetwork of N that does not involve p:

$$\langle N \setminus p, \Sigma, [\![\mathscr{C}]\!] \rangle \xrightarrow{\mu} \langle N' \setminus p, \Sigma', [\![\mathscr{C}]\!] \rangle. \tag{8.6}$$

Let $M = N \setminus p \,|\, p[[\![C'']\!]_p]$. We know that $[\![C]\!] \setminus p = [\![C'']\!] \setminus p$, by Proposition 8.2, and $N \sqsupseteq [\![C]\!]$, by hypothesis. It follows that $M \sqsupseteq [\![C'']\!]$. By rule PAR and (8.6), M can mimic the transition in (8.6):

$$\langle M, \Sigma, [\![\mathscr{C}]\!] \rangle \xrightarrow{\mu} \langle M', \Sigma', [\![\mathscr{C}]\!] \rangle \text{ where } M' \triangleq N' \setminus p \,|\, p[[\![C'']\!]_p]. \tag{8.7}$$

From $M \sqsupseteq [\![C'']\!]$ and (8.7), the induction hypothesis gives us:

$$\langle C'', \Sigma, \mathscr{C} \rangle \xrightarrow{\mu} \langle C''', \Sigma', \mathscr{C} \rangle \text{ for some } C''' \text{ such that } M' \sqsupseteq [\![C''']\!]. \tag{8.8}$$

By (8.8), $p \notin pn(\mu)$, and rule DELAY for choreographies, it follows that

$$\langle C, \Sigma, \mathscr{C} \rangle = \langle p.x := e; C'', \Sigma, \mathscr{C} \rangle \xrightarrow{\mu} \langle p.x := e; C''', \Sigma', \mathscr{C} \rangle.$$

Let C' be the choreography in the derivative just provided – that is, $C' \triangleq p.x := e; C'''$. To reach the thesis, we need to prove that $N' \sqsupseteq [\![p.x := e; C''']\!]$. By Proposition 3.15, $N' = N' \setminus p \,|\, p[N(p)]$. Thus, by Proposition 8.12, the thesis follows if we prove that $N' \setminus p \sqsupseteq [\![p.x := e; C''']\!] \setminus p$ and $N(p) \sqsupseteq [\![p.x := e; C''']\!]_p$. The first fact is obtained as follows.

$$\begin{aligned} N' \setminus p &= M' \setminus p & \text{by (8.7)} \\ &\sqsupseteq [\![C''']\!] \setminus p & \text{by (8.8)} \\ &= [\![p.x := e; C''']\!] \setminus p & \text{by Proposition 8.2} \end{aligned}$$

That leaves us with the final task of showing that $N'(p) \sqsupseteq [\![p.x := e; C''']\!]_p$, which we conclude as follows.

$$\begin{aligned} N'(p) &= N(p) & \text{by } p \notin pn(\mu), \text{ and Proposition 7.3} \\ &\sqsupseteq [\![p.x := e; C'']\!]_p & \text{by hypothesis} \\ &\sqsupseteq [\![p.x := e; C''']\!]_p & \text{by Lemma 8.20.} \end{aligned}$$

Case 3 C starts with a communication, a selection, a procedure call, or a runtime term for a procedure call. The development is similar to Case 2, with the minor differences that sometimes it is necessary to single out two processes in the initial network (for communications and selections) or to invoke properties related to the $\mathbin{\mathrm{\S}}$ operator (for procedure calls and their runtime terms).

Case 4 $C = $ if p.e then C_1 else $C_2; C''$ for some p, e, C_1, C_2, and C''. By (7.13), Proposition 3.15, and definition of merging:

$$N = N \setminus \mathsf{p} \mid \mathsf{p}[\text{if } e \text{ then } P_1 \text{ else } P_2; Q]$$

for some P_1, P_2, and Q such that

$$P_1 \sqsupseteq [\![C_1]\!]_\mathsf{p} \qquad\qquad P_2 \sqsupseteq [\![C_2]\!]_\mathsf{p} \qquad\qquad Q \sqsupseteq [\![C'']\!]_\mathsf{p}.$$

As in the previous cases, we observe that p can either be involved in μ, $\mathsf{p} \in pn(\mu)$, or not, $\mathsf{p} \notin pn(\mu)$.

Case 4.1 Let us deal with the possibility that $\mathsf{p} \in pn(\mu)$ first. Under this assumption, by the semantics of networks, μ, N', and Σ' are determined by either rule COND-THEN or rule COND-ELSE. The reasonings for these different occurrences are very similar. Here, we assume that the transition is due to an application of rule COND-THEN, which gives us:

$$\mu = \tau @\mathsf{p} \qquad \Sigma(\mathsf{p}) \vdash e \downarrow true \qquad \Sigma' = \Sigma \qquad N' = N \setminus \mathsf{p} \mid \mathsf{p}[P_1 \mathbin{\mathrm{\S}} Q].$$

This also implies that $N' \setminus \mathsf{p} = N \setminus \mathsf{p}$. By rule COND-THEN for choreographies, we obtain:

$$\langle \text{if p.}e \text{ then } C_1 \text{ else } C_2; C'', \Sigma, \mathscr{C} \rangle \xrightarrow{\tau @\mathsf{p}} \langle C_1 \mathbin{\mathrm{\S}} C'', \Sigma, \mathscr{C} \rangle.$$

Let us set $C' \triangleq C_1 \mathbin{\mathrm{\S}} C''$. We need to prove that $N' \sqsupseteq [\![C_1 \mathbin{\mathrm{\S}} C'']\!]$. By Lemma 8.20, $[\![C]\!] \setminus \mathsf{p} \sqsupseteq [\![C_1 \mathbin{\mathrm{\S}} C'']\!] \setminus \mathsf{p}$. Therefore, since $N' \setminus \mathsf{p} = N \setminus \mathsf{p}$ and $N \sqsupseteq [\![C]\!]$, we get: $N' \setminus \mathsf{p} = N \setminus \mathsf{p} \sqsupseteq [\![C]\!] \setminus \mathsf{p} \sqsupseteq [\![C_1 \mathbin{\mathrm{\S}} C'']\!] \setminus \mathsf{p}$. It remains to show that $N'(\mathsf{p}) \sqsupseteq [\![C_1 \mathbin{\mathrm{\S}} C'']\!]_\mathsf{p}$, which follows by $P_1 \sqsupseteq [\![C_1]\!]_\mathsf{p}$, $Q \sqsupseteq [\![C'']\!]_\mathsf{p}$, and Lemma 8.16.

Case 4.2 Say now that $\mathsf{p} \notin \mu$, and let $\vec{\mathsf{q}} \triangleq pn(\mu)$. The thesis follows by a similar development as that for the case that covers assignments, with one key difference: if $\vec{\mathsf{q}}$ appear in the branches of the choreographic conditional (C_1 or C_2), then rule DELAY-COND should be used instead of rule DELAY; otherwise, if $\vec{\mathsf{q}}$ do not appear in the conditional at all, rule DELAY should still be used. □

8.5   Consequences of the Correctness of Endpoint Projection

In this section, we present some interesting properties that we can prove by leveraging the correctness of EPP.

We start by showing that the correspondence between choreographies and their EPPs is preserved under executions of arbitrary lengths.

Theorem 8.33 The following statements hold for every well-formed configuration $\langle C, \Sigma, \mathscr{C} \rangle$.

Completeness of Executions For any $\vec{\mu}$ and $\langle C', \Sigma', \mathscr{C} \rangle$, $\langle C, \Sigma, \mathscr{C} \rangle \xrightarrow{\vec{\mu}} \langle C', \Sigma', \mathscr{C} \rangle$ implies $\langle \llbracket C \rrbracket$, $\Sigma, \llbracket \mathscr{C} \rrbracket \rangle \xrightarrow{\vec{\mu}} \langle N, \Sigma', \llbracket \mathscr{C} \rrbracket \rangle$ for some N such that $N \sqsupseteq \llbracket C' \rrbracket$.

Soundness of Executions For any N, $\vec{\mu}$, N', and Σ' such that $N \sqsupseteq \llbracket C \rrbracket$, $\langle N, \Sigma, \llbracket \mathscr{C} \rrbracket \rangle \xrightarrow{\vec{\mu}} \langle N', \Sigma'$, $\llbracket \mathscr{C} \rrbracket \rangle$ implies $\langle C, \Sigma, \mathscr{C} \rangle \xrightarrow{\vec{\mu}} \langle C', \Sigma', \mathscr{C} \rangle$ for some C' such that $N' \sqsupseteq \llbracket C' \rrbracket$.

Proof We prove the two results separately.

For completeness, let $\mathcal{D}$ be the derivation of $\langle C, \Sigma, \mathscr{C} \rangle \xrightarrow{\vec{\mu}} \langle C', \Sigma', \mathscr{C} \rangle$ and proceed by induction on $\mathcal{D}$.

Case 1 $\mathcal{D}$ ends with an application of rule REFL. The thesis follows by reflexivity of $\sqsupseteq$.
Case 2 $\mathcal{D}$ ends with an application of rule STEP-R:

$$\mathcal{D} = \frac{\overset{\mathcal{E}}{\langle C, \Sigma, \mathscr{C} \rangle \xrightarrow{\vec{\mu}'} \langle C'', \Sigma'', \mathscr{C} \rangle} \quad \overset{\mathcal{F}}{\langle C'', \Sigma'', \mathscr{C} \rangle \xrightarrow{\mu} \langle C', \Sigma', \mathscr{C} \rangle}}{\langle C, \Sigma, \mathscr{C} \rangle \xrightarrow{\vec{\mu}', \mu} \langle C', \Sigma', \mathscr{C} \rangle} \text{ STEP-R}$$

for some C'', Σ'', $\vec{\mu}'$, μ, $\mathcal{D}'$, and $\mathcal{D}''$ such that $\vec{\mu} = \vec{\mu}', \mu$. By induction hypothesis,

$$\langle \llbracket C \rrbracket, \Sigma, \llbracket \mathscr{C} \rrbracket \rangle \xrightarrow{\vec{\mu}'} \langle N'', \Sigma'', \llbracket \mathscr{C} \rrbracket \rangle \tag{8.9}$$

for some $N'' \sqsupseteq \llbracket C'' \rrbracket$. By the conclusion of $\mathcal{F}$ and Theorem 8.30,

$$\langle \llbracket C'' \rrbracket, \Sigma'', \llbracket \mathscr{C} \rrbracket \rangle \xrightarrow{\mu} \langle M, \Sigma', \llbracket \mathscr{C} \rrbracket \rangle \tag{8.10}$$

for some $M \sqsupseteq \llbracket C' \rrbracket$. By (8.10), $N'' \sqsupseteq \llbracket C'' \rrbracket$, and Lemma 8.19:

$$\langle N'', \Sigma'', \llbracket \mathscr{C} \rrbracket \rangle \xrightarrow{\mu} \langle N', \Sigma', \llbracket \mathscr{C} \rrbracket \rangle \tag{8.11}$$

for some $N' \sqsupseteq M$. Since $M \sqsupseteq \llbracket C' \rrbracket$, transitivity of $\sqsupseteq$ gives us $N' \sqsupseteq M$. The thesis follows by (8.9), (8.11), and rule STEP-R.

For soundness, let $\mathcal{D}$ be the derivation of $\langle N, \Sigma, \llbracket \mathscr{C} \rrbracket \rangle \xrightarrow{\vec{\mu}} \langle N', \Sigma', \llbracket \mathscr{C} \rrbracket \rangle$ and proceed by induction on $\mathcal{D}$.

Case 1 $\mathcal{D}$ ends with an application of rule REFL. The thesis follows by reflexivity of $\sqsupseteq$.
Case 2 $\mathcal{D}$ ends with an application of rule STEP-R:

$$\mathcal{D} = \frac{\overset{\mathcal{E}}{\langle N, \Sigma, \llbracket \mathscr{C} \rrbracket \rangle \xrightarrow{\vec{\mu}'} \langle N'', \Sigma'', \llbracket \mathscr{C} \rrbracket \rangle} \quad \overset{\mathcal{F}}{\langle N'', \Sigma'', \llbracket \mathscr{C} \rrbracket \rangle \xrightarrow{\mu} \langle N', \Sigma', \llbracket \mathscr{C} \rrbracket \rangle}}{\langle N, \Sigma, \llbracket \mathscr{C} \rrbracket \rangle \xrightarrow{\vec{\mu}', \mu} \langle N', \Sigma', \llbracket \mathscr{C} \rrbracket \rangle} \text{ STEP-R}$$

for some N'', Σ'', $\vec{\mu}'$, μ, $\mathcal{E}$, and $\mathcal{F}$ such that $\vec{\mu} = \vec{\mu}', \mu$. By induction hypothesis,

$$\langle C, \Sigma, \mathscr{C} \rangle \xrightarrow{\vec{\mu}'} \langle C'', \Sigma'', \mathscr{C} \rangle \tag{8.12}$$

for some C'' such that $N'' \sqsupseteq \llbracket C'' \rrbracket$. By $N'' \sqsupseteq \llbracket C'' \rrbracket$, the conclusion of $\mathcal{F}$, and Theorem 8.30,

$$\langle C'', \Sigma'', \mathscr{C} \rangle \xrightarrow{\vec{\mu}} \langle C', \Sigma', \mathscr{C} \rangle \tag{8.13}$$

such that $N' \sqsupseteq \llbracket C' \rrbracket$. The thesis follows by (8.12), (8.13), and rule STEP-R. $\square$

8.5.1 Communication Safety

To formulate communication safety for Recursive Processes, we need to extend the definition of communication errors from Simple Processes to deal with the new constructs.

We say that an instruction I in the language of Recursive Processes *targets* p if it is of the form p!e, p?x, p $\oplus$ L, or p & $\{L_i: P_i\}_{i \in I}$.

Definition 8.34 (Communication Error)   A network N has a *communication error* if there are p and q such that one of the following conditions holds.

1. $N(p) = q!e; P$ and $N(q) = I; Q$, for some e, P, I, and Q such that I targets p and $I \neq$ p?x for all x.
2. $N(p) = q?x; P$ and $N(q) = I; Q$, for some x, P, I, and Q such that I targets p and $I \neq$ p!e for all e.
3. $N(p) = q \oplus L; P$ and $N(q) = I; Q$, for some L, P, I, and Q such that I targets p and $I \neq$ p & $\{L_j : Q_j\}_{j \in J}$ for any J, $\{L_j\}_{j \in J}$, and $\{Q_j\}_{j \in J}$ such that L $\in \{L_j\}_{j \in J}$.
4. $N(p) = q$ & $\{L_j : P_j\}_{j \in J}; P$ and $N(q) = I; Q$, for some J, $\{L_j\}_{j \in J}$, $\{P_j\}_{j \in J}$, P, I, and Q such that I targets p and $I \neq$ q $\oplus L_k$ for all $k \in J$.

A configuration $\langle N, \Sigma, \mathscr{P} \rangle$ has a communication error if N has a communication error.

Essentially, we have a communication error if two processes start with incompatible actions that target each other.

A configuration is communication safe if it can never reach a configuration with a network that has a communication error.

Definition 8.35 (Communication Safety)   A configuration $\langle N, \Sigma, \mathscr{P} \rangle$ is *communication safe* if all its multi-step derivatives do not have communication errors.

Given a well-formed choreographic configuration $\langle C, \Sigma, \mathscr{C} \rangle$, its corresponding network configuration according to EPP $\langle [\![C]\!], \Sigma, \mathscr{C} \rangle$ is communication safe. The proof of this property relies on two auxiliary lemmas: the projection of a well-formed choreography does not have communication errors, and merging cannot add communication errors.

Lemma 8.36   Let $N \sqsupseteq M$. If N does not have communication errors, then M does not have communication errors.

Lemma 8.37   If C is well-formed, then $[\![C]\!]$ does not have communication errors.

The combination of Theorem 8.33, Lemma 8.36, and Lemma 8.37 gives us communication safety for implementations of choreographies generated by EPP.

Theorem 8.38   For any well-formed $\langle C, \Sigma, \mathscr{C} \rangle$, $\langle [\![C]\!], \Sigma, [\![\mathscr{C}]\!] \rangle$ is communication safe.

Exercise 8.15 (!)   Prove Lemmas 8.36 and 8.37, and then use them to write a detailed proof of Theorem 8.38.

8.5.2 Deadlock-Freedom

Differently from the case of Simple Choreographies, the theory of EPP for Recursive Choreographies does not guarantee starvation-freedom. We can write a simple counterexample by reusing procedure *Ping* from Example 7.1. Specifically, consider the configuration $\langle C, \Sigma, \mathscr{C} \rangle$, where Σ is a choreographic store, and C and $\mathscr{C}$ are defined as:

$$C \triangleq Ping(\mathsf{Alice}, \mathsf{Bob}); \mathsf{Bob} \to \mathsf{Carol}[\textsc{done}]$$

$$\mathscr{C} \triangleq \{Ping(\mathsf{p}, \mathsf{q}) = \mathsf{p} \to \mathsf{q}[\textsc{sig}]; Ping(\mathsf{p}, \mathsf{q})\}.$$

In C, Bob can perform the selection with Carol only after the execution of procedure *Ping* terminates, but this can never happen. Thus, Carol is going to be stuck forever.

Instead of starvation-freedom, we can provide a weaker liveness property: EPP for Recursive Choreographies generates *deadlock-free* networks. While starvation-freedom requires that all processes must always be able to eventually progress, deadlock-freedom requires that the system as a whole can always make some progress (ignoring which processes get to act). We can formalise deadlock-freedom for Recursive Networks as follows.

Definition 8.39 (Deadlock-Freedom)   A configuration $\langle N, \Sigma, \mathscr{P} \rangle$ is *deadlock-free* if, for all its multi-step derivatives $\langle N', \Sigma', \mathscr{P} \rangle$, $N' \neq \mathbf{0}$ implies that there exist μ, N'', and Σ'' such that $\langle N', \Sigma', \mathscr{P} \rangle \xrightarrow{\mu} \langle N'', \Sigma'', \mathscr{P} \rangle$.

The key to proving deadlock-freedom for EPP is the next lemma, which guarantees that a well-formed choreography containing instructions can always perform a transition.

Lemma 8.40   Let $\langle C, \Sigma, \mathscr{C} \rangle$ be a well-formed configuration such that $C \neq \mathbf{0}$. Then, there exist μ and $\langle C', \Sigma', \mathscr{C} \rangle$ such that $\langle C, \Sigma, \mathscr{C} \rangle \xrightarrow{\mu} \langle C', \Sigma', \mathscr{C} \rangle$.

Proof   Since $\langle C, \Sigma, \mathscr{C} \rangle$ is well-formed, $\mathcal{D} :: \langle \mathscr{C}, \{\vec{r}\}, C \rangle \checkmark$ for some $\mathcal{D}$ and $\vec{r}$. We proceed by structural induction on $\mathcal{D}$.

Case 1 $\mathcal{D}$ ends with an application of rule WF-END. This case cannot occur, because it would mean that $C = \mathbf{0}$.

Case 2 $\mathcal{D}$ ends with an application of rule WF-LOCAL:

$$\mathcal{D} = \frac{\mathsf{p} \in \{\vec{r}\} \quad \overset{\mathcal{D}'}{\langle \mathscr{C}, \{\vec{r}\}, C'' \rangle \checkmark}}{\langle \mathscr{C}, \{\vec{r}\}, \mathsf{p}.x := e; C'' \rangle \checkmark} \; \text{WF-LOCAL}$$

for some p, x, e, C'', and $\mathcal{D}'$. By rule LOCAL,

$$\langle \mathsf{p}.x := e; C', \Sigma, \mathscr{C} \rangle \xrightarrow{\tau @ \mathsf{p}} \langle C'', \Sigma[\mathsf{p}.x \mapsto v], \mathscr{C} \rangle$$

for some v. Thus the thesis follows for $C' \triangleq C''$.

Case 3 $\mathcal{D}$ ends with an application of rule WF-COM, WF-SEL, or WF-COND. These cases are similar to Case 2 (for conditionals, we might need to apply either rule COND-THEN or rule COND-ELSE depending on how the guard can be evaluated).

Case 4 $\mathcal{D}$ ends with an application of rule WF-CALL:

$$\mathcal{D} = \dfrac{\begin{array}{c} \text{distinct}(\vec{p}) \quad \{\vec{p}\} \subseteq \{\vec{r}\} \\ X(\vec{q}) = C''' \in \mathscr{C} \quad |\vec{p}| = |\vec{q}| \quad \langle \mathscr{C}, \{\vec{r}\}, C'' \rangle \checkmark \end{array}}{\langle \mathscr{C}, \{\vec{r}\}, X(\vec{p}); C'' \rangle \checkmark} \text{ WF-CALL}$$

for some $\vec{p}$, $\vec{q}$, X, C'', and C'''.

The thesis follows by rule CALL-FIRST, which can be applied because of the compatibility check between procedure call and definition performed by rule WF-CALL.

Case 5 $\mathcal{D}$ ends with an application of rule WF-RT-CALL. This case is similar to Case 4, and the thesis follows by rule CALL-ENTER or rule CALL-LAST.   □

Theorem 8.41   Let $\langle C, \Sigma, \mathscr{C} \rangle$ be a well-formed configuration. Then, $\langle [\![C]\!], \Sigma, [\![\mathscr{C}]\!] \rangle$ is deadlock-free.

Proof   The proof is similar to that of Theorem 4.14. For any multi-step derivative of $\langle [\![C]\!], \Sigma, [\![\mathscr{C}]\!] \rangle$, Theorem 8.33 gives us a corresponding choreographic configuration, which we know to be well-formed by Theorem 8.29. We conclude by Lemma 8.40 and Theorem 8.30.   □

8.5.3   Starvation-Freedom

As we exemplified in the previous section, starvation-freedom does not hold for Recursive Choreographies because of procedure calls followed by instructions that need the procedure to terminate. However, we can consider a fragment of the language whereby this situation never occurs: that of *tail-recursive* choreographies. A choreography is tail-recursive if we forbid instructions from appearing after a procedure call.

Definition 8.42   A choreography C is *tail-recursive* if it respects any of the following conditions.

- $C = \mathbf{0}$.
- $C = X(\vec{p}); \mathbf{0}$ for some X and $\vec{p}$.
- $C = $ if $p.e$ then C_1 else $C_2; \mathbf{0}$ for some p, e, C_1, and C_2 such that C_1 and C_2 are tail-recursive.
- $C = I; C'$ for some I and C' such that: I is a value communication, a selection, or an assignment; and C' is tail-recursive.
- $C = \vec{q}: X(\vec{p}).C'; C''$ for some $\vec{q}$, C', X, $\vec{p}$, and C'' such that C' and C'' are tail-recursive.

A choreographic configuration $\langle C, \Sigma, \mathscr{C} \rangle$ is tail-recursive if C is tail-recursive and the bodies of the procedure definitions in $\mathscr{C}$ are tail-recursive.

We now show that EPP maps tail-recursive choreographies to starvation-free implementations. First, we formulate starvation-freedom for Recursive Processes.

Definition 8.43 (Starvation-Freedom)   A configuration $\langle N, \Sigma, \mathscr{P} \rangle$ is *starvation-free* if, for all its multi-step derivatives $\langle N', \Sigma', \mathscr{P} \rangle$ and process names p, $p \in \text{supp}(N')$ implies that there exist $\vec{\mu}$, μ, N'', and Σ'' such that $p \in \text{pn}(\mu)$ and $\langle N', \Sigma', \mathscr{P} \rangle \xrightarrow{\vec{\mu}} \xrightarrow{\mu} \langle N'', \Sigma'', \mathscr{P} \rangle$.

Second, following a similar strategy to the one for deadlock-freedom, we prove that every process in a well-formed, projectable, and tail-recursive choreography can eventually participate in a transition.

Lemma 8.44   Let $\langle C, \Sigma, \mathscr{C} \rangle$ be a configuration and r be a process name such that C is tail-recursive and projectable, $\langle C, \Sigma, \mathscr{C} \rangle$ is well-formed, and r $\in$ pn(C). Then, there exist $\vec{\mu}$, μ, and $\langle C', \Sigma', \mathscr{C} \rangle$ such that $\langle C, \Sigma, \mathscr{C} \rangle \xrightarrow{\vec{\mu}} \xrightarrow{\mu} \langle C', \Sigma', \mathscr{C} \rangle$ and r $\in$ pn(μ).

Proof   Since $\langle C, \Sigma, \mathscr{C} \rangle$ is well-formed, $\mathcal{D} :: \langle \mathscr{C}, \{\vec{r}\}, C \rangle \checkmark$ for some $\mathcal{D}$ and $\vec{r}$. We proceed by structural induction on $\mathcal{D}$.

Case 1 $\mathcal{D}$ ends with an application of rule WF-END. This case is trivial, because pn(C) = $\emptyset$.

Case 2 $\mathcal{D}$ ends with an application of rule WF-LOCAL:

$$\mathcal{D} = \frac{\mathsf{p} \in \{\vec{r}\} \quad \overset{\mathcal{D}'}{\langle \mathscr{C}, \{\vec{r}\}, C'' \rangle \checkmark}}{\langle \mathscr{C}, \{\vec{r}\}, \mathsf{p}.x := e; C'' \rangle \checkmark} \text{ WF-LOCAL}$$

for some p, x, e, C'', and $\mathcal{D}'$. By rule LOCAL,

$$\langle \mathsf{p}.x := e; C'', \Sigma, \mathscr{C} \rangle \xrightarrow{\tau @ \mathsf{p}} \langle C'', \Sigma[\mathsf{p}.x \mapsto v], \mathscr{C} \rangle$$

for some v. Now we have two subcases, depending on whether r is p.

Case 2.1   If r = p, then the thesis follows by rules REFL, STEP-R, and LOCAL, for

$$\vec{\mu} \triangleq \epsilon \qquad \mu \triangleq \tau @ \mathsf{p} \qquad C' \triangleq C'' \qquad \Sigma' \triangleq \Sigma[\mathsf{p}.x \mapsto v].$$

Case 2.2   If r $\neq$ p, then r $\in$ pn(C''). By induction hypothesis, $\langle C'', \Sigma, \mathscr{C} \rangle \xrightarrow{\vec{\mu}'} \xrightarrow{\mu'} \langle C''', \Sigma'', \mathscr{C} \rangle$ for some μ' such that r $\in$ pn(μ'). The thesis follows by rule STEP-L, for

$$\vec{\mu} \triangleq \tau @ \mathsf{p}, \vec{\mu}' \qquad \mu \triangleq \mu' \qquad C' \triangleq C'''.$$

Case 3 $\mathcal{D}$ ends with an application of rule WF-COM or rule WF-SEL. These cases are similar to Case 2.

Case 4 $\mathcal{D}$ ends with an application of rule WF-COND:

$$\mathcal{D} = \frac{\mathsf{p} \in \{\vec{r}\} \quad \langle \mathscr{C}, \{\vec{r}\}, C_1 \rangle \checkmark \quad \langle \mathscr{C}, \{\vec{r}\}, C_2 \rangle \checkmark \quad \langle \mathscr{C}, \{\vec{r}\}, 0 \rangle \checkmark}{\langle \mathscr{C}, \{\vec{r}\}, \text{if } \mathsf{p}.e \text{ then } C_1 \text{ else } C_2; 0 \rangle \checkmark} \text{ WF-COND}$$

for some p, e, C_1, and C_2. (We know that the continuation of the conditional is 0 because C is tail-recursive.) Projectability of C implies that pn(C_1) \ {p} = pn(C_2) \ {p} – otherwise, the process projections of C on all processes but p would not be mergeable. We have two subcases, depending on whether r is p.

Case 4.1   If r = p, then the thesis follows by rules REFL and STEP-R in combination with either rule COND-THEN or COND-ELSE, for

$$\vec{\mu} \triangleq \epsilon \qquad \mu \triangleq \tau @ \mathsf{p} \qquad \Sigma' \triangleq \Sigma.$$

If $\Sigma(\mathsf{p}) \vdash e \downarrow \textit{true}$, then $C' \triangleq C_1$; otherwise, $C' \triangleq C_2$.

Case 4.2   If r $\neq$ p, then by pn(C_1) \ {p} = pn(C_2) \ {p} we know that r appears in both pn(C_1) and pn(C_2). We proceed as follows:

- Say that r $\in$ pn(C_1) \ {p} and $\Sigma(\mathsf{p}) \vdash e \downarrow \textit{true}$. By induction hypothesis, $\langle C_1, \Sigma, \mathscr{C} \rangle \xrightarrow{\vec{\mu}'} \xrightarrow{\mu'} \langle C''', \Sigma'', \mathscr{C} \rangle$ for some μ' such that r $\in$ pn(μ'). The thesis follows by rules STEP-L and COND-THEN, for

$$\vec{\mu} \triangleq \tau @ \mathsf{p}, \vec{\mu}' \qquad \mu \triangleq \mu' \qquad C' \triangleq C'''.$$

- Say that $r \in pn(C_1) \setminus \{p\}$ and $\Sigma(p) \vdash e \downarrow v$ for some $v \neq true$. Recall that $pn(C_1) \setminus \{p\} = pn(C_2) \setminus \{p\}$. By induction hypothesis, $\langle C_2, \Sigma, \mathscr{C} \rangle \xrightarrow{\vec{\mu}'} \xrightarrow{\mu'} \langle C''', \Sigma'', \mathscr{C} \rangle$ for some μ' such that $r \in pn(\mu')$. The thesis follows by rules STEP-L and COND-ELSE, for

$$\vec{\mu} \triangleq \tau @ p, \vec{\mu}' \qquad \mu \triangleq \mu' \qquad C' \triangleq C'''.$$

Case 5 $\mathcal{D}$ ends with an application of rule WF-CALL:

$$\mathcal{D} = \frac{\text{distinct}(\vec{p}) \quad \{\vec{p}\} \subseteq \{\vec{r}\}}{X(\vec{q}) = C'' \in \mathscr{C} \quad |\vec{p}| = |\vec{q}| \quad \langle \mathscr{C}, \{\vec{r}\}, \mathbf{0} \rangle \checkmark}{\langle \mathscr{C}, \{\vec{r}\}, X(\vec{p}); \mathbf{0} \rangle \checkmark} \text{ WF-CALL}$$

for some $\vec{p}$, $\vec{q}$, X, and C''. (As in the previous case, we know that the continuation of the procedure call is $\mathbf{0}$ because C is tail-recursive.)

Since $r \in \vec{p}$, the thesis follows by rules SINGLE and CALL-FIRST, following reasoning similar to the previous cases. Notice that here we know that we can apply rule CALL-FIRST because of the checks performed by rule WF-CALL.

Case 6 $\mathcal{D}$ ends with an application of rule WF-RT-CALL. This case is similar to Case 5. If r is one of the processes waiting to enter the procedure invocation, we apply either rule CALL-ENTER or rule CALL-LAST. Otherwise, the thesis follows by induction hypothesis and rule DELAY-MULTI. □

Finally, we use Lemma 8.44 to demonstrate that tail-recursive choreographies are projected to starvation-free implementations.

Theorem 8.45 Let $\langle C, \Sigma, \mathscr{C} \rangle$ be a well-formed configuration such that C is tail-recursive. Then, $\langle [\![C]\!], \Sigma, [\![\mathscr{C}]\!] \rangle$ is starvation-free.

Proof As for the proof of Theorem 8.41, we follow a strategy similar to that for Theorem 4.14. For any multi-step derivative of $\langle [\![C]\!], \Sigma, [\![\mathscr{C}]\!] \rangle$, Theorem 8.33 gives us a corresponding choreographic configuration, which we know to be well-formed by Theorem 8.29. We conclude by Lemma 8.44 and Theorem 8.33. □

Part III

Extensions and Variations

In this part, we discuss how the theory of Recursive Choreographies can be extended to deal with additional communication patterns of practical interest.

Some of these extensions are *conservative* in the sense that they do not add any new kinds of behaviour. Specifically, we shall formalise them as *syntactic sugar* – that is, we will add new choreographic constructs and present how they can be appropriately translated to terms in the language of Recursive Choreographies. This strategy is conveniently economic: once the 'sugared' choreographies are translated to Recursive Choreographies, we can use the semantics of the latter for modelling execution just as before. Likewise, we do not need to update the theories of processes and endpoint projection to reason about implementations. We discuss some conservative extensions in Chapter 9.

Other extensions are not conservative and instead require going through the recipe that we have followed in the development of the languages in Part II. That is, they might require modifications to the syntax or semantics of the choreographic and process languages and also to the definition of projection. We present two non-conservative extensions in particular: choreographic choice (Chapter 10), which allows for modelling first-come, first-served protocols, and asynchronous communications (Chapter 11), whereby send actions do not require synchronising with the intended receiver (communication happens in two steps). Proving the correctness of these non-conservative extensions follows the same strategy seen in Chapter 8. We do not detail these proofs, but report the interesting definitions and intuition.

We conclude the book in Chapter 12 with a discussion on alternative designs and other features, including pointers to material for further reading.

9 Conservative Extensions

We define the language of Enriched Choreographies, denoted **EnrichedChor**, a conservative extension of Recursive Choreographies obtained by adding new instructions that make choreographies easier to read or to express. These new instructions are given as shortcut notation ('syntactic sugar') for terms in Recursive Choreographies.

For now, the grammar of Enriched Choreographies is exactly that of Recursive Choreographies. The new instructions are presented incrementally in the rest of this chapter. Comprehensiveness is not an objective: we intentionally present a small number of extensions since our aim is to showcase a technique for introducing syntactic sugar. Some suggestions for additional extensions are given at the end of the chapter.

We formalise how they can be interpreted in terms of Recursive Choreographies by defining the translation:

$$\lfloor \rfloor : \textbf{EnrichedChor} \longrightarrow \textbf{RecursiveChor}.$$

Given a choreography C in Enriched Choreographies, we call $\lfloor C \rfloor$ the *desugaring*, or *expansion*, of C. Desugaring tells us how to map terms in Enriched Choreographies to terms in Recursive Choreographies. For terms in Recursive Choreographies, the translation is defined as an identity:

$$\lfloor p.x := e; C \rfloor \triangleq p.x := e; \lfloor C \rfloor$$

$$\lfloor p.e \rightarrow q.x; C \rfloor \triangleq p.e \rightarrow q.x; \lfloor C \rfloor$$

$$\lfloor p \rightarrow q[\text{L}]; C \rfloor \triangleq p \rightarrow q[\text{L}]; \lfloor C \rfloor$$

$$\lfloor \text{if } p.e \text{ then } C_1 \text{ else } C_2; C \rfloor \triangleq \text{if } p.e \text{ then} \lfloor C_1 \rfloor \text{ else} \lfloor C_2 \rfloor; \lfloor C \rfloor$$

$$\lfloor X(\vec{p}); C \rfloor \triangleq X(\vec{p}); \lfloor C \rfloor$$

$$\lfloor 0 \rfloor \triangleq 0.$$

Desugaring of choreographies extends naturally to desugaring of sets of procedure definitions, as follows.

$$\lfloor \{X_i(\vec{p}_i) = C_i\}_{i \in I} \rfloor \triangleq \{X_i(\vec{p}_i) = \lfloor C_i \rfloor\}_{i \in I}$$

In the next sections, we present a few new instructions and their desugaring.

9.1 Request-Reply Interactions

Recall the choreography from (5.6), where Buyer gets the price for a book from Seller:

$$\textsf{Buyer}.title \rightarrow \textsf{Seller}.x; \textsf{Seller}.cat(x) \rightarrow \textsf{Buyer}.price. \tag{9.1}$$

This is an instance of the *Request-Reply* pattern: Buyer is making a request and Seller is replying [Hohpe & Woolf 2004].

Request-Reply is natively supported by several languages for the composition of web services, sometimes under the name of *Request-Response* or *remote procedure call* [OASIS 2007; Montesi et al. 2014; gRPC Authors 2022]. In these applications, the replier might engage in further communications and internal computations in order to produce the reply. We can syntactically capture this pattern by augmenting the syntax of Enriched Choreographies as follows:

$$I ::= \cdots \mid \mathsf{p}.\overset{e}{y} \rightleftarrows \mathsf{q}.\overset{x}{e'}\{C\},$$

where $\cdots$ means that this is an extension to the grammar of I (all options defined before for I in Recursive Choreographies are still available).

A Request-Reply $\mathsf{p}.\overset{e}{y} \rightleftarrows \mathsf{q}.\overset{x}{e'}\{C\}$ consists of three parts:

1. p communicates the request obtained by evaluating e to q, which stores it in variable x.
2. The choreography C is run.
3. Finally, q communicates the response obtained by evaluating e' to p, which stores it in variable y.

We abbreviate $\mathsf{p}.\overset{e}{y} \rightleftarrows \mathsf{q}.\overset{x}{e'}\{0\}$ as $\mathsf{p}.\overset{e}{y} \rightleftarrows \mathsf{q}.\overset{x}{e'}$.

With our syntactic sugar for Request-Reply, the choreography in (9.1) can be expressed as:

$$\text{Buyer.}\overset{title}{price} \rightleftarrows \text{Seller.}\overset{x}{cat(x)}. \tag{9.2}$$

The expansion of Request-Reply is defined by the equation

$$\lfloor \mathsf{p}.\overset{e}{y} \rightleftarrows \mathsf{q}.\overset{x}{e'}\{C\}; C' \rfloor \triangleq \mathsf{p}.e \rightarrow \mathsf{q}.y; (\lfloor C \rfloor \, \mathring{,} \, (\mathsf{q}.e' \rightarrow \mathsf{p}.x; \lfloor C' \rfloor)).$$

Therefore, the expansion of the choreography in (9.2) is the choreography in (9.1):

$$\lfloor \text{Buyer.}\overset{title}{price} \rightleftarrows \text{Seller.}\overset{x}{cat(x)} \rfloor$$

$$= \text{Buyer.}title \rightarrow \text{Seller.}x; \text{Seller.}cat(x) \rightarrow \text{Buyer.}price.$$

The next example refers to the programming paradigm of *microservices*, in which the components of an applications are fine-grained microservices (modelled as processes in the example) that interact by message passing [Dragoni et al. 2017].

Example 9.1   A Client requests information about a movie from a Website, expecting a description of the movie and user ratings. The website adopts a microservice architecture: movie descriptions and ratings are handled by separate services, respectively Descriptions and Ratings. We model this with the next choreography.

$$\text{Client.}\overset{movie}{info} \rightleftarrows \text{Website.}\overset{movie}{mkInfo(desc, ratings)}\{$$

$$\qquad \text{Website.}\overset{movie}{desc} \rightleftarrows \text{Descriptions.}\overset{movie}{description(movie)};$$

$$\qquad \text{Website.}\overset{movie}{ratings} \rightleftarrows \text{Ratings.}\overset{movie}{ratings(movie)} \tag{9.3}$$

$$\}$$

The choreography uses some local functions, for which we assume that: *mkInfo* composes a movie description and user rating data into an information page for Client; *description* returns the description of a movie; and *ratings* returns the user ratings for a movie.

Exercise 9.1   Write the desugaring of the choreography in (9.3).

9.2   Destructuring Messages

Consider the case in which a process p communicates a pair, which consists of a person's name and age, to a process q:

$$p.(\text{"Homer"}, 42) \rightarrow q.x.$$

Process q can then access the two elements of the pair by using a projection function, say π. Here, we assume that $\pi(i, t)$ returns the i-th element of tuple t:

$$q.name := \pi(1, x);$$
$$q.age := \pi(2, x).$$

This method is known as *destructuring*. Destructuring happens so often that many programming languages provide syntactic sugar for it, and we can do the same for Enriched Choreographies. In our case specifically, it makes sense to allow for destructuring right in communication terms, as follows.

$$I ::= \cdots \mid p.(e_1, \cdots, e_n) \rightarrow q.(x_1, \cdots, x_n)$$

Assume that, for any natural number n, there exists a function $mkTuple_n$ for constructing a tuple from the values that it is passed as arguments: for all n and values $v_1, \ldots, v_n$, we require $\vdash mkTuple_n(v_1, \ldots, v_n) \downarrow (v_1, \ldots, v_n)$. Also, let $\vdash \pi(i, (v_1, \ldots, v_i, \ldots, v_n)) \downarrow v_i$ for every i, n, and tuple $(v_1, \ldots, v_i, \ldots, v_n)$. The desugaring of a destructuring communication term can then be formulated as the following equation.

$$\lfloor p.(e_1, \cdots, e_n) \rightarrow q.(x_1, \cdots, x_n); C \rfloor$$
$$\triangleq p.mkTuple_n(e_1, \cdots, e_n) \rightarrow q.y; q.x_1 := \pi(y, 1); \cdots ; q.x_n := \pi(y, n); \lfloor C \rfloor$$

Example 9.2   Recall the choreography from Example 5.1, where a Buyer inquires about the price a book at a Seller:

$$\text{Buyer}.title \rightarrow \text{Seller}.x; \text{Seller}.cat(x) \rightarrow \text{Buyer}.price.$$

We extend the choreography such that:
- The Buyer, in addition to the title, communicates also a possible discount code.
- The Seller, in addition to the price, replies also with the reviews that the book has gotten so far.

The extension follows.

$$\text{Buyer}.(title, code) \rightarrow \text{Seller}.(title, code);$$
$$\text{Seller}.(cat(title, code), reviews(title)) \rightarrow \text{Buyer}.(price, r) \tag{9.4}$$

Exercise 9.2   Write the desugaring of the choreography in (9.4).

9.3   Distributed Conditions

Conditionals allow for choosing between alternative choreographies depending on the state of a single process. An intuitive generalisation of this construct is to allow for conditions that span multiple processes. Here, we consider *distributed and-conditions*, which we obtain by extending the syntax of conditionals as follows.

$$I ::= \cdots \mid \text{if } p_1.e_1 \text{ and } \cdots \text{ and } p_n.e_n \text{ then } C_1 \text{ else } C_2$$

A *distributed conditional* if $p_1.e_1$ and $\cdots$ and $p_n.e_n$ then C_1 else C_2 executes C_1 if, for $i \in [1, n]$, each condition e_i evaluates to *true* in the state of its respective process p_i; otherwise, it executes C_2.

The equation in (9.5) demonstrates how to expand a distributed conditional under the typical *short-circuit evaluation* of mainstream programming languages.

$$
\begin{vmatrix}
\text{if } p_1.e_1 \text{ and } \cdots \text{ and } p_n.e_n \text{ then} \\
\quad C_1 \\
\text{else} \\
\quad C_2; \\
C
\end{vmatrix}
=
\begin{aligned}
&(\text{if } p_1.e_1 \text{ then} \\
&\quad p_1 \rightarrow p_2[\text{T}]; \\
&\quad \text{if } p_2.e_2 \text{ then} \\
&\quad\quad p_2 \rightarrow p_3[\text{T}]; \\
&\quad\quad \text{if } p_3.e_3 \text{ then} \\
&\quad\quad\quad \cdots \\
&\quad\quad\quad \text{if } p_n.e_n \text{ then} \lfloor C_1 \rfloor \text{else } \lfloor C_2 \rfloor \\
&\quad\quad\quad \text{else } p_3 \rightarrow p_4[\text{E}]; \cdots ; p_{n-1} \rightarrow p_n[\text{E}]; \lfloor C_2 \rfloor \\
&\quad\quad \text{else } p_2 \rightarrow p_3[\text{E}]; \cdots ; p_{n-1} \rightarrow p_n[\text{E}]; \lfloor C_2 \rfloor \\
&\quad \text{else } p_1 \rightarrow p_2[\text{E}]; \cdots ; p_{n-1} \rightarrow p_n[\text{E}]; \lfloor C_2 \rfloor); \\
&\lfloor C \rfloor
\end{aligned}
\tag{9.5}
$$

Starting from process p_1, each process evaluates its own condition and communicates the selection of label T (for 'then branch') to the next process. If all conditions evaluate to *true*, C_1 is executed. Otherwise, as soon as a condition does not evaluate to *true*, the current process informs the next process that the entire distributed condition cannot possibly hold. This is done by communicating the selection of label E (for 'else branch') to the next process, which communicates the same to the next, and so forth until all processes are informed.

Example 9.3   Alice, Bob, and Carol are considering whether to purchase together an item from a Store, splitting the expense equally (a third each). After getting the price for the item from the Store, they check if they are all willing to proceed, each using their own decision criteria (respectively *approveA*, *approveB*, and *approveC*). Carol is responsible for informing the Store of the final outcome.

This scenario is modelled by the choreography on the left side of Figure 9.1. The desugaring of the choreography is shown on the right side of the same figure.

Store.*getPrice(item)* → Alice.*price*;
Store.*getPrice(item)* → Bob.*price*;
Store.*getPrice(item)* → Carol.*price*;
if Alice.*approveA*(*price*/3) then
   Alice → Bob[T];
   if Bob.*approveB*(*price*/3) then
      Bob → Carol[T];
      if Carol.*approveC*(*price*/3) ther
         Carol → Store[OK]
      else
         Carol → Store[KO]
   else
      Bob → Carol[E];
      Carol → Store[KO]
else
   Alice → Bob[E];
   Bob → Carol[E];
   Carol → Store[KO]

Store.*getPrice(item)* → Alice.*price*;
Store.*getPrice(item)* → Bob.*price*;
Store.*getPrice(item)* → Carol.*price*;
if Alice.*approveA*(*price*/3)
   and Bob.*approveB*(*price*/3)
   and Carol.*approveC*(*price*/3) then
   Carol → Store[OK]
else
   Carol → Store[KO]

Figure 9.1   A choreography with a distributed condition for a three-party purchase (left side) and its desugaring (right side).

10 Choreographic Choice

We introduce *choreographic choice*, another construct for choosing between alternative choreographies. Differently from conditionals, resolving a choreographic choice might require interaction between processes. In other words, the resolution of the choice might be determined by the emerging behaviour of the system, rather than a local decision by a single process.

Choreographic choice enables the implementation of first-come, first-served behaviours. That is, we are interested in choosing whichever choreography can be started first. These behaviours are very useful in practice, for example in the implementation of patterns such as client-server and producers-consumer [Tanenbaum & van Steen 2007].

10.1 From Local to Choreographic Choice

We discuss the feature that conditionals do not cover with a running example.

So far, we have discussed two mechanisms that can affect the order in which choreographic instructions are executed. On the one hand, out of order execution, formalised by the DELAY-rules, allows for observing communications performed by distinct processes in any order. On the other hand, conditionals allows for writing choreographies where a process can locally decide in which order it will interact with other processes. For instance, in the choreography from Example 6.5, Alice nondeterministically chooses whether to receive some news from Bob or Carol first, as we recall next. We refer to this choreography as C_{coin}.

$$C_{\text{coin}} \triangleq \begin{array}{l} \text{if Alice.}flipCoin() \text{ then} \\ \quad \text{Bob.}news \rightarrow \text{Alice.}x; \text{Carol.}news \rightarrow \text{Alice.}y \\ \text{else} \\ \quad \text{Carol.}news \rightarrow \text{Alice.}y; \text{Bob.}news \rightarrow \text{Alice.}x \end{array} \tag{10.1}$$

Not all interesting nondeterministic choreographies can be expressed by means of local conditionals. In particular, a process cannot choose between instructions depending on which one can be executed first. This makes the choreographic languages seen so far unsuitable for the implementation of first-come, first-served patterns. To illustrate this limitation, consider the following augmentation of the choreography in (10.1).

$$\begin{array}{l} \text{Bob.}news := \text{"Bob likes apples"}; \\ \text{Carol.}news := \text{"Carol likes oranges"}; \\ C_{\text{coin}} \end{array} \tag{10.2}$$

We shall abbreviate "Bob likes apples" as v_{Bob} and "Carol likes oranges" as v_{Carol}. In (10.2), Bob and Carol have to do their respective assignments before they are ready to interact with Alice.

By rules LOCAL and DELAY, any of them could complete their assignment first. Say that Carol goes first:

$$\left\langle \begin{matrix} \text{Bob}.news := v_{\text{Bob}}; \\ \text{Carol}.news := v_{\text{Carol}};, \Sigma, \emptyset \\ C_{\text{coin}} \end{matrix} \right\rangle$$

$$\xrightarrow{\tau \, @\text{Carol}} \left\langle \begin{matrix} \text{Bob}.news := v_{\text{Bob}}; \\ C_{\text{coin}} \end{matrix}, \Sigma[\text{Carol}.news \mapsto v_{\text{Carol}}], \emptyset \right\rangle \quad (10.3)$$

for some Σ. In the derivative shown in (10.3), Carol is ready to communicate with Alice and Bob is not. However, this is not taken into consideration in the choice made by Alice in C_{coin}, and Alice may choose to prioritise communicating with Bob anyway (by rules COND-THEN and DELAY):

$$\left\langle \begin{matrix} \text{Bob}.news := v_{\text{Bob}}; \\ C_{\text{coin}} \end{matrix}, \Sigma[\text{Carol}.news \mapsto v_{\text{Carol}}], \emptyset \right\rangle$$

$$\xrightarrow{\tau \, @\text{Alice}} \left\langle \begin{matrix} \text{Bob}.news := v_{\text{Bob}}; \\ \text{Bob}.news \to \text{Alice}.x; , \Sigma[\text{Carol}.news \mapsto v_{\text{Carol}}], \emptyset \\ \text{Carol}.news \to \text{Alice}.y \end{matrix} \right\rangle. \quad (10.4)$$

The transition in (10.4) reveals that the choreography does not implement a first-come, first-served behaviour: Bob should not be given priority since he still has work to do before he can interact with Alice.

Unfortunately, there is no way of tuning the conditional to guarantee that Alice will choose whichever interaction can be performed first. To do it, Alice would need the ability of checking if any of Bob and Carol is ready to go. But only Bob and Carol know when they are ready, so the only way for Alice to know is to interact with them. Since a conditional uses a local expression, and local expressions cannot interact with other processes, using a conditional is hopeless: we need a new way of composing choreographies that allows for interaction. We achieve this through a new operator, choreographic choice, which we study in the remainder of this chapter.

10.2 Choreographies

We extend the language of Recursive Choreographies with a nondeterministic choice operator, obtaining the language of Nondeterministic Recursive Choreographies. The syntax of this language is given in Figure 10.1.

The new term, $C_1 +_p C_2$, reads 'p chooses between C_1 and C_2'. Crucially, and differently from conditionals, the process p can only choose one of the alternative choreographies if that choreography can immediately perform an action that involves p. This is formalised by the new rules for deriving transitions for choreographic choices, given in Figure 10.2.

Rule CHOICE-L continues with the left choreography of a choice, assuming that such choreography can perform a transition (first premise) that involves the process making the choice (second

$$I ::= \cdots \mid C_1 +_p C_2$$

Figure 10.1 Syntax of Nondeterministic Recursive Choreographies, new term for choices.

$$\dfrac{\langle C_1, \Sigma, \mathscr{C}\rangle \xrightarrow{\mu} \langle C_1', \Sigma', \mathscr{C}\rangle \quad \mathsf{p} \in \mathrm{pn}(\mu)}{\langle C_1 +_\mathsf{p} C_2; C, \Sigma, \mathscr{C}\rangle \xrightarrow{\mu} \langle C_1' \,\mathring{\,\S\,}\, C, \Sigma', \mathscr{C}\rangle} \;\text{\small CHOICE-L} \qquad \dfrac{\langle C_2, \Sigma, \mathscr{C}\rangle \xrightarrow{\mu} \langle C_2', \Sigma', \mathscr{C}\rangle \quad \mathsf{p} \in \mathrm{pn}(\mu)}{\langle C_1 +_\mathsf{p} C_2; C, \Sigma, \mathscr{C}\rangle \xrightarrow{\mu} \langle C_2' \,\mathring{\,\S\,}\, C, \Sigma', \mathscr{C}\rangle} \;\text{\small CHOICE-R}$$

$$\dfrac{\langle C_1, \Sigma, \mathscr{C}\rangle \xrightarrow{\mu} \langle C_1', \Sigma', \mathscr{C}\rangle \quad \langle C_2, \Sigma, \mathscr{C}\rangle \xrightarrow{\mu} \langle C_2', \Sigma', \mathscr{C}\rangle \quad \mathsf{p} \notin \mathrm{pn}(\mu)}{\langle C_1 +_\mathsf{p} C_2; C, \Sigma, \mathscr{C}\rangle \xrightarrow{\mu} \langle C_1' +_\mathsf{p} C_2'; C, \Sigma', \mathscr{C}\rangle} \;\text{\small DELAY-CHOICE}$$

Figure 10.2 Semantics of Nondeterministic Recursive Choreographies, new rules for choices.

premise). Dually, rule CHOICE-R continues with the right choreography of a choice under the same assumptions. Finally, rule DELAY-CHOICE allows for executing instructions that appear inside of a choice but do not actually depend on it. The reasoning behind the rule is essentially the same seen for rule DELAY-COND in Section 6.1.1.

Example 10.1   Let C_1 and C_2 be the two branches of the conditional in (10.2):

$$C_1 \triangleq \mathsf{Bob}.news \to \mathsf{Alice}.x; \mathsf{Carol}.news \to \mathsf{Alice}.y$$
$$C_2 \triangleq \mathsf{Carol}.news \to \mathsf{Alice}.y; \mathsf{Bob}.news \to \mathsf{Alice}.x.$$

Using choreographic choice, we can rewrite the choreography in (10.2) as follows (v_{Bob} and v_{Carol} are as in Section 6.1.1).

$$C \triangleq \begin{array}{l} \mathsf{Bob}.news := v_{\mathsf{Bob}}; \\ \mathsf{Carol}.news := v_{\mathsf{Carol}}; \\ (C_1 +_{\mathsf{Alice}} C_2) \end{array} \tag{10.5}$$

In this choreography, Alice chooses to interact with either Bob or Carol but gives priority to whoever is ready first. Let us verify that by following the same trail seen in Section 10.1.

Let Σ be any choreographic store. An execution of the choreography C might start in two ways: either Bob completes his assignment or Carol does. In the second case, we have this transition:

$$\langle C, \Sigma, \emptyset\rangle \xrightarrow{\;\tau\,@\,\mathsf{Carol}\;} \langle \mathsf{Bob}.news := v_{\mathsf{Bob}}; (C_1 +_{\mathsf{Alice}} C_2), \Sigma', \emptyset\rangle \tag{10.6}$$

where $\Sigma' \triangleq \Sigma[\mathsf{Carol}.news \mapsto v_{\mathsf{Carol}}]$.

Since Carol is ready to interact with Alice now, the latter can resolve the choice in Carol's favour. We show the derivation of the transition to exemplify the interplay between choice and out-of-order execution:

$$\dfrac{\dfrac{\dfrac{\Sigma'(\mathsf{Carol}) \vdash news \downarrow v_{\mathsf{Carol}}}{\langle C_2, \Sigma', \emptyset\rangle \xrightarrow{\;\mathsf{Carol}.v_{\mathsf{Carol}} \to \mathsf{Alice}\;} \langle \mathsf{Bob}.news \to \mathsf{Alice}.x, \Sigma'', \emptyset\rangle}\;\text{\small COM}}{\langle C_1 +_{\mathsf{Alice}} C_2, \Sigma', \emptyset\rangle \xrightarrow{\;\mathsf{Carol}.v_{\mathsf{Carol}} \to \mathsf{Alice}\;} \langle \mathsf{Bob}.news \to \mathsf{Alice}.x, \Sigma'', \emptyset\rangle}\;\text{\small CHOICE-R} \qquad \{\mathsf{Bob}\}\,\#\,\{\mathsf{Carol}, \mathsf{Alice}\}}{\langle \mathsf{Bob}.news := v_{\mathsf{Bob}}; (C_1 +_{\mathsf{Alice}} C_2), \Sigma', \emptyset\rangle \xrightarrow{\;\mathsf{Carol}.v_{\mathsf{Carol}} \to \mathsf{Alice}\;} \langle \mathsf{Bob}.news := v_{\mathsf{Bob}}; \mathsf{Bob}.news \to \mathsf{Alice}.x, \Sigma'', \emptyset\rangle}\;\text{\small DELAY}$$

for $\Sigma'' \triangleq \Sigma'[\text{Alice}.y \mapsto v_{\text{Carol}}]$. Notice that, crucially, this is the only possible transition that involves Alice. Rule DELAY would not allow for resolving the choice in Bob's favour yet, because that depends on a transition that mentions Bob in its label.

An alternative execution from the derivative in (10.6) is the one where we run Bob's assignment, as follows.

$$\langle \text{Bob}.news := v_{\text{Bob}}; (C_1 +_{\text{Alice}} C_2), \Sigma', \emptyset \rangle$$

$$\xrightarrow{\ \tau\,@\text{Carol}\ } \langle \text{Bob}.news := v_{\text{Bob}}; (C_1 +_{\text{Alice}} C_2), \Sigma''', \emptyset \rangle \quad (10.7)$$

where $\Sigma''' \triangleq \Sigma'[\text{Bob}.news \mapsto v_{\text{Bob}}]$. From the derivative in (10.7), the choice can go either way now. That is, it can be resolved in Bob's or Carol's favour since both are ready to interact with Alice.

Exercise 10.1 Let C be the choreography in (10.5) and Σ be a choreographic store. Draw the graphical representation of the lts generated by the configuration $\langle C, \Sigma, \emptyset \rangle$.

Example 10.2 A *barrier* is a synchronisation method for a group of processes: processes reach the barrier in any order and must wait before proceeding in their executions until all processes have reached the barrier [Goetz et al. 2006].

We can define a choreography for this behaviour by using a process, say b, that implements the barrier using choreographic choices. For example, for a barrier that handles a group of two processes (say p_1 and p_2), we can write the following procedure, *Barrier2*.

$$\begin{aligned}
Barrier2(b, p_1, p_2) = &(p_1 \rightarrow b[\text{ENTER}]; p_2 \rightarrow b[\text{ENTER}] \\
&+_b p_2 \rightarrow b[\text{ENTER}]; p_1 \rightarrow b[\text{ENTER}]); \\
&(b \rightarrow p_1[\text{GO}]; b \rightarrow p_2[\text{GO}] \\
&+_b b \rightarrow p_2[\text{GO}]; b \rightarrow p_1[\text{GO}])
\end{aligned} \quad (10.8)$$

Procedure *Barrier2* has two choreographic choices. The first allows the processes p_1 and p_2 to reach the barrier in any order. Reaching the barrier is represented by the selections of label ENTER. The second choice denotes that the barrier makes no preference in which process is informed first that all processes can now go forward.

Observe that no process can receive the GO label from b before all processes arrive at the barrier: all interactions in the first choice involve b, so rule DELAY is not applicable.

Exercise 10.2 Let $\mathscr{C}$ contain the procedure definition in (10.8) and Σ be a choreographic store. Draw the graphical representation of the lts generated by the configuration $\langle Barrier2(b, p_1, p_2), \Sigma, \mathscr{C} \rangle$.

Example 10.3 Suppose that p_1 and p_2 are processes that compete to gain access to a shared resource managed by another process s. We can represent this scenario with the following choreography.

$$(p_1 \rightarrow s[\text{REQ}]; s \rightarrow p_1[\text{OK}]; W(p_1, s); p_2 \rightarrow s[\text{REQ}]; s \rightarrow p_2[\text{KO}])$$
$$+_s \tag{10.9}$$
$$(p_2 \rightarrow s[\text{REQ}]; s \rightarrow p_2[\text{OK}]; W(p_2, s); p_1 \rightarrow s[\text{REQ}]; s \rightarrow p_1[\text{KO}])$$

In (10.9), p_1 and p_2 request access to s by communicating label REQ. Process s communicates the selection of label OK to whichever process wins the race and then the winner and s enter procedure W (the work that the winner and s have to do together). The process that does not win the race receives label KO, so it knows that it lost and that it should not enter procedure W.

Example 10.4 We can modify the choreography in (10.9) such that the shared resource can be used multiple times, for example as in the following recursive procedure definition (X).

$$X(s, p_1, p_2) = (p_1 \rightarrow s[\text{REQ}]; s \rightarrow p_1[\text{OK}]; W(p_1, s); p_2 \rightarrow s[\text{REQ}]; s \rightarrow p_2[\text{KO}]$$
$$+_s p_2 \rightarrow s[\text{REQ}]; s \rightarrow p_2[\text{OK}]; W(p_2, s); p_1 \rightarrow s[\text{REQ}]; s \rightarrow p_1[\text{KO}]); \tag{10.10}$$
$$X(s, p_1, p_2)$$

Example 10.5 In 10.10, each round of the competition p_1 and p_2 can go either way. This means that one of the two processes might win many rounds in a row. If this is not desired, we can enforce that both p_1 and p_2 are guaranteed access to the shared resource in each round, without fixing the order of which of them goes first in each round. We define such behaviour in the following procedure.

$$X(s, p_1, p_2) = (p_1 \rightarrow s[\text{REQ}]; W(p_1, s); p_2 \rightarrow s[\text{REQ}]; W(p_2, s)$$
$$+_s p_2 \rightarrow s[\text{REQ}]; W(p_2, s); p_1 \rightarrow s[\text{REQ}]; W(p_1, s) \tag{10.11}$$
$$X(s, p_1, p_2)$$

10.3 Processes

To support choreographic choice at the process level, we extend the grammar of instructions with a binary operator for choices between processes, written +. We call the resulting language *Nondeterministic Recursive Processes*. The syntax is shown in Figure 10.3.

A (process) choice $P + Q$ behaves as P or as Q. The rules that define the semantics of this operator are similar to those for choreographic choice and are given in Figure 10.4.

In rule CHOICE-L, a choice $P + Q$ is resolved in favour of P if P can perform a transition. If P starts with a communication action, then performing the transition requires an appropriate network context as well. This justifies the inclusion of N in the premise, with the requirement

$$I ::= \cdots \mid P + Q$$

Figure 10.3 Syntax of Nondeterministic Recursive Processes, new term for choices.

$$\frac{\langle \mathsf{p}[P] \mid N, \Sigma, \mathscr{P}\rangle \xrightarrow{\mu} \langle \mathsf{p}[P'] \mid N', \Sigma', \mathscr{P}\rangle \quad \{\mathsf{p}\} \cup \mathrm{supp}(N) = \mathrm{pn}(\mu)}{\langle \mathsf{p}[(P+Q);R] \mid N, \Sigma, \mathscr{P}\rangle \xrightarrow{\mu} \langle \mathsf{p}[P' \,\mathring{,}\, R] \mid N', \Sigma', \mathscr{P}\rangle} \text{ \footnotesize CHOICE-L}$$

$$\frac{\langle \mathsf{p}[Q] \mid N, \Sigma, \mathscr{P}\rangle \xrightarrow{\mu} \langle \mathsf{p}[Q'] \mid N', \Sigma', \mathscr{P}\rangle \quad \{\mathsf{p}\} \cup \mathrm{supp}(N) = \mathrm{pn}(\mu)}{\langle \mathsf{p}[(P+Q);R] \mid N, \Sigma, \mathscr{P}\rangle \xrightarrow{\mu} \langle \mathsf{p}[Q' \,\mathring{,}\, R] \mid N', \Sigma', \mathscr{P}\rangle} \text{ \footnotesize CHOICE-R}$$

Figure 10.4 Semantics of Nondeterministic Recursive Processes, new rules for choices.

that it is minimal with respect to what is needed for the transition (the condition on the top right). Rule CHOICE-R is equivalent, and deals with the case in which the choice is resolved in favour of Q.

Example 10.6 The following network, N, implements the choreography seen in (10.5):

$$N \triangleq \mathsf{Alice}[P+Q] \mid \mathsf{Bob}[R] \mid \mathsf{Carol}[S]$$

where

$$P \triangleq \mathsf{Bob}?x; \mathsf{Carol}?y \qquad\qquad Q \triangleq \mathsf{Carol}?y; \mathsf{Bob}?x$$
$$R \triangleq news := v_{\mathsf{Bob}}; \mathsf{Alice}!news \qquad\qquad S \triangleq news := v_{\mathsf{Carol}}; \mathsf{Alice}!news.$$

The choice at Alice cannot be resolved yet because neither Bob nor Carol is ready to interact. Say that Carol performs her internal assignment first, for some store Σ:

$$\langle N, \Sigma, \emptyset \rangle \xrightarrow{\ \tau\,@\mathsf{Carol}\ } \langle \mathsf{Alice}[P+Q] \mid \mathsf{Bob}[R] \mid \mathsf{Carol}[\mathsf{Alice}!news], \Sigma', \emptyset \rangle$$

where $\Sigma' \triangleq \Sigma[\mathsf{Carol}.news \mapsto v_{\mathsf{Carol}}]$. Now Alice can choose to proceed by executing Q. We show the full derivation to clarify the application of rule CHOICE-R.

$$\frac{\dfrac{\begin{array}{c}\langle \mathsf{Alice}[Q] \mid \mathsf{Carol}[\mathsf{Alice}!news], \Sigma', \emptyset \rangle \\[2pt] \xrightarrow{\ \mathsf{Carol}.v_{\mathsf{Carol}} \to \mathsf{Alice}\ } \langle \mathsf{Alice}[\mathsf{Bob}?y] \mid \mathsf{Carol}[0], \Sigma'', \emptyset \rangle\end{array}\quad \begin{array}{c}\{\mathsf{Alice}\} \cup \{\mathsf{Carol}\} \\[2pt] = \{\mathsf{Alice}, \mathsf{Carol}\}\end{array}}{\begin{array}{c}\langle \mathsf{Alice}[P+Q] \mid \mathsf{Carol}[\mathsf{Alice}!news], \Sigma', \emptyset \rangle \\[2pt] \xrightarrow{\ \mathsf{Carol}.v_{\mathsf{Carol}} \to \mathsf{Alice}\ } \langle \mathsf{Alice}[\mathsf{Bob}?y] \mid \mathsf{Carol}[0], \Sigma'', \emptyset \rangle\end{array}}\ \text{\footnotesize COM} }{\begin{array}{c}\langle \mathsf{Alice}[P+Q] \mid \mathsf{Bob}[R] \mid \mathsf{Carol}[\mathsf{Alice}!news], \Sigma', \emptyset \rangle \\[2pt] \xrightarrow{\ \mathsf{Carol}.v_{\mathsf{Carol}} \to \mathsf{Alice}\ } \langle \mathsf{Alice}[\mathsf{Bob}?y] \mid \mathsf{Bob}[R] \mid \mathsf{Carol}[0], \Sigma'', \emptyset \rangle\end{array}} \begin{array}{l} \\[2pt] \text{\footnotesize CHOICE-R} \\[30pt] \text{\footnotesize PAR}\end{array}$$

where $\Sigma'' \triangleq \Sigma'[\mathsf{Alice}.y \mapsto v_{\mathsf{Carol}}]$.

10.4 Endpoint Projection

Projecting choreographic choices follows the same principle used for projecting conditionals: the process that makes the choice is projected to a choice, whereas all other processes are projected

$$(P + Q) \sqcup (P' + Q') \triangleq (P \sqcup P') + (Q \sqcup Q')$$

$$[\![C_1 +_p C_2; C]\!]_r \triangleq \begin{cases} [\![C_1]\!]_r + [\![C_2]\!]_r; [\![C]\!]_r & \text{if } r = p \\ ([\![C_1]\!]_r \sqcup [\![C_2]\!]_r) \mathbin{;} [\![C]\!]_r & \text{otherwise} \end{cases}$$

Figure 10.5 Merging and process projection for Nondeterministic Recursive Choreographies, new rules.

to the merging of the projections of the two branches. The new rules for merging and process projection are shown in Figure 10.5.

Example 10.7   Let C be as in Example 10.1 and N be as in Example 10.6. Then, $[\![C]\!] = N$.

Exercise 10.3   Let C be as in Example 10.1, N be as in Example 10.6, and Σ be a store. Show that the graphical representations of the labelled transition systems generated by $\langle C, \Sigma, \emptyset \rangle$ and $\langle N, \Sigma, \emptyset \rangle$ are isomorphic.

Exercise 10.4   Write the EPP of the set of procedure definitions that consists exactly of the procedure definition in (10.8).

Exercise 10.5   Write the EPP of the choreography in (10.9).

Exercise 10.6   Write the EPP of the set of procedure definitions that consists exactly of the procedure definition in (10.10).

Exercise 10.7   Write the EPP of the set of procedure definitions that consists exactly of the procedure definition in (10.11).

11 Asynchronous Communication

Communication in Recursive Choreographies is *synchronous*: a sending action blocks the sender until it can interact with a compatible receiving action at the intended receiver. In this chapter, we consider an alternative semantics for interactions: *asynchronous communication*.

Asynchronous communication allows for a sending action to be executed without waiting for the receiver to be ready. The key idea is that the message from the sender can be immediately stored in a *message queue*, from which the intended receiver can later retrieve the message. We shall see that the adoption of asynchronous communication can yield additional executions compared to synchronous communication.

11.1   Choreographies

Let us start by defining Asynchronous Recursive Choreographies: a choreographic language based on asynchronous communication. The syntax for writing choreographies in this language is the same as that of the language of Recursive Choreographies (Figure 11.1). However, in order to define a semantics, we add two runtime terms. Specifically, we extend the syntax of instructions as shown in Figure 11.1.

Runtime terms are used to represent intermediate states of execution, where a process has sent a message but the intended receiver still has to retrieve it. The first runtime term, $p \rightsquigarrow q.x$, reads 'q receives a value that has been previously sent by p, storing it in variable x'. The second runtime term, $p \rightsquigarrow q[L]$, reads 'q receives the selection of label L that has been previously sent by p'.

Function pn is extended to the new terms by adding the following equations, which tell us which process is involved in each term.

$$\mathrm{pn}(p \rightsquigarrow q.x) \triangleq \{q\} \qquad\qquad \mathrm{pn}(p \rightsquigarrow q[L]) \triangleq \{q\}$$

To define a semantics for Asynchronous Recursive Choreographies, we introduce *message queues*. Let m range over *asynchronous messages*, as specified by the grammar in what follows.

$$m ::= (p, v) \mid (p, L)$$

$$I ::= \cdots \mid p \rightsquigarrow q.x \mid p \rightsquigarrow q[L]$$

Figure 11.1   Syntax of Asynchronous Recursive Choreographies, new terms for asynchronous communication.

A message m can be one of the following:

- A value v sent by a process p, denoted (p, v).
- A label L sent by a process p, denoted (p, L).

We model a message queue simply as a sequence of messages, denoted $\vec{m}$. We use the comma notation for composing and extending message sequences, just like we do for sequences of labels. In particular, for any m and $\vec{m}$ such that $\vec{m} = m_1, \ldots, m_n$ for some $m_1, \ldots, m_n$, we have the following equations.

$$\vec{m}, m = m_1, \ldots, m_n, m$$
$$m, \vec{m} = m, m_1, \ldots, m_n$$
$$\vec{m}, \epsilon = \vec{m}$$
$$\epsilon, \vec{m} = \vec{m}$$

Let **Queue** be the set of all message queues. A *messaging state*, denoted K, is a function that maps every process name to a queue:

$$K: \textbf{PName} \longrightarrow \textbf{Queue}.$$

A messaging state keeps track of which messages have been sent and still need to be retrieved by the intended receiver. To update messaging states, we define a notation similar to that for updating stores. Namely, we write $K[p \mapsto \vec{m}]$ for the messaging state that maps p to $\vec{m}$ and otherwise is as K:

$$K[q \mapsto \vec{m}](p) \triangleq \begin{cases} \vec{m} & \text{if } p = q \\ K(p) & \text{otherwise} \end{cases}.$$

The semantics of Asynchronous Recursive Choreographies defines transitions for configurations of the form $\langle C, \Sigma, K, \mathscr{C} \rangle$. The novelty, compared to configurations in Recursive Choreographies, is the presence of messaging states. Transitions labels are different as well. Specifically, the labels $p.v \rightarrow q$ and $p \rightarrow q[L]$ are replaced by labels that represent sending and receiving messages (as separate steps), where we use ! to denote sending and ? to denote receiving (recalling the syntax of processes):

- $p.v \rightarrow q!$, read 'p sends the value v to q'.
- $p.v \rightarrow q?$, read 'q receives the value v from p'.
- $p \rightarrow q[L]!$, read 'p sends the selection of label L to q'.
- $p \rightarrow q[L]?$, read 'q receives the selection of label L from p'.

Function pn for transition labels is updated with the following equations.

$$\text{pn}(p.v \rightarrow q!) \triangleq \{p\} \qquad\qquad \text{pn}(p.v \rightarrow q?) \triangleq \{q\}$$
$$\text{pn}(p \rightarrow q[L]!) \triangleq \{p\} \qquad\qquad \text{pn}(p \rightarrow q[L]?) \triangleq \{q\}$$

According to our new equations for pn, only the sender is involved in a sending action, and only the receiver is involved in a receiving action.

The inference rules for deriving transitions are given in Figure 11.2. Compared to the semantics of Recursive Choreographies, we have the following changes:

$$\frac{\Sigma(p) \vdash e \downarrow v}{\langle p.x := e; C, \Sigma, K, \mathscr{C} \rangle \xrightarrow{\tau@p} \langle C, \Sigma[p.x \mapsto v], K, \mathscr{C} \rangle} \text{ LOCAL}$$

$$\frac{\Sigma(p) \vdash e \downarrow v \quad K(q) = \vec{m}}{\langle p.e \to q.x; C, \Sigma, K, \mathscr{C} \rangle \xrightarrow{p.v \to q!} \langle p \leadsto q.x; C, \Sigma[q.x \mapsto v], K[q \mapsto \vec{m}, (p, v)], \mathscr{C} \rangle} \text{ SEND-VAL}$$

$$\frac{K(q) = (p, v), \vec{m}}{\langle p \leadsto q.x; C, \Sigma, K, \mathscr{C} \rangle \xrightarrow{p.v \to q?} \langle C, \Sigma[q.x \mapsto v], K[q \mapsto \vec{m}], \mathscr{C} \rangle} \text{ RECV-VAL}$$

$$\frac{K(q) = \vec{m}}{\langle p \to q[L]; C, \Sigma, K, \mathscr{C} \rangle \xrightarrow{p \to q[L]!} \langle p \leadsto q[L]; C, \Sigma, K[q \mapsto \vec{m}, (p, L)], \mathscr{C} \rangle} \text{ SEND-SEL}$$

$$\frac{K(q) = (p, L), \vec{m}}{\langle p \leadsto q[L]; C, \Sigma, K, \mathscr{C} \rangle \xrightarrow{p \to q[L]?} \langle C, \Sigma, K[q \mapsto \vec{m}], \mathscr{C} \rangle} \text{ RECV-SEL}$$

$$\frac{\Sigma(p) \vdash e \downarrow \textit{true}}{\langle \text{if } p.e \text{ then } C_1 \text{ else } C_2; C, \Sigma, K, \mathscr{C} \rangle \xrightarrow{\tau@p} \langle C_1 \mathbin{\S} C, \Sigma, K, \mathscr{C} \rangle} \text{ COND-THEN}$$

$$\frac{\Sigma(p) \vdash e \downarrow v \quad v \neq \textit{true}}{\langle \text{if } p.e \text{ then } C_1 \text{ else } C_2; C, \Sigma, K, \mathscr{C} \rangle \xrightarrow{\tau@p} \langle C_2 \mathbin{\S} C, \Sigma, K, \mathscr{C} \rangle} \text{ COND-ELSE}$$

$$\frac{X(\vec{q}) = C \in \mathscr{C} \quad r \in \vec{p}}{\langle X(\vec{p}); C', \Sigma, K, \mathscr{C} \rangle \xrightarrow{\tau@r} \langle \vec{p} \setminus r: X(\vec{p}).C'; C[\vec{p}/\vec{q}] \mathbin{\S} C', \Sigma, K, \mathscr{C} \rangle} \text{ CALL-FIRST}$$

$$\frac{r \in \vec{q} \quad \vec{q} \setminus r \text{ nonempty}}{\langle \vec{q}: X(\vec{p}).C'; C, \Sigma, K, \mathscr{C} \rangle \xrightarrow{\tau@r} \langle \vec{q} \setminus r: X(\vec{p}).C'; C, \Sigma, K, \mathscr{C} \rangle} \text{ CALL-ENTER}$$

$$\frac{}{\langle q: X(\vec{p}).C'; C, \Sigma, K, \mathscr{C} \rangle \xrightarrow{\tau@q} \langle C, \Sigma, K, \mathscr{C} \rangle} \text{ CALL-LAST}$$

$$\frac{\langle C, \Sigma, K, \mathscr{C} \rangle \xrightarrow{\mu} \langle C', \Sigma', K', \mathscr{C} \rangle \quad \text{pn}(I) \mathbin{\#} \text{pn}(\mu)}{\langle I; C, \Sigma, K, \mathscr{C} \rangle \xrightarrow{\mu} \langle I; C', \Sigma', K', \mathscr{C} \rangle} \text{ DELAY}$$

$$\frac{\langle C_1, \Sigma, K, \mathscr{C} \rangle \xrightarrow{\mu} \langle C_1', \Sigma', K', \mathscr{C} \rangle \quad \langle C_2, \Sigma, K, \mathscr{C} \rangle \xrightarrow{\mu} \langle C_2', \Sigma', K', \mathscr{C} \rangle \quad p \notin \text{pn}(\mu)}{\langle \text{if } p.e \text{ then } C_1 \text{ else } C_2; C, \Sigma, K, \mathscr{C} \rangle \xrightarrow{\mu} \langle \text{if } p.e \text{ then } C_1' \text{ else } C_2'; C, \Sigma', K', \mathscr{C} \rangle} \text{ DELAY-COND}$$

Figure 11.2 Semantics of Asynchronous Recursive Choreographies.

- The rules COM and SEL are replaced by rules for asynchronous communication: SEND-VAL, RECV-VAL, SEND-SEL, and RECV-SEL. Their names are underlined in Figure 11.2, to make them easier to spot. The new rules execute communications in two steps (send and receive) rather than one step as before.

- All other rules are adapted to the new format of configurations.

In rule SEND-VAL, a communication instruction $p.e \to q.x$ is transformed into the runtime term $p \rightsquigarrow q.x$ in the derivative. The transition label denotes that the sender has completed its part of the communication. In the derivative, the messaging state is updated such that the queue for q (originally $\vec{m}$) now contains the message from p (at the end of the queue).

Messages are received by applying rule RECV-VAL, in which a receiving term $p \rightsquigarrow q.x$ makes q retrieve a message from p. The premise of the rule requires that the message queue of q starts with a message from p containing a value v. In the derivative, the message is removed from the queue, and the store (Σ) is updated to reflect that q has stored the received value in its local variable x.

The rules SEND-SEL and RECV-SEL follow the same intuition of rules SEND-VAL and RECV-VAL, but applied to the communication of selection labels. The main difference is that, since there is no value to be stored, the store remains unaltered in the conclusion of rule RECV-SEL.

The definition of pn for runtime communication terms and rule DELAY have a crucial interplay, as we show in the next example.

Example 11.1   We consider an adaptation of Example 4.3 (which was given in the language of Simple Choreographies). In the following choreography C, a process representing a postman (p) delivers three letters to their respective recipients. We denote the three letters as some local values l_1, l_2, and l_3, and the recipients as the processes r_1, r_2, and r_3.

$$C \triangleq p.l_1 \to r_1.x; p.l_2 \to r_2.x; p.l_3 \to r_3.x$$

Let Σ be a choreographic store. If we refer to the semantics of Recursive Choreographies (Figure 7.2), the graphical representation of the lts generated by the configuration $\langle C, \Sigma, \emptyset \rangle$ looks as follows.

$$\langle p.l_1 \to r_1.x; p.l_2 \to r_2.x; p.l_3 \to r_3.x, \Sigma, \emptyset \rangle$$
$$\downarrow {\scriptstyle p.l_1 \to r_1}$$
$$\langle p.l_2 \to r_2.x; p.l_3 \to r_3.x, \Sigma[r_1.x \mapsto l_1], \emptyset \rangle$$
$$\downarrow {\scriptstyle p.l_2 \to r_2}$$
$$\langle p.l_3 \to r_3.x, \Sigma[r_1.x \mapsto l_1][r_2.x \mapsto l_2], \emptyset \rangle$$
$$\downarrow {\scriptstyle p.l_3 \to r_3}$$
$$\langle 0, \Sigma[r_1.x \mapsto l_1][r_2.x \mapsto l_2][r_3.x \mapsto l_3], \emptyset \rangle$$

In other words, the synchronous communication semantics of Recursive Choreographies enforces that the three deliveries are received by their intended recipients in sequence. For example, p cannot move on to r_2 until r_1 receives its letter.

Let us see how the same choreography can be executed according to the semantics of Asynchronous Recursive Choreographies. Let K be an empty messaging state, i.e., K is such that $K(q) = \epsilon$ for all q. Initially, there is only one derivable transition: p sends the letter l_1 to r_1.

$$\frac{\Sigma(\mathsf{p}) \vdash l_1 \downarrow l_1 \qquad K(\mathsf{r}_1) = \epsilon}{\left\langle \begin{matrix} \mathsf{p}.l_1 \to \mathsf{r}_1.x; \\ \mathsf{p}.l_2 \to \mathsf{r}_2.x;, \Sigma, K, \emptyset \\ \mathsf{p}.l_3 \to \mathsf{r}_3.x \end{matrix} \right\rangle \xrightarrow{\mathsf{p}.l_1 \to \mathsf{r}_1!} \left\langle \begin{matrix} \mathsf{p} \leadsto \mathsf{r}_1.x; \\ \mathsf{p}.l_2 \to \mathsf{r}_2.x;, \Sigma, K[\mathsf{r}_1 \mapsto (\mathsf{p}, l_1)], \emptyset \\ \mathsf{p}.l_3 \to \mathsf{r}_3.x \end{matrix} \right\rangle} \; \text{SEND-VAL} \qquad (11.1)$$

Let $K_1 \triangleq K[\mathsf{r}_1 \mapsto (\mathsf{p}, l_1)]$. We now have two possibilities for further execution:

- By rule RECV-VAL, r_1 can retrieve the message from p from its queue.

$$\frac{K_1(\mathsf{r}_1) = (\mathsf{p}, l_1)}{\left\langle \begin{matrix} \mathsf{p} \leadsto \mathsf{r}_1.x; \\ \mathsf{p}.l_2 \to \mathsf{r}_2.x;, \Sigma, K_1, \emptyset \\ \mathsf{p}.l_3 \to \mathsf{r}_3.x \end{matrix} \right\rangle \xrightarrow{\mathsf{p}.l_1 \to \mathsf{r}_1?} \left\langle \begin{matrix} \mathsf{p}.l_2 \to \mathsf{r}_2.x; \\ \mathsf{p}.l_3 \to \mathsf{r}_3.x \end{matrix}, \Sigma, K_1[\mathsf{r}_1 \mapsto \epsilon], \emptyset \right\rangle} \; \text{RECV-VAL}$$

Note that $K_1[\mathsf{r}_1 \mapsto \epsilon] = K$: in the derivative, the messaging state is again empty.

- Or, by rules SEND-VAL and DELAY, p can go on and send l_2 to r_2.

$$\frac{\dfrac{\Sigma(\mathsf{p}) \vdash l_2 \downarrow l_2 \qquad K(\mathsf{r}_1) = \epsilon}{\left\langle \begin{matrix} \mathsf{p}.l_2 \to \mathsf{r}_2.x; \\ \mathsf{p}.l_3 \to \mathsf{r}_3.x \end{matrix}, \Sigma, K_1, \emptyset \right\rangle \xrightarrow{\mathsf{p}.l_2 \to \mathsf{r}_2!} \left\langle \begin{matrix} \mathsf{p} \leadsto \mathsf{r}_2.x; \\ \mathsf{p}.l_3 \to \mathsf{r}_3.x \end{matrix}, \Sigma, K_1[\mathsf{r}_2 \mapsto (\mathsf{p}, l_2)], \emptyset \right\rangle} \; \text{SEND-VAL} \qquad \{\mathsf{r}_1\} \,\#\, \{\mathsf{p}\}}{\left\langle \begin{matrix} \mathsf{p} \leadsto \mathsf{r}_1.x; \\ \mathsf{p}.l_2 \to \mathsf{r}_2.x;, \Sigma, K_1, \emptyset \\ \mathsf{p}.l_3 \to \mathsf{r}_3.x \end{matrix} \right\rangle \xrightarrow{\mathsf{p}.l_2 \to \mathsf{r}_2!} \left\langle \begin{matrix} \mathsf{p} \leadsto \mathsf{r}_1.x; \\ \mathsf{p} \leadsto \mathsf{r}_2.x; \;,\, \Sigma, K_1[\mathsf{r}_2 \mapsto (\mathsf{p}, l_2)], \emptyset \\ \mathsf{p}.l_3 \to \mathsf{r}_3.x \end{matrix} \right\rangle} \; \text{DELAY}$$

This possibility exemplifies the key distinction from the synchronous communication semantics of Recursive Choreographies: even if r_1 still has to retrieve its message from p, p can just go ahead with its other actions in the rest of the choreography (in this case, sending a message to r_2). An important consequence is that r_2 might retrieve its message before r_1. The reader can check that, by rule DELAY and rule RECV-VAL, the following transition is derivable.

$$\left\langle \begin{matrix} \mathsf{p} \leadsto \mathsf{r}_1.x; \\ \mathsf{p} \leadsto \mathsf{r}_2.x; \;,\, \Sigma, K_1[\mathsf{r}_2 \mapsto (\mathsf{p}, l_2)], \emptyset \\ \mathsf{p}.l_3 \to \mathsf{r}_3.x \end{matrix} \right\rangle \xrightarrow{\mathsf{p}.l_2 \to \mathsf{r}_2?} \left\langle \begin{matrix} \mathsf{p} \leadsto \mathsf{r}_1.x; \\ \mathsf{p}.l_3 \to \mathsf{r}_3.x \end{matrix}, \Sigma, K_1, \emptyset \right\rangle$$

In general, asynchronous communication can generate many more possible executions than synchronous communication, for two reasons: a sender can proceed in its execution without waiting for the corresponding receiver; and runtime terms for receiving messages at different processes can be executed out of order. We show the complete graphical representation of the lts generated by $\langle C, \Sigma, K, \emptyset \rangle$ in Figure 11.3, where the stores and messaging states are defined as follows.

$$\Sigma_1 \triangleq \Sigma[\mathsf{r}_1.x \mapsto l_1] \qquad\qquad \Sigma_2 \triangleq \Sigma[\mathsf{r}_2.x \mapsto l_2] \qquad\qquad \Sigma_3 \triangleq \Sigma[\mathsf{r}_3.x \mapsto l_3]$$
$$\Sigma_{12} \triangleq \Sigma_1[\mathsf{r}_2.x \mapsto l_2] \qquad\qquad \Sigma_{23} \triangleq \Sigma_2[\mathsf{r}_3.x \mapsto l_3] \qquad\qquad \Sigma_{13} \triangleq \Sigma_1[\mathsf{r}_3.x \mapsto l_3]$$
$$\Sigma_{123} \triangleq \Sigma_{12}[\mathsf{r}_3.x \mapsto l_3]$$

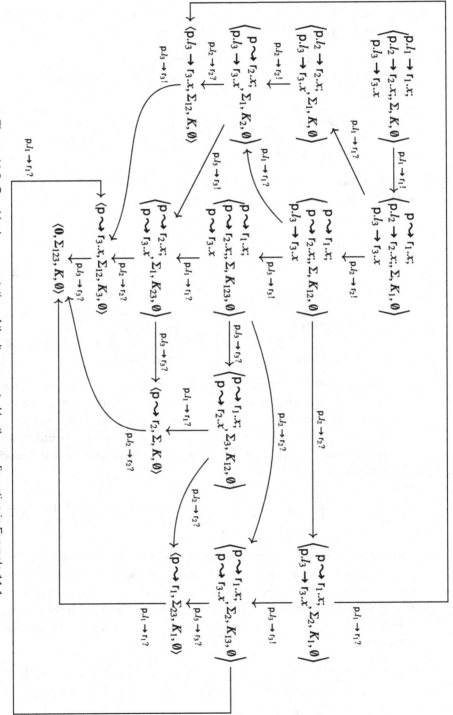

Figure 11.3 Graphical representation of the Its generated by the configuration in Example 11.1.

$$K_1 \triangleq K[r_1 \mapsto (\mathsf{p}, l_1)] \qquad K_2 \triangleq K[r_2 \mapsto (\mathsf{p}, l_2)] \qquad K_3 \triangleq K[r_3 \mapsto (\mathsf{p}, l_3)]$$

$$K_{12} \triangleq K_1[r_2 \mapsto (\mathsf{p}, l_2)] \qquad K_{23} \triangleq K_2[r_3 \mapsto (\mathsf{p}, l_3)] \qquad K_{13} \triangleq K_1[r_3 \mapsto (\mathsf{p}, l_3)]$$

$$K_{123} \triangleq K_{12}[r_3 \mapsto (\mathsf{p}, l_3)]$$

The semantics of Asynchronous Recursive Choreographies preserves message ordering between senders and receivers: a process, say r (for receiver), can receive messages from another process, say s (for sender), only in the order that s has sent these messages to r. This is the case because the sequences of messages ($\vec{m}$) in a messaging state are indeed used like ordered queues. The rules for sending messages (SEND-VAL and SEND-SEL) append messages to the end of the message sequence of the intended recipient, whereas the rules for receiving (RECV-VAL and RECV-SEL) retrieve messages from the other end of the sequence. The next example showcases this aspect.

Example 11.2 Consider the following choreography, where a process s communicates two signals in succession to a process r (SIG1 and SIG2, respectively).

$$C \triangleq \mathsf{s} \to \mathsf{r}[\text{SIG}1]; \mathsf{s} \to \mathsf{r}[\text{SIG}2]$$

Let Σ be a choreographic store and K be a messaging state such that $K(\mathsf{r}) = \epsilon$. Then we have the following execution.

$$\langle C, \Sigma, K, \emptyset \rangle \xrightarrow{\mathsf{s} \to \mathsf{r}[\text{SIG}1]!} \xrightarrow{\mathsf{s} \to \mathsf{r}[\text{SIG}2]!} \left\langle \begin{matrix} \mathsf{s} \rightsquigarrow \mathsf{r}[\text{SIG}1]; \\ \mathsf{s} \rightsquigarrow \mathsf{r}[\text{SIG}2] \end{matrix}, \Sigma, K[\mathsf{r} \mapsto (\mathsf{s}, \text{SIG}1), (\mathsf{s}, \text{SIG}2)], \emptyset \right\rangle \quad (11.2)$$

From the multi-step derivative in (11.2), there is only one possible transition: by rule RECV-SEL, r receives SIG1, as follows.

$$\left\langle \begin{matrix} \mathsf{s} \rightsquigarrow \mathsf{r}[\text{SIG}1]; \\ \mathsf{s} \rightsquigarrow \mathsf{r}[\text{SIG}2] \end{matrix}, \Sigma, K[\mathsf{r} \mapsto (\mathsf{s}, \text{SIG}1), (\mathsf{s}, \text{SIG}2)], \emptyset \right\rangle$$

$$\xrightarrow{\mathsf{s} \to \mathsf{r}[\text{SIG}1]?} \langle \mathsf{s} \rightsquigarrow \mathsf{r}[\text{SIG}2], \Sigma, K[\mathsf{r} \mapsto (\mathsf{s}, \text{SIG}2)], \emptyset \rangle$$

We can then terminate by having r receive SIG2:

$$\langle \mathsf{s} \rightsquigarrow \mathsf{r}[\text{SIG}2], \Sigma, K[\mathsf{r} \mapsto (\mathsf{s}, \text{SIG}2)], \emptyset \rangle \xrightarrow{\mathsf{s} \to \mathsf{r}[\text{SIG}2]?} \langle \mathbf{0}, \Sigma, K, \emptyset \rangle.$$

Exercise 11.1 Draw the graphical representation of the lts generated by the configuration $\langle C, \Sigma, K, \emptyset \rangle$ found in Example 11.2.

11.2 Processes

We now move to modelling asynchronous communication at the level of processes, in a language that we call Asynchronous Recursive Processes.

$$\frac{\Sigma(\mathsf{p}) \vdash e \downarrow v}{\langle \mathsf{p}[x := e; P], \Sigma, K, \mathscr{P} \rangle \xrightarrow{\tau@\mathsf{p}} \langle \mathsf{p}[P], \Sigma[\mathsf{p}.x \mapsto v], K, \mathscr{P} \rangle} \text{ LOCAL}$$

$$\frac{\Sigma(\mathsf{p}) \vdash e \downarrow v \quad K(\mathsf{q}) = \vec{m}}{\langle \mathsf{p}[\mathsf{q}!e; P], \Sigma, K, \mathscr{P} \rangle \xrightarrow{\mathsf{p}.v \rightarrow \mathsf{q}!} \langle \mathsf{p}[P], \Sigma, K[\mathsf{q} \mapsto \vec{m}, (\mathsf{p}, v)], \mathscr{P} \rangle} \text{ SEND-VAL}$$

$$\frac{\Sigma(\mathsf{p}) \vdash e \downarrow v \quad K(\mathsf{q}) = (\mathsf{p}, v), \vec{m}}{\langle \mathsf{q}[\mathsf{p}?x; Q], \Sigma, K, \mathscr{P} \rangle \xrightarrow{\mathsf{p}.v \rightarrow \mathsf{q}?} \langle \mathsf{q}[Q], \Sigma[\mathsf{q}.x \mapsto v], K[\mathsf{q} \mapsto \vec{m}], \mathscr{P} \rangle} \text{ RECV-VAL}$$

$$\frac{K(\mathsf{q}) = \vec{m}}{\langle \mathsf{p}[\mathsf{q} \oplus \mathsf{L}; P], \Sigma, K, \mathscr{P} \rangle \xrightarrow{\mathsf{p} \rightarrow \mathsf{q}[\mathsf{L}]!} \langle \mathsf{p}[P], \Sigma, K[\mathsf{q} \mapsto \vec{m}, (\mathsf{p}, \mathsf{L})], \mathscr{P} \rangle} \text{ SEND-SEL}$$

$$\frac{j \in I \quad K(\mathsf{q}) = \vec{m}}{\langle \mathsf{q}[\mathsf{p} \& \{\mathsf{L}_i : P_i\}_{i \in I}; Q], \Sigma, K, \mathscr{P} \rangle \xrightarrow{\mathsf{p} \rightarrow \mathsf{q}[\mathsf{L}_j]?} \langle \mathsf{q}[P_j \,\mathring{,}\, Q], \Sigma, K[\mathsf{q} \mapsto \vec{m}], \mathscr{P} \rangle} \text{ RECV-SEL}$$

$$\frac{\Sigma(\mathsf{p}) \vdash e \downarrow true}{\langle \mathsf{p}[\text{if } e \text{ then } P_1 \text{ else } P_2; Q], \Sigma, K, \mathscr{P} \rangle \xrightarrow{\tau@\mathsf{p}} \langle \mathsf{p}[P_1 \,\mathring{,}\, Q], \Sigma, K, \mathscr{P} \rangle} \text{ COND-THEN}$$

$$\frac{\Sigma(\mathsf{p}) \vdash e \downarrow v \quad v \neq true}{\langle \mathsf{p}[\text{if } e \text{ then } P_1 \text{ else } P_2; Q], \Sigma, K, \mathscr{P} \rangle \xrightarrow{\tau@\mathsf{p}} \langle \mathsf{p}[P_2 \,\mathring{,}\, Q], \Sigma, K, \mathscr{P} \rangle} \text{ COND-ELSE}$$

$$\frac{X(\vec{r}) = Q \in \mathscr{P}}{\langle \mathsf{p}[X(\vec{\mathsf{q}}); P], \Sigma, K, \mathscr{P} \rangle \xrightarrow{\tau@\mathsf{p}} \langle \mathsf{p}[Q[\vec{\mathsf{q}}/\vec{r}] \,\mathring{,}\, P], \Sigma, K, \mathscr{P} \rangle} \text{ CALL}$$

$$\frac{\langle N, \Sigma, \mathscr{P} \rangle \xrightarrow{\mu} \langle N', \Sigma', K', \mathscr{P} \rangle}{\langle N \mid M, \Sigma, K, \mathscr{P} \rangle \xrightarrow{\mu} \langle N' \mid M, \Sigma', K', \mathscr{P} \rangle} \text{ PAR}$$

Figure 11.4 Semantics of Asynchronous Recursive Processes.

Sending and receiving actions already correspond to dedicated syntactic terms in Recursive Processes. Therefore, the syntax of Asynchronous Recursive Processes is the same as that of Recursive Processes (Figure 7.3).

Regarding semantics, instead, we need to replace rules COM and SEL with other rules whereby communication takes place in two steps, similarly to what we have done for choreographies. Furthermore, we need to adapt all rules to messaging states. The result is presented in Figure 11.4.

The new rules are SEND-VAL, RECV-VAL, SEND-SEL, and RECV-SEL. Notice that, differently from rules COM and SEL in Recursive Processes, the new rules do not require synchronisation between two processes. Rather, executing a sending or a receiving action merely requires interaction with the messaging state.

In rule SEND-VAL, a process p that wishes to send a value to another process q can immediately proceed, in the sense that the action does not need to be matched with a corresponding receiving action at q (in fact, q might not even be present and the rule would still be applicable). The message is then added to the end of the queue for q in the messaging state, as in the rule with the same name in the semantics of choreographies. Rule RECV-VAL is the counterpart to rule SEND-VAL and models how a process can receive a message from its queue. Rules SEND-SEL and RECV-SEL are similar, but deal with the communication of labels rather than values.

Example 11.3 The following network, N, implements the choreography seen in Example 11.1, where a postman p delivers letters to three recipients (r_1, r_2, and r_3).

$$N \triangleq p[r_1!l_1; r_2!l_2; r_3!l_3] \mid r_1[p?x] \mid r_2[p?x] \mid r_3[p?x]$$

Let Σ be a choreographic store and K be a messaging state such that $K(q) = \epsilon$ for all q. By rules PAR and SEND-VAL, we can mimic the first transition of the original choreography, which we derived in (11.1).

$$\dfrac{\dfrac{\Sigma(p) \vdash l_1 \downarrow l_1 \quad K(r_1) = \epsilon}{\langle p[r_1!l_1; r_2!l_2; r_3!l_3], \Sigma, K, \emptyset\rangle \xrightarrow{p.l_1 \to r_1!} \langle p[r_2!l_2; r_3!l_3], \Sigma, K[r_1 \mapsto (p, l_1)], \emptyset\rangle} \text{ SEND-VAL}}{\langle N, \Sigma, K, \emptyset\rangle \xrightarrow{p.l_1 \to r_1!} \langle p[r_2!l_2; r_3!l_3] \mid r_1[p?x] \mid r_2[p?x] \mid r_3[p?x], \Sigma, K[r_1 \mapsto (p, l_1)], \emptyset\rangle} \text{ PAR} \quad (11.3)$$

Indeed, the graphical representation of the lts generated by $\langle N, \Sigma, K, \emptyset\rangle$ is isomorphic to the graph showed in Figure 11.3. The reader is invited to check in the next exercise.

Exercise 11.2 Draw the graphical representation of the lts generated by the configuration $\langle N, \Sigma, K, \emptyset\rangle$ found in Example 11.3.

Exercise 11.3 Write a network that implements the choreography in Example 11.2. Check that the graphical representation of the lts that it generates (in a configuration with Σ and K defined as in Example 11.2) is isomorphic to the graph requested in Exercise 11.1.

11.3 Endpoint Projection

At the level of projection, we need to update the notion of process projection in order to deal with the new runtime terms. The remaining equations that define process projection remain unchanged. In the box, we report both the new rules and the existing ones for communication terms (for reference). The key idea behind projecting a runtime term is that only the sender is skipped since a runtime term represents the state in which the sender has already performed its action.

Process projection for asynchronous runtime terms

$$[\![p \rightsquigarrow q.x; C]\!]_r \triangleq \begin{cases} q!e; [\![C]\!]_r & \text{if } r = p \\ p?x; [\![C]\!]_r & \text{if } r = q \\ [\![C]\!]_r & \text{otherwise} \end{cases}$$

$$[\![p \rightsquigarrow q[L]; C]\!]_r \triangleq \begin{cases} p?x; [\![C]\!]_r & \text{if } r = q \\ [\![C]\!]_r & \text{otherwise} \end{cases}$$

$$[\![p \rightsquigarrow q.x; C]\!]_r \triangleq \begin{cases} q \oplus L; [\![C]\!]_r & \text{if } r = p \\ p \,\&\, \{L : [\![C]\!]_r\}; \mathbf{0} & \text{if } r = q \\ [\![C]\!]_r & \text{otherwise} \end{cases}$$

$$[\![p \rightsquigarrow q[L]; C]\!]_r \triangleq \begin{cases} p \,\&\, \{L : [\![C]\!]_r\}; \mathbf{0} & \text{if } r = q \\ [\![C]\!]_r & \text{otherwise} \end{cases}$$

Example 11.4 Let C and N be the choreography in Example 11.1 and the network in Example 11.3, respectively:

$$C \triangleq p.l_1 \rightarrow r_1.x; p.l_2 \rightarrow r_2.x; p.l_3 \rightarrow r_3.x$$
$$N \triangleq p[r_1!l_1; r_2!l_2; r_3!l_3] \mid r_1[p?x] \mid r_2[p?x] \mid r_3[p?x].$$

Observe that $[\![C]\!] = N$ already by the definition of EPP for Recursive Choreographies, which is sufficient in this case because C contains no runtime terms for asynchronous communication.

Consider now the choreography and network in the first derivatives given in Example 11.1 and Example 11.3, respectively from (11.1) and (11.3), which we call C' and N':

$$C' \triangleq p \rightsquigarrow r_1.x; p.l_2 \rightarrow r_2.x; p.l_3 \rightarrow r_3.x$$
$$N' \triangleq p[r_2!l_2; r_3!l_3] \mid r_1[p?x] \mid r_2[p?x] \mid r_3[p?x].$$

Again, $[\![C']\!] = N'$. In this case, however, it is necessary to use one of the new equations for projecting the runtime term $p \rightsquigarrow r_1.x$.

The strategy for proving that EPP is correct is the same as for the case of Recursive Choreographies. However, deadlock-freedom requires particular care when we update the notion of well-formedness for choreographies. To see the issue, consider the choreography $p \rightsquigarrow q.x$. If this choreography is executed in a configuration where the messaging state does not have a message from p containing a value for q, then process q will get stuck (there is no transition that could be derived, in general). The semantics of Asynchronous Recursive Choreographies is designed such that this situation can never occur, assuming that runtime terms are never written manually (they are only generated by transitions). A way of proving this formally is to update the notion of well-formedness for choreographies to consider messaging states, in addition to procedure definitions and the set of processes that can be used. In particular, the well-formedness rules that regard runtime terms for retrieving messages should require that a compatible message is present in the messaging state.

12 Discussion and Further Reading

In this chapter we outline some of the current lines of research on choreographic languages, give additional considerations on our development, and provide pointers for further reading.

Choreographic Programming

Choreographic programming is a programming paradigm in which programs are choreographies [Montesi 2013]. *Choreographic programming languages* are designed to develop executable code, and typically allow for expressing both the communications and the computations performed by system participants. These languages are usually accompanied by a compiler, which generates executable code for each participant that appears in the input choreography by following the principles of EPP [Carbone and Montesi 2013; Montesi 2013; Dalla Preda et al. 2017; Giallorenzo et al. 2020]. The generated code can be, for example, a library that developers can use to participate correctly in a protocol, or a standalone executable application. The theories that we have seen in Parts II and III can be classified as theories of choreographic programming.

Choreographic programming has been studied in several contexts, including service-oriented computing [Carbone and Montesi 2013; Giallorenzo et al. 2018], cyber-physical systems [López et al. 2016; López & Heussen 2017], parallel algorithms [Cruz-Filipe & Montesi 2016], information-flow control [Lluch-Lafuente et al. 2015], adaptability [Dalla Preda et al. 2017], and security protocols [Bruni et al. 2021]. The starting idea behind these studies is to leverage the knowledge of which communications will take place, which choreographic languages make syntactically manifest. This knowledge can be used to reason about security, liveness, energy consumption, and so forth.

The first implementation of a choreographic programming language is the Chor language, which is described in [Montesi 2013, chapter 7] and follows the language model in [Carbone and Montesi 2013]. Its compiler follows the same ideas behind our definition of process projection: it targets the Jolie programming language and Jolie instructions recall those found in Recursive Processes (e.g., Jolie natively supports branching terms) [Montesi et al. 2014].

An example of how choreographic programming can be applied to mainstream software development is provided by the Choral programming language [Giallorenzo et al. 2020]. In Choral, choreographies are written in an object-oriented choreographic language and the accompanying compiler produces Java code. This code forms modular libraries that software developers can compose to build software that participates correctly in concurrent and distributed systems.

Multiparty Session Types and Behavioural Contracts

In *multiparty session types*, a choreography does not define the internal computations performed by processes, but rather the expected types of their results: the communication primitive in multiparty session types has the form $p \rightarrow q : T$, read 'p communicates a message of type T to q' [Honda et al. 2016]. Choreographies in this setting are called *global types*. Given a global type that expresses the expected communications and the types of their payloads, EPP is used to generate a local specification for each process, called *local type*. Process implementations are then checked to respect their respective local types by means of a type system. (An exception to this workflow is the type system in [Stolze et al. 2021], which checks process implementations directly against a choreography, without going through EPP.) A key property that is usually guaranteed by typing is *session fidelity* – that is, any communication action performed by a well-typed program is allowed by the corresponding local type [Honda et al. 2016].

The key difference between choreographic programming and multiparty session types is that in the former choreographies are seen as programs, whereas in the latter choreographies are seen as types. Both approaches stem from the same concepts: the design of a choreographic language and its related notion of EPP. More specifically, the typical choreographic languages used to write global types can be obtained from Recursive Choreographies with some modifications: local computation is removed, and in particular there are no variables, expressions, and assignments; conditionals have no guards, and the process choosing between two branches does so nondeterministically; and communication is adapted to the simpler form $p \rightarrow q: T$, where T is a constant that does not need to be evaluated. Selection and recursion are instead treated similarly. Applying these restrictions yields a language very similar to the first implementation of multiparty session types, Scribble [Yoshida et al. 2013].

Protocols that have the definition of some computation as an integral part cannot be faithfully expressed with standard global types. An example is the key exchange protocol by Diffie and Hellman [1976] in Example 5.2: the order of communications can be written in a global type, but the essential computation of cryptographic keys cannot. In a sense, global types can be seen as overapproximations of choreographies in choreographic programming. This interpretation was formalised in [Carbone and Montesi 2013], where a type system guarantees that well-typed choreographies written in a choreographic programming language enact only communications prescribed by given global types.

In some settings, the difference between choreographies in choreographic programming and multiparty session types gets much thinner.

One such setting is runtime verification, where the communication actions performed by participants are checked to comply with respective local types during execution [Neykova et al. 2017]. Runtime verification avoids much of the complexity of static verification because it deals with a concrete execution of a program rather than all its possible ones. Consequently, it facilitates the adoption of much more expressive choreographic languages for global types, which can, for example, include assertions on timing and the memories of participants [Bocchi et al. 2017; Neykova et al. 2017]. These languages can include local variables and are much nearer to Recursive Choreographies. In principle, one could take the process projected from a choreography written in a language like Recursive Choreographies and then check at runtime that a program behaves like it.

Another interesting setting is interactive theorem proving, where one could conceive developing a manually written proof that a program behaves like a process projected from a choreography. The same considerations made for runtime verification apply to this setting.

In summary, choreographic programming and multiparty session types share a lot of common ground. The theory that we presented in the previous chapters applies to both, modulo modifications, restrictions, or extensions that depend on the concrete application. Researchers interested in either area should thus be familiar with the developments that regard choreographic languages in both. By contrast, the details on compilation of executable code and typing are more specific to the two respective research lines.

Multiparty session types are also significantly related to choreographic languages for *behavioural contracts*, a theory for the abstract (without computation) description of service behaviours [Bravetti & Zavattaro 2007]. The study of behavioural contracts led to the formulation of several principles for establishing whether process specifications similar to local types are compatible [Bravetti & Zavattaro 2007], and later played an important role in understanding subtle interplays between optimisations in multiparty session types and asynchronous communication [Bravetti et al. 2017; Bravetti et al. 2018; Bravetti & Zavattaro 2018; Ghilezan et al. 2021].

The survey by Hüttel et al. [2016] includes an overview of many of the developments of multiparty session types and behavioural contracts.

Security Protocol Notation

As we discussed in the Preface, the inspiration for the syntax of choreographies comes from the notation introduced by Needham and Schroeder [1978] for security protocols. This notation is known under several names: *security protocol notation*, *Alice and Bob notation*, and *protocol narrations* [Caleiro et al. 2006; Briais & Nestmann 2007]. Security protocol notation is similar to the choreographic languages presented here, but the kind of computation that can be performed by processes is typically restricted to specific cryptographic primitives. Furthermore, distinguishing public and secret values and tracking the knowledge of these values by processes can be important aspects in this setting (and are often captured syntactically with high-level constructs).

Liveness by Design

There are many works on choreographic languages that deal with liveness and prove that implementations of choreographies are deadlock-free [Carbone and Montesi 2013; Honda et al. 2016; Dalla Preda et al. 2017; Cruz-Filipe & Montesi 2020; Hirsch and Garg 2022; Jongmans & Van den Bos 2022]. These proofs typically follow the two-step strategy that we presented in Section 8.5.2 for Theorem 8.41: first prove that a non-terminated choreography can always perform a transition (under assumptions like well-formedness, if necessary), as in Lemma 8.40, and then invoke the correctness of EPP (Theorem 8.33) to obtain the same for the projected network [Carbone and Montesi 2013; Cruz-Filipe & Montesi 2020].

Guaranteeing liveness in programming languages usually requires sophisticated static analyses [Kobayashi 2002; Kobayashi & Sangiorgi 2010; Coppo et al. 2016; Kobayashi & Laneve 2017], and the simpler alternative given by choreographic languages is a standout feature and hallmark of the choreographic method – in addition, of course, to the benefit of making interactions syntactically manifest. The feature led to the slogan of *deadlock-freedom by design* [Carbone and Montesi 2013], which later became popular in choreographic programming [Cruz-Filipe & Montesi 2020; Hirsch and Garg 2022; Jongmans & Van den Bos 2022]. Expanding new choreographic languages that can express more deadlock- or starvation-free networks is a focus of research on choreographies, because it is not always clear how some of the protocols enacted by these networks can be written as choreographies [Kobayashi & Laneve 2017; Scalas & Yoshida 2019; Horne 2020].

We have seen that some choreographic languages can be used to achieve the stronger property of starvation-freedom, in particular including up to tail-recursive choreographies in Recursive

Choreographies (Section 8.5.3). This property is typically not presented in previous works on choreographies. However, it is reasonable to believe that it could be proved for many choreographic languages published so far, and that it was not done because it was not obvious to formulate or see (this is at least the case for some of the works that involved the present author). The reason for which we managed to prove starvation-freedom is not due to a fundamental change in principles but rather a careful design of our semantics, which elicits which processes participate in transitions. In turn, this enables our two-step proof strategy for Theorem 8.45, which is an adaptation of the one for deadlock-freedom: first prove that all processes can progress in the choreography (Lemma 8.44), and then invoke the correctness of EPP to obtain the same for the projected network (Theorem 8.33). Some previous works adopt a similar design for transition labels, for example in [Carbone and Montesi 2013; Montesi & Yoshida 2013; Honda et al. 2016]. One might therefore say that some choreographic languages provide *starvation-freedom by design* – as in some of the previous chapters. Hence, after all, the aptest general slogan for choreographies and liveness might be *liveness by design*.

The liveness properties given by choreographies are also said to be 'by construction' – for example *deadlock-freedom by construction, starvation-freedom by construction, liveness by construction* [Cruz-Filipe & Montesi 2020]. This is in reference to the fact that the transference of these properties to process programs crucially relies on how they are constructed by EPP.

At this point one might ask: should all choreographic languages be designed with the aim of achieving starvation-freedom instead of just deadlock-freedom? Practice brings a negative answer. Consider the following set of choreographic procedures, which involve a client (c), a proxy (p), and a server (s).

$$\left\{ \begin{array}{l} X(\mathsf{c},\mathsf{p},\mathsf{s}) = Y(\mathsf{c},\mathsf{p}); \mathsf{p}.x \to \mathsf{s}.y; \mathsf{s}.f(y) \to \mathsf{c}.z; X(\mathsf{c},\mathsf{p},\mathsf{s}) \\ \quad Y(\mathsf{c},\mathsf{p}) = \mathsf{c}.cmd() \to \mathsf{p}.x; \text{if } \mathsf{p}.allowed(x) \text{ then } \mathsf{p} \to \mathsf{c}[\text{ok}] \text{ else}(\mathsf{p} \to \mathsf{c}[\text{ko}]; Y(\mathsf{c},\mathsf{p})) \end{array} \right\} \quad (12.1)$$

Procedure X illustrates a widespread pattern in distributed computing: the proxy filters incoming requests for the server, which should process only the requests that are allowed through. This pattern is used in various practical scenarios, like access control, data validation, and prevention of server overload [Hohpe & Woolf 2004; Nygard 2007; Montesi & Weber 2018]. In particular, procedure X starts by invoking Y, which involves only the client and the proxy. In Y, the client sends a command (*cmd*(), where *cmd* is a nondeterministic local function) to the proxy. The proxy then decides if the command is allowed: if so, the procedure terminates, and otherwise the client has to send another command. When Y terminates we get back to X, where the proxy forwards the command to the server. The server then finally processes the request using the local function f, and then communicates the result to the client. Procedure X then invokes itself to let the client send further requests.

While procedure X is interesting from a practical viewpoint, it can lead to starvation: if a choreography invokes X and the condition *allowed*(x) can never be evaluated to *true*, then s will starve. In practice, however, this can be acceptable or even wanted: in this case, we do not actually care that the server is used all the time, just that it is used when necessary. Exploring fine-grained liveness properties that pinpoint which processes can remain inactive until needed might be an interesting topic. In some choreographic languages, processes that represent servers are distinguished syntactically and/or with types [Carbone et al. 2012; Carbone and Montesi 2013].

Realisability, Projectability, and Amendment

In the literature, a choreography is said to be *realisable* if there exists a compliant distributed implementation of it [Alur et al. 2005; Kazhamiakin & Pistore 2006; Finkel & Lozes 2017]. In our theory, EPP is defined only for those choreography that we are sure to translate to compliant implementations. Therefore, projectability in our framework implies realisability. The converse does not hold: realisability does not imply projectability. For example, consider the following rewriting of the procedures in (12.1).

$$
\begin{aligned}
Z(\mathsf{c},\mathsf{p},\mathsf{s}) = {}& \mathsf{c}.cmd() \to \mathsf{p}.x; \\
& (\text{if } \mathsf{p}.allowed(x) \text{ then} \\
& \qquad \mathsf{p} \to \mathsf{c}[\text{OK}]; \mathsf{p}.x \to \mathsf{s}.y; \mathsf{s}.f(y) \to \mathsf{c}.z \\
& \text{else} \\
& \qquad \mathsf{p} \to \mathsf{c}[\text{KO}]); \\
& Z(\mathsf{c},\mathsf{p},\mathsf{s})
\end{aligned}
\tag{12.2}
$$

Procedure Z in (12.2) has the same communication behaviour of procedure X in (12.1). It is unprojectable in our theory, because s behaves differently in the two branches of the conditional without appropriate knowledge of choice. However, it is also realisable: the following set of procedure definitions is a compliant implementation.

$$
\left\{
\begin{aligned}
& Z_1(\mathsf{p},\mathsf{s}) = \mathsf{p}!cmd(); \mathsf{p} \,\&\, \{\text{OK}: \mathsf{s}?z, \text{KO}: \mathbf{0}\}; Z_1(\mathsf{p},\mathsf{s}), \\
& Z_2(\mathsf{c},\mathsf{s}) = \mathsf{c}?x; \text{if } allowed(x) \text{ then } \mathsf{c} \oplus \text{OK}; \mathsf{s}!x \text{ else } \mathsf{c} \oplus \text{KO}; Z_2(\mathsf{c},\mathsf{s}), \\
& Z_3(\mathsf{c},\mathsf{p}) = \mathsf{p}?y; Z_3(\mathsf{c},\mathsf{p})
\end{aligned}
\right\}
\tag{12.3}
$$

Improving EPP to make more choreographies projectable is therefore an interesting direction in general. The name 'endpoint projection' was introduced in [Carbone et al. 2006; Carbone et al. 2012], and the first formulation of merging was given by Carbone et al. [2012].

When a choreography is unrelialisable or unprojectable, we can decide to edit it. Let *flipCoin* be the local function from Example 6.4, and consider the following choreography.

$$
C \triangleq \text{if } \mathsf{p}.flipCoin() \text{ then } \mathsf{q}.1 \to \mathsf{p}.x \text{ else } \mathsf{q}.2 \to \mathsf{p}.x
$$

The choreography C cannot be implemented because of (lack of) knowledge of choice: there is no way for q to know whether it should communicate the number 1 or 2 to p. However, we can obtain a realisable (and projectable) choreography by adding appropriate selections:

$$
C' \triangleq \text{if } \mathsf{p}.flipCoin() \text{ then } \mathsf{p} \to \mathsf{q}[\text{THEN}]; \mathsf{q}.1 \to \mathsf{p}.x \text{ else } \mathsf{p} \to \mathsf{q}[\text{ELSE}]; \mathsf{q}.2 \to \mathsf{p}.x.
$$

The act of transforming an unprojectable choreography, like C, into a projectable one, like C', is called *amendment* (or repair). There are automatic procedures for amendment, which typically work by adding interactions as exemplified here [Lanese et al. 2013; Basu & Bultan 2016; Cruz-Filipe & Montesi 2020]. In Dalla Preda et al. [2017], amendment is even part of EPP; for example, C would be projectable because EPP in Dalla Preda et al. [2017] adds the necessary selections from p to q in the generated process terms.

Amendment is not a panacea. It should be used carefully because sometimes it is not obvious how a choreography should be fixed. Consider the choreography:

$$
\text{if } \mathsf{p}.flipCoin() \text{ then } \mathsf{q}.1 \to \mathsf{p}.x; \mathsf{r}.1 \to \mathsf{p}.y \text{ else } \mathsf{q}.2 \to \mathsf{p}.x; \mathsf{r}.2 \to \mathsf{p}.y.
$$

This choreography can be amended in different ways, including

$$
\begin{aligned}
&\text{if } p.\textit{flipCoin}() \text{ then} \\
&\quad p \to q[\text{THEN}]; p \to r[\text{THEN}]; q.1 \to p.x; r.1 \to p.y \\
&\text{else} \\
&\quad p \to q[\text{ELSE}]; p \to r[\text{ELSE}]; q.2 \to p.x; r.2 \to p.y
\end{aligned}
\tag{12.4}
$$

and

$$
\begin{aligned}
&\text{if } p.\textit{flipCoin}() \text{ then} \\
&\quad p \to q[\text{THEN}]; q \to r[\text{THEN}]; q.1 \to p.x; r.1 \to p.y \\
&\text{else} \\
&\quad p \to q[\text{ELSE}]; q \to r[\text{ELSE}]; q.2 \to p.x; r.2 \to p.y.
\end{aligned}
\tag{12.5}
$$

In (12.4), p communicates directly to q and r what they should do. In (12.5), p communicates what to do to q, and then q passes this information on to r. There is no absolute answer to which option is best. It might be that p has better, faster connections to q and r compared to the connection between q and r, which would favour (12.4). Or, q might have a faster connection to r, favouring (12.5). One might not even want q and r to communicate at all, for security or infrastructural reasons, which would favour (12.4) again.

Amendment can be a hard optimisation problem in general, and there might be relevant considerations for its operation that are hard, if not impractical, to formalise. Tools based on amendment should therefore allow choreography designers to inspect (and possibly change) the 'patch' computed for a choreography. Investigating heuristics and optimisations for improving amendment and better support choreography developers is an interesting line of work.

Expressivity of Choreographic Languages

A minimalistic model of choreographic programming, called Core Choreographies, is known to be Turing complete [Cruz-Filipe & Montesi 2020]. Core Choreographies is a simpler language than Recursive Choreographies: conditionals and procedure calls do not have continuations; the processes involved in procedures are statically fixed (procedures are not parameterised); each process can store in its memory only one natural number; and the only computations that a process can perform are calculating the successor of a natural number and checking whether the natural number communicated by another process is the same as the one stored locally.

The proof of Turing completeness encodes partial recursive functions, as defined by Kleene [1952], into choreographies that resemble concurrent versions of programs for register machines (the registers act as distributed processes). These choreographies can then be amended and projected to obtain compliant implementations. Therefore, the image of EPP (the set of all networks that are the EPP of some choreography) in theories like that of Recursive Choreographies is a Turing-complete and deadlock-free process language.

Albeit interesting and well-known, Turing completeness is rather coarse as a property for classifying the expressivity of choreographic languages. For example, it would not distinguish any of the additions to Recursive Choreographies presented in Part III, like choreographic choice and asynchronous communication (all these languages are Turing complete). In the future, it would be interesting to see studies that can distinguish and categorise the expressive power of choreographic languages with respect to what communication patterns they can express.

Extraction and Round-Trip Engineering

Dual to projection is choreography *extraction* [Carbone et al. 2018]. While projection computes a network of process terms from a choreography, extraction computes a choreography from a network of processes [Alur et al. 2003; Lange & Tuosto 2012; Lange et al. 2015; Cruz-Filipe et al. 2017; Carbone et al. 2018]. Extraction is a harder problem than projection because it requires predicting all the possible interactions that a network will enact. Algorithms for extraction typically have superpolynomial worst-case time complexity [Lange et al. 2015; Cruz-Filipe et al. 2017].

Extraction is a very useful operation in practice. Given some process terms that have been written manually, we can extract a choreography to understand what they do as a whole and reason about their correctness. Taken together, projection and extraction have the potential to achieve *choreographic round-trip engineering* for concurrent and distributed systems [Montesi 2013; Carbone et al. 2018]. That is, a development process that offers both choreographic and process-oriented views of the code of a system. Developers can then choose freely whether to edit the choreography (more convenient for changes about interactions) or the process programs (sometimes more convenient for small local changes), leveraging projection and extraction to keep the two views always in sync. There have even been proposals for languages that can describe both views, allowing for choreographic instructions to be mixed with process terms [Montesi & Yoshida 2013; Carbone et al. 2018].

Modularity

Procedures in Recursive Choreographies are parameterised on the processes that they involve, which allows for reusing them in choreographies that involve different processes. Process parameterisation was introduced in [Demangeon and Honda 2012], for multiparty session types. Later, the idea was extended in [Cruz-Filipe and Montesi 2017c] to deal with choreographic programming and general recursion (by using a $\mathring{,}$ operator similar in principle to the one defined here).

The choreographic languages that we have presented can be extended in several ways to better support *modular software development*.

For the sake of simplicity, in Recursive Choreographies all variables are 'global' and the body of an invoked procedure has access to all of them. An immediate improvement for modularity would therefore be to introduce call stacks and parameterise procedures also on local variables. We sketch how this might work. For example, in an extended syntax we could write a procedure like $X(\mathsf{p}(x, y), \mathsf{q}(z)) = C$. In the body C, p could then access only what the invoker of X has passed as arguments for x and y, and q could access only z. The body C could return values at processes, for instance by writing return $\mathsf{p}.v, \mathsf{q}.v'$. This would allow for a procedure call to assign the returned values to variables, for example $\mathsf{p}.w, \mathsf{q}.u := X(\mathsf{p}(e, e'), \mathsf{q}(e''))$. This kind of extensions can be equipped with type systems for checking that procedures are called with values of the right types and return values of the expected types [Carbone and Montesi 2013; Cruz-Filipe and Montesi 2017c].

Another useful extension is higher-order composition – that is, allowing a procedure to take choreographies (or procedure names) as parameters. Higher-order composition was introduced to multiparty session types in Demangeon and Honda [2012], but at the cost of distribution: entering a procedure requires a coordinator. Later, the Choral programming language demonstrated how to achieve higher-order composition with the same level of distribution of Recursive Choreographies (processes enter procedures independently) [Giallorenzo et al. 2020]. Choreographies in Choral are full-fledged objects that can carry state. However, the principles of higher-order choreographic programming in Choral have a simple explanation in terms of a choreographic variation of the λ-calculus, the canonical foundation of functional programming [Cruz-Filipe, Graversen, Lugovic, Montesi & Peressotti 2021]. Interestingly, in higher-order choreographies like those in [Giallorenzo et al. 2020; Cruz-Filipe, Graversen, Lugovic, Montesi & Peressotti 2021], one can write user-defined functions that can be used instead of communication primitives (like $\mathsf{p}.e \to \mathsf{q}.x$). This is useful, for example, in the writing of choreographies that establish secure communication channels and return functions that the programmer can use for secure communication through such channels.

Communication Failures

Most choreographic models, including those presented here, are built on the assumption that communications never fail. Of course, communications can fail in the real world. When models that assume reliable communication are applied in practice, the code generated from a choreography typically throws an unrecoverable error when it encounters a communication error.

Adameit et al. [2017] augmented multiparty session types with optional blocks that can be nondeterministically skipped in case a required communication channel fails. In Montesi and Peressotti [2017], the semantics of choreographies is extended with different kinds of failures: a process might fail in using its own local communication primitives (the network stack or driver, if you like); and the network might lose messages in transit. This extension allows for modelling sophisticated failure recovery strategies in choreographic programming, and writing user-defined robust implementations of communication primitives like those presented in this book.

Mechanisations

Several theories of choreographic languages have been mechanised in interactive theorem provers. A theory of choreographic programming was mechanised in [Cruz-Filipe, Montesi & Peressotti 2021a, 2021b], including proofs of Turing completeness, deadlock-freedom, and correctness of EPP for a variation of Recursive Choreographies where procedures are tail-recursive and parameterless (process names are fixed). Pohjola et al. [2022] explored how to compile choreographies to certified implementations in the functional language CakeML. Castro-Perez et al. [2021] developed a mechanised toolchain for multiparty session types and their compilation to OCaml. Hirsch and Garg [2022] mechanised how type systems for local expressions can be integrated with type systems for higher-order choreographic programming.

Choreographies and Logic

Choreographic languages have a deep connection to linear logic [Girard 1987]. Cut elimination corresponds to a choreographic programming language, and in particular simplifications of cuts correspond to communication terms [Carbone, Cruz-Filipe, Montesi & Murawska 2018; Carbone, Montesi & Schürmann 2018]. Exploring the link between choreographic languages and linear logic led to a new structural rule for linear logic that corresponds to parallel composition in process calculi [Carbone et al. 2018], which is based on hypersequents (collections of sequents) by Avron [1991]. This idea had an interesting spin-off: it later turned out to be important in achieving a strict correspondence between the standard structures of process calculi and proofs (an overview is given in Montesi and Peressotti [2021]). Furthermore, a language of multiparty session types corresponds to *coherence*, a generalisation of the compatibility check of duality found in linear logic from two propositions to many [Carbone et al. 2015; Carbone et al. 2017]. More generally, it has been observed that some languages of global types can be translated directly to proofs in linear logic [Caires & Pérez 2016; Carbone et al. 2016].

Choreographies can also be combined with logical reasoning to prove global properties that span multiple processes, as shown in [Carbone et al. 2010; Jongmans & Van den Bos 2022].

Visual Choreographies, Graphs, and Automata

We have focused on choreographic languages with a *textual* representation.

Some choreographic languages (typically without computation at processes) come with a *visual* representation. Notable examples are Message Sequence Charts [International Telecommunication Union 1996], UML Sequence Diagrams [Object Management Group 2017], and choreographies in the Business Process Modelling Notation (BPMN) [Object Management Group 2011].

A class of choreographic languages with obvious visual representations is that of *graphical choreographic languages*. In these languages, choreographies are given as graphs where edges or nodes are labelled by interactions [Object Management Group 2011; Deniélou & Yoshida 2012; Lange et al. 2015; Basu & Bultan 2016; Finkel & Lozes 2017; Barbanera et al. 2020; Orlando et al. 2021]. Choreographies in this setting can thus be drawn as we usually draw graphs. Operators for composing instructions in these languages are special nodes (sometimes called gates) or edges that have specific semantics (choice, parallel, etc.). Some graphical choreographic languages come with an operational semantics, which is typically developed by borrowing ideas from automata or Petri nets [Peterson 1977]. An interesting language in this category is that presented by Hildebrandt et al. [2019], which supports a declarative approach to the composition of choreographies: interactions are connected by edges that specify constraints, for example, one interaction might require or exclude another.

Networks that correspond to graphical choreographies are typically given in terms of automata that can interact, like communicating finite-state machines [Brand & Zafiropulo 1983].

Network Topology

In our languages, we have assumed that all processes are connected and that the set of processes involved in a choreography is statically determined. Some choreographic languages allow for more sophisticated treatments of network topologies. The connections that allow processes to communicate can be modelled explicitly and processes can interact to change the structure of these connections [Carbone et al. 2012; Carbone and Montesi 2013; Honda et al. 2016; Cruz-Filipe and Montesi 2017c]. Furthermore, the choreographic languages have primitives for creating new processes at runtime [Carbone et al. 2012; Carbone and Montesi 2013; Cruz-Filipe and Montesi 2017c]. Many principles for achieving these features were pioneered by Carbone et al. [2012], which was a significant milestone in the development of choreographic languages: it was the first time that a theory of choreographies could capture the replicated nature of servers. This was part of a significant effort aimed at understanding some of the key principles of the Web Services Choreography Description Language (WS-CDL) by the World Wide Web Consortium (W3C) [W3C 2005; Carbone et al. 2006; Carbone et al. 2007; Carbone et al. 2012]. At the time, and today still, web services represented one of the major application areas for choreographies.

Another interesting extension is to generalise process names in choreographies into collections of process names, say P. This leads to primitives like, for example, $p \rightarrow P[L]$, for the communication of L from p to all the processes in P [Deniélou & Yoshida 2011; Deniélou et al. 2012; Ng & Yoshida 2015; Cruz-Filipe & Montesi 2016; Castro-Perez et al. 2019]. The process instructions used to implement this kind of primitives might have a sophisticated semantics, because in application scenarios like peer-to-peer networks processes can independently join and leave these collections [Deniélou & Yoshida 2011].

Asynchronous Communication

Our runtime terms for asynchronous communication in choreographies are inspired by those in Deniélou and Yoshida [2013] and Cruz-Filipe and Montesi [2017b]. Asynchronous communication can be leveraged to write choreographies that exhibit new behaviours, like asynchronous mutual exchange [Lange et al. 2015; Cruz-Filipe et al. 2017; Cruz-Filipe et al. 2018]. In Cruz-Filipe and Montesi [2017a], asynchronous communication behaviour is simulated in a choreographic language with synchronous communication by spawning processes dedicated to storing messages in transit.

In other works, asynchronous communication is used to allow for some additional behaviours that we have not considered here. Most notably, messages in a queue that are from different senders can be consumed by the receiver in a different order than that in which they appear in the queue [Coppo et al. 2016; Ghilezan et al. 2021]. These reorderings are usually modelled by rewriting laws for message queues. For example, a queue $(p, v), (q, v')$ can be rewritten into $(q, v'), (p, v)$ (and vice versa) for any p, q, v, and v' such that $p \neq q$.

Out-of-Order Execution and Other Composition Operators

Out-of-order execution was introduced in choreographies in Carbone and Montesi [2013], and since then similar ideas have been adopted in other choreographic languages [Deniélou and Yoshida 2013; Honda et al. 2016; Cruz-Filipe & Montesi 2020]. An alternative to out-of-order execution is to have an explicit term for composing interactions in parallel or in unordered groups [Carbone et al. 2012; Cruz-Filipe et al. 2018]. Some theories take this a step further and come with different algebraic operators for the composition of choreographies (usually sequence, parallel, and choice) [Busi et al. 2005; Busi et al. 2006; Bravetti & Zavattaro 2007; Qiu et al. 2007; Lanese et al. 2008].

Unified Communication Primitives

Some choreographic languages feature a unified primitive for value communication and selection, which in our syntax we could write $p.L(e) \rightarrow q.x$ [Montesi 2013; Ng & Yoshida 2015; Dalla Preda et al. 2017; Giallorenzo, Montesi & Gabbrielli 2018; Castro-Perez et al. 2019]. The reason is often pragmatic: in several applications, including web services and object-oriented frameworks, messages carry both a label (the name of an operation or method) and a payload (the communicated value).

Variations of Choreography Compliance

Consider a choreography in which a Client might nondeterministically select label BUY or SELL at a Server:

$$C \triangleq \text{Client} \rightarrow \text{Server}[\text{BUY}] +_{\text{Client}} \text{Client} \rightarrow \text{Server}[\text{SELL}]. \tag{12.6}$$

Projection gives us the following process terms for Client and Server,

$$[\![C]\!]_{\text{Client}} = \text{Server} \oplus \text{BUY} + \text{Server} \oplus \text{SELL}$$
$$[\![C]\!]_{\text{Server}} = \text{Client} \, \& \, \{\text{BUY}: \mathbf{0}, \text{SELL}: \mathbf{0}\},$$

which ensure that the two processes can enact both selections. In the formulation of our correctness results, we used merging to allow branching terms to offer more labels than necessary. For example, the term

$$\text{Client} \, \& \, \{\text{BUY}: \mathbf{0}, \text{SELL}: \mathbf{0}, \text{QUIT}: \mathbf{0}\}$$

can be considered a compliant implementation of Server as well: since label QUIT is not going to be used by Client anyway, there is no risk of introducing interactions that are not prescribed by the choreography. By contrast, removing a branch prescribed by the choreography is not safe because the Client might want to select it.

If we relax the requirement that the implementation of a choreography should support all the prescribed interactions, we can allow for more flexibility also for the sender of a selection. A popular relaxation is permitting implementations that use fewer options than what the choreography prescribes. Under this interpretation of compliance, all the following process terms can be considered safe implementations of Client:

$$\text{Server} \oplus \text{BUY} + \text{Server} \oplus \text{SELL} \tag{12.7}$$

$$\text{Server} \oplus \text{BUY} \tag{12.8}$$

$$\text{Server} \oplus \text{SELL}. \tag{12.9}$$

The idea is that any of these implementations, when put in parallel with $[\![C]\!]_{\text{Server}}$ (or an extension of it with more labels), would be able to progress and enact at least one of the interactions prescribed by the choreography (but not all of them anymore, in the cases of the last two terms). By contrast, extending the implementation of Client such that it could select another label than BUY or SELL would not be safe: sending the selection of a label not prescribed by the choreography could lead to a deadlock (in case that label is not supported by the implementation of Server) or a selection not prescribed by the choreography (in case the implementation of Server supports the label). In general, it is safe for senders of selections to choose from fewer options than prescribed, and for receivers of selections to offer more options than prescribed.

Relaxing compliance to allow for fewer executions than those specified by the choreography has the advantage that an existing process program might be reused in the implementation of different choreographies. However, this relaxation should be a careful and deliberate choice because it makes choreographies less informative about what a system does. For example, if we establish a formal property about the choreography, this property might not hold anymore for an incomplete implementation of it. Choreographic programming typically requires implementations to be complete (since the aim is to compile faithful implementations), whereas multiparty session types do not (since the aim is to verify that a manually written implementation is sound). As we mentioned already, compliance in multiparty session types is called session fidelity [Honda et al. 2016]. Like compliance, the term is overloaded: sometimes fidelity does not include completeness [Honda et al. 2016], and sometimes it does [Castellani et al. 2022].

In practice, protocols may explicitly define some functionalities as required and others as optional – an example is the Internet Relay Chat protocol (IRC) [Oikarinen & Reed 1993]. Say, for example, that in the choreography in (12.6) the possibility of selecting label ʙᴜʏ is required whereas the possibility of selecting label sᴇʟʟ is optional. In this case, only the process terms found in (12.7) and (12.8) would be deemed as compliant implementations of Client. Therefore, in some cases, fine-grained control over the completeness aspect of compliance might be desirable.

Multiparty Languages

Choreographic languages fall under the umbrella term of *multiparty languages*: languages that describe the behaviour of multiple participants [Giallorenzo et al. 2021]. Another family of multiparty languages is *multitier languages*: languages where data can reside at different places and be transparently moved from one place to another [Weisenburger et al. 2020]. Differently from choreographies, multitier languages hide interaction instead of making it syntactically manifest: knowing how data should flow is not the programmer's responsibility. As a consequence, multitier languages are convenient for programming standalone applications, but not for reasoning about protocols. For some choreographic programming languages, it is possible to translate choreographies into multitier programs (by removing information about the concrete data flow) and vice versa (by computing one of the possible communication strategies for a multitier program) [Castro-Perez & Yoshida 2020; Giallorenzo et al. 2021].

Process names are often also called *roles* in choreographic languages, or *places* in multitier languages [Giallorenzo et al. 2021].

Solutions to Selected Exercises

Solution to Exercise 1.3   We construct a derivation of walk(New York, New York). The derivation is displayed in Figure A.1 (rotated to fit within the page).   □

Solution to Exercise 1.7   We first prove an auxiliary lemma.

Lemma A.1   For any A, B, and $\mathcal{D}$, if $\mathcal{D}$ concludes walk($A, B, 1$) then $\mathcal{D}$ contains exactly one application of an axiom.

Proof   The only way to conclude a walk of weight 1 is to apply rule DIR-w. This can be easily proven by showing that every derivable walk-proposition has at least weight 1, and since the conclusion of rule COMP-w has the sum of the weights in the premises, the weight of anything concluded with rule COMP-w is always strictly bigger than 1.
   We now know that $\mathcal{D}$ is structured as follows for some $\mathcal{D}'$.

$$\mathcal{D} = \frac{\begin{array}{c} \mathcal{D}' \\ \text{conn}(A, B) \end{array}}{\text{walk}(A, B, 1)}\ \text{DIR-w}$$

The derivation $\mathcal{D}'$ concludes a connection, and the only way to derive a connection in the system in Figure 1.4 is to apply an axiom. Since axioms do not have premises, $\mathcal{D}'$ must be exactly an application of one axiom.   □

   We now use Lemma A.1 to prove the statement of Exercise 1.7 – that is, for any derivation $\mathcal{D}$ in the system in Figure 1.4, A, B, and n, if $\mathcal{D}$ concludes walk(A, B, n), then $\mathcal{D}$ contains exactly n applications of axioms.
   We proceed by induction on the structure of $\mathcal{D}$. Since $\mathcal{D}$ concludes walk(A, B, n), it must end with either an application of rule DIR-w or an application of rule COMP-w. In the first case, $n = 1$ (since that is the only weight that DIR-w can conclude) and the thesis follows by Lemma A.1. In the second case, for some C, i, j, $\mathcal{E}$, and $\mathcal{F}$, $\mathcal{D}$ has the form:

A.0A.1

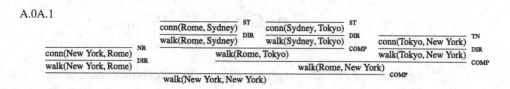

Figure A.1 A derivation of walk(New York, New York) in the system in Figure 1.2.

$$\mathcal{D} = \frac{\overset{\mathcal{E}}{\text{walk}(A, C, i)} \quad \overset{\mathcal{F}}{\text{walk}(C, A, j)}}{\text{walk}(A, B, i + j)} \text{ COMP-W}.$$

By induction hypothesis, $\mathcal{E}$ contains i applications of axioms and $\mathcal{F}$ contains j applications of axioms. Since $\mathcal{D}$ composes the two proofs without any extra axiom applications and rule COMP-W itself is not an axiom, $\mathcal{D}$ contains $i + j$ axiom applications and the thesis follows for $n \triangleq i + j$.   □

Solution to Exercise 1.8   Given any derivation $\mathcal{D}$ of walk(New York, New York), the following is also a valid derivation of the same proposition.

$$\mathcal{E} \triangleq \frac{\overset{\mathcal{D}}{\text{walk(New York, New York)}} \quad \overset{\mathcal{D}}{\text{walk(New York, New York)}}}{\text{walk(New York, New York)}} \text{ COMP}$$

The derivation $\mathcal{E}$ is strictly bigger than $\mathcal{D}$. Let n be the size of $\mathcal{D}$. Then the size of $\mathcal{E}$ is $2n + 1$ (since $\mathcal{E}$ has two distinct copies of $\mathcal{D}$ and an additional application of COMP).   □

Solution to Exercise 2.1   We can formalise the protocol as the choreography

Alice → Bob; Bob → Charlie; Charlie → Alice; 0.   □

Solution to Exercise 3.3   We proceed by showing that all process names in supp($N \mid M$) are necessarily in supp(N) ∪ supp(M) and vice versa.

For the first direction, let p be a process name in supp($N \mid M$). By definition of parallel composition, this is the case only if p ∈ supp(N) or p ∈ supp(M), so the thesis follows.

For the second direction, let p be a process name in supp(N) ∪ supp(M). By definition of set union, this implies that p ∈ supp(N) or (not exclusive) p ∈ supp(M). In the first case (p ∈ supp(N)), we have that ($N \mid M$)(p) = N(p) ≠ **0**, so p ∈ supp($N \mid M$). In the second case, (p ∈ supp(M)), we have that ($N \mid M$)(p) = M(p) ≠ **0**, so p ∈ supp($N \mid M$).   □

Solution to Exercise 3.7   Let n be the length of $\vec{r}$. We proceed by induction on n.

Case 1 $n = 0$, and therefore $\vec{r} = \epsilon$. The case is trivial because $N \setminus \epsilon = N$ and $N' \setminus \epsilon = N'$, so the thesis follows from the hypothesis $N \overset{\mu}{\to} N'$.

Case 2 $n = k + 1$ for $k \geq 0$, and therefore $\vec{r} = $ p, $\vec{q}$ for some p and $\vec{q}$. By induction hypothesis, $N \setminus \vec{q} \overset{\mu}{\to} N' \setminus \vec{q}$. By Lemma 3.10, $N \setminus \vec{q} \setminus $ p $\overset{\mu}{\to} N' \setminus \vec{q} \setminus $ p.   □

Solution to Exercise 4.2   We prove the two results separately.

The completeness part is proven by induction on the derivation of $C \overset{\vec{\mu}}{\twoheadrightarrow} C'$, denoted $\mathcal{D}$.

Case 1 $\mathcal{D}$ ends with an application of rule REFL. In this case, $C = C'$, therefore $[\![C]\!] = [\![C']\!]$ and the thesis follows by rule REFL.

Case 2 $\mathcal{D}$ ends with an application of rule STEP-R:

$$\mathcal{D} = \frac{\overset{\mathcal{E}}{C \overset{\vec{\mu}'}{\twoheadrightarrow} C''} \quad \overset{\mathcal{F}}{C'' \overset{\mu'}{\to} C'}}{C \overset{\vec{\mu}', \mu'}{\twoheadrightarrow} C'} \text{ STEP-R}$$

for some $\mathcal{E}$, $\mathcal{F}$, C'', $\vec{\mu}'$, and μ'. By induction hypothesis on $\mathcal{E}$, there exists $\mathcal{E}' :: [\![C]\!] \overset{\vec{\mu}'}{\twoheadrightarrow} [\![C'']\!]$. By the conclusion of $\mathcal{F}$ and Theorem 4.7, there exists $\mathcal{F}' :: [\![C'']\!] \overset{\mu}{\to} [\![C']\!]$. The thesis follows by rule STEP-R:

$$\dfrac{\overset{\mathcal{E}'}{[\![C]\!] \xrightarrow{\bar{\mu}'} [\![C'']\!]} \quad \overset{\mathcal{F}'}{[\![C'']\!] \xrightarrow{\mu} [\![C']\!]}}{[\![C]\!] \xrightarrow{\bar{\mu}'\mu'} [\![C']\!]} \; \text{STEP-R} \; .$$

Moving to the soundness part, let $\mathcal{D}$ now be the derivation of $[\![C]\!] \xrightarrow{\bar{\mu}} N$. We proceed by induction on the structure of $\mathcal{D}$.

Case 1 $\mathcal{D}$ ends with an application of rule REFL. In this case, the thesis follows immediately by rule REFL.

Case 2 $\mathcal{D}$ ends with an application of rule STEP-R:

$$\mathcal{D} = \dfrac{\overset{\mathcal{E}}{[\![C]\!] \xrightarrow{\bar{\mu}'} M} \quad \overset{\mathcal{F}}{M \xrightarrow{\mu'} N}}{[\![C]\!] \xrightarrow{\bar{\mu}'\mu'} N} \; \text{STEP-R}$$

for some $\mathcal{E}$, $\mathcal{F}$, M, $\bar{\mu}'$, and μ' such that $\bar{\mu} = \bar{\mu}', \mu'$. By induction hypothesis on $\mathcal{E}$, there exists $\mathcal{E}'$ such that $C \xrightarrow{\bar{\mu}'} C''$ for some C'' such that $[\![C'']\!] = M$. By the conclusion of $\mathcal{F}$ and Theorem 4.7, there exist C' and $\mathcal{F}'$ such that $\mathcal{F}' :: C'' \xrightarrow{\mu} C'$ and $N = [\![C']\!]$. The thesis follows by rule STEP-R:

$$\dfrac{\overset{\mathcal{E}'}{C \xrightarrow{\bar{\mu}'} C''} \quad \overset{\mathcal{F}'}{C'' \xrightarrow{\mu} C'}}{C \xrightarrow{\bar{\mu}'\mu'} C'} \; \text{STEP-R} \; . \qquad \square$$

Solution to Exercise 6.1

Identity Element The equation $0 \, \fatsemi \, C = C$ holds by definition of $\fatsemi$. For $C \, \fatsemi \, 0 = C$, we proceed by induction on the structure of C. We get two cases.

  Case 1 $C = 0$. In this case, $0 \, \fatsemi \, 0 = 0$.

  Case 2 $C = I; C'$ for some I and C'. By definition of $\fatsemi$, $(I; C') \, \fatsemi \, 0 = I; (C' \, \fatsemi \, 0)$. By induction hypothesis on C', $C' \, \fatsemi \, 0 = C'$. Hence, $(I; C') \, \fatsemi \, 0 = I; C'$.

Associativity We proceed by structural induction on C_1.

  Case 1 $C_1 = 0$. By the equations for the identity element, $0 \, \fatsemi \, (C_2 \, \fatsemi \, C_3) = C_2 \, \fatsemi \, C_3$ and $(0 \, \fatsemi \, C_2) \, \fatsemi \, C_3 = C_2 \, \fatsemi \, C_3$.

  Case 2 $C_1 = I; C_1'$ for some I and C_1'. The following equations show that $I; C_1' \, \fatsemi \, (C_2 \, \fatsemi \, C_3) = (I; C_1' \, \fatsemi \, C_2) \, \fatsemi \, C_3$.

$$
\begin{aligned}
I; C_1' \, \fatsemi \, (C_2 \, \fatsemi \, C_3) &= I; (C_1' \, \fatsemi \, (C_2 \, \fatsemi \, C_3)) &&\text{by definition of } \fatsemi \\
(I; C_1' \, \fatsemi \, C_2) \, \fatsemi \, C_3 &= (I; (C_1' \, \fatsemi \, C_2)) \, \fatsemi \, C_3 &&\text{by definition of } \fatsemi \\
&= I; ((C_1' \, \fatsemi \, C_2) \, \fatsemi \, C_3) &&\text{by definition of } \fatsemi \\
&= I; (C_1' \, \fatsemi \, (C_2 \, \fatsemi \, C_3)) &&\text{by i.h.} \qquad \square
\end{aligned}
$$

Solution to Exercise 8.3 We prove each property separately.

Reflexivity We have to prove that $P \sqcup P = P$. This follows directly from the idempotency property of the $\sqcup$ operator (Proposition 8.3).

Antisymmetry This result follows by commutativity of $\sqcup$:

$$P = P \sqcup Q \qquad \text{by } P \sqsupseteq Q \text{ and Definition 8.4}$$
$$= Q \sqcup P \qquad \text{by Proposition 8.3, commutativity}$$
$$= Q \qquad \text{by } Q \sqsupseteq P \text{ and Definition 8.4.}$$

Transitivity We have to prove that $P \sqcup R = P$. We proceed by induction on the structure of P.

Case 1 $P = 0$. In this case, by definition of merging, both Q and R are necessarily 0 (were they not, $P \sqcup Q$ and $Q \sqcup R$ would be undefined).

Case 2 $P = I; P'$ for some P' and I that is not a conditional or a branching. By definition of merging, $Q = I; Q'$ for some Q' – otherwise, $P \sqcup Q$ would be undefined. Likewise, $R = I; R'$ for some R'.

By definition of merging and the structures of P and R, $P \sqcup R = I; (P' \sqcup R')$, so we have to prove that $I; (P' \sqcup R') = P$.

By hypothesis, $P = P \sqcup Q$. By the definition of merging and the structures of P and Q, $P \sqcup Q = I; (P' \sqcup Q')$. We thus have the following system of equations.

$$P = I; P'$$
$$P = P \sqcup Q$$
$$P \sqcup Q = I; (P' \sqcup Q')$$

These equations imply that $P' = P' \sqcup Q'$, and therefore $P' \sqsupseteq Q'$. Following a similar reasoning applied to Q and R, we get $Q' = Q' \sqcup R'$ and thus $Q' \sqsupseteq R'$.

By $P' \sqsupseteq Q'$, $Q' \sqsupseteq R'$, and the induction hypothesis, we have that $P' \sqsupseteq R'$. Hence, $P' \sqcup R' = P'$.

Case 3 $P = \text{if } e \text{ then } P_1 \text{ else } P_2$ for some e, P_1, and P_2. This case is similar to the previous one, starting from the observation that merging requires $Q = \text{if } e \text{ then } Q_1 \text{ else } Q_2$, for some Q_1 and Q_2, and $R = \text{if } e \text{ then } R_1 \text{ else } R_2$, for some R_1 and R_2. The rest is a straightforward adaptation of the development for the previous case.

Case 4 $P = \text{p} \& \{L_i : P_i\}_{i \in I}; P'$ for some p, I, and $\{P_i\}_{i \in I}$. This case is similar to the previous two, but the reasoning on subterms needs to be iterated in order to cover all the branches in P that are present also in Q and R. In particular, by definition of merging, $Q = \text{p} \& \{L_j : Q_j\}_{j \in J}$ for some J and $\{Q_j\}_{j \in J}$, and $R = \text{p} \& \{L_k : R_k\}_{k \in K}$ for some K and $\{R_k\}_{k \in K}$.

The key observation is that $P \sqsupseteq Q$ implies $I \supseteq J$ and $Q \sqsupseteq R$ implies $J \supseteq K$. Transitivity of $\supseteq$ yields $I \supseteq K$. By following a similar development to the one for the second case of this proof by induction ($P = I; P'$), we get for every $k \in K$ that $P_k \sqsupseteq R_k$, which allows us to derive the thesis by applying the induction hypothesis and the definition of merging.   □

Solution to Exercise 8.4 For the first item, we have to prove that $(P \sqcup Q) \sqcup P = P \sqcup Q$ and $(P \sqcup Q) \sqcup Q = P \sqcup Q$. These equalities follow by rewriting the left-hand sides by using the laws of commutativity, associativity, and idempotency for $\sqcup$.

For the second item, by hypothesis we know that

$$P \sqcup Q = P \tag{A.1}$$

and

$$P \sqcup R = P. \tag{A.2}$$

We have to prove that $P \sqcup (Q \sqcup R) = P$, which we obtain as follows.

$$
\begin{aligned}
P \sqcup (Q \sqcup R) = (P \sqcup Q) \sqcup R & \qquad \text{by associativity of } \sqcup \\
= P \sqcup R & \qquad \text{by (A.1)} \\
= P & \qquad \text{by (A.2)} \qquad \Box
\end{aligned}
$$

Solution to Exercise 8.7 By induction on P.

Case 1 $P = 0$. In this case, $R = 0$. Therefore, $P \,\fatsemi\, Q = Q$ and $R \,\fatsemi\, S = S$. The thesis follows by the hypothesis $Q \sqsupseteq S$.

Case 2 $P = I; P'$ for some I and P'.

Suppose that I is neither a conditional nor a branching. Then, by the definitions of $\sqcup$ and $\sqsupseteq$, it must be that $R = I; R'$ for some R' such that $P' \sqsupseteq R'$. We obtain

$$
\begin{aligned}
P \,\fatsemi\, Q &= I; (P' \,\fatsemi\, Q) \\
R \,\fatsemi\, S &= I; (R' \,\fatsemi\, S),
\end{aligned}
$$

and the thesis follows by induction hypothesis.

Suppose that I is a conditional – that is, $I = $ if e then P_1 else P_2 for some P_1 and P_2. By the definition of $\sqcup$ and $\sqsupseteq$, $R = $ if e then R_1 else R_2 for some R_1 and R_2 such that $P_1 \sqsupseteq R_1$ and $P_2 \sqsupseteq R_2$. We obtain

$$
\begin{aligned}
P \,\fatsemi\, Q &= \text{if } e \text{ then } P_1 \text{ else } P_2; (P' \,\fatsemi\, Q) \\
R \,\fatsemi\, S &= \text{if } e \text{ then } R_1 \text{ else } R_2; (R' \,\fatsemi\, S),
\end{aligned}
$$

and the thesis follows from the induction hypothesis and the definition of $\sqcup$.

Suppose that I is a branching term – that is, $I = \mathsf{p}\&\{\mathsf{L}_j : P_j\}_{j \in J}$ for some p, set of labels $\{\mathsf{L}_j\}_{j \in J}$, set of processes $\{P_j\}_{j \in J}$, and set of indices J. The reasoning is similar to the one for conditionals, observing that by the definitions of $\sqcup$ and $\sqsupseteq$, $R = \mathsf{p} \& \{\mathsf{L}_k : R_k\}_{k \in K}$ for some $\{\mathsf{L}_k\}_{k \in K}$, $\{P_k\}_{k \in K}$, and K such that $K \subseteq I$ and $P_k \sqsupseteq R_k$ for all $k \in K$. $\qquad \Box$

Solution to Exercise 8.8 By induction on C.

Case 1 $C = 0$. The thesis follows from the definitions of projection and $\fatsemi$, since in this case $C \,\fatsemi\, C' = C'$ and $[\![C]\!]_r \,\fatsemi\, [\![C']\!]_r = [\![C']\!]_r$.

Case 2 $C = I; C_1$, for some I and C_1 such that I is an assignment, a value communication, or a selection. We have a subcase for each possible shape that I can take. We show the reasoning for the first one.

Suppose that $I = \mathsf{p}.x := e$ for some p, x, and e. Then,

$$C \,\fatsemi\, C' = \mathsf{p}.x := e; (C_1 \,\fatsemi\, C').$$

By induction hypothesis,

$$\llbracket C_1 \,\fatsemi\, C' \rrbracket_r = \llbracket C_1 \rrbracket_r \,\fatsemi\, \llbracket C' \rrbracket_r.$$

Now we have two possibilities, depending on whether r is p or not. If r = p, then

$$\llbracket C \,\fatsemi\, C' \rrbracket_r = (x := e; \llbracket C_1 \,\fatsemi\, C' \rrbracket_r)$$
$$\llbracket C \rrbracket_r \,\fatsemi\, \llbracket C' \rrbracket_r = (x := e; \llbracket C_1 \rrbracket_r) \,\fatsemi\, \llbracket C' \rrbracket_r = x := e; (\llbracket C_1 \rrbracket_r \,\fatsemi\, \llbracket C' \rrbracket_r),$$

and the thesis follows by induction hypothesis. Otherwise, if r ≠ p,

$$\llbracket C \,\fatsemi\, C' \rrbracket_r = \llbracket C_1 \,\fatsemi\, C' \rrbracket_r.$$

Here as well, the thesis follows by induction hypothesis.

If I is a value communication of a selection, the reasoning is similar to the one for assignments.

Case 3 $C = \text{if } p.e \text{ then } C_1 \text{ else } C_2; C_3$. In this case,

$$C \,\fatsemi\, C' = \text{if } p.e \text{ then } C_1 \text{ else } C_2; (C_3 \,\fatsemi\, C').$$

We now proceed differently depending on whether r = p or r ≠ p.
If r = p, then

$$\llbracket C \,\fatsemi\, C' \rrbracket_r = \text{if } e \text{ then} \llbracket C_1 \rrbracket_r \text{ else} \llbracket C_2 \rrbracket_r; \llbracket C_3 \,\fatsemi\, C' \rrbracket_r$$
$$\llbracket C \rrbracket_r \,\fatsemi\, \llbracket C' \rrbracket_r = (\text{if } e \text{ then} \llbracket C_1 \rrbracket_r \text{ else} \llbracket C_2 \rrbracket_r; \llbracket C_3 \rrbracket_r) \,\fatsemi\, \llbracket C' \rrbracket_r$$
$$= \text{if } e \text{ then} \llbracket C_1 \rrbracket_r \text{ else} \llbracket C_2 \rrbracket_r; (\llbracket C_3 \rrbracket_r \,\fatsemi\, \llbracket C' \rrbracket_r).$$

The thesis follows by induction hypothesis.
Otherwise, if r ≠ p, then

$$\llbracket C \,\fatsemi\, C' \rrbracket_r = (\llbracket C_1 \rrbracket_r \sqcup \llbracket C_2 \rrbracket_r) \,\fatsemi\, \llbracket C_3 \,\fatsemi\, C' \rrbracket_r$$
$$\llbracket C \rrbracket_r \,\fatsemi\, \llbracket C' \rrbracket_r = ((\llbracket C_1 \rrbracket_r \sqcup \llbracket C_2 \rrbracket_r) \,\fatsemi\, \llbracket C_3 \rrbracket_r) \,\fatsemi\, \llbracket C' \rrbracket_r$$

By associativity of $\fatsemi$, we can rewrite the right-hand side of the second equation as follows.

$$((\llbracket C_1 \rrbracket_r \sqcup \llbracket C_2 \rrbracket_r) \,\fatsemi\, \llbracket C_3 \rrbracket_r) \,\fatsemi\, \llbracket C' \rrbracket_r = (\llbracket C_1 \rrbracket_r \sqcup \llbracket C_2 \rrbracket_r) \,\fatsemi\, (\llbracket C_3 \rrbracket_r \,\fatsemi\, \llbracket C' \rrbracket_r)$$

We thus need to prove that $\llbracket C_3 \,\fatsemi\, C' \rrbracket_r = \llbracket C_3 \rrbracket_r \,\fatsemi\, \llbracket C' \rrbracket_r$, which follows by induction hypothesis. □

References

Adameit, M., Peters, K. & Nestmann, U. [2017], 'Session types for link failures', *in* A. Bouajjani & A. Silva, eds., *FORTE '17: Formal Techniques for Distributed Objects, Components, and Systems: International Federated Conference on Distributed Computing Techniques, Proceedings*. Vol. 10321 of Lecture Notes in Computer Science. Springer, pp. 1–16.

Alur, R., Etessami, K. & Yannakakis, M. [2003], 'Inference of message sequence charts', *IEEE Trans. Software Eng.* **29**(7), 623–33.

Alur, R., Etessami, K. & Yannakakis, M. [2005], 'Realizability and verification of MSC graphs', *Theor. Comput. Sci.* **331**(1), 97–114.

Ancona, D., Bono, V., Bravetti, M. et al. [2016], 'Behavioral types in programming languages', *Found. Trends Program. Lang.* **3**(2–3), 95–230.

Appel, A. W. & Palsberg, J. [2002], *Modern Compiler Implementation in Java*. 2nd ed. Cambridge University Press.

Autili, M., Salle, A. D., Gallo, F., Pompilio, C. & Tivoli, M. [2020], 'Chorevolution: Service choreography in practice', *Sci. Comput. Program.* **197**, 1–11.

Avron, A. [1991], 'Hypersequents, logical consequence and intermediate logics for concurrency', *Ann. Math. Artif. Intell.* **4**, 225–48.

Barbanera, F., Lanese, I. & Tuosto, E. [2020], 'Choreography automata', *in* S. Bliudze & L. Bocchi, eds., *COORDINATION '20: Coordination Models and Languages, Proceedings*. Vol. 12134 of Lecture Notes in Computer Science. Springer, pp. 86–106.

Basu, S. & Bultan, T. [2016], 'Automated choreography repair', *in* P. Stevens & A. Wasowski, eds., *Fundamental Approaches to Software Engineering, Proceedings*. Vol. 9633 of Lecture Notes in Computer Science. Springer, pp. 13–30.

Bocchi, L., Chen, T., Demangeon, R., Honda, K. & Yoshida, N. [2017], 'Monitoring networks through multiparty session types', *Theor. Comput. Sci.* **669**, 33–58.

Brand, D. & Zafiropulo, P. [1983], 'On communicating finite-state machines', *J. ACM* **30**(2), 323–42.

Bravetti, M., Carbone, M. & Zavattaro, G. [2017], 'Undecidability of asynchronous session subtyping', *Inf. Comput.* **256**, 300–20.

Bravetti, M. & Zavattaro, G. [2007], 'Towards a unifying theory for choreography conformance and contract compliance', *in* M. Lumpe & W. Vanderperren, eds., *International Symposium on Software Composition, Revised Selected Papers*. Vol. 4829 of Lecture Notes in Computer Science. Springer, pp. 34–50.

Bravetti, M. & Zavattaro, G. [2007], Towards a unifying theory for choreography conformance and contract compliance, *in* M. Lumpe & W. Vanderperren, eds., *Software Composition – 6th International Symposium, SC@ETAPS 2007, Braga, Portugal, March 24-25, 2007, Revised Selected Papers*. Vol. 4829 of Lecture Notes in Computer Science. Springer, pp. 34–50.

Bravetti, M. & Zavattaro, G. [2018], 'Foundations of coordination and contracts and their contribution to session type theory', *in* G. D. M. Serugendo & M. Loreti, eds., *COORDINATION '18: Coordination*

Models and Languages, Proceedings. Vol. 10852 of Lecture Notes in Computer Science. Springer, pp. 21–50.

Briais, S. & Nestmann, U. [2007], 'A formal semantics for protocol narrations', *Theor. Comput. Sci.* **389**(3), 484–511.

Bruni, A., Carbone, M., Giustolisi, R., Mödersheim, S. & Schürmann, C. [2021], 'Security protocols as choreographies', *in* D. Dougherty, J. Meseguer, S. A. Mödersheim & P. D. Rowe, eds., *Protocols, Strands, and Logic: Essays Dedicated to Joshua Guttman on the Occasion of His 66.66th Birthday*. Vol. 13066 of Lecture Notes in Computer Science. Springer, pp. 98–111.

Busi, N., Gorrieri, R., Guidi, C., Lucchi, R. & Zavattaro, G. [2005], 'Choreography and orchestration: A synergic approach for system design', *in* B. Benatallah, F. Casati & P. Traverso, eds., *ICSOC '05: International Conference on Service-Oriented Computing, Proceedings*. Vol. 3826 of Lecture Notes in Computer Science. Springer, pp. 228–40.

Busi, N., Gorrieri, R., Guidi, C., Lucchi, R. & Zavattaro, G. [2006], 'Choreography and orchestration conformance for system design', *in* P. Ciancarini & H. Wiklicky, eds., *Coordination Models and Languages, Proceedings*. Vol. 4038 of Lecture Notes in Computer Science. Springer, pp. 63–81.

Buss, S. R., ed. [1998], *Handbook of Proof Theory*. Vol. 137 of Studies in Logic and the Foundations of Mathematics. Elsevier.

Caires, L. & Perez, J. A. [2016], 'Multiparty session types within a canonical binary theory, and beyond', *in* E. Albert & I. Lanese, eds., *FORTE '16: Formal Techniques for Distributed Objects, Components, and Systems: International Federated Conference on Distributed Computing Techniques, Proceedings*. Vol. 9688 of Lecture Notes in Computer Science. Springer, pp. 74–95.

Caleiro, C., Viganò, L. & Basin, D. A. [2006], 'On the semantics of alice&bob specifications of security protocols', *Theor. Comput. Sci.* **367**(1–2), 88–122.

Carbone, M., Cruz-Filipe, L., Montesi, F. & Murawska, A. [2018], 'Multiparty classical choreographies', *in* F. Mesnard & P. J. Stuckey, eds., *LOPSTR '18: International Symposium on Logic-Based Program Synthesis and Transformation, Revised Selected Papers*. Vol. 11408 of Lecture Notes in Computer Science. Springer, pp. 59–76.

Carbone, M., Grohmann, D., Hildebrandt, T. T. & López, H. A. [2010], 'A logic for choreographies', *in* K. Honda & A. Mycroft, eds., *PLACES '10: Workshop on Programming Language Approaches to Concurrency and Communication-cEntric Software, Proceedings*. Vol. 69 of Electronic Proceedings in Theoretical Computer Science, pp. 29–43.

Carbone, M., Honda, K. & Yoshida, N. [2007], 'A calculus of global interaction based on session types', *Electron. Notes Theor. Comput. Sci.* **171**(3), 127–51.

Carbone, M., Honda, K. & Yoshida, N. [2012], 'Structured communication-centered programming for web services', *ACM Trans. Program. Lang. Syst.* **34**(2), 8.

Carbone, M., Honda, K., Yoshida, N. et al. [2006], 'A theoretical basis of communication-centred concurrent programming', W3C working note. www.w3.org/2002/ws/chor/edcopies/theory/note.pdf.

Carbone, M., Lindley, S., Montesi, F., Schürmann, C. & Wadler, P. [2016], 'Coherence generalises duality: A logical explanation of multiparty session types', *in* J. Desharnais & R. Jagadeesan, eds., *CONCUR '16: International Conference on Concurrency Theory*. Vol. 59 of Leibniz International Proceedings in Informatics. Schloss Dagstuhl Leibniz Center for Computer Science, pp. 33:1–15.

Carbone, M. & Montesi, F. [2013], 'Deadlock-freedom-by-design: Multiparty asynchronous global programming' *in POPL '13: Principles of Programming Languages*. Association for Computing Machinery, pp. 263–74.

Carbone, M., Montesi, F. & Schürmann, C. [2018], 'Choreographies, logically', *Distributed Comput.* **31**(1), 51–67.

Carbone, M., Montesi, F., Schürmann, C. & Yoshida, N. [2015], 'Multiparty session types as coherence proofs', *in CONCUR '15: Conference on Concurrency Theory*. Leibniz International Proceedings in Informatics. Schloss Dagstuhl Leibniz Center for Computer Science, pp. 412–26.

Carbone, M., Montesi, F., Schürmann, C. & Yoshida, N. [2017], 'Multiparty session types as coherence proofs', *Acta Informatica* **54**(3), 243–69.

Cardelli, L. & Gordon, A. D. [2000], 'Mobile ambients', *Theor. Comput. Sci.* **240**(1), 177–213.

Castagna, G., Dezani-Ciancaglini, M. & Padovani, L. [2012], 'On global types and multi-party session', *Log. Methods Comput. Sci.* **8**(1).

Castellani, I., Dezani-Ciancaglini, M. & Giannini, P. [2022], 'Event structure semantics for multiparty sessions', *CoRR* **abs/2201.00221**.

Castellani, I., Dezani-Ciancaglini, M. & Pérez, J. A. [2016], 'Self-adaptation and secure information flow in multiparty communications', *Formal Aspects Comput.* **28**(4), 669–96.

Castro-Perez, D., Ferreira, F., Gheri, L. & Yoshida, N. [2021], 'Zooid: A DSL for certified multiparty computation. From mechanised metatheory to certified multiparty processes', *in* S. N. Freund & E. Yahav, eds., *ACM SIGPLAN '21: Association for Computing Machinery Special Interest Group on Programming Languages International Conference on Programming Language Design and Implementation*. Association for Computing Machinery, pp. 237–51.

Castro-Perez, D., Hu, R., Jongmans, S., Ng, N. & Yoshida, N. [2019], 'Distributed programming using role-parametric session types in go: Statically-typed endpoint APIs for dynamically-instantiated communication structures', *Proc. ACM Program. Lang.* **3**(POPL), 29:1–30.

Castro-Perez, D. & Yoshida, N. [2020], 'Compiling first-order functions to session-typed parallel code', *in* L. Pouchet & A. Jimborean, eds., *CC '20: International Conference on Compiler Construction*. Association for Computing Machinery, pp. 143–54.

Clarke, E. M. & Grumberg, O. [1987], 'Avoiding the state explosion problem in temporal logic model checking', *in* F. B. Schneider, ed., *Proceedings of the Annual Association for Computing Machinery Symposium on Principles of Distributed Computing*. Association for Computing Machinery, pp. 294–303.

Clarke, E. M., Klieber, W., Nováček, M. & Zuliani, P. [2011], 'Model checking and the state explosion problem', *in* B. Meyer & M. Nordio, eds., *Tools for Practical Software Verification, LASER, International Summer School, Revised Tutorial Lectures*. Vol. 7682 of Lecture Notes in Computer Science. Springer, pp. 1–30.

Cooper, K. & Torczon, L. [2011], *Engineering a Compiler*. Elsevier.

Coppo, M., Dezani-Ciancaglini, M., Yoshida, N. & Padovani, L. [2016], 'Global progress for dynamically interleaved multiparty sessions', *Math. Struct. Comput. Sci.* **26**(2), 238–302.

Cormen, T. H., Leiserson, C. E., Rivest, R. L. & Stein, C. [2022], *Introduction to Algorithms*. MIT Press.

Cruz-Filipe, L., Graversen, E., Lugovic, L., Montesi, F. & Peressotti, M. [2021], 'Choreographies as functions', *CoRR* **abs/2111.03701**.

Cruz-Filipe, L., Larsen, K. S. & Montesi, F. [2017], 'The paths to choreography extraction', *in* J. Esparza & A. S. Murawski, eds., *Foundations of Software Science and Computation Structures, Proceedings*. Vol. 10203 of Lecture Notes in Computer Science, Springer, pp. 424–40.

Cruz-Filipe, L. & Montesi, F. [2016], Choreographies in practice, *in Formal Techniques for Distributed Objects, Components, and Systems: International Federated Conference on Distributed Computing Techniques, Proceedings*. Vol. 9688 of Lecture Notes in Computer Science. Springer, pp. 114–23.

Cruz-Filipe, L. & Montesi, F. [2017a], 'Encoding asynchrony in choreographies', *in* A. Seffah, B. Penzenstadler, C. Alves & X. Peng, eds., *SAC '17: Proceedings of the Symposium on Applied Computing*. Association for Computing Machinery, pp. 1175–7.

Cruz-Filipe, L. & Montesi, F. [2017*b*], 'On asynchrony and choreographies', *in* M. Bartoletti, L. Bocchi, L. Henrio & S. Knight, eds., *ICE '17: Proceedings of the Interaction and Concurrency Experience*. Vol. 261 of Electronic Proceedings in Theoretical Computer Science, pp. 76–90.

Cruz-Filipe, L. & Montesi, F. [2017*c*], 'Procedural choreographic programming', *in* A. Bouajjani & A. Silva, eds., *FORTE '17: Formal Techniques for Distributed Objects, Components, and Systems: International Federated Conference on Distributed Computing Techniques, Proceedings*. Vol. 10321 of Lecture Notes in Computer Science. Springer, pp. 92–107.

Cruz-Filipe, L. & Montesi, F. [2020], 'A core model for choreographic programming', *Theor. Comput. Sci.* **802**, 38–66.

Cruz-Filipe, L., Montesi, F. & Peressotti, M. [2018], 'Communications in choreographies, revisited', *in* H. M. Haddad, R. L. Wainwright & R. Chbeir, eds., *ACM '18: Proceedings of the Annual Association for Computing Machinery Symposium on Applied Computing*. Association for Computing Machinery, pp. 1248–55.

Cruz-Filipe, L., Montesi, F. & Peressotti, M. [2021*a*], 'Certifying choreography compilation', *in* A. Cerone & P. C. Ölveczky, eds., *ICTAC '21: International Colloquium on Theoretical Aspects of Computing, Proceedings*. Vol. 12819 of Lecture Notes in Computer Science. Springer, pp. 115–33.

Cruz-Filipe, L., Montesi, F. & Peressotti, M. [2021*b*], 'Formalising a Turing-complete choreographic language in coq', *in* L. Cohen & C. Kaliszyk, eds., *ITP '21: International Conference on Interactive Theorem Proving*. Vol. 193 of Leibniz International Proceedings in Informatics. Schloss Dagstuhl Leibniz Center for Computer Science, pp. 15:1–18.

Dalla Preda, M., Gabbrielli, M., Giallorenzo, S., Lanese, I. & Mauro, J. [2017], 'Dynamic choreographies: Theory and implementation', *Log. Methods Comput. Sci.* **13**(2).

Davey, B. A. & Priestley, H. A. [2002], *Introduction to Lattices and Order*. 2nd ed. Cambridge University Press.

Demangeon, R. & Honda, K. [2012], 'Nested protocols in session types', *in* M. Koutny & I. Ulidowski, eds., *CONCUR '12: International Conference on Concurrency Theory*. Vol. 7454 of Lecture Notes in Computer Science. Springer, pp. 272–86.

Deniélou, P. & Yoshida, N. [2011], 'Dynamic multirole session types', *in* T. Ball & M. Sagiv, eds., *Proceedings of the Association for Computing Machinery Special Interest Group on Programming Languages (SIGPLAN) Symposium on Principles of Programming Languages*. Association for Computing Machinery, pp. 435–46.

Deniélou, P. & Yoshida, N. [2012], 'Multiparty session types meet communicating automata', *in* H. Seidl, ed., *Programming Languages and Systems: 21st European Symposium on Programming*. Vol. 7211 of Lecture Notes in Computer Science. Springer, pp. 194–213.

Deniélou, P. & Yoshida, N. [2013], 'Multiparty compatibility in communicating automata: Characterisation and synthesis of global session types', *in* F. V. Fomin, R. Freivalds, M. Z. Kwiatkowska & D. Peleg, eds., *International Colloquium on Automata, Languages, and Programming, Proceedings, Part II*. Vol. 7966 of Lecture Notes in Computer Science. Springer, pp. 174–86.

Deniélou, P., Yoshida, N., Bejleri, A. & Hu, R. [2012], 'Parameterised multiparty session types', *Log. Methods Comput. Sci.* **8**(4).

Diffie, W. & Hellman, M. E. [1976], 'New directions in cryptography', *IEEE Trans. Inf. Theory* **22**(6), 644–54.

Dragoni, N., Giallorenzo, S., Lafuente, A. L. et al. [2017], 'Microservices: Yesterday, today, and tomorrow', *in* M. Mazzara & B. Meyer, eds., *Present and Ulterior Software Engineering*. Springer, pp. 195–216.

Finkel, A. & Lozes, É. [2017], 'Synchronizability of communicating finite state machines is not decidable', *in* I. Chatzigiannakis, P. Indyk, F. Kuhn & A. Muscholl, eds., *ICALP '17: International Colloquium on Automata, Languages, and Programming*. Vol. 80 of Leibniz International Proceedings in Informatics. Schloss Dagstuhl Leibniz Center for Computer Science, pp. 122:1–14.

Franklin, J. & Daoud, A. [2010], *Proof in Mathematics: An Introduction*. Kew.

Ghilezan, S., Pantovic, J., Prokic, I., Scalas, A. & Yoshida, N. [2021], 'Precise subtyping for asynchronous multiparty sessions', *Proc. ACM Program. Lang.* **5**(POPL), 16:1–28.

Giallorenzo, S., Lanese, I. & Russo, D. [2018], 'Chip: A choreographic integration process', *in* H. Panetto, C. Debruyne, H. A. Proper et al. eds., *On the Move to Meaningful Internet Systems: Confederated International Conferences, Proceedings, Part II*. Vol. 11230 of Lecture Notes in Computer Science. Springer, pp. 22–40.

Giallorenzo, S., Montesi, F. & Gabbrielli, M. [2018], 'Applied choreographies', *in* C. Baier & L. Caires, eds., *Formal Techniques for Distributed Objects, Components, and Systems: International Federated Conference on Distributed Computing Techniques, Proceedings*. Vol. 10854 of Lecture Notes in Computer Science. Springer, pp. 21–40.

Giallorenzo, S., Montesi, F. & Peressotti, M. [2020], 'Choreographies as objects', *CoRR* **abs/2005.09520**.

Giallorenzo, S., Montesi, F., Peressotti, M. et al. [2021], 'Multiparty languages: The choreographic and multitier cases (pearl)', *in* A. Møller & M. Sridharan, eds., *ECOOP '20: European Conference on Object-Oriented Programming*. Vol. 194 of Leibniz International Proceedings in Informatics. Schloss Dagstuhl Leibniz Center for Computer Science, pp. 22:1–27.

Girard, J.-Y. [1987], 'Linear logic', *Theor. Comput. Sci.* **50**, 1–102.

Girard, J.-Y., Lafont, Y. & Taylor, P. [1989], *Proofs and Types*. Vol. 7 of Cambridge Tracts in Theoretical Computer Science. Cambridge University Press.

Goetz, B., Peierls, T., Bloch, J., et al. [2006], *Java Concurrency in Practice*. Pearson Education.

gRPC Authors [2022], 'gRPC'. https://grpc.io/.

Hennessy, M. [2007], *A Distributed Pi-Calculus*, Cambridge University Press.

Hildebrandt, T. T., Slaats, T., López, H. A., Debois, S. & Carbone, M. [2019], 'Declarative choreographies and liveness', *in* J. A. Pérez & N. Yoshida, eds., *Formal Techniques for Distributed Objects, Components, and Systems: International Federated Conference on Distributed Computing Techniques, Proceedings*. Vol. 11535 of Lecture Notes in Computer Science. Springer, pp. 129–47.

Hirsch, A. K. & Garg, D. [2022], 'Pirouette: Higher-order typed functional choreographies', *Proc. ACM Program. Lang.* **6**(POPL), 23:1–27.

Hohpe, G. & Woolf, B. [2004], *Enterprise Integration Patterns: Designing, Building, and Deploying Messaging Solutions*. Addison-Wesley Professional.

Honda, K., Yoshida, N. & Carbone, M. [2016], 'Multiparty asynchronous session types', *J. ACM* **63**(1), 9.

Hopcroft, J. E., Motwani, R. & Ullman, J. D. [2003], *Introduction to Automata Theory, Languages, and Computation: International Edition*. 2nd ed. Addison-Wesley.

Horne, R. [2020], 'Session subtyping and multiparty compatibility using circular sequents', *in* I. Konnov & L. Kovács, eds., *CONCUR '20: International Conference on Concurrency Theory*. Vol. 171 of Leibniz International Proceedings in Informatics. Schloss Dagstuhl Leibniz Center for Computer Science, pp. 12:1–22.

Hüttel, H., Lanese, I., Vasconcelos, V. T. et al. [2016], 'Foundations of session types and behavioural contracts', *ACM Comput. Surv.* **49**(1), 3:1–36.

International Telecommunication Union [1996], 'Recommendation Z.120: Message sequence chart'.

Jongmans, S. & Van den Bos, P. [2022], 'A predicate transformer for choreographies: Computing preconditions in choreographic programming', *in* P. Müller, ed., *ESOP '22: Programming Languages and Systems: 31st European Symposium on Programming, Proceedings*. Vol. 13240 of Lecture Notes in Computer Science. Springer, pp. 520–47.

Kazhamiakin, R. & Pistore, M. [2006], 'Analysis of realizability conditions for web service choreographies', *in* E. Najm, J. Pradat-Peyre & V. Donzeau-Gouge, eds., *Formal Techniques for Distributed Objects, Components, and Systems: International Federated Conference on Distributed Computing Techniques, Proceedings*. Vol. 4229 of Lecture Notes in Computer Science. Springer, pp. 61–76.

Kleene, S. C. [1952], *Introduction to Metamathematics*. D. van Nostrand Company.

Kobayashi, N. [2002], 'A type system for lock-free processes', *Inf. Comput.* **177**(2), 122–59.

Kobayashi, N. & Laneve, C. [2017], 'Deadlock analysis of unbounded process networks', *Inf. Comput.* **252**, 48–70.

Kobayashi, N. & Sangiorgi, D. [2010], 'A hybrid type system for lock-freedom of mobile processes', *ACM Trans. Program. Lang. Syst.* **32**(5), 16:1–49.

Lanese, I., Guidi, C., Montesi, F. & Zavattaro, G. [2008], 'Bridging the gap between interaction- and process-oriented choreographies', *in* A. Cerone & S. Gruner, eds., *SEFM: '08: Institute of Electrical and Electronics Engineers International Conference on Software Engineering and Formal Methods*. IEEE Computer Society, pp. 323–32.

Lanese, I., Montesi, F. & Zavattaro, G. [2013], 'Amending choreographies', *in* A. Ravara & J. Silva, eds., Proceedings of the *International Workshop on Automated Specification and Verification of Web Systems*. Vol. 123 of Electronic Proceedings in Theoretical Computer Science, pp. 34–48.

Lange, J. & Tuosto, E. [2012], 'Synthesising choreographies from local session types', *in* M. Koutny & I. Ulidowski, eds., *International Conference on Concurrency Theory*. Vol. 7454 of Lecture Notes in Computer Science. Springer, pp. 225–39.

Lange, J., Tuosto, E. & Yoshida, N. [2015], 'From communicating machines to graphical choreographies', *in* S. K. Rajamani & D. Walker, eds., *Proceedings of the Association for Computing Machinery Special Interest Group on Programming Languages (ACM SIGPLAN) International Conference on Programming Language Design and Implementation*. Association for Computing Machinery, pp. 221–32.

Leesatapornwongsa, T., Lukman, J. F., Lu, S. & Gunawi, H. S. [2016], 'TaxDC: A taxonomy of non-deterministic concurrency bugs in datacenter distributed systems', *in ASPLOS '16: Proceedings of the 21st International Conference on Architectural Support for Programming Languages and Operating Systems*. Association for Computing Machinery, pp. 517–30.

Lluch-Lafuente, A., Nielson, F. & Nielson, H. R. [2015], 'Discretionary information flow control for interaction-oriented specifications', *in* N. Martí-Oliet, P. C. Ölveczky & C. L. Talcott, eds., *Logic, Rewriting, and Concurrency: Essays dedicated to José Meseguer on the Occasion of His 65th Birthday*. Vol. 9200 of *Lecture Notes in Computer Science*. Springer, pp. 427–50.

López, H. A. & Heussen, K. [2017], 'Choreographing cyber-physical distributed control systems for the energy sector', *in* A. Seffah, B. Penzenstadler, C. Alves & X. Peng, eds., *SAC '17: Proceedings of the Symposium on Applied Computing, Marrakech, Morocco, 3–7 April*. Association for Computing Machinery, pp. 437–43.

López, H. A., Nielson, F. & Nielson, H. R. [2016], 'Enforcing availability in failure-aware communicating systems', *in* E. Albert & I. Lanese, eds., *Formal Techniques for Distributed Objects, Components, and Systems: International Federated Conference on Distributed Computing Techniques, Proceedings*. Vol. 9688 of Lecture Notes in Computer Science. Springer, pp. 195–211.

Lu, S., Park, S., Seo, E. & Zhou, Y. [2008], 'Learning from mistakes: a comprehensive study on real world concurrency bug characteristics', *in* S. J. Eggers & J. R. Larus, eds., *ASPLOS '08: Architectural Support for Programming Languages and Operating Systems, Proceedings*. Association for Computing Machinery, pp. 329–39.

Lynch, N. A. & Tuttle, M. R. [1987], 'Hierarchical correctness proofs for distributed algorithms', *in* F. B. Schneider, ed., *Proceedings of the Sixth Annual ACM Symposium on Principles of Distributed Computing, Vancouver, British Columbia, Canada, August 10-12, 1987*. Association for Computing Machinery, pp. 137–51.

Mendling, J. & Hafner, M. [2008], 'From WS-CDL choreography to BPEL process orchestration', *J. Enterp. Inf. Manag.* **21**(5), 525–42.

Merro, M. & Sangiorgi, D. [2004], 'On asynchrony in name-passing calculi', *Math. Struct. Comput. Sci.* **14**(5), 715–67.

Milner, R. [1980], *A Calculus of Communicating Systems*. Vol. 92 of Lecture Notes in Computer Science. Springer.

Milner, R. [1989], *Communication and Concurrency*. PHI Series in Computer Science. Prentice Hall.

Miu, A., Ferreira, F., Yoshida, N. & Zhou, F. [2021], 'Communication-safe web programming in typescript with routed multiparty session types', *in* A. Smith, D. Demange & R. Gupta, eds., 'CC '21: *Association for Computing Machinery Special Interest Group on Programming Languages (ACM SIGPLAN) International Conference on Compiler Construction*. Association for Computing Machinery. pp. 94–106.

Montesi, F. [2013], Choreographic programming, PhD Thesis, IT University of Copenhagen. www.fabriziomontesi.com/files/choreographic-programming.pdf.

Montesi, F., Guidi, C. & Zavattaro, G. [2014], 'Service-oriented programming with Jolie', *in* A. Bouguettaya, Q. Z. Sheng & F. Daniel, eds., *Web Services Foundations*. Springer, pp. 81–107.

Montesi, F. & Peressotti, M. [2017], 'Choreographies meet communication failures', *CoRR* **abs/1712.05465**.

Montesi, F. & Peressotti, M. [2021], 'Linear logic, the π-calculus, and their metatheory: A recipe for proofs as processes', *CoRR* **abs/2106.11818**.

Montesi, F. & Weber, J. [2018], 'From the decorator pattern to circuit breakers in microservices', *in* H. M. Haddad, R. L. Wainwright & R. Chbeir, eds., *Proceedings of the Annual Association for Computing Machinery Symposium on Applied Computing*. Association for Computing Machinery, pp. 1733–5.

Montesi, F. & Yoshida, N. [2013], 'Compositional choreographies', *in CONCUR 2013: Concurrency Theory*. Vol. 8052 of Lecture Notes in Computer Science. Springer, pp. 425–39.

Needham, R. & Schroeder, M. [1978], 'Using encryption for authentication in large networks of computers', *Commun. ACM* **21**(12), 993–9.

Neuman, B. & Ts'o, T. [1994], 'Kerberos: An authentication service for computer networks', *IEEE Communications Magazine* **32**(9), 33–8.

Neykova, R., Bocchi, L. & Yoshida, N. [2017], 'Timed runtime monitoring for multiparty conversations', *Formal Aspects Comput.* **29**(5), 877–910.

Ng, N. & Yoshida, N. [2015], 'Pabble: Parameterised scribble', *Serv. Oriented Comput. Appl.* **9**(3–4), 269–84.

Nygard, M. [2007], *Release It! Design and Deploy Production-Ready Software*. Pragmatic Bookshelf.

OASIS [2007], 'Web services business process execution language version 2.0', http://docs.oasis-open.org/wsbpel/2.0/OS/wsbpel-v2.0-OS.html.

Object Management Group [2011], 'Business process model and notation', www.omg.org/spec/BPMN/2.0/.

Object Management Group [2017], 'Unified modelling language, version 2.5.1', www.omg.org/spec/UML/2.5.1/.

O'Hearn, P. W. [2018], 'Experience developing and deploying concurrency analysis at Facebook', *in* A. Podelski, ed., *Static Analysis: International Symposium, Proceedings*. Vol. 11002 of Lecture Notes in Computer Science. Springer, pp. 56–70.

Oikarinen, J. & Reed, D. [1993], 'Rfc1459: Internet relay chat protocol', www.rfc-editor.org/rfc/rfc1459.

OpenID [2021], 'OpenID specifications', http://openid.net/developers/specs/.

Orlando, S., Pasquale, V. D., Barbanera, F., Lanese, I. & Tuosto, E. [2021], 'Corinne, a tool for choreography automata', *in* G. Salaün & A. Wijs, eds., *Formal Aspects of Component Software: International Conference, Proceedings*. Vol. 13077 of Lecture Notes in Computer Science. Springer, pp. 82–92.

Peterson, J. L. [1977], 'Petri nets', *ACM Comput. Surv.* **9**(3), 223–52.

Peterson, W. W. & Brown, D. T. [1961], 'Cyclic codes for error detection', *Proceedings of the IRE* **49**(1), 228–35.

Pfenning, F. [2012], 'Lecture notes on deductive inference', https://www.cs.cmu.edu/~fp/courses/15816-f16/lectures/01-inference.pdf

Pierce, B. C. [2002], *Types and Programming Languages*. MIT Press.

Plotkin, G. D. [2004], 'A structural approach to operational semantics', *J. Log. Algebr. Program.* **60–61**, 17–139.

Pohjola, J. Å., Gómez-Londoño, A., Shaker, J. & Norrish, M. [2022], 'Kalas: A verified, end-to-end compiler for a choreographic language', *in* J. Andronick & L. de Moura, eds., *ITP '22: International Conference on Interactive Theorem Proving.* Vol. 237 of Leibniz International Proceedings in Informatics. Schloss Dagstuhl Leibniz Center for Computer Science, pp. 27:1–18.

Qiu, Z., Zhao, X., Cai, C. & Yang, H. [2007], 'Towards the theoretical foundation of choreography', *in WWW '07: Proceedings of the 16th International Conference on World Wide Web.* Association for Computing Machinery, pp. 973–82.

Rivest, R. L., Shamir, A. & Adleman, L. [1978], 'A method for obtaining digital signatures and public-key cryptosystems', *Commun. ACM* **21**(2), 120–6.

Rosen, K. H. & Krithivasan, K. [2012], *Discrete Mathematics and Its Applications: With Combinatorics and Graph Theory.* Tata McGraw-Hill Education.

Sangiorgi, D. [2011], *Introduction to Bisimulation and Coinduction.* Cambridge University Press.

Scalas, A., Dardha, O., Hu, R. & Yoshida, N. [2017], 'A linear decomposition of multiparty sessions for safe distributed programming', *in* P. Müller, ed., *ECOOP '17: European Conference on Object-Oriented Programming.* 19–23 June, Barcelona, Spain. Vol. 74 of Leibniz International Proceedings in Informatics. Schloss Dagstuhl Leibniz Center for Computer Science, pp. 24:1–31.

Scalas, A. & Yoshida, N. [2019], 'Less is more: Multiparty session types revisited', *Proc. ACM Program. Lang.* **3**(POPL), 30:1–29.

Scalas, A., Yoshida, N. & Benussi, E. [2019], 'Effpi: Verified message-passing programs in Dotty', *in* J. I. Brachthäuser, S. Ryu & N. Nystrom, eds., *ACM SIGPLAN '19: Association for Computing Machinery Special Interest Group on Programming Languages International Conference on Scala.* Association for Computing Machinery, pp. 27–31.

Stolze, C., Miculan, M. & Gianantonio, P. D. [2021], 'Composable partial multiparty session types', *in* G. Salaün & A. Wijs, eds., *FACS '21: International Conference on Formal Aspects of Component Software, Proceedings.* Vol. 13077 of Lecture Notes in Computer Science. Springer, pp. 44–62.

Tanenbaum, A. S. & Van Steen, M. [2007], *Distributed Systems: Principles and Paradigms.* 2nd ed. Pearson Education.

Valmari, A. [1996], 'The state explosion problem', *in* W. Reisig & G. Rozenberg, eds., *Lectures on Petri Nets I: Basic Models, Advances in Petri Nets.* Vol. 1491 of Lecture Notes in Computer Science. Springer, pp. 429–528.

W3C [2005], 'Web services choreography description language version 1.0', www.w3.org/TR/ws-cdl-10/.

Weisenburger, P., Wirth, J. & Salvaneschi, G. [2020], 'A survey of multitier programming', *ACM Comput. Surv.* **53**(4), 81:1–35.

Yoshida, N., Hu, R., Neykova, R. & Ng, N. [2013], 'The scribble protocol language', *in* M. Abadi, A. L. Lafuente, eds., *TGC '13: International Symposium on Trustworthy Global Computing.* Vol. 8358 of Lecture Notes in Computer Science. Springer, pp. 22–41.

Index